Luciano Bardi | Wojciech Gagatek
Carine Germond | Karl Magnus Johansson
Wolfram Kaiser | Silvia Sassano

# The European Ambition

## The Group of the European People's Party and European Integration

Nomos

**The Deutsche Nationalbibliothek** lists this publication in the Deutsche Nationalbibliografie; detailed bibliographic data are available on the Internet at http://dnb.d-nb.de

ISBN 978-3-8487-6767-0 (Print)
978-3-7489-0871-5 (ePDF)

**British Library Cataloguing-in-Publication Data**
A catalogue record for this book is available from the British Library.

ISBN 978-3-8487-6767-0 (Print)
978-3-7489-0871-5 (ePDF)

**Library of Congress Cataloging-in-Publication Data**
Bardi, Luciano / Gagatek, Wojciech / Germond, Carine / Johansson, Karl Magnus / Kaiser, Wolfram / Sassano, Silvia
The European Ambition
The Group of the European People's Party and European Integration
Luciano Bardi / Wojciech Gagatek / Carine Germond / Karl Magnus Johansson / Wolfram Kaiser / Silvia Sassano
380 pp.
Includes bibliographic references and index.

ISBN 978-3-8487-6767-0 (Print)
978-3-7489-0871-5 (ePDF)

Onlineversion
Nomos eLibrary

1st Edition 2020

# Contents


| | | |
|---|---|---|
| Preface | | 7 |
| Introduction | | 11 |
| Chapter 1 | Shaping institutions and policies: The EPP Group in the European Communities<br>*Wolfram Kaiser* | 23 |
| Chapter 2 | Constitutionalising the Union: The Role of the EPP Group<br>*Karl Magnus Johansson* | 89 |
| Chapter 3 | Co-Shaping the Internal Market: The EPP Group and EU Internal Policies<br>*Carine Germond* | 131 |
| Chapter 4 | Values, Strategies, Actions: The EPP Group and EU External Relations<br>*Wojciech Gagatek* | 201 |
| Chapter 5 | The Heart of the Core: The EPP Group in the EU Institutional and Political Framework<br>*Luciano Bardi* | 255 |
| The Authors | | 335 |
| General Appendix | | 337 |
| List of Figures | | 369 |
| List of Tables | | 373 |
| Index of Names | | 375 |

# Preface

This book presents the results of the research project "The European ambition – The Group of the European People's Party and European integration". With the aim of contributing not only to scholarly debate but also to the general public's knowledge, it focuses on the impact of the Group of the European People's Party (EPP) in the European Parliament on European integration following the first direct European elections in 1979. The book begins with an account of co-operation models of Christian Democrats in the Common Assembly, which had been established with the European Coal and Steel Community in 1951. It then covers four decades of the EPP Group's input in the shaping of parliamentary debates, formulation of European policies and stimulation of the development of an institutional framework and a European party system. Interdisciplinary research on the Group's impact on the democratic integration of Europe is long overdue given that it will enrich the current understanding of the European Parliament's history. This book strives to close this gap and is the result of a series of initiatives launched with the EPP Group and the European University Institute working in partnership.

The EPP Group's ambition for a united Europe was a decisive stimulus in the post-war history of European integration. Two founders of the European Communities and early members of the Group had been elected as President of the predecessor to the European Parliament: Alcide De Gasperi in 1952 and Robert Schuman in 1958. 70 years ago, on 9th May 1950, the French Foreign Minister Robert Schuman gave impetus to the idea of a European Community with his ground-breaking declaration. After his election as President of the European Parliament on 19th March 1958, he presented to the plenary his view on the political role of the Parliament and his political group's European ambition:

> "...elle [l'Assemblée parlementaire dans l'Europe des Six] a été le banc d'essai d'une vie démocratique élargie à l'échelle européenne, ce qui lui a permis de renforcer constamment son influence politique en exerçant un contrôle parlementaire sur l'action de la Haute Autorité. Elle a rendu vaines les craintes souvent exprimées d'une prédominance technocratique dans les institutions économiques européennes. Certes, l'Assemblée consultative du Conseil de l'Europe avait ouvert l'histoire des assemblées internationales où l'opinion parlementaire ne s'inspire

> pas de la seule défense des intérêts nationaux, mais relève essentiellement des options politiques fondamentales. Mais il faut souligner que c'est à l'Assemblée commune que la formation des groupes politiques a permis, dès ses premières sessions, de développer ce sentiment européen au-delà des particularismes nationaux ... Le fait d'avoir été le candidat unique des trois groupes politiques de cette Assemblée est pour moi un honneur inespéré et en même temps un engagement pour l'avenir. Mon appartenance au groupe politique le plus nombreux a pu justifier ce choix en vertu d'une tradition parlementaire et démocratique, mais je le déclare hautement, je ne serai, ici, ni le représentant d'un parti, ni celui d'un pays."[1]

The research project was officially created on 12th July 2017, marking the EPP Group's call for a study on the Group's impact on European integration. The Alcide De Gasperi Research Centre on the History of European Integration, a joint undertaking of the History Department and the Historical Archives of the European Union at the European University Institute, responded to this call with a research proposal, which was carried out by an interdisciplinary and transnational team of scholars.

The Historical Archives of the EU and the Alcide De Gasperi Research Centre worked together closely in the past years with the former contributing its unique archival memory of European integration, which consists of the EU institutional archives, numerous private papers, and the archives of Federalist movements, European organisations and political groups in the European Parliament.

The EPP Group in the European Parliament and the Historical Archives have developed their fruitful co-operation over many years, starting with privileged electronic access to the Brussels-based EPP Group archives for researchers in Florence. This was followed by the introduction of an annual postgraduate grant programme on "Christian Democracy and European Integration", encouraging research which would make use of the Group's archival patrimony held in the Konrad-Adenauer-Stiftung in Sankt Augustin and in the Brussels office.

This book was achieved thanks to a number of key actors, partners and contributors. Thanks must therefore go firstly to the EPP Group in the European Parliament; its Secretary-General Martin Kamp, the Group's longest serving Secretary-General, who prompted and supported the project with an open mind and interest in academic research; former Di-

1 *Assemblée Parlamentaire Européenne*, 1 (Mai 1958), Débats, Compte rendu in extenso des sèances, Session constitutive mars 1958, 31.

rector of the EPP Group's Presidency Johan Ryngaert, who energised the project with questions and comments based on his deep insight into the Group's policies; Emma Petroni who has framed and managed the Group's archives with dedication for many years; and the various members of the Group, who participated in the series of interviews conducted for the project. Thanks must also go to the Konrad-Adenauer-Stiftung for providing access to the EPP Group's archival deposit and supporting the consultation by digitising relevant documents.

The results of the research were presented in a conference held at the EUI on 14th-15th November 2019. Thanks go to the discussants, who contributed their respective knowledge to the research, namely Sandro Guerrieri, Alfredo De Feo, Lorenzo Cicchi, Angela Romano, Martin Bull and Carlos Closa. Our gratitude must also go to the former Members of European Parliament, who enriched the debate with their personal testimonies, namely President Hans-Gert Pöttering and MEPs Jo Leinen and Andrew Duff.

At the Alcide De Gasperi Research Centre of the EUI, special thanks go to Prof. Luciano Bardi, Jacopo Cellini, Johannes Karremans and Silvia Sassano, who laid the project's foundations, co-ordinated the research team and liaised with the EPP Group. Finally, thanks go to the authors who contributed their knowledge and insight to the book, namely Wojciech Gagatek, Carine Germond, Karl Magnus Johansson and Wolfram Kaiser.

*Florence, 30th April 2020*

Dieter Schlenker
Director
Historical Archives of the European Union
European University Institute

# Introduction

*Luciano Bardi and Silvia Sassano*

This book is a study on the Group of the European People's Party (EPP). It traces the Group's origins in the European Coal and Steel Community (ECSC) Assembly and concentrates on its evolution throughout the four decades following the first universal suffrage elections of the European Parliament (EP), held in 1979. The stimulus for an academic research study investigating the EPP Group's objectives, strategies, actions, achievements and failures was provided by the Group itself. In response, this book aims to trace the Group's institutional, organisational and political trajectory in pursuit of what prominent exponents of the Group itself defined as its 'European ambition': the step-by-step achievement of levels of European awareness, commonality of values and co-operation, capable of enabling once arch-inimical nation states to live in peace and speak with one authoritative voice with the rest of the world. The expression 'European ambition' echoed the one used by EPP Group Chair Wilfried Martens when he referred to European political union in his speech at the XIII EPP Congress, held in Brussels in 1999.[1]

This volume uses a dynamic approach to deepen the public's knowledge of the impact of the EPP Group's actions on European integration and on the EP. It also intends to provide an original contribution to the study of all political groups in the EP with a multidisciplinary perspective that does not currently exist in the literature. As the book aims to engage practitioners and the wider public as well as the scientific community, it presents descriptive and qualitative narratives besides quantitative analyses and hermeneutical outputs. It is divided into five chapters, which trace and assess the elements of the 'European ambition'. At the same time, it focuses on the political and organisational evolution of the EPP Group and its strategic view of Europe from 1979 onwards, within the framework of international Christian democratic co-operation since the end of World War II. The methodology used in this book follows a multidisciplinary approach based on history, political science, European law and political sociology.

1 EPP Group Archives (1994-1999), President EPP – Group – Martens – Speeches.

Each chapter discusses the relevant literature within the legal framework regulating the European Union (EU) and the EP as well as European political parties. Each makes use of multiple archival sources, drawing upon the Historical Archives of the European Union (HAEU), the EPP Group's archives, the Archive for Christian-Democratic Policy (ACDP) and EU official documentation and data. All chapters rely on selected interviews with relevant actors (current and past EPP members and the EPP Group's support staff as well as other informed observers and experts).

The first chapter, authored by Wolfram Kaiser, discusses the history of the EPP Group in the European Parliament from its origins to the Maastricht Treaty, beginning with Christian Democracy's (CD) transnational co-operation after the end of the Second World War. Next, the author focuses on the Group's composition and internal governance from 1958 to 1992 as well as its evolving relationships with the EPP's central party organisation and other political groups in the EP. The chapter's final sections are devoted to the Group's 'European ambitions' of shaping two crucial functions of the EP: system-building and policy-making.

The second chapter, written by Karl Magnus Johansson, explores the role of the EPP Group in regards to EU treaty and institutional reform through an overview of six significant cases: the Single European Act and the Maastricht, Amsterdam, Nice, Constitutional and Lisbon Treaties.

In the third chapter, Carine Germond sets out to explore the EPP Group's contribution to and role in shaping the development of the internal policies of the European Union. She focuses on four internal policy areas of strategic importance: agricultural, economic and monetary, social, and environmental policy.

The fourth chapter, authored by Wojciech Gagatek, encompasses a broad area of the EU's external policies, including foreign policy, security and defence policy, development policy, commercial policy (external trade) and EU enlargement.

The fifth and final chapter, written by Luciano Bardi, concentrates on the Group's role as a crucial component in the EP party system and its core. Through an analysis of quantitative data, it also assesses the Group's institutional impact and positioning within the EPP party's wider organisation. Finally, it explores the Group's role in the relationship between the EP and other EU institutions, namely the Commission and the Council(s).

This study is justified due to the interest it can elicit in a wider pool of potential readers and due to the significance of the scientific contribution it can provide. Its relevance for anyone interested in European political phenomena as regards the EPP Group, especially in comparison with other political groups, is evident. For more than four decades, the EPP Group has played an important role in shaping the EP and the EU's institutional and democratic development. European elections have no doubt enhanced the strength and legitimacy of the political groups in the EP and have fostered the development of a party system at European level, at least in the parliamentary arena, defined as consisting of the political groups it includes, their relative strength and their structured interactions. At European level, a structured party system only exists in the parliamentary arena, whilst it is fragmented into 27 different national ones in the electoral arena and has yet to develop in the governmental arena (Bardi, Katz and Mair 2015). This explains the importance of political groups in the EP. Moreover, genuine European political parties, with complex parliamentary and extra-parliamentary organisations, have developed as well.

The EPP and its Group have long been at the centre of this process (Hix and Lord 1997; Kreppel 2002). In particular, the EPP, along with the Liberal (ALDE, now Renew Europe) and the Socialist (S&D) Groups, forms what is referred to as the European party system's core (see Bardi in Chapter 5 of this book). The core shares a common imperative mission: to strengthen the EP vis-à-vis the other EU institutions and enhance the supranational dimension of the EU in the process. This common objective has led the three groups to collaborate on institutional and constitutional matters, no doubt accelerating the EP's acquisition of significant powers (see Johansson in Chapter 2 and Bardi in Chapter 5 of this book).

Thus, the political groups of the EP continue to have a fundamental role in the institutional development of the EP and the EU. This is particularly true of the EPP Group due to several factors, not least the numerical primacy that the Group has enjoyed for the last five EP terms. However, as the analysis in the rest of this volume reveals, the long-standing Europeanist and institutionalist legacy inherited from the Christian Democratic Group and the commitment and competence of EPP MEPs are equally important. The Group has had a strong institutional presence throughout its history, which, in turn, has always allowed it to be a protagonist in the drafting and approval of the norms that regulate the functioning of the EP. This does not necessarily result in any direct advantages being gained but certainly ensures that the EP's institutional evolution follows a path which is consistent with the Group's objectives.

For a long time, the EP's political groups were, politically and organisationally, the most relevant component of European political parties and instrumental in the latter's growth. European political parties are indeed strong within the European Parliament where the groups have exhibited high levels of cohesiveness and inclusiveness (the ability to incorporate new national party delegations). Conversely, they are weak outside the EP, as demonstrated by the comparative irrelevance of their extra-parliamentary organisational structures, which consisted of loose federations of national parties with very few resources (Bardi 1994; Hix and Lord 1997; Kreppel 2002; Hix and Roland 2007).

This brief discussion has highlighted the objective centrality of the EPP Group and the system of political groups in which it operates: Both appear to be relevant foci of scientific research as well. Indeed, European political parties, as named and defined in Regulation EU 1141/2014, have been the object of keen interest in academic literature. They are, after all, important actors in the development of the European Communities (EC) and subsequently the EU. This has been true at least since Ernst Haas' suggestion (in 1958) that European political parties' growth provides an essential analytical focus for the assessment of the EU's political system. Since the EP's first universal suffrage elections, scholarly interest in the development and potential role of EU-specific political parties has grown considerably. The political groups in the European Parliament have not been the object of comparable attention. Moreover, even the most relevant study of a single EP political group (Fontaine 2009), which was an impressively informative and detailed account of the EPP Group, did not provide a systematic analysis of its intra-party and interinstitutional relations.

The few years leading up to the first elections of the European Parliament saw a revamping of the Europeanist drive that gave European integration a solid start in the early 1950s after the failure of a more ambitious project in the late 1940s. That success, often attributed to the pragmatism and realism of Jean Monnet's gradualist intuition, was also massively idealistic, as the project was shared and owned by other important European leaders, most of them Christian Democrats. Monnet broke the stalemate caused by the scepticism surrounding the federalist idea of the United States of Europe as a supranational institutional entity to be formed in one step with a single treaty. He conceived of a gradualist approach that would lead to a European federation in successive constitutional steps, starting with the creation of institutions for the integration of one crucial economic sector (the coal and steel industry). This method, which was termed neo-functionalist because of its sectoral nature (Haas 1958), was accepted by Schuman and the other 'founding fathers' and applied through the approval of a succession of treaties. During the 1970s, the EPP and its Group embraced the institutionalist and supranationalist traditions respectively embedded in Jean Monnet's and Robert Schuman's approaches (for the latter see Schlenker in the Preface of this book).

From a scientific perspective, a dedicated study of the EPP Group is therefore necessary, not only because it will fill an obvious gap in the literature, but also because it is an opportunity to investigate the impact on the elected Parliament of the very same Europeanist and federalist tradition that was a driving force in the establishment of the European Communities. The 1976 Manifesto of European Christian Democracy envisaged "a personalist, communitarian society, rooted in Christian values and founded on the dignity of the human being" whilst also stating "its commitment to the political integration of the [European] continent, with the goal of setting up a European government with independent powers and a parliament resulting from general and direct elections" (Cellini 2018: 86). Although the values and ideals at the Manifesto's core were universalistic, the concern for the creation of instruments for their affirmation in Europe was explicit. The European People's Party was founded mere months after the Manifesto was approved. European Christian Democrats felt that the implementation of their idea of Europe required effective institutional and political means, such as those provided by an integrated party at European level. This organisation would potentially overcome the limitations and shortcomings of both the European Union of Christian Democrats (EUCD) and CD Group in the European Parliament.

Promoting European Christian values and European political integration were therefore one and the same. One could even surmise that the pursuit by the EPP, as a Party and a Group, of more secular/political objectives, including the EU's institutionalisation, was tantamount to claiming the relevance of European Christian roots. As was consistently the case with these principles and their very *raison d'être*, the CD Group, followed by its EPP successor, took positions that clearly aimed to strengthen an institutional approach to European integration, as recommended by various reports on the state of EU institutions over the course of the 1970s. Moreover, the Group took strong stances in favour of the conferral of budgetary powers to the EP and, prominently, the completion of the operational process that would lead to the first universal suffrage election of the EP. In some of these cases, the CD and EPP Groups acted as veritable driving forces, whereas they limited themselves to taking favourable positions in other cases.

Be that as it may, the analysis in this volume demonstrates that the Group, as is consistent with the foremost objective of its 'European ambition', contributed strongly to the breaking of the institutional stalemate afflicting the EC in the 1970s. In the decades that followed, this legacy allowed the Group to pursue an integrationist strategy towards a supranational Union, despite the progressive, albeit relative, erosion of its Christian democratic identity. This was determined by the crisis faced by many traditional Christian democratic parties in Western Europe and the momentous historical events following the fall of the Berlin Wall as well as the subsequent expansion of the EU to East-Central and South-Eastern Europe. The ultimate, yet still very remote, objective of the 'ambition' could be the creation of a common European identity based on personalistic and universalistic values rooted in the notion of human dignity. Such values are part of the Christian tradition. However, as they are also present in secular visions, they are compatible with many of the parties that were more recently incorporated into the Group.

The study will therefore analyse how the EPP Group has pursued its 'European ambition'. Analytically but also conceptually, the 'European ambition' is much more than a simple idea about European integration. It consists of the following different but connected values/ideals, objectives and means/instruments.

*Values* – Christian values, principles and ideals as understood in a universalistic manner (based on human dignity) and, more specifically, in a supranational way.

*Institutional objective* – European federal state through a gradual approach. Intermediate institutional objective which is also a means of achieving the primary one – institutional strengthening and empowerment of the EP.

*Political means/strategy* – achievement of hegemony in the EP through a strong institutional presence/activism and political alliances (creation of a core group with S&D and ALDE; selective collaboration with the Greens).

*Organisational means* – achievement and maintenance of numerical prevalence in the EP and a presence in all Member States, mainly via its ability to attract sister (or at least 'cousin') parties across successive EU enlargements.

The relevance of the components of the EPP Group's European ambition can be traced through this volume's five chapters. As the previous discussion has revealed, Christian values are the foundation of the Group's Europeanist vocation. Although this is a separate theme, analytically, it is closely intertwined with the Group's primary institutional objective: the gradual creation of a European federal state. The connection between the two emerges clearly in Chapter 1 as Wolfram Kaiser's historical analysis focuses on the role played by the Christian Democrats in the debate on the future progress of European integration since the early post-war period. Although the analysis concentrates specifically on the ECSC and the European Economic Community (EEC), it goes as far as to include Altiero Spinelli's acceptance of the relevance of Christian Democracy's European roots during the debate on the Draft Treaty on the European Union (1984). This compatibility of values is also demonstrated by the EPP Group's decision to support Spinelli's initiative despite the fact that he belonged to the Communist Group (see Bardi in Chapter 5 of this book). Similarly, the Christian tradition appears in subsequent discussions on treaty reform (see Johansson in Chapter 2 of this book). Specifically, proposals for including references to the Christian heritage of Europe were part of the debate on the Constitutional Treaty (see Gagatek in Chapter 4 of this book).

In her chapter, Carine Germond outlines, amongst various successful proposals for inclusion in the text of the Maastricht Treaty by the EPP Group, the subsidiarity principle and describes it as "an integral part of a Christian vision of Europe". Germond also focuses on the Christian notion of solidarity, responsibility, respect and social justice in the context of social policy. This is not surprising as these chime perfectly with traditional Christian values. Conversely, the relevance of Christian views in shaping the EPP Group's position on environmental policy and even EU financial and budgetary governance is less expected, even if it is limited to its social dimension.

Likewise, Wojciech Gagatek repeatedly refers to values or ethical attitudes that can cement or break apart positions on key external policies in his analysis. For example, values such as freedom, democracy and human rights are discussed as foundations of a possible convergence between the United States and the EU in the Transatlantic Trade and Investment Partnership (TTIP). As regards development policy, however, the discussion juxtaposes issues such as abortion and freedom of religion with policy actions, such as the effort to ensure access to drinking water. In other words, the EPP Group considers a free trade area as an opportunity rather than a danger given its ideological orientation in favour of the defence of human dignity and peace and against poverty and war. Finally, Christian values also emerge as important elements in the analysis of the evolving EPP Group's cohesiveness and identity (see Bardi in Chapter 5 of this book), as successive EU enlargements have required the incorporation of parties coming from traditions that are not explicitly Christian.

The EPP Group's primary institutional objective, the achievement of a European federal state, is a theme running through all five chapters. In Chapter 1, Wolfram Kaiser juxtaposes the EPP Group's outstanding role in promoting EC/EU constitutionalisation with the lack of unity on this matter on the part of the PES. In Chapter 2, Karl Magnus Johansson illustrates how the EPP Group's statement that the Draft Treaty should be used as a basis for further EU integration and constitutionalisation found a concrete application in successive treaty reforms, beginning with the Single European Act. The gradualist nature of the EPP's approach to EU constitutionalisation is thus confirmed by the Group's role in promoting successive treaty reforms. After the Nice Treaty (2001), the EPP Group played a crucial role in establishing the Convention for the elaboration of a Constitutional Treaty (2004) and its outcomes. After this initiative's failure, the Group continued to encourage the adoption of a new treaty, an effort which came to fruition with the 2007 Lisbon Treaty.

The Group's position on the 'deepening vs. widening' dilemma, which animated the debate at European level after the collapse of Communist regimes in Central and Eastern Europe, was that the latter is not possible without the former, as is well argued by Wojciech Gagatek in his discussion of enlargement policy. As expected, institutional deepening is not the main focus of Carine Germond's dissection of treaty reform. Given her chapter's focus on policy, she highlights, amongst other things, the timetable set for the Economic and Monetary Union (EMU) and the creation of an independent European Central Bank (ECB) whilst discussing the Maastricht Treaty.

Luciano Bardi concentrates on the EPP Group's role in promoting the parliamentarisation and democratisation of the EU through non-constitutional means. In particular, he discusses the Group's changing positions on its assessment of the potential impact of electoral reform, especially as concerns the creation of transnational lists in EP elections, the Europeanisation of political parties and representation at EU level. In his analysis, this assessment is partially connected to a discussion of the *Spitzenkandidaten* initiative as a means of modifying the political balance between supranational and intergovernmental institutions in favour of the former.

The main intermediate objective of the EPP Group's 'European ambition' is the empowerment and institutional strengthening of the EP, yet it is not only a goal but also an instrument by which the Group may exert influence in the EU. Indeed, in this book's analysis, the EPP Group's commitment to EU constitutionalisation and institutional deepening goes hand in hand with a commitment to a more powerful EP. In Wolfram Kaiser's chapter, the CD/EPP Group's idea that the empowerment of the EP is a "*conditio sine qua non*" for a federal Europe is clearly spelled out. At the same time, Kaiser demonstrates that the CD Group was convinced that a more powerful Parliament would pave the way for a more active and influential role of political parties in EC/EU integration.

This aspect is addressed in each chapter. According to Karl Magnus Johansson, the extension of the EP's powers of co-decision through various treaties and growing tendencies toward EU parliamentarism strengthen the partisan dimension of EU politics. In Chapter 3, Carine Germond connects the political groups' ability to influence legislation with the legislative empowerment of the EP in those internal policy areas in which it gained new competences after 1979. Conversely, Wojciech Gagatek's chapter discusses how the relative lack of EP powers in some specific policy fields can make membership of the corresponding EP committees less attractive to MEPs. In a counter-intuitive way, this confirms the importance of the connection between EP empowerment and partisan activism at EU level. In Chapter 5, Luciano Bardi stresses the role of EP party groups, and that of the EPP Group in particular, in the EP's empowerment through their initiatives and support for treaty reforms and other, less direct methods. An important case in point is the use by political groups of the EP's budgetary powers to exercise parliamentary political control over the executive during the Santer Commission resignation, even if the EPP Group was more of a bystander than a protagonist.

The pursuit of the intermediate and primary objectives of the EPP Group's 'European ambition' requires a vision and strategy for the acquisition of the necessary political resources. The diversity of political opinions across Europe ensures that no political group can obtain an absolute majority in EP elections. This can be compensated for with adequate institutional strategies, political alliances and networking within the EP and beyond. Luciano Bardi discusses the relationship between the political groups' electoral strength and their ability to obtain relevant institutional positions in the EP at length. He also presents original data to demonstrate that this relationship is far from being a linear one. In fact, it is connected with a group's ability to form solid alliances, such as the one that includes the parties belonging to the EU party system's core.

Furthermore, transnational party networks, informal channels and personal relations are important resources for groups in the context of negotiations and policy discussions. Wolfram Kaiser pays particular attention to this matter and points out how the EPP Group tried in the past to compensate for the lack of EP formal powers through informal networking mechanisms. Moreover, he describes the transnational Christian democratic networks' impact on the EPP Group's internal constitution as well as on its ideological orientation and programmatic commitments. Likewise, Johansson draws attention to the ways in which the EPP Group promotes initiatives outside the EP by involving parties and civil society representatives at national level as well as how it uses party networks within and around the European Council to influence treaty reforms. Luciano Bardi addresses another aspect of this strategy: the constitutionalisation, through the approval of a specific statute, of political parties at European level and the strengthening of their links with civil society through the establishment of corresponding political foundations.

The relevance of networks also emerges in policy-making. Carine Germond stresses the EPP Group's reliance on contact between its members and fellow Christian Democrats holding office in the governments or parliaments of the Member States for the purpose of shaping internal policies. Germond also highlights their role in articulating, mediating and promoting civil society's interests in the EP and other institutional contexts. This analysis continues with a description of EPP MEPs' actions to influence discussions within the EP committees and in plenary sessions as far as key economic, social and environmental issues are concerned. Finally, Gagatek uses his chapter to describe the role of formal and informal mechanisms and committee members, especially Chairs, Rapporteurs or shadow Rapporteurs, in the promotion of the Group's positions.

This study shows how the EPP Group's 'European ambition' has influenced EU integration. At the same time, EU development, via institutional deepening and successive enlargements, has changed the Group's own organisation and political features. The Group's ability to influence the EP and EU politics is closely linked to its internal structures and dynamics. Adequate organisational characteristics are essential resources for reaching objectives. The impact of the entry of new parties and other factors on the EPP Group's cohesion and balance of power between national delegations is analysed in this study as an element of the EPP Group's organisational strength or weakness. Wolfram Kaiser looks at how direct elections, the progressive strengthening of the EP's legislative powers and the Group's activism in EC reform impacted upon its own voting cohesiveness in the EP.

The impact of incoming parties following several EU enlargements on the Group's organisational structure is addressed in various chapters of this volume. Kaiser examines how the Northern and Southern enlargements affected the EPP Group's internal composition and cohesion as well as its influence in the European Parliament. Gagatek's analysis concentrates on the effect of new members in the EP after the 2004/2007 enlargement on the voting cohesiveness of the main EP political groups. Bardi looks at the impact of all EU enlargements on the Group's identity and composition in terms of its history, ideology and values. He also analyses changes in the Group's own institutional balance and political orientation as well as its capacity to maintain unity and easily reach common positions on crucial questions.

Throughout this book, the EPP Party and Group's converging tradition of Christian values and European vocation are treated as identitarian elements that the Group ostensibly seeks to preserve, albeit with various levels of success. These elements can also be seen as assets to be used by the Group in the pursuit of political objectives and its own consolidation. Christianity has long been recognised as one of the fundamental elements of the European value structure even in countries without a proper Christian democratic political tradition. Politically, values such as the importance of family as a cornerstone of society and the equidistance between the aspirations of groups belonging to different societal strata overlap considerably with those of ostensibly secular, moderate to conservative parties across Europe. This, as well as the power and influence that comes with the Group's size, has attracted sister parties from all EU expansion Member States as successive enlargements have increased the number of EU Member States to 27 after having reached a maximum of 28. However, this successful process has come at a price. The Group's internal composition has become increasingly fragmented following the three-fold increase in the number of national delegations since 1979. At the same time, the Group's ideological make-up has been modified and is no longer based exclusively on Christian values. Both circumstances are potential internal governance problems facing the Group's leadership.

Besides coping with internal changes, the EPP Group now faces more potentially menacing external challenges. Sovereignist and anti-EU sentiments have emerged in several Member States and are, according to some, threatening the EU's very existence. The objectives of the Group's 'European ambition' must be recast. It may be necessary to balance progress towards European integration with the preservation of what has already been achieved. As is consistent with the gradualist approach that has always characterised its actions, the EPP Group seems to have identified a new intermediate step in the empowerment of the EP: the acquisition of a new co-decisional role with the Commission and the European Council in long-term budgetary and financial planning.

At the time of completion of this manuscript in spring 2020, in a letter to the (Christian democratic) President of the Commission, Ursula von der Leyen, and the President of the European Council, Charles Michel, the EPP Group's Chair, Manfred Weber, and Vice-Chair, Siegfried Mureşan, advanced a request for the EP to be "*fully involved in the decision-making process and the adoption and implementation of the Recovery Plan*" (emphasis in the original). Their contention was that the coronavirus recovery plan "cannot be an exception to this basic rule of democracy and legitimacy". They went as far as listing the conditions under which the EPP Group would approve the Multiannual Financial Framework (MFF) and the Recovery Fund (EPP Group 2020a). Whilst the letter was characterised on the EPP Group's own website and reported by the online media as an ultimatum (EPP Group 2020b; Express 2020), supported by the threat to veto the MFF, the EPP Group representatives also expressed the hope that the "Commission and the Council would share the same level of *ambition*" (emphasis ours) as the Group.

# Chapter 1 Shaping institutions and policies: The EPP Group in the European Communities

*Wolfram Kaiser*

The political parties of the Left should have comprehensively won the first free elections in (Western) Europe in 1944-45 after the experience of fascism and national-socialism, as well as conservative and Catholic nationalist collaboration as in the case of Vichy France. After all, even in the unoccupied United Kingdom, the Labour Party defeated the Conservative wartime leader Winston Churchill in the general election in July 1945 to win a parliamentary majority for the first time ever. However, it was not to be. The Left's relative electoral failure to gain majority support in free elections after the war was to preoccupy historian sympathisers for a long time. Mirroring the debate about the fate of the German Reich after 1918-19, they tended to argue that the Socialists should have dedicated themselves to far more revolutionary change of the social and political institutions and socio-economic policy-making to achieve a more decisive break with the past (de Graaf 2019; Judt 2005).

Instead of the Social Democrats, the Socialists and Communists, the more centrist and centre-right Christian Democrats became the strongest electoral force in continental Western Europe after 1945. They revived interwar political party traditions largely untainted by collusion with fascism as in the case of Luxembourg, Belgium, and the Netherlands, or they created new formally non-confessional or inter-confessional parties as in France, Italy, and Western Germany. At the time of the negotiation of the Treaty of Paris, that resulted in the creation of the European Coal and Steel Community (ECSC) in 1951-2, the Christian Democrats were in power in all of these six founding Member States – together with the Labour Party in the Netherlands, temporarily ruling with an absolute majority in Belgium, and leading coalition governments as far and away the largest single party in all other countries. They continued to dominate continental Western European politics as well as the politics of European integration well into the 1960s (Gehler and Kaiser 2004a; Buchanan and Conway 1996).

The emerging Cold War greatly facilitated the rise and political hegemony of these parties. After all, pronounced anti-communism had characterised both political Catholicism and more secular conservative political tendencies since Karl Marx first advocated socialist class struggle and revolution in the middle of the nineteenth century. Conveniently for the Christian Democrats, the Cold War greatly simplified ideological and political choices once more: this time between parliamentary democracy and private ownership in a predominantly market economy on the one hand, and class dictatorship and centrally planned collectivised production on the other. Aligning themselves strongly with the United States as the protector of Western Europe's democracies, the Christian Democrats successfully presented themselves as the only effective bulwark against bolshevism externally as well as internally: in France and Italy where the Communists did very well in free elections, with the Socialists allying themselves with them in Italy; and in Western Germany in opposition to the newly formed Eastern German communist state effectively set up and protected by the Soviet Union.

The Cold War alone does not sufficiently explain the durability and adaptability of centre-right political parties in Western Europe after 1945, however (Botsiou 2009: 175). As Martin Conway (2004) has pointed out, the key tenets of political Catholicism remained quite stable from the interwar period into the 1960s. It retained a 'fortress mentality' until the death of Pope Pius XII in 1958 and beyond. Crucially, however, political Catholicism still achieved greater success at escaping the confessional political ghetto of practising Catholics than the Socialists did at overcoming class barriers. As a result, it was able to ally itself increasingly with protestant, liberal and moderate conservative political forces as in the Netherlands, where the two traditional protestant political parties initially continued to exist alongside the Catholic People's Party, and in Western Germany, where new Christian democratic parties overcame the Centre Party's confessional limitations.

After 1945 the Christian Democrats developed a political vocabulary of human dignity, individual freedom, social rights and subsidiarity that loosely drew on a combination of personalism and Catholic social teaching. At the same time, the Christian Democrats built bridges to liberal concepts of political pluralism, private enterprise and market economy. This in turn allowed the creation of broad centre-right political groupings as in the case of the Western German Christian Democratic Union (CDU) and its Bavarian sister party, the Christian Social Union (CSU), and the Italian Democrazia Cristiana (DC). The parties' evolving doctrines and programmes were adapted to specific national contexts, traditions and structures of party competition. However, all Christian democratic parties sought to connect Christian values with secular political causes. They also advocated different versions of a socio-economic 'third way'. Depending on national circumstances, their programmatic preferences could flexibly be made compatible with a diverse range of economic policies, from indicative planning in France to ordo-liberal competition policy in Western Germany.

With their pronounced anti-communism, advocacy of a 'third way' for European societies and middle-of-the-road-policies in government, the Christian Democrats shaped the post-war consensus about the developing welfare state to a large degree. Their European ambitions were designed to sustain these programmatic preferences. They also developed a life of their own, with the Christian Democrats adopting strong advocacy of European integration as one of their core ideological and programmatic tenets after 1945. They strongly influenced many core features of the present-day European Union (EU), and did so not just through intergovernmental bargaining, but also via their transnational party co-operation, which was both formalised and highly informal (Kaiser 2007). In addition to private personal and bilateral contacts, this cooperation mainly took place in the Nouvelles Equipes Internationales (NEI) formed in 1948, the informal Geneva Circle and – from 1949 onwards – in the Consultative Assembly of the Council of Europe.

In 1952–3, the ECSC Common Assembly for the first time constituted a formal institutional platform for a more exclusive cooperation among the Christian democratic parties from its six founding Member States. They formed the largest common transnationally constituted parliamentary group, alongside those of the Socialists and Liberals. In 1958, they remained the largest group by a significant margin in the integrated Parliamentary Assembly of the European Economic Community (EEC), which renamed itself the European Parliament (EP) in 1962. In conjunction with its first direct election in 1979, the Christian Democratic Group (CD Group) renamed itself the European People's Party (EPP) Group following the transnational organisation of parties from the by now institutionally integrated European Communities (EC) in 1976.

This first chapter analyses and discusses the European cooperation and joint political action of the CD/EPP Group in the EC into the 1980s before its transformation into the EU in the Treaty of Maastricht, when the EP acquired legislative co-decision powers. When the EP was first directly elected in 1979, the EPP Group's political activism was strongly influenced by long-term vectors (Kaiser and Patel 2017), or what historical institutionalists call path-dependencies (e.g. Pierson 2000), both in terms of its internal organisation and practices and its political preferences. For this reason, the chapter's first section traces the origins of the transnational and parliamentary co-operation of the Christian democratic parties (hereafter CD parties) until 1958 to sketch these long-term continuities and to facilitate an assessment of what actually changed with the direct elections during the 1980s.

The second section then analyses the CD/EPP Group's changing composition and internal governance over time. This includes how the Group allocated posts internally and how it organised its policy-making before and after the first direct elections. As we will see, while the Group grew in size and the administration became professionalised, key practices – such as the close cooperation between the German and Italian Christian Democrats – at least initially survived the direct elections.

The third section then addresses the Group's evolving relations with the EPP as its EC-level party organisation and with the other political parties within the EP. This section seeks to understand why and how the Christian Democrats laid the groundwork for becoming the largest and most influential Group in the EP once again, having lost the position in 1975; and how it co-operated with other groups in the EP – especially the Socialists – to decide the distribution of posts and influence budgetary and legislative action.

Sections four and five of the chapter are devoted to the CD/EPP Group's European ambitions for shaping two crucial functions of the EP: system-building and policy-making. In the period covered in this chapter, the CD/EPP Group's greatest contribution to European integration was arguably its consistent approach to system-building based on its broadly federalist agenda, and its relatively united approach to making the EC/EU institutions both more efficient and more democratic – the latter primarily by working towards a significant strengthening of the EP's role and powers broadly in line with the national template of parliamentary democracy.

In contrast, regarding socio-economic policy issues that lay at the heart of European integration in the EC, the CD/EPP Group was generally more heterogeneous than the Socialists. Section five focusses on the Group's policy-making by selectively discussing three key policy challenges: the integration of agricultural policy, which was dear to the Christian Democrats; issues of economic integration from the common market to competition, monetary cooperation and regional policy; and the origins of EC environmental policy – a policy that the CD Group somewhat surprisingly co-shaped in the 1970s as one of several new policy areas that evolved in response to new societal challenges and pressures from new social movements from the 1960s onwards.

On this basis, the chapter's conclusion draws out some larger questions of continuity and discontinuity across the first direct elections in 1979, which the EP itself usually assumes to mark a watershed in its own history and that of the EC/EU. In doing so, the conclusion also pinpoints some of the CD/EPP Group's core structural and policy challenges that continued to inform its later parliamentary organisation and actions as addressed in chapters two to five in this book. They included the Group's – and the EP's – great difficulty in going beyond the system-building and policy-making functions to act as intermediaries between EU institutions and citizens to strengthen their political engagement for European integration, to foster European identity, and to enhance the legitimacy of the EU and its institutions.

### *Shaping European integration: transnational party cooperation after 1945*

Political Catholicism as it evolved in the nineteenth century was transnational primarily in the sense that it sought to organise Catholics against the modern secular ideologies of liberalism, socialism and anticlericalism in defence of the Church as a global institution (Clark 2003). Organised transnational networks were largely limited to the so-called Black International dominated by Catholic aristocrats (Lamberts 2002), which unsuccessfully tried to protect the Vatican's temporal powers after the occupation of the Papal States by the liberal Kingdom of Italy. After the First World War, politicians from the Italian Partito Popolare created in 1919 first initiated bilateral contacts with the German Centre Party. The Italians began to advocate a thorough revision of the Versailles Treaty, including territorial changes with the aim of the full integration of the Weimar Republic into the post-war international order of the League of Nations (Gualerzi 1959).

When the Italian party's founder Luigi Sturzo went into exile after the usurpation of power by Benito Mussolini, he started to work towards organised cooperation among Catholic parties to strengthen moderate political Catholicism against the authoritarian and fascist threat from the Right as well as communism from the Left. He made contact with the French Parti Démocrate Populaire (PDP) which broke ranks with the nationalist Right when it voted for the ratification of the Locarno Treaty. Keen on developing a more conciliatory approach towards Germany, the PDP sought to establish contacts with other Catholic parties and in December 1925 launched the Sécretariat International des Partis Démocratiques d'Inspiration Chrétienne (SIPDIC) in Paris, with full German Centre Party participation (Kaiser 2007: 72–118).

This limited interwar Catholic party cooperation was dominated by left-Catholics who often had close links to Catholic trade unions and charities.

In policy terms, these politicians were primarily concerned with issues of industrial, social, and education policy that even within the present-day EU have largely remained a national competence. As a result, their policy debates focused on the exchange of information and learning from foreign examples in these policy domains. They were not geared towards developing plans for European economic integration, as advocated at the time particularly by the French Socialist foreign minister Aristide Briand and liberal political parties. When the National-Socialists took power in Germany in 1933, SIPDIC effectively became defunct. The only loosely organised co-operation among Catholics in exile in the United Kingdom and in the United States subsequently failed to produce blueprints for a European post-war order, as the German question continued to polarise participants (Kaiser 2000).

Despite strong continuities in the social organisation, political beliefs and cultural practices of Catholics, the end of the Second World War fundamentally changed the conditions for party organisation and transnational co-operation. To begin with, while they still supported more neo-corporatist forms of societal organisation, the new Christian democratic parties were reconciled to parliamentary democracy. When discussing transnational party co-operation with Catholics from neutral Switzerland in 1946, DC representatives stated, and other Christian democratic party representatives concurred, that "democracy [is] the sole political system compatible with Christian beliefs", categorically excluding participation by representatives of Franco's Spain, for example.[1] As a result, the Christian democratic parties favoured co-operation with anti-communist clerical regimes and military dictatorships during the Cold War. However, they also aligned themselves with socialist and liberal preferences for the protection of human rights (Duranti 2017) and supported the exclusion of non-democratic regimes like Franco's Spain from Western European integration organisations with clear political objectives such as the ECSC/EEC.

Moreover, liberal-conservative party elites largely came to dominate the CD parties and their developing transnational cooperation in parliamentary forums as well as in the NEI and the Geneva Circle, with a more marginal role for Christian trade unionists. These liberal-conservative elites quickly came to see European economic integration as the only suitable structure for defending private ownership and a mixed economy; for what Alan S. Milward (1992) has called the "European rescue of the nation-state" through creating large more efficient markets and European welfare

1 Bundesarchiv, CVP-Archiv JII.181, 2659, Meier to Rosenberg, 29 October 1946.

policies in sectors like coal and steel and agriculture; and for maintaining peace in Europe. Moreover, they were able to draw on a new repertoire of cross-party constitutional visions for a united Europe, which were already developed during the war and fostered by various federalist organisations and the European Movement, as witnessed at its congress at The Hague in May 1948.

Lastly, the Christian Democrats also benefitted in different ways from how the Cold War shaped the external conditions for European integration. The division of Europe, first of all, excluded the German-Polish conflict from cooperation among the Western European political parties, which had severely complicated the work of SIPDIC in the interwar period. Moreover, the division of Germany allowed the Christian Democrats to develop a simplistic narrative in relation to a Prussian-communist German East in their party co-operation after 1945 and, in contrast, a Western German culture and society with connections to Latin-Roman culture, which could be democratised, Westernised, and successfully integrated in European organisations, as was indeed the overriding objective of Konrad Adenauer, the first German CDU Chancellor after 1949. Even better, the division of Germany also militated against the possible danger of a German domination of European integration organisations – a wide-spread latent fear in Western Europe put in a nutshell much later by the Italian DC politician Giulio Andreotti, when he said that he loved Germany so much that he preferred when there were two (Trocini 2012).

The Cold War additionally guaranteed that the United States strongly supported European integration, for political as well as economic reasons. Finally, the United Kingdom, where the Christian Democrats had no sister party, refused to participate in more meaningful economic, let alone political, integration (Kaiser 1999). This in turn strengthened the Christian Democrats' political hegemony in continental 'core Europe' until the first EC enlargement in 1973. In these changing circumstances after 1945, the Christian Democrats now saw their party co-operation not just as a forum for the exchange of ideas, but as an essential mechanism for discussing and somewhat aligning their programmatic objectives on key shared policy challenges, and for influencing the politics of European integration.

The Christian Democrats formally founded the NEI at its first official congress in Liège in Belgium in May 1947 (Gehler and Kaiser 2004b: 97–100). With its weak secretariat, bureau meetings and annual congress, the NEI were institutionally ineffective, primarily due to opposition from the French and Belgians to formalising them as an organisation of political parties. The French Mouvement Républicain Populaire (MRP), which was essential to NEI cooperation, sought to establish itself as a non-clerical centrist party in French politics, and was initially keen to avoid too close an association with what could be presented by the French Left as more clerical or conservative parties elsewhere in Western Europe. The NEI were also weakened by their broad membership, including the Swiss and Austrian political parties. While both shared a strongly anti-communist orientation, the Austrians could not commit to participation in Western European integration with Soviet troops still in Eastern Austria until 1955, and the Swiss did not want to do so due to their established policy of neutrality. Moreover, the NEI even had exile groups from Eastern Europe and Spain. The 'core Europe' parties from the founding Member States of the ECSC/EEC remained rhetorically loyal to Christian Democrats in and from Eastern Europe (Kaiser and Kosicki 2021). However, under the conditions of the deepening Cold War, they were keen to concentrate on the integration of continental Western Europe.

In contrast to the NEI, cooperation in the so-called Geneva Circle from 1947 was much more informal, and was even kept secret initially to avoid compromising its participants in domestic politics (Gehler 2001). Initiated by Georges Bidault, the MRP foreign minister and Prime Minister to establish links with reliable German Christian Democrats like Adenauer, the meetings primarily created a platform for bilateral Franco-German co-operation, albeit with broader participation, which seemed especially useful before the Federal Republic was created and governmental contact became possible in 1949. While the NEI meetings and annual congresses focused more on fundamental ideological and policy issues, the encounters in the Geneva Circle were geared closely towards the concertation of policy on concrete issues, such as the constitutional future of West Berlin within the Federal Republic of Germany.

Moreover, despite his apparent Atlantic orientation, Bidault strongly agreed with Adenauer and other participants during the meetings in 1948–49 that Britain's self-exclusion from European integration was highly desirable to allow deeper economic and political integration in 'core Europe' – a position that quickly became prevalent in the MRP and other Christian democratic parties with the partial exception of the Dutch protestant parties that only joined the NEI in 1954. Supporting Bidault, P.J.S. Serrarens from the Dutch Catholic People's Party (KVP) argued in the Geneva Circle in June 1949: "There is a British tendency to limit Europe to inter-state negotiations, if not to create no Europe at all. If England dominates, nothing will be achieved."[2] Paolo Emilio Taviani (1954, 248), a close confidant of

2 ACDP, 01–009–017, Geneva Circle, 10 June 1949.

the Italian DC Prime Minister Alcide De Gasperi, claimed that the English had an "insular mentality, which can never be extinguished". At best, or so Ernest Pezet from the MRP phrased it, the British could accept facts and might eventually join, but "we must play the role of the engine".[3] This prevailing scepticism regarding the United Kingdom's role in Europe also characterised the CD/EPP Group's attitudes to the British Conservatives as a necessary but not always easy ally in the EP after 1973.

When the Consultative Assembly of the Council of Europe met for the first time in Strasbourg in August 1949, therefore, the Christian Democrats, despite their institutional limitations, operated fairly dense networks of transnational contacts – both bilateral and multilateral in nature – in the NEI and the Geneva Circle. Co-operation in the new parliamentary forums of the Council of Europe and, from 1952–53 onwards, the Common Assembly of the ECSC, became informally integrated with these networks to a large extent. For example, the MRP leader Pierre-Henri Teitgen and Heinrich von Brentano, the CDU/CSU parliamentary party leader in the German Bundestag, met and worked closely with each other in the Geneva Circle before they played a leading role in the Constitutional Committee of the ECSC Ad Hoc Assembly, which drafted the European Political Community (EPC) proposal in 1953.

On occasion, the Christian Democrats also drew upon these informal networks to support their governmental co-operation, such as when they convinced the MRP to pass the treaty creating the Western European Union in late December 1954 during a hastily arranged, last-minute mission to Paris (Kaiser 2007: 277–81). The overlap between party and parliamentary networks continued later, when the NEI were transformed into the European Union of Christian Democrats (EUCD) in 1965 and the EPP was founded in 1976. Over time, however, the CD/EPP Group acquired a far more dominant coordinating position and, as we will see below, frequently complained about the ineffectiveness of the EC-level party organisation.

The fact that the ECSC had a parliamentary assembly at all can, in fact, largely be attributed to pressure from the Christian Democrats at political party and government levels. After all, Jean Monnet's original proposal for integrating the coal and steel industries had not even mentioned such a parliamentary dimension. Monnet's objective was to institutionalise what Pezet in the Geneva Circle called a "para-political" institution run by inde-

3 KADOC, Archief CEPESS, 3.1.11, Geneva Circle, 12 June 1950.

pendent appointed experts –[4] individuals who in Monnet's vision would then act in "the interests of all", free from pressures by national governments or interest groups (Duchêne 1994, BBC 1971). In contrast, the Christian Democrats were wary of such forms of technocratic government. They were initially flexible regarding the precise institutional form of European integration, but united in their advocacy of a popular parliamentary dimension, which would create a link with citizens and strengthen the legitimacy of European integration. Their debates about integration in the early post-war period created a strong ideological vector for their later advocacy of constitutionalising the EC in a European parliamentary system.

When the Common Assembly started its work, its first Rules of Procedure from January 1953 mentioned committees, but not political groups. Three transnational groups formed regardless, which became formalised in a revision of the Rules of Procedure five months later, in June 1953 (Mittag 2011). However, the delegates from national parliaments initially sat in alphabetical order. Seating according to group membership was only introduced in the new EP formed for the EEC, Euratom and the ECSC in 1958. The CD Group officially constituted itself in June 1953.[5] It came close to an absolute majority of members, comprising 38 of 78 national delegates (Guerrieri 2015). The CD Group created an executive Bureau which was initially headed up by the Dutch KVP politician Emmanuel Sassen and comprised eight other members; this Bureau started to hold regular meetings in Brussels and Strasbourg. When the Belgian Robert Houben demanded at the end of 1954 that the Group "define its political programme more clearly so that we can accomplish our task better",[6] its members began to discuss concrete policy issues more and more. However, despite the transnational organisation of the political groups, nationality continued to matter in the Common Assembly (Mittag 2011, 20).

The Christian Democrats were not only keen on the inclusion of a meaningful parliamentary dimension in European integration. The decision to start with economic integration in one sector – coal and steel – also very much reflected their political preferences and followed their close transnational co-ordination, before the French foreign minister Robert Schuman adopted Monnet's initiative for the French government and made it public on 9 May 1950 (Lynch 1997). Functional reasons for start-

---

4 Ibid.

5 EPP Group Archives, E.1, Déclaration de constitution, 23.6.1953.

6 ACDP, 09–001–009/1, Houben to Opitz, 12.11.1954, Note au groupe démocrate-chrétien de l'assemblé commune.

ing with integration in coal and steel included its importance for European, and not merely nationally focused reconstruction; the need under combined US and British pressure to replace the ineffective and discriminatory Allied control of German heavy industry through the Ruhr Authority; and the sector's symbolic value for European integration as a peace project (Kaiser and Schot 2014: 219–58). In addition, however, some Christian democratic parties had especially strong links to the industry. This was true for the German CDU, which initially lacked mass membership and was largely reliant on funding from German heavy industry (Bösch 2001). Industry also mattered immensely for some regions such as Wallonia in Belgium, the largest German state of North Rhine-Westphalia where the CDU led a coalition government from 1946 onwards, and Alsace-Lorraine, which was an electoral stronghold of the MRP.

Adenauer repeatedly suggested joint control over coal and steel in some form of sector integration in meetings in the NEI and the Geneva Circle, highlighting the fact that he had already made a similar proposal as early as 1923, when French and Belgian troops had occupied the Ruhr Area. At a meeting of the Geneva Circle in November 1949, von Brentano propagated the idea once more as a way to guarantee "effective French control over the production of German companies".[7] In a letter to French Prime Minister Bidault dated 22 March 1950, Adenauer again suggested starting European integration with the coal, steel and chemical industries – an initiative that guaranteed that Bidault was prepared for the idea when Schuman got the French government to support it in its meeting on 8 May 1950. However, leading Christian Democrats also discussed integration in coal and steel in many forums between 1948 and 1950, for example during a study visit by a French Senate commission to North Rhine-Westphalia in the spring of 1949, with meetings between Pezet and von Brentano and Karl Arnold, the state's CDU minister president (Kaiser 2007: 223–227).

The ECSC effectively developed quite neo-corporatist forms of governance, which later informed the sector's carefully negotiated restructuring in the EC in the late 1970s and 1980s. For the Christian Democrats it was clear in any case that European integration in one sector would have to be broadened as soon as possible to horizontal market integration in a customs union and common market. In its public message for 1949, the NEI for the first time committed publicly to treating the Benelux customs union, which was under construction at the time, as a template for wider

7 ACDP 01–009–017, Geneva Circle, 21 November 1949.

European economic integration.[8] With their advocacy of market integration the Christian Democrats pursued three main goals. The first was to utilise the German economic potential as an industrial powerhouse and importer of agricultural products for European reconstruction. The second was to strengthen national economies, enhance growth and raise the welfare of citizens to counter the appeal of the communist ideology and political parties and thus enhance the security of Western Europe more generally. Finally, the third objective was to turn the to-be-created European common market into a third-way transnational market-based societal model between liberal capitalism and Soviet communism – a model that would have to cater for the needs of the core electoral constituencies of Christian democratic parties, especially the middle classes and farmers.

In these different ways, the Christian Democrats – through their cooperation in the NEI, the Geneva Circle and the CD Group in the Common Assembly – created long-term vectors for the later work of the CD/EPP Group in the EP. These concern the CD/EPP Group's broad political and more concrete policy preferences for the EC's institutional deepening and common policies. They also characterise key elements of its internal organisation and practices as well as its relations with other political parties in the EP, as we will now see.

## *Italo-German dominance: composition and governance*

The CD/EPP Group was made up of MEPs from six Member States until 1973, seven (of nine Member States) until 1981 and eight (of ten Member States) until 1986. Until 1973 and again from when first the Spanish Partido Popular (PP) and then the British Conservatives joined in 1992, until 2009, the CD/EPP Group had members from all EC/EU states (see Bardi in Chapter 5 of this book). However, its percentage of MEPs and its internal composition by nationality changed significantly during the 35 years until the EC's transformation into the EU. In 1958, the CD Group had 67 of 142 delegated MEPs, with 38 Socialists and 35 Liberals. By 1968, the CD Group was marginally down to 65 MEPs. Between the 1973 Northern enlargement and the 1979 EP elections, it only had 52 of 189 MEPs, with the Socialists on 66 when Labour Party members joined after the British 1975 membership referendum to remain in the EC.

8 Österreiches Staatsarchiv, Archiv der Republik, BKA/AA, II-pol., Int.14, Zl80.755-pol/49, Botschaft der NEI für 1949.

The CD/EPP Group's relative decline was due in large measure to the electoral decline of Christian democratic parties as seen in the Benelux countries, and the fact that it had no MEPs from the United Kingdom and Denmark. However, the EPP parties did well in the first direct elections in 1979 (Bomsdorf 1980). They gained the largest percentage of the popular vote and ended up with 107 MEPs of 410, only marginally behind the Socialists on 113. However, throughout the 1980s, the gap with the Socialists widened significantly once more. In 1984, the EPP Group won 110 of 434 seats and in 1989, 121 of 518 seats. In 1989, this constituted only 23 % compared to the Socialists' 35 % of all seats (European Parliament 2009a; Fontaine 2009: 593–597).

Compared to the composition of the EP generally, and broader patterns of policy-making in the EC, the CD/EPP Group was characterised by two key features which impacted directly on its internal dynamics. The first concerned the low representation of French parties, which resulted from the Fifth Republic majoritarian voting system, the decline and subsequent dissolution of the MRP in the 1960s, and the shifting party organisation and transnational allegiances in the centre of French politics. In 1968, for example, only two of 65 members of the CD Group were from France. In 1989 six of 81 elected French MEPs joined the EPP Group. This constituted just 5 % of its total of 121 MEPs, which was barely more than in 1968. For historical, economic and political reasons, Franco-German bilateralism heavily dominated intergovernmental relations and bargaining in the EC, however (e.g. Germond and Türk 2008). The low French representation and influence meant that, in contrast to the great importance of bilateral Franco-German co-operation in multilateral party networks in the early post-war period, the CD/EPP Group could do very little to support Franco-German co-ordination at government level later. This was especially true while the German CDU/CSU was out of power at the federal level between 1969 and 1982.

The second key feature was the strong representation of the Italian DC. This was only in part down to its electoral strength. Additionally, the DC profited heavily from the pro-Western centrist parties' decision to exclude the neo-fascist Italian Social Movement (MSI) as well as the Italian Communist Party (PCI) and (initially) the Italian Socialist Party (PSI), who were allied to them until 1956, from the Italian representation in European parliamentary assemblies (Guerrieri 2011). In 1953, the PCI and PSI together gained 35 % of the popular vote in the Italian elections but had no members in the ECSC's Common Assembly. The issue became embroiled in the DC's vociferous internal debate in the 1960s regarding its political opening to the Left. In 1966, DC leader Benigno Zaccagnini still claimed that his party was blocking communist representation in the EP (as in France) out of "political responsibility" (Guerrieri 2011: 54). In contrast, the PCI argued that their exclusion was undemocratic and could obviously not be maintained anyway once the EP was directly elected (Feld 1967). The issue was only resolved in 1969 after the PCI had completed its turn towards Europe and gained nearly 27 % of the popular vote in the 1968 Italian elections (Pons 2010).

As a result of the DC's anti-communist policy, the Italians, with 18 of 38 members, nearly had an absolute majority in the CD Group in the Common Assembly. Initially, the numbers were similarly skewed towards the DC in the EP. In 1968, out of 65 MEPs, 28 were Italian and only 18 German, eight Dutch and six Belgian; there were also three from Luxembourg and two from France.[9] The internal composition only became normalised after 1969. After the first direct elections, the 42 German CDU/CSU MEPs constituted 40 % of the EPP Group and the Italians with 30 members, 28 %. In 1989, when the CDU/CSU did badly in the third direct elections just before the end of the Cold War and German unification, the 32 CDU/CSU MEPs constituted 27 % of the EPP Group and the Italian 27 MEPs 23 %.

Against this background, the CD Group initially developed an informal tripartite relationship between the Italian, German and Benelux groups of MEPs, which strongly influenced its internal governance, including the allocation of the Group and EP posts as well as recruitment for the Group's administration. The Group's working patterns were also characterised by a strong bilateralism between the Germans and Italians, who together formed a numerical majority in the CD/EPP Group, which could greatly facilitate internal policy-making. This bilateralism became especially pronounced during the long reign of Egon Klepsch as Chair of the EPP Group from 1977 to 1982 and again from 1984 to 1992. As early as November 1975, Klepsch wrote to the CDU leader Helmut Kohl that one should aim to make close informal co-operation between the CDU/CSU and the DC before any meeting of the CD Group or the EUCD a habitual, regular practice, to facilitate policy-making.[10] More generally, for Klepsch and the CD/EPP Group, the DC constituted a European bulwark against the challenge from the Left during the 1970s and 1980s. At a meeting between the CD Group, members of the EUCD's Political Bureau and leading DC po-

9 EPP Group Archives, E.3.1, Il Gruppo Democratico Cristiano del Parlamento Europeo, 6.11.1968.

10 ACDP, 01–641–003/1, Klepsch, Persönlich-Vertraulich [für Kohl], 3.11.1975.

liticians like Amintore Fanfani in Rome in May 1976, for example, the CDU Secretary-General Kurt Biedenkopf claimed that the DC was "the only party in Italy to uphold the European idea".[11]

Transcending nationality, the members of the CD/EPP Group were largely united in their strong support for further integration. The notion of self-selection of Europhile delegated and elected MEPs fits particularly well for the members of this Group (Kerr 1973, 79). The CD parties did initially face internal scepticism or opposition against their strong preference for a spatially limited 'core Europe' without the United Kingdom based around the creation of a common market and the dismantling of trade barriers. This is true of some on the MRP Left, who disliked NEI party cooperation and 'core Europe' integration as collusion with Catholic conservatives to protect industry cartels and interests; for nationalists in the CDU like Jacob Kaiser, who wanted to prioritise German unification, if necessary at the expense of Western integration; or Dutch Catholics and Protestants who were initially afraid that supranational integration could jeopardize the interests of small states that could be better defended through intergovernmental negotiation. By the late 1950s, however, such forms of internal dissent were marginal to the point of extinction in most Christian democratic parties creating a climate that was highly conducive to strong support for the further deepening of integration in the direction of 'ever closer union'. As a result, the most pro-integration politicians, who often had formal or informal links with federalist organisations, frequently became members of the EP.

Their shared European integration ideology acted as strong glue that helped the CD/EPP Group transcend internal transnational social, political and cultural divides. These divides included the latent tensions between Christian trade unionists and MEPs close to industry, in particular the farming lobby, which was extremely well-organised within the Group and integrated into the policy community that developed and defended the Common Agricultural Policy (CAP). Their shared European ideology also made it easier for the CD/EPP Group to ignore the Nazi past of several German members, who were in fact at the forefront of propagating federalist solutions for the EC after the war. These members included Hans Furler, who had joined the SA in 1934 and the Nazi party in 1938 and was EP President from 1960 to 1962, and Hans Edgar Jahn, who had become a Nazi party member as early as 1932. After the 'reworking' of the German

11 ACDP, 01–641-004/1, Protokoll der Sitzung der CD-Fraktion unter Teilnahme von Mitgliedern des Politischen Bureaus der EUCD am 6.5.1976 in Rom.

past had started, he resigned his EP mandate in June 1979 after it became known that he had published a heavily anti-Semitic treatise in 1943 (Meyer 2012).

The shared ideological commitment to deeper European integration also made it easier for the Christian Democrats to grapple with the practical problems of inter-cultural communication. Until the 1973 enlargement, the CD Group mainly used French and German for purposes of internal communication.[12] Despite the relatively low number of MEPs in the Group who spoke it as their first language, French was the most important EC language and the first foreign language for most Italian MEPs, if they had one. German in turn was spoken by many MEPs from the Benelux countries, in addition to the CDU/CSU members. English only slowly became more important as the main language of internal communication throughout the 1980s and 1990s. At times, informal communication between Group members remained impossible. Hans-Gert Pöttering, who was first elected to the EP in 1979, for example, recalls (Interview Pöttering, 26.06.2018) that he only ever smiled at a certain Italian DC member as they did not share even a rudimentary knowledge of any one language. As had been the case in the Geneva Circle, the CD/EPP Group leadership drew on the linguistic versatility of cultural mediators to facilitate informal communication. Thus, Klepsch worked closely with Maria Louisa Cortivo from South Tyrol, who was fully bilingual in German and Italian, to manage his cooperation with Italian members and the DC.

The internal composition of the CD/EPP Group made it necessary to strike a delicate balance in the allocation of posts. Until the 1980s, this balance largely reflected the interests of the German, Italian, and Benelux delegations, with some scraps left over for the Irish Fine Gael members after 1973 and the Greek New Democracy MEPs after 1981. The Group leadership sought to achieve such a balance by combining internal posts – especially the Chairmanship – with those available to the Christian Democrats in the EP, especially the prestigious Presidency and the Chairmanships of parliamentary committees (see Bardi in Chapter 5 of this book). The presidencies of the EUCD and – from 1976 onwards – the EPP became more loosely connected to such package deals.

The controversy about the Group Chairmanship in the spring of 1975 shows how challenging it could be to maintain the internal power balance.

---

12 ACDP, 01–641–005/2, Egon A. Klepsch, Arbeit an der Europäischen Einigung. Zum Beitrag der EVP-Fraktion in der 1. Wahlperiode des direkt gewählten Europäischen Parlamentes, Januar 1984.

By this time, Hans August Lücker from the Bavarian CSU had led the Group for five years. When it became clear that he was interested in continuing in this post, the DC issued an informal veto and Giovanni Bersani demanded a 'rejuvenation' of the Group leadership and a change in nationality. The Group should agree 'guidelines' for guaranteeing some form of alternation in the position of Chair. Lücker nonetheless stood for election. However, he only received 24 votes, putting him well short of an absolute majority of members, with 22 ballot papers left blank in protest against the CDU/CSU's support for Lücker.[13]

Jahn then threatened the DC, stating that any new arrangement would have to comprise all relevant posts including the Chairmanship of the EP's hugely influential Political Affairs Committee, which had become a kind of ancestral estate of the DC ever since De Gasperi's proposal for the EPC in the 1950s. In the end, the CD Group opted for the Belgian Alfred Bertrand as a compromise candidate who had made a name for himself in the debates in the EP about institutional reform. Over the course of the following two years, the pieces of the internal power puzzle fell into place once more. The Belgian Leo Tindemans became the first EPP leader in 1976, Emilio Colombo from the DC became EP President in 1977 and Bertrand moved sideways to become Chair of the Political Affairs Committee. As a result, the German delegation was able to reclaim the Group Chairmanship once more, this time for Klepsch, who – as leader of the German delegation from 1975 to 1977 – had played a crucial role in negotiating all of these arrangements.

As the two largest national delegations in the CD/EEP Group until the transformation of the EC into the EU, comparing the distribution of the most important posts between the Italians and Germans reveals interesting preferences and career and behavioural patterns. From 1952 to 1992, the CDU/CSU with Joseph Illerhaus (1966–69), Lücker (1970–75) and Klepsch held the Group Chairmanship for 20 out of 40 years and the DC with Paolo Barbi for only two-and-a-half years from 1982–84. In contrast, the DC had four EP Presidents, with De Gasperi in 1954 and Giuseppe Pella from De Gasperi's death to 1956, Mario Scelba from 1969 to 1971 and Colombo from 1977 to 1979, compared to the one held for the CDU/CSU by Furler. Until 1977, DC politicians also continuously filled the position of Chair of the EP's Political Affairs Committee.

13 EPP Group Archives, A.1.23.4, Protokoll der Fraktionssitzung vom Mittwoch, den 14. Mai 1975 in Strasbourg.

Italian DC politicians tended to regard the EP as a forum for propagating and fostering their broadly federalist agenda for the EC – hence their interest in the Chairmanship of the Political Affairs Committee, which was responsible for institutional issues until the formation of a separate Institutional Affairs Committee in 1982. They also saw it as a suitable means to gain popularity and legitimacy for a national or European career outside of the EP. Their relatively low attendance in the EP and lack of effectiveness in the CD/EPP Group is partly explained with greater difficulties in travelling to Strasbourg and Brussels, especially in the early years. It was also down to the need to participate in the time-consuming internal strife within and between the different *correnti*, the political factions of the DC, to secure their position within their national party. Lastly, it also resulted from the particularities of the Italian electoral system that encouraged physical and media presence in the constituency and in Italy. Their preoccupation with DC and Italian politics – with its peculiar combination of great structural stability paired with frequent government changes and policy activism – made it near impossible for Italian MEPs to invest sufficient time into the demanding managerial role of Group Chair.

Indeed, when the Italians criticised the German Chairmanship in 1975, they suggested Giulio Andreotti, who at that time was Italian economics minister, for the post. Bersani believed that Andreotti could deal with the demands of the Group Chairmanship on the side – something that the other delegations rejected out of hand, especially in the run-up to the first direct elections of the EP originally scheduled for 1978. When Barbi became Group Chair in 1982 in anticipation of Klepsch's election to the Presidency of the EP, which then failed, he did not invest much time and energy into his new post. In fact, Giampaolo Bettamio, the EPP Group's Italian Secretary-General at the time, recalls (Interview Bettamio, 9.11.2018) Barbi's 'absenteeism' and chaotic style, which annoyed the MEPs so much that they were glad to see Klepsch return to the post after the second direct elections in 1984.

At the same time, DC politicians helped to connect the CD/EPP Group with national politics and other EC institutions through their variegated career paths. Thus, Mario Scelba, who had already been Italian Prime Minister in 1954–55 and interior minister, was elected to the Italian Senate in 1968, became President of the DC's National Council in 1971 and acted as EP President from 1969 to 1971. In another example of a political career across the national level and EC institutions, Carlo Scarascia-Mugnozza was a DC member of the CD Group from 1961 to 1972, chaired the Energy and Political Affairs committees and then became one of two Italian members in the European Commission from 1972 to 1977.

The German members on the whole focused more on their EP role both before and after the first direct elections. The likes of Furler, Illerhaus and Lücker never held ministerial posts in Germany. Furler was only briefly Chair of the Foreign Affairs Committee of the German Bundestag during 1959–60. Lücker saw his vocation in fostering European integration and creating and protecting the CAP as its showpiece through his work in the EP. In the regional Bavarian CSU, which was somewhat more pragmatically European with some Gaullist tendencies in the 1960s, Lücker represented the federalist wing. Lücker was strongly influenced by Robert Schuman, the French MRP politician and first EP President from 1958 to 1960, who was a devout Catholic. After the end of his political career, Lücker played a leading role in the campaign for Schuman's beatification in the Catholic Church.

Other German MEPs also had strong European policy expertise, which drew them to their EP work. One excellent example of this is Arved Deringer, a leading European integration lawyer who co-founded the law firm Tessin-Deringer in Bonn/Cologne in 1962, which merged with the international law firm Freshfields in 2000. Deringer was a member of the EP from 1958 to 1970 and he chaired the influential Legal Affairs Committee from 1966 to 1970. As European integration specialists, these German MEPs were given space by their parties to invest time in EP matters, but they never played an influential role in the CDU/CSU.

Moreover, after 1979, many German MEPs had a political career in the EP only. First elected in 1979, Hans-Gert Pöttering, for example, was re-elected as an MEP until 2014. He was EPP Group Chair from 1999 to 2007 and EP President from 2007 to 2009. Elmar Brok, who first entered the EP in 1980, stayed as MEP until 2019. He became one of the most influential EPP MEPs in foreign affairs (see also Gagatek in Chapter 4 of this book). This strong continuity based on a combination of the CDU/CSU's relative electoral stability and EP-centred career paths allowed many German MEPs to develop an excellent understanding of EP politics and extensive networks within the EP and the wider EC/EU institutional system.

All the while, the Group Chair and the MEPs operated in a political structure that largely remained unchanged until 1979 and beyond. The Group was coordinated by its Bureau and led by the Chair. In 1968, for example, alongside Illerhaus the Bureau included, as Vice-Chairs, the Italian Aldo Moro, the Frenchman André Colin and four other MEPs, as well as the three Christian Democrats in the EP Presidium at the time, EP President Alain Poher and the Vice-Presidents Furler and Bersani.[14] Decision-making took place in the meetings of the Group, which were regularly organised in Brussels and Strasbourg. The Group meetings decided the Group's positions on policy issues and its speakers in plenary debates, for example. To facilitate policy formation and decision-making the Group organized so-called Study Days from the beginning. These events could last between two and four days and were devoted to one or more political themes or policy issues, which were chosen to feed into the EC's and EP's evolving agenda. In Oostende in November 1965, for example, the CD Group focused entirely on the ongoing 'Empty Chair' crisis (Bajon 2012) to put pressure on the other five governments not to yield to demands for formal treaty changes by the French President Charles de Gaulle.

Crucially, the Group often organised these Study Days and select Group meetings in the Member States, to align with national political events like elections to enhance publicity both for the national party and the Group. In 1977, the CD Group met in London for the first time, although it had no British members, to inform the British public about its work and create a platform for meetings with Europhile British Conservatives (Fontaine 2009: 609–11). The speeches, papers and results of the Study Days were published in the series *Cahiers Européens* about three times a year. The third issue was devoted to the Commission's proposals for the CAP and published in early 1960, for example. Additionally, the Group put out *DC Europa* to publicise its parliamentary activities more regularly. Later on, the press service *Flash* informed journalists in Strasbourg and Brussels about CD/EPP Group activities, statements and resolutions. The Group's initial interest in creating more publicity was in fact stirred up by competition with the Socialists, who had begun putting out similar – albeit very rudimentary – information to the media reporting on European integration[15] in the early 1960s.

At the administrative level, the Group Secretary-Generals played an influential role in working closely with the Chairmen and Bureau from the beginning. The first in this role was the German Hans-Joachim Opitz, who was appointed in the Common Assembly in 1954 before moving to work for the EP administration after 1959. At this point, the German delegation nominated Carl Otto Lenz, the son of the deceased former state-secretary in the German chancellery and Adenauer confidant, Otto Lenz. Lenz re-

14 EPP Group Archives, E.1, Constitution and rules of the EPP Group.

15 EPP Group Archives, A.4.6, Procès-verbal de la réunion du Bureau du Groupe, 16.11.1959.

mained in this position until 1965 when he was elected to the German Bundestag and later became attorney general at the European Court of Justice (ECJ). However, Lenz's appointment on Adenauer's recommendation provoked a minor controversy. Some members argued that no position could or should be reserved "for candidates from a single country".[16] Shortly afterwards, as a quid pro quo, the Italian Arnaldo Ferragni was appointed Deputy Secretary-General with special responsibility for liaising with the NEI, where he was already active; he then succeeded Opitz in 1965.[17]

At around this time, while the EP was struggling to make political progress in the face of resistance regarding its future direct election – especially from French President Charles de Gaulle – the CD Group's administration was quite small. The delegated MEPs still relied mainly on their respective parliamentary group, administration and personal offices in the national capital and their constituencies both for policy advice and secretarial support, which also prevented any language obstacles for them. Their use of support services in the EP was mainly directed at the secretariats of their parliamentary committees, which slowly began to develop legal and policy expertise on issues of EEC/EC policy-making.

In this environment, at a time when their EP work remained of secondary importance to most delegated MEPs, Ferragni stayed on as Secretary-General until 1972, when he was succeeded by Alfredo di Poi. From 1976 until 1986, Bettamio then worked closely with Group Chairmen Bertrand, Klepsch, Barbi and again Klepsch before he was succeeded by Sergio Guccione (1986–1990) who in turn made space for the German Gerhard Guckenberger (1991–1997). Di Poi and Bettamio both moved on to positions in the EP administration. In contrast, Guccione was recruited back from his role as director with responsibility for the budget in the EP administration.

Thus, for a period of 25 years from 1965 to 1990, the CD/EPP Group administration was headed up by four Italians. Bettamio in particular left his mark by working closely with Klepsch from 1977 to 1982 to professionalise the EPP Group's organisation and practices in the transition to the directly elected parliament. In preparation for the 1979 elections, the EPP Group had already moved to create four permanent Working Groups,

---

16 EPP Group Archives, A.4.6. Procès-verbal de la réunion du Bureau du Groupe, 9.9.1959.

17 EPP Group Archives, A.4.7, Procès-verbal de la réunion du Bureau du Groupe, 13.5.1960.

which replaced the older tradition of ad hoc organisation of groups for the discussion of topical issues. Each of the four new Working Groups covered the work of several EP committees. Each was headed up by an MEP who coordinated the EPP Group's policy-making across the various EP committees interested and involved in a particular issue, the preparation of common positions and voting in the plenary. Now, when the EPP Group did not fill the role of Rapporteur for a new issue in a committee, it appointed a shadow Rapporteur to enhance the Group's expertise and influence on policy-making across all issues.

To give one example, after an overhaul of the Working Group structure in 1982, Working Group A for Political Affairs – which had been numbered C before, but no longer covered budgetary issues – was mainly responsible for foreign policy and institutional matters. It was chaired by Lambert Croux from Belgium with Achillefs Gerokostopoulos from Greece as his deputy. Otto von Habsburg from the Bavarian CSU led on political affairs and Jean Seitlinger from France on institutional matters, with which he had been familiar going back to his leading role in the NEI in the 1950s. Within the EP committee structure, Mariano Rumor from Italy held the Chairmanship of the Political Affairs Committee and Sjouke Jonker from the Netherlands was one of the Vice-Chairs of the newly created Institutional Affairs Committee.[18] Thus, all key constituent groups of the CD/EPP Group – the German, Italian and Benelux parties – plus the Greek and French parties had leading roles in the field of political affairs either within the Group or the EP committee structure.

All policy-making staff were associated with one of the four Working Groups and covered the work of one or more EP committees liaising with their counterparts in the other larger EP Groups and with the officials in the committee secretariats. Moreover, when the EP unblocked the budget for 1980, the EPP Group was able to use its substantially increased budget to grow its administration and to enhance its policy-making competence very significantly. By 1982–83, the Group employed 16 staff with university degrees and responsibility usually for one policy area or committee, in addition to the personal staff of the Group Chair and secretarial staff.[19] Some of the Group's administrators stayed on for a long time, creating a high degree of continuity in terms of personnel, networks and practices. Beatrice Scarascia Mugnozza, the daughter of the Italian MEP and Commissioner Carlo, was initially responsible for institutional matters in the

18 ACDP, 09–001–222.

19 EPP Group Archives, L. Dossier confidentiel, Staff/Organigramme 1982–83.

1980s (Interview Scarascia Mugnozza, 26.06.2018). By 2019, she was still working for the EPP Group, but now had responsibility for relations with national parliaments. Other staff went on to work for the EP administration, including Riccardo Ribera d'Alcalá, who also joined the EPP Group in the 1980s, initially with responsibility for social affairs (Interview Ribera d'Alcalá, 26.09.2018); at the time of writing, Ribera was Director General for Internal Policies of the Union in the EP administration.

Giving the EPP Group a permanent and professional operational structure at the political and administrative levels in this way constituted a crucial internal precondition for effective policy formation and decision-making. This in turn proved essential for the rising voting cohesion in the EPP Group which has been observed in the political science literature about the EP after 1979 (Hix, Noury and Roland 2007: 231). Interestingly, this happened at a time when the EP still had no legislative powers and thus lacked one key institutional incentive for a high level of integration and voting cohesion.[20]

Almost as important as the EPP Group's structural professionalisation were its leadership and informal cooperation and decision-making culture and practices. These aspects were also strongly shaped in the transition from the delegated to the directly elected EP by Klepsch and Bettamio. As Bettamio has recalled (Fraktion EVP/ED 2000: 60), "in Brussels people said that we were a good team. Egon was the most 'Italian' of Germans and I was the most 'German' of the Italians." Building on the new structures, Klepsch proved to be a "very clever manager of crises and opinion formation in the Group", as Thomas Jansen recalls (Interview Jansen, 13.06.2018). As EPP Secretary-General, Jansen worked closely with Klepsch from 1983 to 1994. According to Jansen, Klepsch knew "all procedural rules of the Group and the EP extremely well" (Interview Jansen, 13.06.2018) and led the Group as a "quite tamer", as the German journalist Jürgen Wahl had already called him after his election as Group Chair in 1977.[21] As such, Klepsch invested a lot of time into holding informal conversations with influential MEPs from national delegations to understand their positions and prepare suitable compromise solutions (Kaiser 2020).

Klepsch was perceived as 'Italian' mainly in the sense that he seemed to understand the finesses of Group and EP politics even better than many

20 On these organisational changes and their internal impact, see also Klepsch' review of the first parliamentary term after the 1979 direct elections: ACDP 01-641-005/2, Egon A. Klepsch, Arbeit an der Europäischen Einigung.

21 Kein Platz für Indianerspiele, *Rheinischer Merkur*, 20.5.1977.

Italian MEPs, who should have known them from their national political system and DC party experience. Klepsch had a fine sense for the crucial importance of close co-operation between the German and Italian delegations (Interview Bettamio, 9.11.2018). He learned to speak Italian quite well and worked with the bilingual Cortivo to cultivate his DC contacts. He went to Italy for EPP events, some DC party congresses and Italian elections[22] and he became a close advisor to Chancellor Kohl on DC and Italian politics from the mid-1970s onwards. However, as German MEP Horst Langes (Fraktion EVP/ED 2000: 51) has recalled, Klepsch also sought to outmanoeuvre Italian MEPs or the entire Italian delegation on policy matters, where necessary, for example by starting meetings early and deciding the most important matter straight away, even before all attendees were present.

Thus, despite important long-term continuities as seen in the close co-operation between the German and Italian delegations in the CD/EPP Group, the 1979 direct elections also marked major change in terms of internal organisation and working practices. To begin with, the Group roughly doubled in size and the vast majority of its members already were, or soon became, exclusively members of the EP. As a result of the end of the dual mandate they could devote far more time and energy to EC matters in the EP. They also needed to find themselves something useful to do at a time when the EP already had substantial budgetary powers, but no legislative powers at all. Much of the further increased policy activism in the EPP Group and the EP after 1979 derived from this internal structural incentive, as well as the perceived 'Eurosclerosis' that needed to be overcome.

However, to translate the wide-spread desire among EPP MEPs for greater internal cohesion and increased influence in the EP and beyond into practical politics required entrepreneurial leadership that carefully took the Group's political and cultural heterogeneity into account. Klepsch and Bettamio in particular provided this leadership in the transition from the delegated to the directly elected EP, thus preparing the EPP Group for co-operation and competition in the EP in the fight over positions, influence and the future of European integration more generally. Moreover, they could now build on a much enlarged and professionalised administrative structure with growing policy competence – something that helped the EPP Group and its members to become more independent both from the EP committee secretariats and from national sources of policy advice.

22 See e.g. Egon Klepsch, *Il Popolo*, 3.11.1978.

*Forging alliances: co-operation and competition with other political groups*

In its quest for greater autonomy and influence as a key protagonist in EC policy formation and decision-making, the EPP Group hoped for a long time that the EPP as its associated party organisation could increasingly act as an effective ally in Europeanising EC politics beyond the prevailing patterns of intergovernmental co-operation and limited citizen engagement. At the personal level, working relations were often quite good – for example between Klepsch during his long reign and Bettamio and Guckenberger in the EPP Group, and the EPP leaders Tindemans (1976–85), Piet Bukman (1985–87), Jacques Santer (1987–90) and Wilfried Martens after 1990, as well as Jansen as EPP Secretary-General. However, the EPP as an EC-level political party organisation remained weak. It had small financial resources, had to be cross-subsidised by the EPP Group, and it also suffered from limited political cohesion.

By the early 1980s, the CD/EPP Group had been complaining about the lack of effectiveness, first of the NEI and then of the EUCD after 1965, and finally of the EPP after 1976, for some time. At a meeting of the CD Group Bureau on 6 May 1960 attended by NEI President Théo Lefèvre and Secretary-General Seitlinger, it was decided to enhance co-operation through the appointment of Ferragni for relations with the NEI.[23] Poher, the leader of the CD Group, also demanded that MEPs participate more regularly in NEI Bureau meetings. It was essential to turn the NEI into "a political organisation that can develop a common policy line in economic and social matters".[24]

When the EPP was founded in 1976, it finally created a forum for political parties from the EC only. The choice of name – with the singular 'party' in the title – appeared to indicate a strong European vocation. However, the preparation of the EPP programme for the first direct elections showed the limits of consultation within the EPP and of agreement on socio-economic issues. Its drafting was "almost entirely a German-Belgian affair" and it formulated clear demands only in relation to the institutional issue of "federalisation of the Community", but otherwise remained quite vague (Claeys and Loeb-Mayer 1979: 462). Writing to Kohl at the start of January 1987, Klepsch commented that the EPP's "contribution to EC-level integration of opinion and policy formation" among the Christian

23 EPP Group Archives, A.4.7, Procès-verbal de la réunion du Bureau du Groupe, 13.05. 1960.

24 Ibid.

Democrats remained "practically nil", despite all efforts. It contributed nothing to "forging consensus for practical politics". It was entirely left to the EPP Group to "clarify and integrate national interests".[25]

For a long time, the EPP party organisation had been neglected by the member parties as they were in power most of the time in most EC Member States. With EC policy-making de facto remaining quite intergovernmental during the 1960s and beyond, not least under the influence of de Gaulle, it seemed pointless to invest too much time into transnational party co-operation. In addition, the Christian Democrats' party organisation had been created before the formation of the ECSC and the EEC. Its origins created vectors in terms of structures and membership that proved difficult to break. Some member parties felt a strong allegiance to the Swiss and Austrian parties, who had played a leading role in fostering transnational party co-operation after 1945, and a moral obligation to support Christian Democrats in exile – whether from Eastern Europe or the Basque country and other regions of Spain (Kaiser and Kosicki 2021). However, even when the birth of the EPP created an EC-level platform for party co-operation, the functional incentives for greater integration of policy formation and decision-making were much stronger for the EPP Group than the EPP, which helps explain the continued dysfunctionality in their organisations and relations.

The EPP Group also acutely felt the decline in its numerical and percentage representation in the EP resulting from its parties' declining vote share in national and then, from 1979, European elections, and of the northern enlargement. As it had no members from the United Kingdom, the CD Group was relegated to second place in the EP in 1975, when the Labour Party MEPs joined the EP after the British referendum about continued membership. The situation got significantly worse for the EPP Group with the Southern enlargement to include Spain and Portugal. At the start of 1987, Klepsch calculated that the Socialists' far greater number of Spanish MEPs meant that, even together with the European Democrats (ED) led by the British Conservatives, the Liberals and the Progressive Democrats with the French Gaullists, the EPP Group could no longer muster a majority in the EP. At least, Klepsch added, there was no majority of left-wing parties in the newly constituted EP either.[26]

Additionally, the EPP Group – unlike the EPP as a party – was preoccupied with policy matters with an EC competence only, from institutional

25 ACDP, 01–641–017/2, Klepsch to Kohl, 6 January 1987.
26 ACDP, 01–641–017/2, Klepsch to Kohl, 6 January 1987.

deepening to budgetary matters and other policy issues like the CAP or regional policy. In contrast, the EPP member parties had broader political concerns that also touched on domestic matters and what later became known as sharing 'best practice' in dealing with similar policy challenges. Moreover, until the early 1990s, the national parties did not realise the full potential of their more effective cooperation for steering intergovernmental negotiations within the EC through prior co-ordination of their negotiating positions – something that co-shaped the Intergovernmental Conference that led to the Treaty of Maastricht (see also Johansson in Chapter 2 of this book).

The CD Group first felt its declining status and influence in the EP even before northern enlargement when the German Social Democrat Walter Berendt was elected to the EP Presidency with the support of the Liberals in 1971. Coming a mere two years after the CDU/CSU had been ousted from power in Germany and replaced by the same alliance between Social Democrats and Liberals, this experience constituted a nasty wake-up call for the CD Group. In fact, the election of EP Presidents serves as a good indicator for the increased politicisation of EP politics in anticipation of the first direct elections and especially afterwards, which provided the strongest incentive yet for greater EPP Group cohesion. In 1953, the Belgian Socialist Spaak had been elected to the Presidency with the votes of Christian Democrats from the Benelux countries. In 1960, the Christian Democrat Furler became the office-holder with the votes of the German Social Democrats. However, Berendt's election in 1971 already reflected the greater political polarisation in some EC countries, such as Germany, during the 1970s.

From 1977 on, the politicisation of the elections to the EP Presidency became even stronger. At this point, the CD Group under the new leadership of Klepsch was increasingly concerned about being pushed "into a minority role" in the EP, with the Socialists apparently establishing a "hegemonic position in the parliamentary hierarchy". In Klepsch's view, it was necessary to break the "socialist dominance" by constructing an alliance with the Liberals and the British Conservatives. For this to work, however, it was necessary to make the Liberals "an attractive offer".[27] At this point, Klepsch's close co-operation with Martin Bangemann, a leading member of the Liberal Group, paid off in the form of an agreement that led to the election of Colombo to the EP Presidency for 1977–79 and then of the

27 ACDP 01–641–003/1, Klepsch, Notiz über die Wahl des Präsidenten des Europäischen Parlaments, 9.5. 1977.

French liberal Simone Veil as the first President of the directly elected EP during 1979–81.

When Klepsch spectacularly lost the EP Presidency election to the Dutch social democrat Piet Dankert in 1982, this experience had a profound impact on his own strategic thinking, as we will see below. In fact, while Klepsch's internal organisational and leadership skills were beyond doubt, many members of the EPP Group – including several of his German colleagues – believed that he lacked stature within the EP, let alone in the European public, to qualify to follow Veil in the office of EP President. Among the CDU MEPs, Hans Katzer, a former German minister in the 1960s, encouraged Tindemans to stand against Klepsch arguing that the EP needed "a personality with intellectual and statesmanlike charisma, not an executive director" – like Klepsch.[28] Within the EPP Group, Klepsch narrowly secured his candidature by 56 to 48 votes against Tindemans.[29] Of the 42 German MEPs, twelve voted for Tindemans.

In the end, Klepsch lost to Dankert because many British conservative MEPs voted against him and for the Dutch Socialist contrary to the advice of the Conservative Central Office and British Prime Minister Margaret Thatcher (Crowson 2007: 205–6). They were annoyed by Klepsch's support for the continued use of Strasbourg as a seat of the EP, which they regarded as a waste of taxpayers' money. James Scott-Hopkins, the ED Group leader, also believed that the British Conservatives had received informal assurances from Klepsch back in 1977 that they and not the EPP could fill the EP Presidency in 1982 in return for voting for Colombo in 1977 and Veil in 1979. Finally, Klepsch was a red rag for some Conservative MEPs, partly because he had once been seen to operate the newly established electronic voting system in the EP for an absent EPP colleague – an obviously illegal practice that subsequently became known in the EP as 'klepschen'.

Klepsch's defeat led to bitter recriminations within the EPP and the ED Groups. Klepsch replaced Katzer as one of the Vice-Presidents of the EP. In the ED Group, Lord Plumb, the later EP President, compiled a list of 'traitors' who had voted for a socialist as EP President – an absolute horror for Thatcher – and Scott-Hopkins was stripped of the Chairmanship.[30] What was perhaps the greatest voting disaster for the EPP Group in the history of the EP accentuated the extreme need for internal unity. More-

28 Schließlich wollten die Linken Mitterrand nicht weh tun, *Frankfurter Rundschau*, 10.7.1981.

29 Chance für einen Deutschen, *Rheinischer Merkur*, 18.9.1981.

30 Der CDU-Fuhrmann Hans Katzer verlor den letzten Zügel, *Hamburger Abendblatt*, 22.1.1982.

over, it also demonstrated – not just in Klepsch's mind – the strategic objective of maximising the EPP Group's own size and voting power, as well as its ability to form cross-party alliances.

This dual functional need for increasing its size and voting power and making the Group central to EP politics and policy-making clashed with concerns about a potential German hegemonic role. After all, Kohl had already pushed hard for the creation of the EPP in 1976 to create a broader centre-right alliance in Western European politics in the image of the CDU as a people's party. What was widely seen as an attempted opening to the Right by the more centrist parties in the Benelux countries and Italy had even led to the DC's initial refusal to join such a new EC-level party organisation (Kaiser 2013: 13). Alongside concerns about an ideological shift to the Right, other member parties also feared that the creation of the EPP in this form could foster German dominance in the new organisation, which would be accentuated further by the financial prowess of the CDU/CSU and its associated Konrad Adenauer Foundation.

Enlarging the EPP Group to include traditionally conservative parties could potentially raise similar concerns in the EP. After all, ideologically the German contingent would be best placed to act as a hinge between the more centrist CD parties and new member parties that were not steeped in the traditions of political Catholicism and Catholic social teaching. Moreover, as we saw in the previous section, many German MEPs had their political career in the EP only, which made it easier for them collectively to act as an anchor point in the EPP Group and to give it much-needed stability beyond its enlargements. More generally, as academic studies demonstrated at the time, the German delegation of 81 MEPs in the EP, despite being the same size as those from France, Italy, and the United Kingdom, was "more homogeneous". As the German MEPs were concentrated in the two largest EP Groups, the delegation was in a "more dominant position than numerical parity ... would indicate" (Fowler and Pohuis 1983: 172).

During the period of Kohl's leadership of the CDU, he and Klepsch were very sensitive to the resulting fears about German hegemony in the EPP Group and party organization. In fact, when Kohl attended a meeting of the CD Group in Bonn in March 1976 in the run-up to the German federal elections, which the CDU/CSU lost only very narrowly, he explicitly emphasised that the CDU did not aim for a hegemonic role at all when recommending closer co-operation with the British Conservatives.[31] During the 1980s, this continued sensitive approach guaranteed that the strong

31 EPP Group Archives, A.1.24, Procès-verbal de la réunion du groupe, 4.-5.3.1976.

functional incentives for increasing the EPP Group's size and effectiveness in forming cross-party alliances overrode residual concerns about possible German hegemony more easily than in the EPP as a party organisation.

These functional incentives to maximise power and policy influence exercised considerable pressure on the EPP Group and its leadership not just to increase its internal integration and voting cohesion, but also, first and foremost, to increase its size. Throughout the 1980s, the EPP Group's greatest strategic challenge remained not having any member from the United Kingdom as one of four EC countries with equal representation in the EP. At party level, the German CDU/CSU had well-established contacts with the British Tories since the 1960s, which were mainly fostered and maintained by protestant and Northern German members. Upon becoming CDU leader in 1973, however, the Catholic Kohl also invested much time and energy into developing closer links with the Tories and Thatcher, their new leader after 1975. The two parties' international offices coordinated the inter-party contacts (Kaiser 2013).

On the British side leading Catholic party members usually felt greater affinity with the continental European Christian democratic intellectual and programmatic traditions (Crowson 2007). Chris Patten, an official in the Conservative Research Department – where he worked on the party's international links – from 1966 onwards, is a case in point. Elected to the House of Commons in 1979 he was one of the most vocal supporters of close co-operation with the EPP and the EPP Group. The EPP and EPP Group also had close connections with other leading pro-Europeans like Geoffrey Howe, Michael Heseltine, Douglas Hurd and Malcolm Rifkind. As Minister for Europe, Rifkind visited the EP in April 1985, for example, to discuss the ongoing work of the Dooge Committee on the EC's institutional reform. He held several meetings with Klepsch and other EPP politicians, alongside MEPs from his own party and from the Institutional Affairs Committee (Kaiser 2018a, 40).

Even more importantly from the perspective of the EPP Group, however, the British Conservative contingent in the ED Group on the whole had more strongly pro-integration attitudes as long as the self-recruitment of pro-Europeans still operated until well into the 1990s, than Thatcher and the national party – something that was regularly reflected in how they voted in the EP or abstained from voting to avoid challenging Thatcher directly, especially over institutional questions such as the 1984 DTEU (Kaiser 2018a). Moreover, after the debacle of the 1982 elections for the EP Presidency, the EPP Group worked hard to restore good relations with the Tories, leading to the division of the Presidency between the Group itself (Pierre Pflimlin) and the ED Group (Lord Plumb) after the second direct elections. Analysing the EPP Group's relations with other Groups in the EP at the start of January 1984, Klepsch concluded that the ED Group was quite cohesive internally and reliable in parliamentary co-operation. Both groups also had much in common in major policy areas, especially European foreign policy co-operation and economic policy. Relations were more difficult regarding the budget and the CAP, where the Conservatives were keen tightly to control expenditure.[32]

Thatcher's resignation and her replacement as party leader and British Prime Minister with the more Europhile John Major in November 1990 finally paved the way for a realignment between the Conservatives and the EPP Group. After many months of confidential talks managed by Klepsch until his election to the EP Presidency in January 1992, and then by Tindemans, the Tories applied for the special status of 'allied membership' in the EPP Group without actually joining the EPP as a party organisation.[33] The new rule 5b of the EPP Rules of Procedure stipulated that such an allied membership was possible if a party subscribed "to the basic policies of the Group of the European People's Party and if they accept the Rules of Procedure" – a solution that, in their perspective at the time, allowed the Conservatives to maintain sufficient ideological distance from the EPP, particularly with regard to its essentially federalist objectives for European integration, which were not popular among the Tory rank-and-file or in the British public more generally. At the same time, the EPP Group and the British Conservatives together could maximise their influence in the EP.

The EC's Southern enlargement constituted a different but similarly difficult challenge for the EPP Group. Faced with the prospect of EC accession by Greece, Spain and Portugal, Klepsch already warned in a meeting of the EPP Group on 19 September 1979 that further EC enlargements "will pose structural problems for us", as Christian Democracy as a postwar intellectual and political party phenomenon was largely confined to the EC founding Member States.[34] In Greece, the EPP Group struggled to find a partner, as the New Democracy founded by Konstantin Karamanlis after the end of the military dictatorship in 1974 initially wavered between allying itself with the EPP or the ED Group. However, its strong pro-integration stance greatly facilitated its eventual accession to the EPP Group,

32 ACDP, 01–641–005/2, Egon A. Klepsch, Arbeit an der Europäischen Einigung. Zum Beitrag der EVP-Fraktion in der 1. Wahlperiode des direkt gewählten Europäischen Parlamentes, Januar 1984.

33 EPP Group Archives, L. Dossier confidentiel, Membership EPP Group, 31.3.1992.

34 ACDP, 01–641–007/1, Rede von Egon A. Klepsch anlässlich der Fraktionssitzung der EVP am 19.9.1979 in Brüssel.

alongside its much greater size and influence in the EP compared to the ED Group.

The EPP Group had even greater difficulty in identifying electorally successful strong partners on the Iberian peninsula after the collapse of the Salazar and Franco regimes there in 1974–75. In fact, since 1966, Spanish exiles comprising various Catholics and Christian Democrats opposed to the Franco regime, as well as the Basque and Catalan regionalists, had formed a disparate group in the EUCD.[35] In the run-up to the first free elections in Spain in 1977, two national-level Christian democratic parties and three regionalist parties created an electoral alliance, the Equipo Demócratico Cristiano (EDC). However, despite the financial and political backing of the EPP Group and several EPP member parties (Kaiser and Salm 2009), it only gained a dismal 1.3 % of the vote. Anticipating this outcome, Fernando Álvarez de Miranda, a leading member of the left-wing Christian Izquierda Democrática, left to create a breakaway group and allied himself with Adolfo Suárez, formerly a leading member of the Falange, who won the elections. Further to the Right, Manuel Fraga Iribarne, a minister from 1962–67, founded the Alianza Popular (AP) in 1976, which was initially a party of Francoists.

Co-opting the Spanish Christian Democrats into the EUCD in the 1960s created a long-term vector that largely determined the CD/EPP Group's response to the regime change in the mid-1970s. Alongside the German parties and their associated political foundations, the Group played a leading role in strengthening transnational networks and providing external support for the EDC's organisation and preparation for the 1977 elections. However, when Suárez's heterogenous coalition collapsed in 1981–2 and the Socialists came to power, the CD/EPP Group was left with the prospect of having no significant representation after the forthcoming accession by Spain as the fifth-largest Member State. Klepsch and the EPP Group thus played a key role in establishing closer links with the AP during its transformation into the PP in 1989 – an attempt to modernise its programme and break out of the Francoist electoral ghetto. This in turn greatly facilitated its accession to the EPP and EPP Group under the new leadership of José Maria Aznar.

Poaching the PP from the ED Group that it had initially joined in 1987 followed the earlier decision by the Bavarian CSU and its associated Hanns Seidel Foundation to work with the AP and introduce it to the conserva-

35 ACDP, 09–007–030, UEDC/EUCD, Procès-verbal de la réunion du bureau, Rome, 17.12.1966.

tive European Democratic Union (Gehler et al. 2018; Kaiser 2013). The PP's switch to the EPP and EPP Group not only symbolised its transformation into a more mainstream centre-right party; it also – together with the Tories' accession – reflected the EPP Group's transformation from a Christian democratic organisation with a conservative Greek annex to a centre-right people's party in line with the CDU/CSU's nature and role in German politics and ambition at the time of the EPP's creation in 1976. It is not surprising, then, that the effectively liberal-conservative Portuguese Social Democratic Party also moved from the Liberal Group to the EPP Group in 1996. In Portugal, the EPP Group had played a leading role in facilitating the democratic transition and constitution of political parties to the right of the Socialists in the mid-1970s. Lücker and Bertrand had led trips to explore the situation in Portugal and identify partners during the Carnation Revolution in July and December 1974.[36] However, like in Spain, the EPP and EPP Group had been unable to build an electorally strong EPP-style party in the country.

The integration of the Greek, Spanish, UK and Portuguese parties between 1981 and 1996 clearly marked a shift to the Right within the originally much more centrist CD/EPP Group. Crucially, the EPP Group's simultaneous turn towards closer cross-party co-operation with the Socialists after 1984 and especially after 1989, when the two Groups began to operate an informal grand coalition, assuaged concerns among the Benelux and Italian parties and MEPs about the effects of its enlargement on the Group's programmatic orientation.

The rise of grand coalition politics in the EP also had clear functional motivations. In fact, political science research at the time predicted (Rattinger 1982: 146) that fragmented parliaments were likely to produce coalitions of large parties as they minimised the coordination needs and maximised political benefits. In the case of the EP, co-operation between the two largest groups promised to facilitate the distribution of posts in the Praesidium and the committees. Both Groups also essentially agreed on expanding the EC budget, especially the non-compulsory expenditure, and progress in new EC policy fields like environmental protection to demonstrate the positive impact of the EC and the EP on citizen's everyday lives. Finally, the EP's involvement in the legislative process following the SEA

---

36 ACDP, 009–004–025, K.J. Hahn, Rapport sur un voyage au Portugal, 2, 3 et 4 mai 1974, no date; K.J. Hahn, Bref rapport sur la visite de la délégation de groupe démocrate-chrétien du Parlement Européen, accompagnée du secrétaire général adjoint de l'UEDC, au Portugal les 16, 17, et 18 décembre 1974, 14.1.1975.

also required closer cooperation, if the EP as an institution wanted to maximise its influence on EC politics.

Moreover, neither the Socialists nor the EPP Group could rely on stable alternative coalition arrangements in the medium-term. On the Left, the Communists were a disparate bunch and unreliable partners for the Socialists on a number of occasions, such as when the Italian PCI voted with the EPP Group for Colombo as EP President in 1977, during the historic Italian compromise between 1976 and 1980. From 1984 onwards, the even more disparate Rainbow Group was initially quite hostile to the EC, especially the German Greens. At the same time, from the EPP Group's perspective, the Liberal Group contained Left-liberals who could be tempted by centre-left co-operation, and the French Gaullists still had strong intergovernmental preferences for European integration. With the French Socialists ending their domestic experiment of cooperation with the Communists in 1983 and increasingly supporting the EC's institutional deepening and the British Labour Party moderating its own Eurosceptic stance after Neil Kinnock's election to the leadership in 1983, cross-party cooperation with the Socialists no longer faced any insurmountable ideological barriers.

The process of rapprochement between the two largest Groups after 1984 was additionally facilitated by the fact that both had large German contingents. These German MEPs largely agreed on the EC's institutional deepening. They were also keen to overcome the previous ideological polarisation from the times when Kohl had used the election slogan "Freedom or Socialism" in the 1976 German elections. The influence of the German contingents was symbolised by the simultaneous Group leadership of Rudi Arndt, who was close to Willy Brandt, the leader of the Socialist International, and Klepsch from 1984–89. The pair worked together closely, and were known in the EP as "the two big Germans" (Interview Dastoli, 10.10.2017). Arndt was the archetypical pragmatic Social Democrat. In a position paper for the Socialist Group he had already asked their leftist internal component the rhetorical question back in 1980: "Does the majority of the group want Parliament to be a debating club for world affairs or does it view Parliament more as a forum in which realistic socialist demands should be put forward and carried?"[37] At the same time, Klepsch continuously warned Kohl against what he called the "theory centre-right"

37 HAEU, GSPE-69, Paper on the position of the Socialist Group in the European Parliament, Draft by Rudi Arndt, 25.08.1980.

and insisted that the EPP Group had to keep all options for co-operation open, including with the Socialists.[38]

This rapprochement and the resulting grand coalition politics facilitated pragmatic decisions such as the division of the EP Presidency after 1989, with Klepsch getting elected in 1992 following the Spanish Socialist Enrique Barón Crespo. Furthermore, it strengthened the EP's hand within the new treaty framework and legislative process of the SEA. Crucially, it also facilitated the convergence between the two Groups, their member parties and national governments in terms of their constitutional preferences, which was a precondition for the successful negotiation of the Treaty of Maastricht as a great reform package (see also Johansson in Chapter 2 of this book).

In addition to the EPP Group's numerical growth in terms of MEPs and administration, its professionalisation and increased policy-making capacity discussed in the previous section, the 1979 direct elections had other impact: on the increased politicisation of the EPP Group and its positioning in relation to other parties and the search for cross-party consensus in the EP's centre. Faced with the erosion of its previously dominant role in the EP after the first and second EC enlargements, and with the looming perspective of the direct elections and the possible later increase in the EP's powers, the EPP Group became much more concerned about its own share of formal posts and roles and its informal influence on EP policy- and decision-making patterns.

At first, the EPP Group responded to the dual challenge of the rise of Socialist parties and its own historical, intellectual and organisational limitation to continental Western Europe by trying to form a centre-right alliance in the EP. However, this alliance proved to be fragile, as the 1982 elections to the EP Presidency showed. Under Klepsch's leadership the EPP Group subsequently focused on transforming and absorbing electorally successful partners in the new Member States and creating a formal alliance with the British Conservatives with the long-term aim of becoming the largest Group in the EP again. At the same time, however, it sought to buttress its central position in EP politics by working with the Socialist Group in an informal grand coalition – something that Klepsch prepared carefully with Arndt from 1984 onwards. With this dual strategy, the EPP Group succeeded in becoming the key power broker in the EP (see Bardi in Chapter 5 of this book). 'Governing' without or against the EPP Group eventually became practically impossible.

38 ACDP, 01–641–017/2, Klepsch to Kohl, 6.1.1987.

### Federalist vocation: deepening European integration

The EPP Group's professionalisation after 1979, and its strategic focus on its own enlargement and buttressing its role in the EP, contributed greatly to making it central to the EP's system-building function: demanding and facilitating the EC's institutional deepening, including endowing the EP with greater budgetary and legislative powers. For the EPP Group, the end-point of the process of constitutionalising the EC was a European parliamentary system in which the EP would – grosso modo – have the same powers and fulfil the same functions as national parliaments did in the Member States.

In the prevailing political language at the time, the EPP Group supported a dual strategy of combining 'small steps' to enhance the EC's decision-making effectiveness and strengthen the EP's role within the scope of the existing treaties, with demanding substantial treaty reform. The CD Group effectively agreed on such a dual strategy as early as 1972, when it set up an ad hoc Working Group in co-operation with the EUCD, which met several times. It comprised influential MEPs including the former Commission President Walter Hallstein. Its task was to discuss institutional reform questions in response to the debate that Member State governments were now beginning to engage with, about creating some form of European 'union'. At one of the meetings, the CD Group Chair Lücker admitted that one "would have to work with the current treaties and existing institutional set-up for some time". Scelba, formerly EP President, expressed his belief that it was both necessary and possible to improve the EP's role without treaty changes. Lücker also insisted, however, that "in the long-run, the EC's enlargement makes treaty change inevitable".[39] In the resolution resulting from the Working Group deliberations, the EPP Group demanded "greater EP powers", both regarding the budget and its "legislative participation in the production of EC legal norms generally and especially those with fiscal implications". The EC would have to transform into a "community 'sui generis' of a federal character". At that point, a European government would have to depend on parliamentary support.[40]

Although the EPP Group played a key role in shaping it, the policy of 'small steps' enjoyed broad inter-party support in the EP, even among

39 ACDP, 09/001/071/1, Arbeitsgruppe Institutionelle Probleme, 11.2.1972.

40 ACDP, 09–001–110/4, Entschließung der Arbeitsgruppe UEDC-CD-Fraktion des Europäischen Parlaments zur konstitutionellen und institutionellen Fortentwicklung der Europäischen Gemeinschaft, 4.04.1972.

those who were sceptical or hostile to the EC's constitutionalisation. The limited approach generated some successes. These included enhancing the EP's influence on the EC budget; somewhat strengthening its weak position in policy-making; and expanding its practice of own initiative reports to propose common solutions to new policy challenges and to demand the expansion of EC powers over new policy fields.

The Luxembourg Treaty of 1970 and the Brussels Treaty of 1975 created the basis for the EP's role in the EC's budgetary process (Corbett 1998, 93). In a 1969 report to influence the Luxembourg Treaty, which was drafted by Furler as Rapporteur, the EP had already demanded full budgetary co-decision powers.[41] In a 1972 follow-up report again written by Furler, the EP complained that it had only gained significant powers over the EC's non-compulsory expenditure. Here, it could overrule the Member States with a three-fifths majority. However, this type of expenditure only made up 3 % of the budget in the beginning. Furler and the EP castigated this rule as an "intolerable limitation" of its powers (European Parliament 1972). The Brussels Treaty, which came into force in 1978, only slightly modified the budgetary process. Within existing ceilings, the EP at least had the final say on allocating funding between competing budget lines – something that became more relevant as the percentage of non-compulsory expenditure continued to rise during the 1980s.

The EPP Group worked closely with the Liberals and Socialists to fight these limitations tooth and nail. In the autumn of 1979, the directly elected EP rejected the budget for 1980 (Corbett 1998: 97–113). In the end, it passed the budget in July 1980, not least to get sufficient resources for itself, in what was little more than a face-saving exercise. After this experience, the Budget Committee adhered to what became known internally as the Adonnino doctrine (Fontaine 2009: 212), named after Pietro Adonnino, the Italian Christian Democrat MEP and EP Rapporteur for the 1981 budget. From then onwards, the EP successfully fought a war of attrition with the Council to increase non-compulsory expenditure. The MEPs were keen to demonstrate to EC citizens that they could make a tangible difference, not just institutionally, but also through creating European funding programmes in policy areas like education and culture (Calligaro 2013; Patel 2013). As Richard Corbett has argued, however, the conflict over the 1980 budget also radicalised many MEPs who had invested greater hopes

41 HAEU, PE0–1022, Bericht im Namen des Politischen Ausschusses, über die Entwicklung der Befugnisse des Europäischen Parlaments, insbesondere auf haushaltsrechtlichem Gebiet, 3.10.1969.

into a policy of small steps (Corbett 1998: 99; see also Bardi in Chapter 5 of this book).

Incremental change through small steps also characterised the EP's involvement in the legislative process in the early 1980s. Under the EEC Treaty, the EP had a right to be consulted on some legislative texts, a provision that the Council agreed under pressure from the EP to generalise to all legislative and non-legislative texts during the 1960s. In 1973, the Commission consented to consult the EP on all policy proposals. It also promised to send all formal proposals for legislation to the EP as well as the Council, and to express its views in the EP's plenary on amendments put forward by the EP. The Commission and Council also agreed to reconsult the EP in the event of major changes to the legislative text. For the case of legislation with possible budgetary implications, a joint declaration by Parliament, Council and the Commission dated 4 March 1975 instituted the 'conciliation procedure', which promised to open up wider opportunities for the EP to influence the legislative process (Corbett 1998: 113–116).

The ECJ handed the EP a potentially more powerful weapon in its 1980 'Isoglucose' ruling (Leopold 1982: 454–459). The Court decided that consultation of the EP constituted "the means which allows the Parliament to play an actual part in the legislative process of the Community. Such a power represents an essential factor in the institutional balance intended by the treaty." In revising its own Rules of Procedure following the first direct elections, the EP eagerly took up this ECJ invitation to strengthen its role by delaying or blocking a proposal. Henceforth, according to its new rules, it could decide to delay its final vote on a proposal until the Commission took a position on its amendments, and if it rejected one or more of the amendments, the EP could refer the proposal back to the responsible committee. It could thus delay the entire legislative process. While the EP was still lacking the power to make law, it at least compelled the Commission and the Council to treat its involvement in the legislative process as more than a meaningless routine procedure (Nicolas 1981).

Initiative reports constituted the last of the three types of small steps to enhance the EP's role in EC politics after 1979. Endowed with greater policy-making capacity it promoted several policy ideas that were subsequently taken up by the Commission, such as the introduction of a European passport or enfranchising EC citizens for European elections, wherever they lived (Lodge 1985: 51). The EPP Group also used such initiative reports to kick-start new policy developments in the EC.

In contrast to the policy of 'small steps', which largely united EP Groups, the EPP Group played an outstanding role in promoting treaty reform for constitutionalising the EC (see Johansson in Chapter 2 of this book). In part, it assumed this role by default, as the Socialists were for a long time disunited on the issue of the constitutional future of European integration. While many Socialists in countries such as Italy and Belgium supported the notion of a federal Europe – at least as a long-term objective – the Dutch Labour Party initially followed a much more pragmatic institutional approach after 1945, and the German Social Democrats even boycotted the work of the Ad Hoc Assembly on the EPC in 1953 for fear that it would jeopardise German unification. Later, the French Socialists increasingly turned into sceptical Europeans, when François Mitterrand as party leader put the ideological objective of creating what he called a 'socialist Europe' through EC-level welfare policies above the question of its political-institutional future. Moreover, as a result of the British Labour Party's continuous drift to the Left during the 1970s, its new leader Michael Foot, elected in 1980, even demanded a British exit from the EC. Consequently, views in the Socialist Group on treaty reform after 1979 initially ranged from support for federal union among Italian and other federalists to the British Anti-marketeers' fundamentalist opposition to any institutional deepening, preventing the largest EP Group from playing a meaningful collective role in the debate about the future of the EC.

At the same time, however, the Christian Democrats had played such a role in the debate about, and the practical politics of, European integration from the beginning – a role that it cultivated as the core component of its own remembrance discourse. The CD/EPP Group's habitual references to the post-war political heritage of Schuman, Adenauer and De Gasperi constituted a distinctly Christian democratic version of the 'founding father' narrative. This narrative served as discursive glue to paper over the Group's pronounced heterogeneity on socio-economic issues, socialize new member parties into its pro-integration consensus, and attract electoral support in times of strong permissive consensus on the desirability of further European integration.

In the early post-war period, the continental Western European Christian Democrats strongly supported forms of 'core Europe' integration as in the ECSC and the EEC. However, regarding its most desirable institutional set-up, some were pragmatic while others supported federalist solutions. In discussions in the informal Geneva Circle in December 1948, for example, some participants agreed with the French MRP politician Georges Bidault that "results [are more important] than their legal form".[42] Earlier in the

42 Archives Nationales, AP10/519, Geneva Circle, 22 December 1948.

same year, however, François de Menthon, another leading MRP politician, had prepared the first draft of a constitution for a united Europe following the European Movement's congress at The Hague. Large sections of the Italian DC were also enthusiastic federalists. In September 1948, the NEI passed a political resolution at its congress in The Hague, envisaging a bicameral system as a long-term institutional solution. This system would have a directly elected chamber of deputies and a second chamber of Member State representatives.[43]

Once the ECSC became operational, the Christian Democrats took a pragmatic approach to institutional issues at the intergovernmental level, for example when negotiating the EEC Treaty. Later, during the 1960s, they had no other choice because of de Gaulle's preferences, if they wanted to maintain the EEC, implement the policies foreseen in the Treaty and secure its legal integrity while making pragmatic concessions in the Luxembourg compromise of January 1966 (Bajon 1966). At the same time, the CD Group upheld the constitutionalisation paradigm. As Sandro Guerrieri (2015) has shown, not only was EPC article 38 inserted in the European Defence Community Treaty on the initiative of Taviani on behalf of De Gasperi, but the Christian Democrats subsequently also dominated the proceedings of the ECSC's Ad Hoc Assembly that drafted the EPC Treaty during 1952–53; not just in terms of numbers, but also its political agenda. Among its leading members were two lawyers, Heinrich von Brentano, CDU/CSU parliamentary party leader in the Bundestag and later foreign minister, and Pierre-Henri Teitgen, the MRP leader at the time.

The CD Group created a strong vector from post-war party networks and existing constitutional blueprints to the EPC and beyond. Taviani, von Brentano, and Teitgen had all been highly active in the NEI and the Geneva Circle. They shared a broadly Catholic continental vision of reconciliation and European integration. They made sure to introduce many elements into the draft EPC Treaty of the constitutional blueprint prepared by de Menthon in 1948. As a result of the activism of CD Group members, the draft EPC Treaty contained the provision, for example, that the EPC would have a two chamber system: one directly elected parliament and a 'senate' constituted of members appointed by the national parliaments, who would, by majority vote, elect the EPC's executive (Scalingi 1980) – a constitutional solution that has cropped up in different forms in debates about treaty reform ever since (Judge and Earnshaw 2003: 278).

---

43 ACSP, Nachlass Josef Müller, Entschließung, Politischer Ausschuss, NEI-Kongress, The Hague, 17–19 September 1948.

After the failure of the European Defence Community (and with it, the EPC) in the French Assemblée Nationale at the end of August 1954, the CD Group was also at the forefront of EP efforts to push for some form of relaunch of European integration, as it was frequently called at the time. After the death of De Gasperi on 19 August 1954, leading CD Group members such as Teitgen, Poher, the German CDU politician Hermann Kopf, the Dutch female member Margaretha Klompé and the Belgian Pierre Wigny, who later became a member of the first EEC Commission, supported the election of another Italian, Pella, to the Presidency of the EP as a symbol of its continued federalist vocation. Moreover, long before the official initiatives by the Benelux and German governments in the spring of 1955, the CD Group debated restarting European integration in the economic field in October 1954.[44] As Christian Salm (2017) has shown, the CD Group subsequently played the leading role in the Political Affairs Committee, too, with Rapporteur Klompé and a resulting EP resolution demanding a European relaunch. As Klompé insisted in the EP, "We must never forget we are a political institution, and not an Assembly of technocrats" (Guerrieri 2015: 398). In January 1955, Pella then travelled to the ECSC capitals to promote the EP's proposals for a relaunch – a process that fed into the subsequent government proposals, the Messina conference and the intergovernmental negotiations that led to the signing and ratification of the EEC Treaty.

The CD/EPP Group continued to play the role of federalist engine in European Christian Democracy after the creation of the EEC. During the period of no formal institutional reform, which endured until 1970, the CD Group's Italian Chairmen of the Political Affairs Committee – Teresio Guglielmone, Emilio Battista, Edoardo Martino, Mario Scelba and Carlo Scarascia Mugnozza – pushed the reform agenda strongly. Several prominent CD Group members acted as Rapporteurs for key EP reports. Christian Democrats also used the Presidency to promote their agenda. Upon being elected as EP President in April 1960, for example, Furler warned against "overbearing bureaucracies" that could develop "technocratic lives of their own". Instead, it was essential to "hear the heart-beat of politics" in European integration.[45] Whereas de Gaulle wanted to hear this heart-beat in national capitals only, the CD Group advocated European-level parlia-

44 ACDP, 09–001–001/1, Procés-verbal de la réunion du Bureau du Groupe qui a eu lieu le samedi 30 octobre 1954; ACDP 09–001 002/2, Procès-verbal de la réunion du Bureau du Groupe qui a eu lieu le samedi 30 octobre 1954.

45 Bewegende Kraft für Europas Entwicklung, *Das Parlament*, 20 April 1960.

mentarization as the key component of what Bertrand in the mid-1970s termed the Christian Democrats' strategy for the EC's "fundamental democratisation".[46]

As Umberto Tulli (2017) and Daniele Pasquinucci (2013) have traced in some detail, the CD Group, the Political Affairs Committee, and the EP in its entirety focused first, on making proposals on how to implement the EEC Treaty provision for the EP's direct elections. The CD Group promoted the use of a uniform system of proportional representation for these elections, which would take place on the same day throughout the EC as would befit a parliament in a federal system. It made a major contribution to the Dehousse report adopted by the EP in May 1960 which inter alia, drew on work by the Dutch Christian Democrat Willem Schuijt on "questions relating to the electoral system of the parliament". However, compromise was required. While the report recommended the switch to a uniform electoral system after a transition period, it also advocated an EP composed of two-thirds directly elected and one-third delegated national parliamentarians to avoid a confrontation between the EP and national parliaments. However, the report did adopt the CD Group's parliamentarisation paradigm, by insisting that it was "high time ... that the peoples be drawn into this venture [of European integration]".

In the end, all MEPs were directly elected in 1979, but not according to a uniform procedure or on the same day. In the 1960s, the CD Group recognised the need to get de Gaulle on board for the direct elections, which proved to be impossible, and to create a broad EP majority for reform proposals to exercise meaningful pressure on the Member State governments. In the 1970s, it proved difficult enough to gain the support of the French, British and Danish governments for the direct elections, resulting in the CD/EPP Group's demands for a uniform electoral system and voting on one day as well as for more legislative powers for the EP initially falling by the wayside.

The CD/EPP Group continued to advocate for EC constitutionalisation during the debate about European 'union' in the 1970s. It thus largely shaped the EP's 1975 Bertrand Report, named after the Belgian Rapporteur and CD/EPP Group leader 1975–77. However, in times of strong intergovernmentalism that saw the informal institutionalisation of the European Council in 1974, the CD/EPP Group put somewhat greater emphasis on two points for which it expected more support from the Commission and the Council: new EC policies to address transnational challenges such

46 EPP Group Archives, C.1.16, Study Days, *Cahiers Européens* 37 (May 1976).

as pollution, and increased institutional efficiency to overcome blockages in the Council.

Although its own ambitions for EC constitutionalisation remained far greater, the CD/EPP Group as a result supported the moderate findings of the report for the Council submitted by Tindemans, the Christian democratic Belgian Prime Minister and later EPP president, in January 1976 (de Schoutheete 1986). At a Group meeting on 28 January 1976, Bertrand explained that Tindemans himself only saw his proposals as a 'medium-term' attempt to address the most pressing institutional issues. Klepsch agreed with Tindemans that the future directly elected EP would have to formulate demands for strengthening its own powers in a reformed EC.[47] Two years later, at the EPP congress in March 1978, Klepsch called upon the Christian Democrats to take on Socialists like Mitterrand and the British Foreign Minister David Owen, who were planning to let even the Tindemans Report with its moderate demands "go mouldy".[48]

Once the EP was directly elected the EPP Group immediately set out to discuss EC reform. Initially this discussion primarily took place in the Political Affairs Committee's newly created institutional sub-committee and later, from 1982, in the separate Institutional Affairs Committee. The work of the institutional sub-committee resulted in several reports adopted in plenary session (Palmer 1983, 188–193). They included three by Christian Democrat MEPs, one by the Frenchman André Diligent, on relations between the EP and national parliaments (European Parliament 1981a), one by the Italian Dario Antoniozzi on relations between the EP and the European Council (European Parliament 1981b), and one by the German Erik Blumenfeld on the role of the EP in the negotiation and ratification of accession treaties and treaties with third countries (European Parliament 1981c). These reports largely dealt with the EP's role in inter-institutional relations. They led to some changes in practices including the Council's agreement for the presidents of the specialised Councils to attend EP committee meetings occasionally (Kaiser 2018a). However, none of the reports' recommendations would have fundamentally changed the EC's institutional set-up.

At this point, the Italian MEP and former Commissioner Altiero Spinelli claimed in the EP plenary that "the Community is practically paral-

---

47 ACDP, 01–641–004/1, Procès-verbal de la réunion jointe du Groupe démocrate-chrétien du Parlement européen et des membres du Comité Politique des Partis démocrates-chrétiens de la Communauté, 28 January 1976.

48 ACDP, 01–641–005/3, Rede von Dr. Egon A. Klepsch, I. Kongress der Europäischen Volkspartei, 6./7. März 1978, Brussels.

ysed".[49] He took the initiative and set up the cross-party Crocodile Club to bring about fundamental constitutional change by creating an ad hoc EP committee to prepare a draft constitution to be ratified by the parliaments of the Member States.[50] By the end of October 1980, Spinelli had recruited 78 members for the Crocodile Club.[51] Interestingly, 35 members were Socialists and only 15 were Christian Democrats. Unlike the Liberal Group Chair Bangemann, Klepsch neither joined nor encouraged others from the CD/EPP Group to do so. As a result, the Crocodile Club initially only included the most committed federalists from the CD/EPP Group, such as Lücker and Tindemans. Elected to the EP in 1979, however, Tindemans remained sceptical about Spinelli's overriding objective. In an interview on German radio in March 1981 he proclaimed that the notion of a constitution for the EC was "a dream, and we need dreams in Europe, but we all know that it has absolutely no chance if we suggest it now".[52]

The Crocodile Club initiative posed a serious challenge for the EPP Group in several ways. Ideologically, as one of the founding fathers of European federalism, Spinelli – who had broken with Stalinism in the 1930s – largely shared the EPP Group's programmatic preference for constitutionalising the EC. Nevertheless, although not a party member, he had been elected to the EP on the list of the Italian Communists, which made it much harder for Christian Democrats to sell cross-party cooperation with him to their staunchly anti-communist members in countries like Germany.

Politically, Spinelli's initiative also threatened to undermine the EPP Group's stand-alone identity in the EP as the strongest promoter of deepening European integration since 1945. This meant that, even when the Group agreed to make a full contribution to the work of the newly constituted Institutional Affairs Committee charged with drafting the DTEU, it remained concerned about its own identity and visibility in the process. On 12 February 1982, the Group submitted a resolution as the first step to realising a 'federal constitution' as the end goal, prepared by the Dutch MEP Sjouke Jonker, who was Vice-Chair of the new committee (European

49 HAEU, AS-356, Altiero Spinelli, Der Augenblick der Wahrheit für Rat und Parlament, 21.5.1980 [translation from German text].

50 HAEU, AS-356, Spinelli to MEPs, 25.06.1980 [translation from German text].

51 HAEU, AS-356, Adesioni al Crocodile, 23 October 1980.

52 HAEU, GSPE-72, Marcel Gärtner, Der Klub „Krokodil“ – ein umstrittener Versuch, *WDR*, 10.3.1981, 22.20 – 22.30.

Parliament 1982a).[53] His plan foresaw, among other points, overcoming the unanimity practice in the Council and awarding the EP more powers, including its greater involvement in the legislative process. With this and similar initiatives, the EPP Group sought to buttress its continued leadership in the EP on constitutionalising the EC.

Institutionally, the EPP Group feared that its leading role on EC reform could be undermined by changes in the EP's committee structure. After 1979, the Italian Mariano Rumor, who had also led the EUCD for many years, chaired the Political Affairs Committee. Spinelli's demand for the creation of a new 'ad hoc' committee threatened his committee's control over the EC reform agenda in the EP (Interview Dastoli, 10.10.2017). Moreover, once the Institutional Affairs Committee was set up at the start of 1982, the EPP Group complained that Spinelli was acting in public as if he had a prominent formal role over and above the other Rapporteurs, when his actual agreed position was that of 'co-ordinating Rapporteur' only. At a meeting of the EPP Group's Working Party A in March 1982, Blumenfeld also criticised the fact that the new committee's secretariat consisted of four "Socialists only", including the then very junior later British Labour Party MEP Richard Corbett.[54]

Thus, on the day when the Crocodile Club presented EP President Veil with its demands on 10 February 1981, the EPP Group put out a press statement. It agreed with the thrust of the Crocodile resolution but insisted that institutional proposals should continue to be prepared in the Political Affairs Committee.[55] In the fourth Crocodile newsletter, Spinelli addressed the issue of the EPP's reluctance head-on. It was of great strategic importance to him as he was keen to secure the largest possible majority for the resolution in the EP to impress European citizens and the national governments. It seemed bizarre, Spinelli argued, that the EPP of all political groups should create such procedural problems. After all, it prided "itself on being the most homogeneous on European matters, and especially institutional questions". Referring the motion for a resolution back to the Political Affairs Committee, Spinelli claimed, would amount to a "silent burial". It was necessary to create a different institutional trajectory

53 See also ACDP, 09–001–222, Sjouke Jonker, Persönliche Anmerkungen zu einigen aktuellen institutionellen und politischen Fragen, no date [1981].

54 ACDP, 09–001–222, Protokoll Nr. 1 der Sitzung des Arbeitskreises A vom Mittwoch, 3. März 82 in Kopenhagen.

55 Cited in Krokodile am Werk, *Das Parlament*, 25 April 1981.

in the form of a committee solely devoted to debating treaty reform and preparing a coherent project for the EP to debate and decide upon.[56]

Spinelli took great pains to convince the EPP Group to come around to supporting the setting up of such a separate committee. On 7 May 1981, he took the unusual step of writing a letter to Klepsch and the EPP Group. Referring to the Christian Democrats' own narrative about their "European roots going back to Schuman, De Gasperi and Adenauer", Spinelli emphasised the need to treat institutional reform as a cross-party matter. The constitutional question "gives rise to political divisions which are different from the usual ones". Moreover, the reports of the Political Affairs Committee "do not and cannot tackle the central problem of the Community's constitutional crisis". Developing a new draft treaty would have to be done by "the groups' top experts in political and institutional affairs" in a new institutional setting.[57]

Following up on the letter, Spinelli had two private conversations with Klepsch, who he believed agreed to the creation of a new committee for drafting proposals. However, this committee would not be set up straight away, but only at the start of 1982, to coincide with the election of the new EP President and the reallocation of positions in the new revised committee structure. But some MEPs from the EPP Group continued to resist this compromise. As one of his collaborators from the committee secretariat recalls, the simmering conflict between Spinelli and the EPP Group became "unpleasant" (Interview Nickel, 27.10.2017).

In the end, Klepsch overruled the internal dissent so that the resolution for European union was eventually adopted in plenary with full EPP Group support, by 161 votes to 24 with twelve abstentions on 9 July 1981 (European Parliament 1981d).[58] In a diplomatic gesture, it explicitly referred to the EPP Group's 1979 resolution on European union.[59] From then onwards, the EPP Group constituted the backbone of parliamentary support for the Spinelli initiative and the DTEU. It fully supported the EP initiative as a "new federalist approach" to a "constitution-developing pro-

56 HAEU, AS-356, Crocodile Numéro 4, 4 March 1981 [translation from French text].

57 HAEU, AS-356, Spinelli to EPP Group, 7 May 1981.

58 Le Parlement européen entend se transformer en constituante, *Le Soir*, 11 July 1981.

59 Resolution (Abens et consorts), *Europe. Agence Internationale d'Information pour la Presse*, 6 August 1981; HAEU, AS-037, Crocodile, Letter to the Members of the European Parliament, September 1981.

cess".[60] The EPP Group also met with the parliamentary parties of the national EPP parties at the end of June 1982 to gain their support and get them to pressurise national governments into action.[61]

Initially, the EPP Group was keen to take control of what they regarded as the two key reports for the DTEU, namely those on institutional matters and economic integration.[62] This proved overly ambitious, when Jacques Moreau – a French Socialist and close confidant of Delors' – was charged with the economic report. The EPP Group was given two reports, but one was on social policy by Gero Pfennig in addition to institutional matters by Ortensio Zecchino. Working closely with Spinelli, the Italian DC politician initially sought to insert the old EPC idea, of a Senate of delegated national parliamentarians to replace the existing Council, into the DTEU, but this was dropped later on.

All the while, individual MEPs in the EPP Group kept up the pressure on Spinelli and the Institutional Affairs Committee with maximalist federalist demands. Thus, the CDU politician Pfennig, one of the DTEU Rapporteurs and Rudolf Luster, with the support of Friedrich Fugmann, the Group's Deputy Secretary-General,[63] drafted a "constitution for a federal State" to coincide with the debate about the DTEU draft in the EP in September 1983 (Fontaine 2009, 189; Luster 1988). They forcefully argued the need to overcome the EC's existing mixed institutional structure in favour of a properly federal constitutional design. However, there was no majority in the EP for a federal constitution, so that compromise was inevitable. Therefore, once the final DTEU text was agreed, the EPP Group opposed all amendments directed at merely modifying the existing treaties.[64] In the end, the EP adopted the DTEU by a large margin in February 1984, with 237 MEPs voting for and 31 against, with 43 abstentions.

Although the final version of the DTEU marked a constitutional compromise and was never ratified, the process leading up to the EP vote on it in the end nevertheless played a crucial role first, in sustaining the EPP

---

60 ACDP, 09–001–082/2, Friedrich Fugmann, die Debatte über die institutionelle Frage, 6.7.1982, 13.7.1982.

61 ACDP, 09–001–082/2, Fugmann to Luster and Pfennig, Berlin, 23.7.1982.

62 ACDP, 09–001–222, Protokoll Nr. 2 der Sitzung der Arbeitsgruppe "A" in Brüssel, 14.4.1982.

63 See also Fugmann's papers on a European constitution and his correspondence with the two CDU MEPs in ACDP, 09–001–078, and ACDP, 09–001–082/2.

64 ACDP, 09–001–222, Protokoll der Sitzung der Arbeitsgruppe "A" in Bonn, 9.2.1984, vom Donnerstag, 9. Februar 1984, in Bonn.

Group's leadership role on institutional deepening despite its origins in the Spinelli initiative; second, in facilitating cross-party consensus on the need for endowing the EP with substantial powers and for overcoming blockages in the Council by stopping the unanimity practice; and third, by creating a repertoire of constitutional ideas for EC/EU reform which the EPP Group, national parties and EPP-controlled governments could later draw upon (see Johansson in Chapter 2 of this book). As a result, the DTEU for the first time legally defined the principle of subsidiarity that was later inserted in the Treaty of Maastricht (Interview Jacqué, 17.10.2017). Originally derived from Catholic social teaching and thus chiming nicely with the EPP's programmatic commitments, this constitutional principle served to allay fears about an overbearing European 'superstate' and to protect the rights of localities and regions in the future EU.

Leading up to the transformation of the EC into the EU, the CD/EPP Group consistently played the role of engine in the institutional reform debate, both within European Christian Democracy and in the EP, in the different ways discussed in this section. The origins of the Christian Democrats' drive for European constitutionalisation lay in post-war transnational party networking. The national parties in government took the first steps in that direction, as they had in the creation of the ECSC. After the new European institutions were set up, however, the CD/EPP Group protected the Christian Democrats' constitutional 'acquis' in times of prevailing intergovernmentalism, loss of power in key Member States like Germany, and EC enlargements that temporarily reduced it to second place in the EP. The Group's EC reform activism enhanced its internal cohesion, incentivised cross-party cooperation, and led it to pressurise national parties and governments to support major change in a broadly federal direction. Thus, the EPP Group played a leading role in creating and consolidating a strong trajectory for the further deepening of European integration.

### *Farmers, markets, and new challenges: policy-making in the Communities*

Its commitment to such a deepening of European integration featured prominently, when the EPP prepared its first political programme in the run-up to the 1979 elections, which it passed at its congress in Brussels in March 1978.[65] At its next congress in February 1979, the EPP also adopted

65 EPP Group Archives, N.1., EPP Party, Political Programme 1978.

a shorter "electoral platform" for use in the election campaign, which was generally phrased as a lowest common denominator document.[66] Like the EPP programme, this platform summarised key Christian democratic policy aims for the EC's future. It first of all listed generic Christian democratic norms such as its commitment to protecting the family and the necessary focus of social policy on ensuring that individuals can help themselves, as well as its opposition to "individualism without moral constraints". An integrated Europe, the platform document argued, would have to contribute to this agenda, for example by protecting "human rights and fundamental freedoms"; striving for "a more equitable and human economic order" within Europe and in its relations with other parts of the world; and by accepting "its moral and human responsibility towards the countries of Eastern Europe".

The electoral platform went on to defend a "democratic Europe" with a "pluralist democracy" and decentralised power based "on the principle of subsidiarity". It also confirmed EPP support for the accession of Greece, Portugal and Spain to the EC "in order to consolidate our common democratic ideals". Moreover, the document set out the EPP's expectation that the EP – strengthened by "amendments to the treaty" – would enhance "democratic control over Community institutions" and "the smooth working of the Community" through improved decision-making, progressively moving towards a "European Union" that in future could "speak with one voice" to strengthen "freedom and solidarity, justice and peace" in global affairs.

Finally, the electoral platform also included a reference to the "social market economy", which had still been contested during the EPP's formation. While emphasising the "free responsibility and enterprise of the individual" as this model's core element, the document nevertheless talked at length about safeguards: a "vigorous regional, structural and social policy", which would have the objective of eliminating "regional imbalances"; a European Charter of Employees' Rights aimed at an "improvement in working conditions" to result from Europe-wide "collective agreements" to cover such issues as working hours and equal pay for men and women; "adequate protection for small and medium-sized undertakings, craftsmen and the middle classes"; and finally, support for the "modern family farm".

The EPP's programmatic demands as condensed in the electoral platform for the 1979 election enshrined fundamental policy objectives and created vectors that basically shaped EPP Group preferences until the Lis-

66 EPP Group Archives, N.1., EPP Party, Electoral Platform 1979.

bon Treaty. Alongside institutional reform demands, these objectives mainly pertained to 'domestic' EC affairs. Foreign policy cooperation in the EC was limited and purely intergovernmental. The EP could and did discuss global issues, but it did not substantially influence policy. As a result, global policy matters remained marginal to the EPP Group's work during the Cold War, with the exception of the EC competences for trade and aid (see Gagatek in Chapter 4 of this book). 'Foreign' affairs were dominated by relations with international organisations like the European Free Trade Association and the Organisation for Economic Co-operation and Development (OECD), as well as issues pertaining to democratic transition and EC enlargement.

Regarding domestic EC matters, the 1979 electoral platform was a bland document designed to please all constituencies and to paper over fundamental differences within and across the EPP Group and EPP member parties, especially on socio-economic policy. In fact, the EPP Group encompassed a significantly broader ideological range on socio-economic issues than the Socialists (Klingemann et al. 2006: 43). Its internal programmatic diversity was down to three main factors. The first of these consisted of the significant differences in the political economy and socio-economic policy traditions of the Member States, ranging from the German social market economy to the Dutch consociational model of institutionalised consensus-seeking and the statist French system. These differences played a large role in the continuous ideological debate on the role of EC and Member State institutions in steering the economy. Thus, in 1962, CDU member Hallstein as Commission President defended the recommendations for economic planning in the Commission's Action Programme, which were largely copy-pasted from the French notion and practice of indicative planning. He was sharply attacked for this by the German Economics Minister Ludwig Erhard from the same party (Dyson 1994: 71). The ensuing debate in the CD Group reflected a range of views, from Leopoldo Rubinacci's support for 'programmation' to fix obligatory economic performance goals in several economic sectors, to Hans Dichgans' resolute ordo-liberal insistence on the maximum liberal competition with minimum interference by the state or, for that matter, EC institutions (Forsyth 1964: 34).

The second factor that helps to explain the EPP Group's internal fragmentation is intra-party politics, especially the relative influence in the national catch-all parties of representatives close to constituencies like farmers, trade unionists or industry. As early as 1953–54, when the CD Group in the ECSC's Common Assembly began to debate policy issues in the coal and steel sector, it found a great diversity of views especially on the questions of cartels and the use of European level social policy funding for sectoral structural adjustments (Guerrieri 2015: 403). At a meeting of a Working Group charged with applying the Christian democratic doctrine to problems of the ECSC, those like de Menthon and Bertrand – with ties to the Christian trade unions – were closer to socialist views on the need to eradicate cartels comprehensively than others like Wolfgang Pohle from the CDU, who defended the interests of the German coal industry in maintaining its vertical integration with steel production, for example.[67] While the ECSC Treaty outlawed domestic cartels, Christian Democrats played a key role working through the High Authority, the CD Group and national governments in maintaining and legitimising close industry relations and persisting cartel-like practices, including the 1953 ECSC export cartel and the 1966 domestic cartel, which was obviously illegal under the Treaty (Kaiser 2018b).

Finally, different and changing coalition preferences constituted the third factor that helps explain the EPP Group's ideological diversity on socio-economic policy issues. In Germany, the CDU/CSU followed a staunchly anti-socialist course during the Cold War. With the exception of a short period from 1966 to 1969, it only formed coalitions at the national level with the liberal Free Democrats. At the opposite end of the spectrum, the Italian DC forged the historic compromise with the PCI. These different preferences indirectly impacted on ideological positions, too, such as when the DC initially refused to join a future EPP in 1975 or to endorse the notion of a social market economy – something that it rightly identified at the time with a strong German ordo-liberal economic policy tradition.

When individual MEPs or the EPP Group as a whole sought to influence legislative policy-making before the EP acquired formal powers in the SEA and the Treaty of Maastricht, they could basically use three different routes. The first was working with the Commission at the EC level. This concerned, in the first instance, the Christian Democrats in the Commission who often attended Study Days or Group meetings. Several of these Christian Democrats, including Wigny, Scarascia Mugnozza and Hallstein, had experience as MEPs before or after their mandate in the Commission, thus contributing to close ties between the institutions at the political level. One case in point is the cooperation between Arved Deringer, the co-

67 ACDP, 09–001–002/2, Procès-verbal de la réunion du Groupe qui a eu lieu mercredi 1er décembre 1954. See also ACDP 09–001–009/1, Robert Houben, Note au groupe démocrate-chrétien de l'Assemblée commune. Comment préciser la doctrine politique?

founder of law firm Deringer-Tessin in 1962, and Hans von der Groeben. As MEP from 1958 to 1970 and Chair of the EP's Legal Committee from 1966 to 1970, Deringer worked closely with the German Commissioner in developing and drafting Regulation 17/62, which structured EC competition policy for forty years (Warlouzet 2016; Leucht and Seidel 2008).

Influencing national parties and governments constituted a second avenue for the CD/EPP Group and individual MEPs to influence EC policy-making. Access via the national route was especially important in policy areas with entrenched national policy communities. It was for this reason that Lücker, when he was appointed EP Rapporteur in July 1958, worked closely with national farm groups to ensure that the future CAP would have market regulations for more product groups than originally foreseen and strong financial support mechanisms for farmers and high intervention prices, thus moderating the socialist Dutch Agriculture Commissioner Sicco Mansholt's quest for a faster modernisation of the sector (Knudsen 2009; Patel 2009).

Lastly, the EPP Group and individual MEPs could also appeal to the public to encourage the Commission and Council to act at the EC level. When concerns regarding transnational air and water pollution, as well as other issues of environmental degradation became very wide-spread in the late 1960s and early 1970s, the EP used reports and public appeals to get the EC to agree measures in policy fields that were not yet formally covered as such by the EEC Treaty.

Arguably, the creation, implementation, and protection of the CAP initially had the greatest strategic importance for the CD Group after 1958 (see Germond in Chapter 3 of this book). Embedded in personalist notions of human dignity and 'healthy' rural communities and based on the inter-war experience of many farmers moving over to far-right political parties, the Christian Democrats prioritized keeping farmers happy after 1945. Crucially, they constituted a core electoral constituency, too, with some 90 % of them voting for the CDU/CSU in Germany, for example. The Europeanisation of agricultural policy as originally proposed by Pflimlin as French agriculture minister in 1950 (Thiemeyer 1999; Griffiths and Girvin 1995), was a key building block for the Christian Democrats' strategy for the sector. The CD Group strongly supported the notion of the 'family farm' not just as an economic model, but also as a social model for the EEC and its Member States – a powerful narrative that Lücker also introduced into his first report for the EP's Agriculture Committee,[68] although the CAP's funding mechanisms later actually favoured large-scale farming and multinational food companies.

In his report, which was adopted by the Agriculture Committee with 15 votes to one, Lücker emphasised the need to consider the actual production costs for farm produce, to facilitate greater specialisation in the customs union, and to replace national minimum prices with a new EEC-wide system as soon as possible. The report also demanded European market regulation for products ranging from sugar to milk and grain. It justified the switch to an EEC-level protectionist agricultural policy with general principles such as European self-sufficiency, the promotion of welfare and equal living conditions, and the maintenance of established forms of production and living for "the free-thinking farmer".[69]

The majority of the CD Group worked across the party divide with others who were close to the farm policy community that made up roughly one third of the Agriculture Committee (Forsyth 1964: 32). In this way, it could dominate the policy debate in the committee and in the EP. The CD Group's allies included, for example, Roland Boscary-Monsservin, French agriculture minister from 1957–8 and an MEP and Chair of the Agriculture Committee from 1959–71, who was also a member of the National Centre of Independents and Farmers. In a supplementary report, Boscary-Monsservin demanded that stabilising prices and raising family farm incomes should be the CAP's primary objectives. Any costs of restructuring the sector needed to be fully compensated, and external levies would have to be so high as to fully cover the internal support mechanisms.[70]

Throughout the formation of the CAP, the majority of the CD Group pushed the Commission and the Member States to develop the most comprehensive, protectionist, and also expensive CAP subsidy regime that would comply with these policy principles. On some issues, the more liberally-minded MEPs from the Netherlands, which had the most efficient farms in relative terms, deserted the Group,[71] for example when the Agri-

---

68 HAEU, PE0–44, Bericht im Namen des Ausschusses für Fragen der Landwirtschaft über die Landwirtschaftspolitik in der Europäischen Wirtschaftsgemeinschaft, von Hans August Lücker, Berichterstatter, June 1959.

69 Ibid.

70 HAEU, PE0–111, Rapport complémentaire fait au nom de la commission de l'agriculture sur l'orientation de la politique agricole commune, par M. Boscary-Monsservin, Président de la commission, Rapporteur, 5.10.1960.

71 For internal differences see also EPP Group Archives, C.1.1, *Cahiers Européens* 3 (Mai 1960).

culture Committee and the CD Group asked the Commission to prepare a more comprehensively protectionist system of import quotas than it was envisaging at the time (Houdbine and Vergès 1966: 106–9). Once the CAP was completed, the CD/EPP Group initially defended it as the EC's greatest political achievement. In the CSU and in Germany more widely, Lücker claimed, for example, that the CAP – contrary to media reports – was not too costly. While it did foster structural change in the sector, he said, German farmers had become more competitive and increased their exports very substantially.[72]

At EC level, despite growing overproduction and rising costs, the CD/EPP Group continued to defend the CAP as "a cornerstone of the whole construction" of the EC.[73] When the EPP prepared its political programme under the strong influence of Klepsch and the EPP Group, it continued to repeat the same basic principles established in the early 1960s. It even justified subsidies for overproduction and exporting inefficiently produced foodstuffs with the need "to supply the world with agricultural produce". The EPP demanded an extension of the existing market regulations and an increase in regional and structural policy spending to support family farms.[74] In its Electoral Platform for the 1979 elections the EPP told the same story about the family farm, the need to secure food production, and the desirability of greater structural funding for rural communities.[75]

The EPP Group only began to revise its policy on the CAP in the 1980s. This change was due to a number of factors including the decline of the farm vote, the CAP's rising costs, as well as demands from agricultural export countries in the Cairns Group to reduce EC agricultural protectionism in return for the liberalisation of trade in goods and services. Crucially, the EPP Group also had to face the stark fact that it was impossible to convince national governments to expand the EC budget above agreed ceilings. As a result, more CAP spending meant less money for non-compulsory expenditure on new EC policies that the EPP Group hoped would bolster its own legitimacy and that of the EP in the EC system. Looking back on the first five years of the directly elected EP, Klepsch noted in January 1984 that the CAP clearly needed to be reassessed and revised. The EC

72 Hans August Lücker, EWG-Finanzen und Landwirtschaft, *Bayern-Kurier*, 26 July 1969; Hans August Lücker, Auf dem Weg in neue Dimensionen, *Bayern-Kurier*, 13 June 1970.

73 EPP Group Archives, C.1.15, *Cahiers Européens* 35 (Mai 1975).

74 EPP Group Archives, N.1., EPP Party, Entwurf des Politischen Programms, 9.12.1977.

75 EPP Group Archives, N.1., EPP Party, Electoral Platform 1979.

had to prevent growing surpluses and the destruction of foodstuffs. The CAP had to remain "functional and fundable" –[76] basic facts recognised at the national level, where Member State governments were increasingly keen to keep budget and state deficits in check (see also Germond in Chapter 3 of this book).

The structure of the CAP effectively put farmers on a Europe-wide welfare system (Knudsen 2009). During the 1960s and 1970s, the CD/EPP Group also favoured more Community spending for other welfare policies. Thus, when Keynesian economics reached its peak in Western Europe at the start of the 1970s, it propagated greater state interventionism, EC-level fiscal mechanisms for regional redistribution and increased EC-level funding for investment programmes designed to strengthen infrastructures, foster growth and employment in backward regions, and to create comparable living conditions, as referred to in the German Basic Law constitution. Far from being solely a demand by Britain in its accession negotiations, the CD/EPP Group also argued for a powerful EC regional policy to address regional imbalances (Kaiser 2013). After the 1979 elections, Klepsch reminded his newly elected colleagues that the Group would not budge in its demand for providing more funding for EC regional policy.[77]

Despite the ideological differences among the member parties, the CD/EPP Group did not see EC-level funding for farmers and rural and old industrial regions in transition as a waste of taxpayers' money. To the Christian Democrats at the time this EC-level expenditure constituted the Europeanisation of redistributive policies that were well-established at national level before, in the form of subsidy policies for farmers and regional policies such as the Italian Cassa del Mezzogiorno or the German financial equalisation mechanism among the federal states. Moreover, this was a form of Europeanization, that they regarded as necessary to counter-balance the effects of economic liberalisation in the customs union and as beneficial for enhancing the political legitimacy of the EC. At the national level the late 1970s and the early 1980s saw a shift among EPP parties and governments towards policies of liberalisation and deregulation that also affected the EC. Importantly, however, this process impacted on the CD/EPP Group belatedly, as it initially remained preoccupied with expanding the EC's policy remit and financial scope for action.

---

76 ACDP, 01–641–005/2, Egon A. Klepsch, Arbeit an der europäischen Einigung. Zum Beitrag der EVP-Fraktion in der 1. Wahlperiode des direkt gewählten Parlamentes, Januar 1984.

77 ACDP, 01–641–007/1, Rede von Egon A. Klepsch anlässlich der Fraktionssitzung der EVP am 19.9.1979 in Brüssel.

The Christian Democrats had advocated the creation of a common market from the start of 'core Europe' integration, both for its expected economic benefits and as a stepping stone to greater political integration. However, the successful completion of the customs union on 1 July 1968 was only one building block of such a common market. In the early 1960s, the CD Group made a significant contribution to the debate surrounding competition policy as a second building block. Commissioner von der Groeben acknowledged at the time that the Internal Market Committee's work leading to the Deringer report influenced the shape of Regulation 17/1962 (Houdbine and Vergès 1966: 100). The EP mainly pleaded for a simplified administration of the notification requirement for mergers and acquisitions imported into the EEC from the existing German system, which did indeed result in immediate administrative gridlock in 1962 (Cini and McGowan: 18). However, once set up, the administration of competition policy became increasingly de-politicised. For some time, it appeared to be a technical policy field best left to lawyers, until the ECJ turned the existing Regulation into an instrument for liberalisation with key decisions such as those of the 1974 Dassonville case and the 1979 Cassis de Dijon case, which established the principle of mutual recognition (Leucht 2018; Patel and Schweitzer 2013).

The third building block in creating a common market was the abolition of non-tariff barriers (Warlouzet 2018). Member States sometimes deliberately, sometimes inadvertently used such non-tariff barriers like technical norms and standards to protect domestic producers from foreign competition. With the Commission making no significant progress to tackle this problem during the 1970s, industry circles increasingly lobbied for a more comprehensive approach to complete the internal market which eventually resulted in the 1987 SEA and the Single Market Programme. This process was largely shaped by Member States like the United Kingdom which pushed the liberalisation agenda for the EC (Moravcsik 1998); the industry lobby, especially the European Round Table of Industrialists (Ramirez 2013; Green Cowles 1995); and the European Commission, especially British Commissioner Lord Cockfield and President Delors, who exploited the political opportunity of connecting the internal market with the EC's institutional reform in the SEA.

The EPP Group collectively, which (as was also reflected in its electoral platform for the 1979 election) was still more stuck in the Europeanisation of Keynesian redistribution, played a supportive, but not a decisive role in this process (Warlouzet 2020), which was initially mainly backed by liberal Conservatives in the EPP and among the British Tories as well as many in the Liberal Group in the EP. In 1979, the German CDU MEP Karl von

Wogau created the Kangaroo Group together with the British Conservative Basil de Ferranti, one of the EP Vice-Presidents. The Kangaroo Group – named after the Australian animal for its ability to make huge forward leaps – initially consisted of MEPs only. Later, it became a broader international forum aiming to promote the completion of the internal market and progress on monetary cooperation and integration within the EP and beyond. Von Wogau had been a manager at the Swiss company Sandoz before working as a lawyer, and Ferranti was an industrialist. Other early members of the Kangaroo Group also had connections to industry or experience with economic policy-making. The Christian Democrat Fernand Herman had been Belgian economics minister and the Gaullist Christine Scrivener French consumer affairs minister in the 1970s.

Much like Spinelli working across party divides to unite the EP behind his institutional reform agenda, von Wogau sought to create broad parliamentary support for the completion of the internal market. In 1981, he recruited Dieter Rogalla, a new German Social Democrat MEP, to the Kangaroo Group. Rogalla subsequently worked hard to convince the Socialist Group of the benefits of the abolition of non-tariff barriers. Von Wogau established a close rapport with the French Socialist Moreau, too, who was close to Delors and also involved in the preparation of the DTEU. Eventually, the two MEPs together were responsible as joint Rapporteurs for the Committee on Economic and Monetary Affairs' "Report on the Need to Implement the Internal European Market" which they submitted in March 1984 (Warlouzet 2020). When he became Commission President at the start of 1985, Delors welcomed such broad parliamentary backing for his White Paper on the completion of the internal market. What he really needed to do, however, was to strike a bargain with the Member State governments on his proposal to combine further economic integration with institutional reform.

Questions of economic integration in the broadest sense were evidently at the heart of European integration. The EEC Treaty demanded the creation of a common market and a competition policy. Questions of monetary cooperation were also intimately linked to the functioning of integrated markets and as a result became a prominent topic of debate for the EPP Group and the EP more generally, especially after the 1970 Werner Report and the turmoil following the US decision to end the Bretton Woods system (Mourlon-Druol 2012). The CD/EPP Group, in line with the EP majority (Jacobs 1991: 362), supported the abolition of capital controls as well as the general objective of monetary union, including the creation of a single currency as its end goal. At the same time, as the CD/EPP Group also noted,[78] how to implement this general objective "in practice" was highly contested within and across the Member States and political parties, including the Christian Democrats, in times of continuing great divergences of socio-economic preferences and policies during the 1970s and early 1980s (see Germond in Chapter 3 of this book). This was also the reason why Tindemans left monetary integration out of his 1976 report to the Member State governments and why the 1984 DTEU still only included generalities on the topic (Kaiser 2018a).

Going beyond core issues of economic integration included in or derived from the Treaty, the CD/EPP Group created space for the policy entrepreneurship of individual MEPs keen to advance a political agenda and get the EC to become active in emerging policy fields. This was the case for what could be called soft foreign policy issues, especially human rights and democracy promotion, which became intimately linked, among other issues, to the suspension of the association agreement with Greece after the military took power there in 1967 (Fernandez 2017). Questions of human rights also became connected to development aid policy leading on to the conditionality debate and policy (Garavini 2012), as well as the internal drive for an EC-level bill of rights of sorts.

Initially focussed on domestic EC, rather than external policy, the environment was another policy field that saw strong policy entrepreneurship by individual MEPs including members of the CD/EPP Group, confounding the notion of environmental protection as only a concern of the political Left in this period. While other international organisations such as the OECD had already put issues such as air and water pollution on their agenda during the 1950s and 1960s (Kaiser and Meyer 2017), the European Commission only became actively engaged under the influence of Commissioners Spinelli and Mansholt, as well as officials like Petra Kelly, the later co-founder of the German Green Party, from February 1971 onwards. By this point, however, the EP had already been promoting EC-level environmental protection for some time, pushing the Commission and Member States to address their growing concerns. In June 1969, the poisoning of the river Rhine with the pesticide Thiodan had raised multiple linked concerns about fishing stock, the livelihood of fishermen and the safety of citizens swimming in rivers. The Dutch and German Christian Democrats Jacob Boersma and Hans Jahn subsequently worked on reports and EP res-

78 ACDP, 01–641–004/1, Procès-verbal de la réunion jointe du Groupe démocrate-chrétien du Parlement européen et des membres du Comité Politique des Partis démocrates-chrétiens de la Communauté, 28.1.1976.

olutions on water and air pollution that were passed in 1970 and 1972, the year of the United Nations' Stockholm conference on the environment, respectively (Meyer 2011: 78–80).

The environmental activism of Boersma and Jahn and their two reports then fed into the EP Committee on Public Health and the Environment's 1973 report about the first Environmental Action Programme.[79] In it, the EP demanded "effective action" by the Member States. It was high time to "achieve a rapid reduction of existing environmental pollution and nuisances". Moreover, the Commission needed to be empowered to set "binding deadlines" for the implementation of pollution reduction measures. The EP Committee also introduced the notion of necessary "preventive action", a concept that helped pave the way for the later precautionary principle (Meyer 2017). Furthermore, the EP aggressively challenged the legal basis on which the Commission had drafted the Environmental Action Programme and how the Council had discussed it without comprehensive EP consultation. In one of many such incidences of disagreements between the EP and the Council in this period about the legal need and political desirability of consulting the EP, the MEPs took the view that the Treaty strictly demanded such consultation on an "obligatory basis".

During the 1970s, Jahn continued to invest a great deal of time into taking up new environmental concerns within the CD/EPP Group and in the responsible EP committee. Thus, in 1979 he drew up a report for what was now the Committee on the Environment, Public Health and Consumer Protection, on compounds that could pollute the environment and cause cancer.[80] His report set out a strong rationale for EC activism and the EP's involvement in addressing environmental degradation: like other environmental issues, the spread of such carcinogens was transnational in nature and had a direct impact on citizens, and these citizens expected the EC to take action against such threats. In these different ways, the activism of Jahn and other MEPs in the early stages of EC environmental policy helped ensure the incorporation of this new policy field in the SEA and as an exclusive EU competence in the Maastricht Treaty, with full EP co-decision powers (Meyer 2014).

79 HAEU, PE0–1630, Report on behalf of the Committee on Public Health and the Environment, on the proposal from the Commission of the European communities to the Council (Doc 62/73) on the programme of environmental action.

80 HAEU, PE0–2975, Report drawn up on behalf of the Committee on the Environment, Public Health and Consumer Protection on environmental carcinogens, Rapporteur M. H.E. Jahn, 2.5.1979, Doc. 99/79.

Jahn rode another political hobby horse that was even more dear to him during the 1970s: the protection of birds, especially migratory birds, which eventually started at EC level with the 1979 Birds Directive – an environmental concern that constitutes a great example for how individual MEPs, the CD/EPP Group and the EP more generally were able, even before the 1979 elections, to work closely with political actors outside of the EP to create what social scientists have called advocacy coalitions, appealing to the European public to demand EC-level action and thus legitimise their political cause (Meyer 2013). In this case, migratory birds were increasingly threatened by traditional hunting patterns in the Mediterranean including EC Member States Italy and France, as well as by the loss of wetlands, excessive use of pesticides, and the spread of electricity lines. Jahn worked closely with bird protection organisations such as the British Royal Society for the Protection of Birds, as well as the European Environmental Bureau created in 1974, to raise awareness for the problem. Media reports by well-known conservationists like Bernhard Grzimek helped to further raise awareness of the issue among the European public further. The Commission began to seek and build scientific expertise to corroborate the need for EC-level action for what was clearly a transnational issue. While the debate about the EC's institutional reform largely failed to agitate EC citizens, the fate of migratory birds clearly did. Public outrage at their suffering and the decline of populations, combined with media reporting, decisively facilitated EC action in this field.

Thus, although the CD/EPP Group was ideologically more heterogeneous than the Socialists regarding socio-economic policy, the Group as a whole and individual MEPs already succeeded in co-shaping ideological vectors and buttressing paths for some emerging EC policies before the first direct elections let alone the SEA and the Maastricht Treaty. At times, new EC policy fields once more lost political importance for the EPP Group and its programmatic profile relative to other policy areas. Despite its integration into the SEA with the support of the EPP Group, and the adoption of majority voting for it in the Maastricht Treaty, this was the case for environmental protection, when the newly formed Green parties made it their ideological core from the late 1970s onwards. They radicalised this policy agenda to the point where it seemed to threaten other competing core EPP Group preferences, for example restoring the competitiveness of European industry, which could be hampered by very costly environmental regulation.

The EPP Group sought to exercise influence through formal channels like written and oral questions to the Commission (Forsyth 1964: 53–54), EP initiative reports and meetings with national parliamentary parties and committees, commissioners and national governmental policy-makers. Informal network-type contacts – largely overlooked by early political science work on European integration until the 1980s (Dinan 2018) – were quite effective in impacting EC-level policy-making (van Schendelen 1984).

The CD/EPP Group and individual MEPs fulfilled three main functions in the period before the EP acquired stronger legislative powers in the SEA and the Maastricht Treaty. First, they contributed to setting policy agenda, particularly in fields such as the environment, where the EC lacked formal policy competence and where demand by citizens for EC-level action was strong. Secondly, individual MEPs from the CD/EPP Group, with strong informal links to key organised constituencies such as farmers or specialist expertise in areas such as competition law, were able to influence the framing and technical details of actual EC policies. It appears that German Christian Democrats were especially successful at influencing EC-level policy-making, most likely because they had no leading roles in their national parties or parliaments and were much more focussed on their EP work than the Italian MEPs, for example. Thus, Lücker was very active in the creation and defence of the CAP, Deringer had strong legal expertise and contributed to the framing of competition policy, and Jahn helped to shape advocacy coalitions for EC-level environmental policy action. Thirdly, the CD/EPP Group could lend additional political legitimacy to the Commission and the Member States, when they did take action on issues such as the creation of an EU level regional policy, for example.

Moreover, with its strong ideological commitment to European integration and primary networks and cooperation in continental Western Europe, the CD/EPP Group was more than any other in the EP, principally keen to advance the EC's policies as well as its institutional deepening even in policy fields where it was difficult to achieve internal consensus. As a result, as a Group it was arguably most focussed on finding practical solutions to the EC's challenges. In contrast, the EP as a whole was still sometimes characterised after 1979 by what the French newspaper *Le Monde* at the time called a form of "disorganised cosmopolitanism", with "a tendency to discuss all problems in the world" in the absence of ordinary parliamentary powers.[81] Moreover, its key role within the EP's party system did mean, that the EPP Group put increasing emphasis on its internal cohesion and capacity to form stable alliances with other Groups during the 1980s, not least to shape legislative politics and policy-making after the

81 *Le Monde*, 2 August 1980.

EP's acquisition of greater formal powers in the SEA and the Treaty of Maastricht – something that in turn left less space for the 'individual' entrepreneurial leadership by Christian Democrats like Lücker, Deringer and Jahn.

## *Conclusion*

This chapter has shown how the CD/EPP Group with its European ambitions succeeded in playing a central role in EP politics and policy-making from the creation of the ECSC through to the EC's transformation into the EU in the early 1990s – and did so even after 1975, when it was no longer numerically the largest Group. The Christian democratic parties' early transnational networking and their cooperation in the ECSC's Common Assembly and in the EP after 1958 created long-term vectors, or what historical institutionalists call path-dependencies, which shaped its internal constitution and practices as well as its ideological orientation and programmatic commitments for a long time, and in several ways actually beyond the first direct elections.

As we saw in sections one and two, one of the most important structural continuities consisted of the emergence and maintenance of strong ties among Christian Democrats from the six ECSC founding Member States. From Taviani, Teitgen, von Brentano, and Wigny during the 1950s through to Colombo, Pflimlin, Lücker, Bertrand and others during the 1970s, these Christian Democrats were highly committed to European integration. While pragmatic in adverse circumstances like de Gaulle's aggressive advocacy of intergovernmentalism during the 1960s, they essentially shared a broadly federalist agenda for the EC.

The second most important structural continuity lay in the weakness of Franco-German ties in the CD/EPP Group compared to the great importance of this bilateral engine in the Council, which sometimes stuttered badly, but was nevertheless indispensable for European integration. In view of the organisational and electoral weakness of Christian Democracy in France after 1958, the CD/EPP Group was characterised instead by an informal trilateralism of the Italian, German and Benelux delegations. As became clear in section two, these delegations largely determined the distribution of key positions in the Group and in the EP Presidency and committee structure, with Belgian Christian Democrats like Bertrand, Herman and Tindemans often acting as political and cultural mediators.

From the 1970s, the CD/EPP Group was increasingly dominated by an Italo-German bilateralism, which was personified in the cooperation between Klepsch as long-time Group leader after 1977 and two Italian Secretary-Generals. Both delegations together had an absolute majority of seats. Their effective cooperation gave stability not just to the Group, but also to the EC more generally, with Klepsch often acting as interlocutor between German Chancellor Kohl and the DC leadership – something that has largely been overlooked by literature that has focussed on the importance of Franco-German cooperation at the intergovernmental level.

Alongside these structural continuities, sections three and four have also highlighted how early post-war ideological commitments, which became loosely formalised in the EPP programme and platform for the 1979 elections, informed the CD/EPP Group's European ambitions and created strong long-term vectors for its political and policy preferences. This concerned, most importantly, the Group's overriding commitment to the EC's constitutionalisation and the normalisation of the EP as a federal level parliament with full budgetary and legislative powers. The process that led to the drafting of the 1984 DTEU made abundantly clear just how important this commitment was; not just for the EPP Group's ideological identity and cohesion, but also for its position within the EP.

Additionally, the Group was also committed from the start of European integration to the creation of a common market with associated policies such as competition and monetary cooperation – economic liberalisation that had to be combined with the full or partial Europeanisation of redistributive welfare policies – especially for agriculture, but also for rural and old industrial regions in the form of structural funds and the new regional policy in the 1970s.

At the same time, the first direct elections also marked a turning point in other important ways. Structurally, the EPP Group roughly doubled in size in 1979. The end of the dual mandate also meant that its MEPs could now fully focus on their EP work and wanted something important to do on a daily basis. This in turn created a very strong functional incentive for working towards the EC's institutional deepening, including far greater powers for the EP on top of Christian Democracy's commitment to the long-term aim of a federal Europe. Moreover, from 1980 onwards, the EPP Group controlled a much larger budget which it used for a process of professionalisation by employing – by 1982 – 16 officials with policy responsibility. This professionalisation reduced the MEPs' previous dependence on the support of the EP committee secretariats or their national parties and parliamentary parties. The direct elections in this sense set off a process of what could be called autonomisation – or the much greater independence of the EPP Group not just within the EP, but also as an actor in the complex institutional network of national and European level political parties and parliaments, as well as national governmental and supranational institutions.

While the Christian Democrats' general ideological and policy commitments remained quite stable until the Maastricht Treaty, the EPP Group also needed to respond to new previously unforeseen challenges. One of these was the growing importance of non-tariff barriers to trade, which set off the renewed quest for the completion of an internal market – a process that the EPP Group supported during the 1980s, but did not influence decisively. Similarly, while the Christian Democrats had already discussed monetary cooperation in the late 1940s and early 1950s, the US-induced collapse of the Bretton Woods system in the early 1970s made such cooperation more urgent. However, it also exposed that the Christian Democrats were much more united on general economic policy goals than on their actual implementation, which in this case was largely left to the national governments and central banks – a lack of agreement about core objectives of monetary union that was (as in other policy fields) due to different national experiences and policy traditions (Marks and Wilson 2000) and has come back to haunt not just the EPP Group, but also the EU more generally. Despite continued dissonance within the Group in this and some other policy fields, the direct elections, as well as the anticipation and actual acquisition by the EP of substantive legislative powers in the SEA and the Maastricht Treaty created strong functional incentives for maximising internal cohesion and voting strength in the EP to influence law making effectively.

Over the course of the forty years between the creation of the ECSC and the EC's transformation into the EU in the early 1990s, the EPP Group was able to influence not just EP politics and policy-making, but also the development of the EC in ways that have largely been overlooked in the older political science literature, which was still focussed on explaining formal institutions and their powers. What the EP lacked in formal powers, the EPP Group and individual MEPs sought to compensate as much as possible through informal mechanisms of networking: with the national parties and parliamentary parties, the Christian democratic Commissioners and Christian democrat-led governments as well as – occasionally – non-governmental organisations as in the case of the emergent EC environmental policy.

Alongside its growing formal powers to influence the EC budget and later, EC legislation, the CD/EPP Group and individual MEPs were a source of expertise in fields like competition policy, as the example of Deringer's close collaboration with von der Groeben and the Commission's Directorate-General IV shows. They were also at the centre of strong policy communities as in the case of agriculture, which was especially dear to the CD/EPP Group, helping to link the national and EC levels as well as state and non-state actors to Europeanise this policy effectively. Moreover, they started to form, or at least to contribute to, advocacy coalitions, whether for the EC's institutional reform or new EC-level solutions to transnational policy challenges.

While this chapter has provided ample evidence of CD/EPP Group and individual MEP policy activism, their actual influence was largely informal and is difficult to measure precisely in relation to other factors because of a lack of written sources or of comprehensive studies of policy fields that include source material from the EP, its Groups and individual MEPs as well as the Member States or the Commission.

Nonetheless, it has become clear that the EPP Group to varying extents fulfilled the system-building and policy-making functions. It contributed core ideas to the process of EC constitutionalisation in a federal direction including the normalisation of the EP as a federal level parliament with full budgetary and legislative powers. It also sought to shape opinion and policy-making not just in the EP, but in the EC system more generally – and did so quite successfully. It is therefore unsurprising that, when the Cold War ended in 1989–90 and the Soviet Union collapsed in the following year, this momentous change marked a kind of 'end of history' for the EPP: its values of democracy, human rights, social market economy and European integration appeared to have prevailed for good, not just over communism, but any form of socialism.

However, the resulting enthusiasm for the EPP and EPP Group's fast enlargement and for deepening the EU quickly based on existing federalist templates posed great challenges, that the alliance of centre-right parties did not foresee, and that were perhaps not foreseeable at the time. The first of these concerned the EPP's ability to absorb many more new parties during the EU's Northern and Eastern enlargements. The ambition to socialise new East-Central and South-Eastern European parties into the postwar Christian democratic consensus proved to be particularly difficult (Kaiser 2012, Dakowska 2009a) and created internal strife (see Bardi in Chapter 5 of this book). The second concerned the increasingly pervasive discourse about the EC's 'democratic deficit' from the 1970s onwards – a discourse that ironically, the EPP Group had fostered in order to strengthen its claim to more powers for the EP as apparently the only remedy to this fundamental problem. After the end of the Cold War and the Maastricht Treaty, however, populist parties on the Right and Left of the spectrum increasingly radicalised this 'democratic deficit' discourse to discredit long-standing EPP Group ambitions for the EU as well as the entire European 'project'.

# Chapter 2 Constitutionalising the Union: The Role of the EPP Group[1]

*Karl Magnus Johansson*

## *Introduction*

The purpose of this chapter is to explore the role of the European People's Party (EPP) Group in the European Union's (EU) constitutional reform and the overall process of constitutionalisation.[2] The chapter addresses three interrelated research questions. Firstly, what did the Group want? Secondly, how did the Group attempt to achieve its goals? Thirdly, what did it achieve? The chapter addresses this topic and these questions empirically through a focus on how the EPP Group sought to influence, either directly or indirectly, the course and outcome of the negotiations leading to the adoption of the successive treaties over the past three decades.

In this context, influence means successful attempts to change an outcome from what it otherwise would have been in the absence of the action. Influence is difficult to observe and measure in practice. However, attempts can be made to identify the prime movers behind influence attempts, even if this too may be difficult considering the multiplicity of actors and the complexity of chains of causation or causal networks.

The chapter covers six attempts at political group influence in constitutional reform from the 1980s to the 2000s: the negotiations leading to the adoption of the Single European Act (SEA, 1986), the Treaty of Maastricht

---

1 Earlier versions of this chapter were presented at the project workshops at the European University Institute in Florence in November 2018 and March 2019, as well as at the final conference held there in November 2019. For helpful comments and suggestions, I wish to thank Alfredo De Feo, my fellow project participants, in particular Luciano Bardi, and the two research assistants Jacopo Cellini and Johannes Karremans for their valuable readings of my drafts and for their editorial and research assistance. I also wish to thank Martin Kamp and Johan Ryngaert of the EPP Group Secretariat for their valuable input, as well as Emma Petroni at the EPP Group archives for her support.

2 For simplicity the chapter uses the abbreviation EPP Group, even for the period (1999-2009) during which the Group was called the European People's Party and European Democrats (EPP-ED).

or the Treaty on European Union (TEU, 1992), the Amsterdam Treaty (1997), the Nice Treaty (2001), the Constitutional Treaty (2004) and the Lisbon Treaty (2007). The chapter also discusses the Draft Treaty establishing a Constitution for Europe, which was adopted by the European Convention in 2003, but treats it mainly as a prelude to the analysis of the EPP Group and the Constitutional Treaty and the Lisbon Treaty. The story begins in Dublin, where the EPP – both the party and the Group – gathered in 1984; it ends in Lisbon in 2007, when the current treaty was adopted.

The chapter purports to document the role of the EPP Group and its networks in the context of treaty negotiations in Intergovernmental Conferences (IGCs), which have resulted in wide-ranging constitutional and institutional changes since the mid-1980s (Laursen 2012a, 2016a, 2016b and references therein). This analysis will pick up the thread where Wolfram Kaiser left off in Chapter 1, after the discussion of the Draft Treaty of the European Union (DTEU). Since the mid-1980s and into the late 2000s, the politics of the European Communities (EC)/EU have amounted to a near-permanent IGC. IGCs constitute milestones in the history, process and long-term patterns of European integration, and they have resulted in wide-ranging treaty changes, considered to be 'history-making' decisions (Moravcsik 1998).

While treaty reforms in the EU involve a complex set of actors, and the complexity of IGCs also reflects the complexity of the broader EU system, general EU bargaining and decision-making, the existing literature on IGCs often treats these processes as unique and as mainly involving national players representing governments. However, there is a much wider range of actors involved and the significance of their role in the treaty reform process is a matter of empirical research. While the growing impact of the European Parliament (EP) has already been addressed by the literature (e.g. Christiansen and Reh 2009), the role of political groups has generally not been taken into consideration.

This chapter examines the effects of the EPP Group's role on treaty reform in these instances, drawing on a combination of primary and secondary material and relying on complementary forms of primary material. For reasons of space, the chapter does not cover in detail the content of every treaty or the positions of Member States. Instead, the focus is on the informal and the formal relationship between the treaty-making process, the EPP Group and its networks. These are actors who handle inputs into the policy process by operating through transnational transmission systems at the interface between the national and the European levels. How informal integration interacts with formal integration is the central question in this research (Christiansen and Piattoni 2003; Johansson 2017; Middlemas

1995; van Heumen and Roos 2019; Wallace 1990). By drawing also on previous research on the history of European Christian Democracy (e.g. Kaiser 2007), the chapter aims to demonstrate that transnational partisanship is one dimension or category of informality in European integration. In doing so, an analytic-narrative approach will be adopted (Bates et al. 1998). Such analysis seeks to draw broad, applicable theoretical generalisations from specific historical examples or particular cases, from explanations of political outcomes in case studies. It uses close analysis of cases to illuminate important general issues.

The chapter thus attempts to recount the EU's constitutionalisation through the microcosm of politico-individual ties. It concludes that, while the EPP Group has been able to shape treaties, its influence is bounded insofar as it is conditional on favourable circumstances in general and particularly on government links and the standing of government leaders. This finding, developed in the concluding discussion of this chapter, has important implications for our understanding of the mechanism through which political actors affect the process and outcome of EU decision-making and treaty negotiations. It also contributes to the literature on the 'constitutionalisation' of the EU, the reasons for integration and the logic of pooled sovereignty.

The chapter is divided into seven sections. The next six sections present the results of the exploration of the influence of the EPP Group on the treaties, addressing the main question of what collective influence the EPP Group had over the content of these treaties. The chapter concludes by summarising the findings and discussing the broader implications of the chapter for existing and future research.

### *The EPP Group and the Single European Act (1986)*

In February 1984, the EP had passed the DTEU with the pivotal contribution of the EPP Group, after a long negotiating process (see Kaiser in Chapter 1 of this book). However, for its provisions to be enacted, the agreement of the Member States and the ratification of national parliaments was necessary, and this was soon regarded as an extremely unlikely outcome. Instead, the process of EC reform took another route. At the Fontainebleau summit in June 1984, the Member States decided to set up a committee to discuss treaty reform. The committee, known as the Dooge Committee after its Irish chairman, former Minister for Foreign Affairs James Dooge, consisted of personal representatives of the Heads of State and Government plus one representative of the Commission, and was modelled on the Spaak Committee, which had paved the way for the negotiation of the EEC Treaty in the 1950s (Corbett et al. 2016: 436). Belgium's Christian democratic Prime Minister Wilfried Martens nominated EPP MEP Fernand Herman, a former Minister of Economic Affairs (1975-1977) and now member of the Committee on Institutional Affairs, who was in favour of working out a European constitution along federal lines and later became heavily involved in the EP's drive for institutional reform (Kaiser 2018: 39). His name will appear often over the following pages.

The Dooge Committee was clearly of great potential importance in the path towards a much more integrated Community. It was useful in bringing people together and creating momentum for the duration of its work and beyond. It presented an interim report for the Dublin European Council of December 1984, and a final report, often referred to as the Dooge Report, in Brussels in March 1985.[3] This report is credited with paving the way for the Single European Act and the Maastricht Treaty, with much of the language used in the latter being the same.

In view of the Dublin European Council meeting, the EPP Bureau and the EPP Group held a joint meeting in the Irish capital on 5 December 1984, in the presence of Christian democratic party and government leaders.[4] In a resolution adopted unanimously, it was stated that the EP's 1984 DTEU should be used as a basis for further considerations and decisions on such a union. It was stressed as necessary to take quick and irreversible steps in the direction of its foundation, without awaiting the minority of governments that were not prepared to follow suit (in EU jargon, this amounts to 'flexible integration' or 'enhanced co-operation'). Finally, it was suggested that the heads of government affiliated with the EPP and the chairmen of EPP member parties and of their parliamentary groups come together before the Milan summit of June 1985. They should do so in order to express their political will to found the European Union and together seize the necessary initiatives and measures.

On 17 April 1985, the EP adopted a resolution based on the report by Belgian Christian democratic MEP Lambert Croux, Vice-Chair of the Institutional Affairs Committee and member of the Political Affairs Committee. The report reiterated the EP's demand that the governments speedily convene an IGC no later than June 1985, before the forthcoming Milan summit. An EPP Conference meeting was held in Luxembourg on 23

3 UCD Archives, Papers of Professor James Dooge, P270/222, 29-30 March 1985.

4 ACDP, 009-007-044/2, Erklärung, Dublin, den 5. Dezember 1984.

April 1985, with a working dinner the previous evening.[5] The Conference was attended by four heads of government: FitzGerald, Kohl, Lubbers and Santer (Martens was in China at the time). The Italian Deputy Prime Minister Forlani was also present, along with Andreotti, Tindemans and representatives of the EPP and of the EPP Group. In a communiqué, the EPP linked the need for institutional reform to the enlargement of the Community to 12 Member States. In view of the Milan summit and in light of the conclusions drawn in the Dooge Report and of the EP's Draft Treaty, the EPP demanded that an IGC should be convened. The view was expressed that its duration should be as limited in time as possible, and preferably finalised before November 1985. With the exception of the governments of the Member States, it was proposed that representatives of the future Member States of Spain and Portugal should be invited to take part in the IGC, along with the Presidents of the Commission and the EP. Finally, it was stated that another EPP Conference would meet to prepare the Milan summit.

The EPP Conference was held at Palazzo Barberini in Rome on 20 June 1985, one week before the subsequent Milan European Council.[6] Once again, party and group worked together, on the basis of a text drafted by Fernand Herman. The Group was represented at a high level by people like Chairman Egon Klepsch (DE), Vice-Chairmen Panayotis Lambrias (GR), Giovanni Giavazzi (IT) and Willem Vergeer (NL), and Secretary-General Giampaolo Bettamio (IT). Of the five Christian democratic heads of government who would attend the Milan summit, the following were present at the Rome EPP Conference: Garret FitzGerald, Helmut Kohl and Jacques Santer (Martens was absent and Lubbers had to stay in The Hague because of a visit by the Spanish Prime Minister). Arnaldo Forlani, Deputy Prime Minister of Italy, was there, and so were the two Foreign Ministers Guilio Andreotti (Italy) and Leo Tindemans (Belgium). Other participants included Pierre Pfimlin, President of the EP, Siegbert Alber, Vice-President of the EP, Emilio Colombo from Italy and the EPP Presidency, Paolo Barbi (Italy), a former Chairman of the EPP Group, James Dooge, and Fernand Herman.

5 ACDP, 009-004-018/4, Aide-Mémoire, der EVP-Arbeitsgruppe 'Europäische Union' für die Konferenz der Partei- und Regierungschefs am 23. April 1985 in Luxemburg; Communiqué de la Présidence du PPE à l'occasion du Sommet-PPE du 23 avril à Luxembourg; Erklärung des EVP-Präsidiums anläßlich des EVP-Gipfeltreffens am 23. April 1985 in Luxemburg.

6 ACDP, 09-007-017/2.

In the final declaration issued at the end of the Conference, Christian democratic leaders were unequivocal about their priorities for the further development of European integration towards a political union, following the recommendations of the EP and the Dooge Committee. A new treaty must be established for the European Union, in particular to organise effective co-operation in relation to foreign and security policy. Under the heading of "new areas of activity", the declaration called for the completion of the internal market and for the EC to hold the necessary powers, in particular in the sectors of research, technology and protection of the environment. The reinforcement of the convergence of economic policies must go hand-in-hand with the development of the monetary system. Provisions must be made for the reduction of the economic and social disparities between Member States. The creation of a European judicial area was regarded as essential. In conclusion, the leaders of the Christian democratic parties meeting in Rome pleaded that the Milan European Council "should take irreversible decisions concerning the matters set out above and, on this basis, should convene an inter-governmental conference with a precise mandate to achieve these objectives". The EP, through its President, must take part in the conference. The conference "should moreover conclude its work this year". This was deemed as "necessary so as to enable the community of 12 to retain the capacity for action and to permit the pursuit of the objective of integration".[7]

Testimonies suggest that the EPP meeting in Rome contributed to a push for a major treaty reform. As Thomas Jansen testifies: 'I agree fully with your considerations concerning the role of the EPP with respect to the 85 Milano European Council. In fact, the EPP heads of government and party leaders had agreed, a couple of days before in Rome, to follow the strategy proposed by Andreotti; there was a very strong feeling among the participants that 'die Stunde der Wahrheit' (Kohl) had come, and that therefore one had to go ahead, hoping and being rather sure that others would follow.'[8] According to Jansen, Andreotti forced Craxi to move ahead with an IGC (Interview Jansen, 27.10.1995).

Indeed, at the Milan European Council, which marked the end of the Italian Presidency of the EC, the prime ministers and heads of state decided by an unprecedented majority vote to convene an IGC to revise the existing treaties. This event was a turning point and a crucial step forward in the history of European integration. The vote was not hastily and unex-

7 Ibid.
8 Personal letter to the author, dated 4 February 1996.

pectedly arrived at: it had been prepared and was a matter of great priority within the Christian democratic network (Johansson 2002b).

The Luxembourg Presidency of the second half of 1985 launched the IGC, which opened in September of that year. The acting President of the European Council during the second half of 1985 was a Christian Democrat, Jacques Santer, Prime Minister of Luxembourg. During the period of the IGC, the Christian Democrats continued their deliberations with a view to shaping the detailed agenda of the IGC in the lead-up to the Luxembourg European Council in December 1985 (Corbett 1987: 243). In view of that meeting, the EPP Conference of party leaders and heads of government convened in Brussels on 9 November 1985 "with the aim of elaborating a common position" for their governments and to advance progress in the IGC (Budden 1994: 341; Budden 2002). At the Luxembourg European Council, there was an agreement on the text that would become the SEA. By adopting the SEA, the governments had achieved the objective of setting a deadline for completing the internal market on the basis of the Commission's White Book. For the time being, they left the question of a single currency hanging in the air. However, a brief reference in the treaty "at least planted a seed for further reference" (Corbett 1993: 3; see also Dyson and Featherstone 1999: 318-19, and Germond in Chapter 3 of this book). Monetary union, including a single currency, required further treaty amendments and thus another IGC. The legislative role of the EP was the final outstanding issue in the IGC, with Kohl favouring a form of co-decision between the EP and the Council (Dinan 2012: 139).

The convergence of preferences and positions over the priorities that led to the SEA was, at least partly, the product of mobilisation through transnational party networks, particularly the EPP, which arranged caucus meetings and sustained the networks. At the time, the EPP Conference brought together some 30 persons. They included heads of government, the chairmen of EPP member parties and the chairmen of national parliamentary groups. The Presidencies of the EPP and of the EPP Group were represented, along with Commissioners and leading politicians from the EP. Occasionally, as we have seen, members of the EPP Group took part in high-level talks, notably when the EPP Conference met in Rome in June 1985. MEP Fernand Herman was especially influential in contributing to the success of the negotiations.

In his foreword to the EPP Group's 1985/1986 activity report, Egon Klepsch noted that the Group enjoyed close contact with the Council Presidency, as well as with the other Christian democratic governments and the national parliamentary groups. In addition, the EPP Group maintained close contacts with political friends in the Commission. More specifically, according to Klepsch, the Group

> played a decisive role in preparing the government conference that finally led to the adoption of the Luxembourg decisions and the Single European Act. Owing to the co-ordination measures based to a large extent on proposals drawn up by the Group with the help of the Federation of the EPP, the efforts of Italy and Luxembourg as Presidents of the Council and the support of the Christian Democratic heads of government of the Federal Republic of Germany, Belgium, Ireland and the Netherlands the final result can serve as a starting point for the further development of the Community.[9]

However, the EPP Group wanted more integration. In an extended comment on the SEA and the results of the IGC, the EPP Group stated: "Much could be said about flaws and shortcomings in the Single Act when compared with the EP's draft treaty. ... The Single European Act is not and cannot be the end of the road – with a little goodwill it can be seen as a beginning".[10] For one, the formal legal power of the EP should be extended further: although the new procedure introduced by the treaty, the cooperation procedure, enabled the Parliament for the first time to participate in the process of forming European law, the Council still held the bulk of the powers.

At the same time, EPP Group Chairman Klepsch was self-congratulatory about how influential the group had been. In the 1986/1987 annual report, he wrote that the SEA was "the most important reform since the signature of the Treaties of Rome thirty years ago", and that it

> marks the beginning of a new chapter in the history of the Community. For European Christian Democrats its greatest merit is that, after numerous unsuccessful attempts, our governments have finally succeeded in taking a first decisive step towards European Union. Consequently, there are high expectations attached to the implementation of this reform on all sides. From the outset our Group has been aware that the decisive factor will be the contribution that *we, the initiators of the Act*, make to its implementation.[11] (Emphasis added)

9 EPP Group Archives, D.5.7, Activity Report, Yearbook, July 1985–July 1986, p. 7.
10 EPP Group Archives, D.5.7, Activity Report, Yearbook, July 1985-July 1986, p. 35.
11 EPP Group Archives, D.5.8, Activity Report, Yearbook, July 1986–July 1987, p. 5.

In summary, the EPP Group had actual influence on the outcome of this treaty reform. Members belonging to the EPP Group were to some extent able to influence the direction and outcome of the process of constitutionalisation and European integration. The EPP – both the party and the group – had established a common position on an institutional strategy and a broad support for a new treaty. Pressure for an IGC and a major treaty reform in a federalist direction was built up in the EPP network. The EPP party and group sustained interest in these integrationist proposals through informal networks linking national parties and parliamentarians and their European counterparts to each other.

Although the EP considered the results to be insufficient, it nevertheless accepted them. After all, it was the first major revision of the treaties since 1957. The SEA was signed on 17 February 1986 in Luxembourg. It came into force in July 1987. It paved the way for the more substantial negotiations on the Treaty of Maastricht concluded five years later, and for subsequent IGCs.

### *The EPP Group and the Treaty of Maastricht (1992)*

Although the SEA was a significant step forward in the history of European integration, European union had not yet been achieved. The Christian Democrats therefore continued to push for a major treaty reform. In the interval between the adoption of the SEA in December 1985 and the launch in December 1990 of the two IGCs on Economic and Monetary Union (EMU) and European Political Union, the EPP, party and group, set out its objectives and federalist blueprint for a true union.

In the 1986/1987 annual report, EPP Group Chairman Klepsch emphasised the goal of federal union and wrote, "we intend to pursue more radical initiatives based on the draft Treaty adopted by the European Parliament in 1984 and the draft constitution produced by our Group, with a view to amending the Treaty to achieve 'European Union'."[12] He referred to the Herman report on the strategy of the EP for achieving European union, which was adopted by the Committee on Institutional Affairs on its meeting of 29 October 1986. It made the point that the transition from the SEA to the European Union required the commitment of the institutions standing for democratic legitimacy at national and European level.

12 EPP Group Archives, D.5.8, Activity Report, Yearbook, July 1986-July 1987, p. 5.

Based on the Herman report, the EP adopted a resolution in June 1987 (European Parliament 1987). The resolution called on European political groups to take all necessary steps to secure governmental agreement. It also called on the Committee on Institutional Affairs to establish suitable contacts with the national governmental and parliamentary authorities, the confederation of political parties at European level, the national parties and the economic, social and cultural agencies. The Committee was also asked to stimulate public awareness of the urgent need to establish a European Union and to submit to the Parliament a final report.[13] This was shortly before the entry into force of the SEA, on 1 July 1987.

In this way, the EPP Group and its members outlined the EP's strategy as regards to European union. In the foreword to the 1987/1988 activity report, EPP Group Chairman Klepsch wrote: 'In accordance with its twin-track strategy, the Group seized every opportunity for institutional development, in co-operation with the other parliamentary and Community bodies, partly with a view to creating the best possible conditions for the intergovernmental conference to review the treaties in the early 1990s.'[14]

The resolution adopted by the EP in February 1989 drew upon the work carried out by Herman, especially in the report submitted to the Committee on Institutional Affairs: it declared the EP's intention, after the June elections and with a view to 1992, to draw up comprehensive proposals based in the main on its Draft Treaty of 1984 to create the necessary institutional basis for the EU. It called on the heads of state and government meeting in the European Council held on 26 and 27 June in Madrid to recognise the need for this project and to undertake to support it. If Europe was to speak with one voice, it would need one government, and the formation of that government would require institutional reforms (European Parliament 1989a). The EP proposed a wider agenda, not just on economic union but on political union.

Outside of the Parliament, too, the EPP continued to push for European integration. At the Dublin Congress in November 1990, the party characteristically portrayed itself as the federalist inheritor of the legacy of the Christian democratic founding fathers of European integration. The document adopted at the Congress called for a federal constitution and major institutional reform.[15] It served as the EPP's contribution to the IGCs, and

---

13 EPP Group Archives, D.5.8, Activity Report, Yearbook, p. 314.

14 EPP Group Archives, D.5.9, Activity Report, Yearbook, Report on the activities 1987–1988, p. 6.

15 EPP Group Archives, N.1.1.4, EPP Party, "For a Federal Constitution of the European Union". Congress Document, Dublin, November 1990.

it was quoted by Klepsch as "a reference point for all our political activities."[16] However, the Group also did its part to pursue its ambition for the European construction, toward a federal type union organised on the basis of democracy and the principle of subsidiarity.

The European elections held on 15 June 1989 changed both the EP geography and the Group's internal composition. The EPP Group continued to be the second-largest group in the EP, but the gap with the Socialists increased to 59 seats, mostly due to the effect of Spain and Portugal joining the EC (see Bardi in Chapter 5 of this book). Socialist Enrique Barón Crespo was elected EP President for the first half of the term. At the same time, new MEPs joined the EPP Group's ranks, including the Spanish members Marcelino Oreja and José María Gil-Robles y Gil-Delgado, and Frenchman Jean-Louis Bourlanges, who would become influential players in institutional matters. Oreja became Chairman of the Committee on Institutional Affairs, which counted among its EPP members Emilio Colombo and Fernand Herman; among the deputies were Bourlanges, Elmar Brok and Leo Tindemans, creating a mix between the old and new guard. The Committee aimed to bring about European union and institutional reform "aimed at changing the legal institutional basis of the European Community, not least by defining the Community's future powers and responsibilities."[17] In 1990, the EP adopted (on 11 July) a resolution on its guidelines for a draft constitution for the EU, as well as a resolution (on 12 December) on the constitutional basis of the EU, with Colombo (EPP) serving as Rapporteur in both cases (European Parliament 1990a; European Parliament 1990b).

In the meantime, the EPP Group also organised initiatives outside the EP to push for constitutional reform. In particular, its Study Days held in Funchal from 10 to 14 July 1989 resulted in the 'Funchal Appeal', which proposed a strategy: "a tripartite preparatory conference, bringing together the Council, Parliament and the Commission, should be held to determine the content and procedure of the intergovernmental conference. The main aims here were to extend the scope of reform to embrace the consequences of economic and monetary union, and to strengthen the powers of Parliament in order to reduce the democratic deficit."[18] An objective was to involve Parliament in the drawing up of a new treaty. The activity report further stated that the "federalist goal of European unity can be

16 EPP Group Archives, D.5.12, Activity Report, Yearbook 1990-1991, p. 5.
17 EPP Group Archives, D.5.11, Activity Report, Yearbook 1989-1990, p. 241.
18 EPP Group Archives, D.5.11, Activity Report, Yearbook 1989-1990, p. 10.

achieved only on the basis of a common currency and a common defence policy".

The initiatives undertaken by the EP in order to widen the agenda of the future IGC, not just on economic union (as agreed in the June 1989 Madrid European Council) but also on political union, gradually gained support from Member States. Chancellor Kohl was sympathetic to the involvement of MEPs in the discussions on further European integration. Although Bonn was the major target for MEP lobbying, the links between the EPP Group and national Christian democratic parties appear to have influenced the governments in Rome, Brussels and The Hague alike. Even if the EPP Group requests merely caused sympathetic governments to submit proposals in line with policy preferences that already existed, the chronology suggests that the Group and individual members influenced the timing and presentation of these interventions. The Belgian memorandum of 20 March 1990 was, for example, prepared in consultation with MEPs (Corbett 1993: 9).

In April 1990, Chancellor Kohl and President Mitterrand sent a joint message to the President of the European Council proposing an IGC on 'political union' of the existing EC, as well as that already planned on economic and monetary union. If there was to be monetary union, political union was also necessary. Kohl wanted to show that Germany, also in the context of reunification, was firmly anchored in Europe.

In December 1990, two IGCs were finally launched, one on Economic and Monetary Union and the other on European Political Union. During the two IGCs, the EP maintained its involvement through an inter-institutional conference, which continued in parallel with the IGCs, involving monthly meetings between the 12 ministers, 12 MEPs and four Commissioners (Corbett et al. 2016: 438). The EP's delegation also toured the national capitals holding individual meetings with each head of government.

In this crucial period, institutional matters dominated the Group's agenda. At their Study Days in Santiago de Compostela on 8-12 April 1991, the EPP Group adopted a memorandum on the two IGCs stating the need for "a Union before the end of the century, with a deepened and complete internal market, a two-House legislative power, a government, a single federal Constitution, on the basis of a constituent mandate attributed to the EP"[19].

On 3-4 June 1991 in Luxembourg, with a view to the European Council meeting there later that month, there was a parliamentary seminar of the

19 *Agence Europe* 15-16 April 1991.

EPP Group, with a particular focus on the two IGCs. The final document, adopted by the Group on 6 June, sets out its "absolute priorities" – including "a federal Constitution" and "a federal Europe" – for the two IGCs, and was forwarded to the heads of government and the parties that met at the EPP Conference on 21 June 1991.[20]

The Conference brought together several party leaders and all six Christian democratic heads of government. Klepsch took part in this and other EPP Conference meetings. In 1991, he attended all three EPP Conference meetings – in Brussels in April, in Luxembourg in June and the one held in The Hague in December prior to the Maastricht summit – as well as the informal get-together of the Prime Ministers in Brussels in November 1991.

During the Dutch Presidency in the second half of 1991, Prime Minister Ruud Lubbers also exchanged views with the EPP Group. Lubbers had two meetings with the Group Bureau, in October and December 1991, and he received a list of priorities, which was summed up in seven items.[21] They covered unity of the procedures for economic union, political union and judicial co-operation, democratic legitimacy, decision-making efficiency, EMU, social dimension and economic and social cohesion, foreign and security policy, federal-type union and a treaty revision in 1996 with parliamentary representation. Lubbers evoked these key items for discussion at the EPP Conference meeting and added a few, notably the strengthening of the statutes of the Court of Auditors and the number of German MEPs. Hence there was a clear pattern of interaction involving the Group, the party, national party leaders and also EPP representatives at the head of European institutions (Johansson 2002a). As Fontaine (2009: 303) observes:

> The Party and the Group worked closely together during this intense phase that everyone felt was changing the European context. … The preparations for the Maastricht summit prompted intense collaboration between the Group and the Party, bolstered by a shared conviction. The objectives were clear and well-defined: pushing forward political union and Economic and Monetary Union, extending the Community's competences and qualified majority voting, making the Union more democratic, and agreeing on a single Treaty …

---

20 EPP Group Archives, C.6.5, What Institutions for the European Community? Parliamentary Seminar of the EPP Group, Luxembourg, 3-4 June 1991. See also *Agence Europe*, 6 June 1991.

21 EPP Group Archives, D.5.13, Activity Report, Yearbook 1991-1992, p. 310.

Agreement on the Treaty on European Union was finally reached on 10 December 1991 in Maastricht, and the treaty was officially signed in the same city on 7 February 1992. It brought about a further extension of the powers of the EP through co-decision with the Council of Ministers and two further pillars, which were primarily intergovernmental: the second pillar, Common Foreign and Security Policy (CFSP), and the third pillar, Justice and Home Affairs (JHA).

The EP – which by then had a new President, longstanding EPP Group Chairman Egon Klepsch, who finally succeeded in being elected to the highest post of the Assembly (see Kaiser in Chapter 1 of this book) – discussed the results of the IGCs on 7 April 1992. It could give only an advisory opinion, given that the treaty had not conferred on it power of assent (in other words the right to reject), but the Belgian, German and Italian national parliaments stated that they would ratify only if the EP approved it. Fernand Herman was Rapporteur together with David Martin (PES) for the resolution on the results of the IGCs (European Parliament 1992). Here, the EP invited the national parliaments to ratify the treaty on account of its positive aspects, but drew up a long list of its shortcomings, such as the role that the EP and the Commission were to play in the intergovernmental 'pillars' and economic and social policy.

The EPP Group voiced the same reservations during the plenary debate. The speaker was the new EPP Group Chairman, Belgian Leo Tindemans, who replaced Klepsch. Tindemans explained:

> I do, however, wish to make it clear that we shall vote in favour of Maastricht, in spite of our disappointment or our criticisms of certain decisions. … I should like to issue a warning: we hear even serious politicians say that the Community must not be enlarged until the democratic deficit has been overcome. Why not say that it should not be enlarged until a constitution has been adopted for Europe …[22]

In a document issued in June 1992, meant to inform about and analyse the new treaty, the Group further emphasised that the Treaty of Maastricht is a text that "merely represents a staging post on the road to European Union along federal lines".[23] In his foreword to the activity report for 1991/1992, Tindemans also stressed that the fight for a "European Constitution" would go on and "armed with its convictions and commitment, the Group

22 EPP Group Archives, C.8.11, The Maastricht Treaty, June 1992, p. 36.
23 EPP Group Archives, C.8.11, The Maastricht Treaty, June 1992, p. 3.

of the European People's Party, which sets out to be in the political vanguard, has the resources to win the battle".[24]

In summary, the EPP Group sought to influence – including through the EPP party networks – the outcome of the treaty negotiations and was able to do so to some extent. While it had set out higher expectations, expressing strongly pro-federalist sympathies, it contributed to the momentum towards institutional and treaty reform that had been generated by the SEA. They were pushing to solve the 'democratic deficit' by increasing the powers of the EP.

The Treaty of Maastricht provided that a further IGC should be convened in 1996 to review the treaty, thereby already identifying some specific issues for consideration and possible reforms (e.g. Vanhoonacker 2012: 183-184). These included, among other things, a review of the two intergovernmental pillars of CFSP and JHA, the scope of co-decision – that is, a possible extension of the number of areas in which the EP acts in co-decision with the Council of Ministers and the weighting of the votes of Member States there – as well as of qualified majority voting (QMV) and of the competences of the Union.

### *The EPP Group and the Amsterdam Treaty (1997)*

Part of the overall compromise signed off in Maastricht was an agreement written into the text to re-examine some issues in a further IGC in 1996. Thus, the agenda of the IGC was largely predetermined or foreseen by the TEU and to focus on the Maastricht leftovers.

The new treaty had barely been adopted when the preparations for the next IGC were taking off in the EPP and in the EPP Group. Successive EPP Congresses reiterated the demand for a federal European union. In November 1992, the EPP Congress in Athens adopted a new programme. At the December 1993 Congress in Brussels, the EPP adopted its 1994-1999 action programme. These programmes pushed for a federalist solution, just like the EPP manifesto for the June 1994 European elections.

Once again, party and group acted in sync: although their relationship was occasionally tense, there was a shared integrationist agenda (Johansson 2015, 2016). Looking to 1996 and the IGC due to start that year, EPP Group Chairman Tindemans, while welcoming Parliament's new and wider powers, stressed the need for "thoroughgoing reform", not least in

24 EPP Group Archives, D.5.13, Activity Report, Yearbook 1991-1992, p. 8.

view of enlargement: "Careful, painstaking preparations for the Intergovernmental Conference must begin immediately, in order to make 1996 a decisive year."[25]

As Fontaine (2009: 308) notes, the Treaty of Maastricht had "scarcely been ratified" when the EP went back to the subject of a draft Constitution for the European Union through its adoption, on 9 February 1994, of the Herman report (European Parliament 1994), which called for a treaty reform for the consolidation of the various treaties into a single constitutional text. This was in part necessary to tackle the institutional challenge of future enlargements towards Central and Eastern Europe. However, there was still a long way to go before a definitive text could be achieved, especially since not everyone believed that a written constitution was essential. It was for the next elected Parliament to consider the text in an in-depth political debate and decide what action to take.[26]

The European elections held in June 1994 confirmed the Party of European Socialists (PES) and the EPP as the two largest groups in the EP. German Social Democrat Klaus Hänsch was elected President of the Parliament for the first mid-term; he would be replaced by Gil-Robles (EPP) in 1997. The elections brought about critical changes in the internal composition of the EPP Group, notably the size of the Italian delegation was much reduced because of the collapse of the Italian Democrazia Cristiana (see Bardi in Chapter 5 of this book). EPP President Wilfred Martens was elected Group Chairman, becoming the first person to simultaneously hold the Presidency of the party and the group.

Martens was one of the members of the Committee on Institutional Affairs, together with Elmar Brok (DE), Hanja Maij-Weggen (NL) and Íñigo Méndez de Vigo (ES), Vice-Chairman of the Committee. José Maria Gil-Robles Gil-Delgado, a federalist and future EP president, became Chairman of the Committee on Institutional Affairs in July 1993. EPP Group members in the committee were co-ordinated through the person who served as Co-ordinator of the EPP Group members in the Committee – successively Bourlanges, Froment-Meurice, Gil-Robles Gil-Delgado and Méndez de Vigo. In 1995, the Committee prepared a set of proposals on the EU Treaty and IGC. The preparations for the 1996 IGC involved the Bourlanges and Martin report on the functioning of the Treaty on European Union. The report was adopted as a resolution by the EP on 17 May 1995 (European Parliament 1995). The report was then sent to the Reflec-

25 EPP Group Archives, D.5.15, Activity Report, Yearbook 1993-1994, pp. 7-8.
26 EPP Group Archives, D.5.15, Activity Report, Yearbook 1993-1994, p. 275.

tion Group, which had been set up to prepare the IGC by the European Council at its Corfu meeting in June 1994. The Reflection Group was composed of a representative of each Member State's foreign minister and two MEPs.

The EP appointed Elmar Brok, a German Christian Democrat, and Elisabeth Guigou, former French European Affairs Minister (Socialist), as its two representatives in the Reflection Group. Brok and Guigou also represented the EP in the subsequent IGC, with the status of closely associated observers. Brok, a noted federalist, enjoyed the confidence of, and had a direct line to, Chancellor Kohl.[27]

The Reflection Group met from June to December 1995, and prepared a report which served as a platform for the subsequent IGC. In the Turin European Council on 29 March 1996, the fifteen Member States convened the IGC, which, under the successive Presidencies of Italy, Ireland and the Netherlands, drew up a draft treaty that was adopted by the Amsterdam European Council on 16 and 17 June 1997. Each one of the Member States' heads of state or government nominated a negotiating team; together, these teams formed the IGC negotiating group. The European Council agreed that the EP could have its two representatives, Brok and Guigou, and they would meet monthly with the IGC negotiating group. The President of Parliament would have an exchange of views with the EU Foreign Ministers each time they discussed the IGC. In practice, according to the Belgian representative in the IGC Philippe de Schoutheete, while the British and French governments were opposed to their presence in the room during the IGC negotiations, in the end Brok and Guigou were there almost all the time (Interview de Schoutheete, 8.04.1999).

According to Corbett et al. (2016: 441), Brok and Guigou were able to discuss every subject with the IGC negotiators, obtain every document, table their own proposals and counter-proposals and join in informal dinners and conclaves. The two Parliament representatives were able to play a substantial agenda-setting role. Priestley (2008: 36) emphasises "the efficiency of Parliament's representations; the main institutional change at Amsterdam was to put Parliament and Council on an equal footing in the legislative co-decision procedures and to extend the number of areas cov-

27 Brok said he certainly knew Kohl but that his first priority, as a member of the Reflection Group, was to take care of the "interests of the Parliament" (Interview Brok, 25.02.1998). As a representative of the EP in the context of the Amsterdam Treaty negotiations Brok was told by Kohl: "I trust you" (Interview Brok, 23.03.2018).

ered by them, thus rapidly correcting an imbalance imported into the Maastricht Treaty".

In March 1996, the EP adopted a resolution on Parliament's opinion on the convening of the IGC, an evaluation of the work of the Reflection Group and a definition of the political priorities of the EP with a view to the IGC, with Raymonde Dury (PES/BE) and Hanja Maij-Weggen (EPP/NL) as Rapporteurs (European Parliament 1996).

The EPP network closely followed the negotiations leading to the Amsterdam Treaty, and contributed to the discussion through several initiatives and documents, including document or position paper "Ability to Act, Democracy and Transparency – the European Union on the Road to a United Europe" adopted at the EPP Congress held in Madrid in November 1995. This document advocated a federal EU and served as the EPP's contribution to the debate on the forthcoming IGC, with a particular emphasis on institutional reform in the EU (Jansen 2006: 200). The paper was based on deliberations in the EPP ad hoc Working Group 'Preparation for the 1996 Intergovernmental Conference', which was set up by the EPP Bureau in 1994. The Working Group was chaired by Hans-Gert Pöttering, German MEP and Vice-Chairman of the EPP Group and later to become Chairman of the EPP Group and President of the EP, assisted by the EPP secretariat, and consisted of representatives of member parties (see also Pöttering 2016: 145-157). The paper constituted a transnational policy contribution by the EPP. The proposals put forward by the EPP Working Group were co-ordinated with and discussed in a working party on the IGC set up by the EPP Group. According to Pöttering, the EPP had a position and this was reflected in the Madrid document (Interview Pöttering, 25.02.1998).

The EPP strategy was further discussed at meetings of the EPP Council, a new body within the EPP, where the IGC was among the agenda items and to which Brok reported (EPP/EUCD 1997).[28] The EPP Council met several times in 1996 and during the period of the IGC itself. The same was true of the EPP Summit, previously known as the EPP Conference, which was comprised of heads of government. It convened six times during the period of the IGC: three times in 1996 – in June, July and December – and three times in 1997 – in March, May and June (EPP/EUCD 1997). Moreover, the positions taken by the governments in the IGC, most notably the German one, would be closely co-ordinated with the policies of the EPP

28 The EPP Council was to be composed mainly of party leaders and Secretary-Generals of member parties.

(Hix and Lord 1997: 194) as well as, directly or indirectly, with the EPP Group. As it happened in the negotiations that led to the Treaty of Maastricht, the synergy between party, group, national governments and European institutions allowed the Christian Democrats to make an effective contribution to treaty reform.

The EP's report on the Amsterdam Treaty was drawn up by the Spanish MEP Íñigo Méndez de Vigo, together with the Greek social democratic MEP Dimitris Tsatsos, as Co-rapporteurs. The report was adopted as a resolution by the EP on 19 November 1997 (European Parliament 1997a).

On behalf of the Group, Martens noted the achievements in some areas, such as the new co-decision-making powers, but again stressed the shortcomings: "However, the EPP Group has already expressed its concern about the limits of the Amsterdam Treaty as regards the institutional arrangements under which the future enlargement of the Union to more than ten Central and Eastern European and Mediterranean countries is to take place".[29]

When asked about the EPP position and co-ordination, Martens said the Amsterdam outcome was a disappointment to him, especially as demands in the institutional fields were abandoned (Interview Martens, 30.03.2000). Although several of the EPP demands were satisfactorily met, the Amsterdam outcome was thus a disappointment to the EPP and EPP Group President. "Amsterdam was not of the same calibre as Maastricht", writes Martens (2008: 137). The employment chapter was one of the most difficult issues for the EPP in the IGC (Interview Welle, 24.02.1998), since EPP governments were divided on the issue (Van Hecke 2004: 50, n. 38). In spite of the challenges faced, some 'degree of success' could be achieved; for example, the expansion of co-decision and strengthening of the EP's control over the Commission (Martens 2008: 138).

In the end, a comparison between the Pöttering document for the EPP Congress in Madrid in November 1995, the EP resolution in March 1996 (the Maij-Weggen report), and the Amsterdam Treaty, shows that the agenda and list of aims identified by the EPP bears a significant similarity to the contents of the new treaty. On a number of points, the demands of the EPP were therefore satisfactorily met.

In the media and in subsequent academic works the Amsterdam outcome has largely been scorned as a failure and as mediocre; this assessment became a "conventional wisdom" (Monar and Wessels 2001). However, more was achieved than has generally been recognised, and outcomes were

29 EPP Group Archives, D.5.20, Activity Report, Yearbook 1998-1999, p. 6.

broadly in line with the EPP demands. Notably, what was actually agreed on the provisions of flexibility/differentiated integration, closer/enhanced co-operation, the extension of QMV and co-decision and thus, with strong German backing too, an increase in EP powers, as well as areas in which the treaty provisions should be strengthened such as employment and third pillar issues, subsequently transferred to the first pillar and thus moving beyond intergovernmental co-operation, implied that the result clearly was significant. Importantly, it all laid a basis for the next IGC. A momentum was built for yet another treaty reform, to begin after the 1999 European elections.

Notwithstanding the divisions inside the EPP and its relative numerical weakness in the European Council, where the balance had shifted further towards the Socialists, the EPP network reached a common position on many of the issues and was able, directly or indirectly, to influence the agenda during the IGC and the outcome of the Amsterdam European Council. The same was true of the EPP Group, a part of the EP which emerged as a winner (e.g. Hix 2002a; Rittberger 2005). Corbett et al. (2016: 450) conclude: "By the time of the 1996 IGC, Parliament was accepted as a partner in the preparatory process, if only partly in the IGC itself, and set a large part of the agenda of the IGC. In terms of the final result, many called Parliament the big winner from the Amsterdam Treaty, which considerably enhanced its power".

### *The EPP Group and the Nice Treaty (2001)*

After the June 1999 European elections, the EPP Group became the biggest group in the EP for the first time in the history of the elected EP. From this dominant position, it was able to pursue its European ambition and shape the EP's line of action more effectively. The EPP's Nicole Fontaine became President of the Parliament, while Hans-Gert Pöttering began his eight-year stint as Chairman of the Group. The new Parliament was to deal with another round of treaty reform that, as decided by the June 1999 Cologne European Council, would take place in the year 2000 through a new IGC. Unlike previous treaty reforms, this time the agenda was largely limited to institutional issues: the re-weighting of votes in the Council; the increased use of Qualified Majority Voting (QMV) in the Council; and the size and composition of the Commission (e.g. Laursen 2006, 2012b). The agenda of the IGC thus encompassed important subjects, such as more majority voting and co-decision. All of these issues are related and raise delicate questions of balancing the power of countries and of institutions. The drive to extend QMV presupposed more co-decision power for the EP.

In preparing its resolution on the preparation of the reform of the treaties and the next IGC, the EP largely relied on the report by Giorgos Dimitrakopoulos (EPP/GR) and Jo Leinen (PES/DE) from the Committee on Constitutional Affairs, which called for a constitutionalisation of the treaty and adopted the report by a large majority (20 to 3) (European Parliament 1999). When the EP stated its view on the report in plenary on 18 November 1999, a large majority of members called for an IGC with a broad agenda. The EP adopted the report and thereby an outline programme for the IGC. However, the Helsinki European Council summit in December 1999 decided that a narrow agenda would be set for next year's IGC to review how, in preparation for its expansion, the EU's main institutions function. This was met with criticism from EPP Group Chairman Pöttering who, in December 1999, insisted on the necessity of in-depth institutional reform, emphasising that his group would like to see the IGC also address the questions of the extension of majority decision-making, the EU's legal personality and ratification by the EP of treaty changes.[30]

The Helsinki European Council of December 1999 confirmed the launch of the IGC for the following year, asserting that the Foreign Ministers would have overall political responsibility. Preparatory work was to be the responsibility of a Group composed of a representative of each Member State government, plus representatives from the Commission and the EP; this Group would also be fully involved in the IGC. The IGC ran from February 2000 until December 2000, when the Nice European Council concluded the negotiations.

Two representatives of the EP were to take part in the work of the Preparatory Group. The EP President represented the EP at IGC engagements at ministerial level (Ministers for Foreign Affairs) and, of course, at the level of heads of state or government, as with the EP's participation at the European Council. Both the Portuguese and the French Presidency of the Council fully involved the EP, on the basis of this approach, in the preparatory work on the Treaty of Nice. According to the EPP Group, the EP's representatives, Elmar Brok (EPP/DE) und Dimitris Tsatsos (PES/GR), as well as EP President Nicole Fontaine (EPP/FR), were therefore "able not only to present the Group's ideas, which had shaped the Parliament's resolutions, to the Ministers for Foreign Affairs and the Heads of State or Government, but also to translate those ideas emphatically into

30 *Quotidien Europe* 7614, 13-14 December 1999.

practical measures in the preparatory phase of the Intergovernmental Conference."[31] The demands of the Group were set out in its motions for resolutions on the IGC and in proposals made by Brok, the Group's representative, at the working level of the IGC on the reform of the treaties, and by EP President Fontaine at the level of heads of state and government in the European Council.

One of these demands related to the introduction of an effective body of rules for closer co-operation between a certain number of Member States. In the report by Gil-Robles to the Committee on Constitutional Affairs, the Group laid down clear requirements regarding the criteria for activating the procedure, the scope of application, the minimum number of members, conformity with the treaty, last resort and, in particular, regarding its capacity to operate within a Community framework (European Parliament 2000a).

Moreover, the Group paid particular attention to the future legal status of the Charter of Fundamental Rights. The Charter was important, also symbolically, in the constitutional development of the Union. The body entrusted to draft the Charter was called a Convention. The text should be ready for the European Council meeting scheduled for December 2000. Maij-Weggen and Méndez de Vigo were among the EPP Group members of the EP delegation charged to draw up the Charter of Fundamental Rights, with Méndez de Vigo appointed Chair of the EP delegation in November 1999. At the time, Méndez de Vigo was the EPP Group Coordinator or spokesman in the Committee on Constitutional Affairs.

In 2000, the EP prepared and adopted a series of resolutions in order to influence the negotiations and broaden the IGC agenda (European Parliament 2000b, 2000c). In the debate in the EP on 12 April 2000 on its proposals for the IGC, EPP Group Chairman Pöttering warned: "If the extension of majority decision-making does not occur then the IGC will fail".[32] For the EPP Group, the extension of majority decision-making in the Council was the key to success. It meant, of course, an extension of EP powers as well.

Brok and Tsatsos presented a report to the EP just before the Feira European Council in June 2000, on the IGC's progress (or lack thereof) to date. Among other things, they requested a radical extension of QMV and for the application of the co-decision procedure to all QMV decisions. The EP wanted to broaden the agenda, including issues such as the reallocation of

31 EPP Group Archives, D.5.21, Activity report, Yearbook 2000, p. 120.
32 EPP Group Archives, D.5.21, Activity report, Yearbook 2000, p. 124.

seats per Member State in the EP, the integration of the Western European Union, the size and working methods of the Courts, enhanced co-operation, the statute of European political parties and the protection of fundamental rights. The Commission, too, wanted a wider IGC agenda, including but also beyond the Amsterdam Treaty's unfinished business, such as flexibility and the Charter of Fundamental Rights.

After four days of non-stop negotiations, a final agreement was reached at Nice European Council in December 2000. Ultimately, there was progress on the party statute regulating the recognition and funding of European political parties (Johansson and Raunio 2004, 2005, 2019). The legal basis for the Europarties was provided by the Nice Treaty (Article 191, paragraph two) but some governments remained opposed to the regulation. An initial attempt with Germany's Ursula Schleicher, a member of the EPP Group and Vice-Chairman of the Committee on Constitutional Affairs, as Rapporteur foundered in the course of 2001. A second attempt by Parliament, with the German Socialist member Jo Leinen as Rapporteur and also sponsored by the Greek EPP Group member Giorgos Dimitrakopoulos, was finally successful. The EP approved the statute in June 2003. At the end of 2003, the Council approved the regulation with a qualified majority. This meant a further constitutionalisation of Europarties (see also Bardi in Chapter 5 of this book).

In his statement on the outcome of the Nice Summit, EPP Group Chairman Pöttering said he was disappointed insofar as the extension of QMV in the Council and parallel co-decision with the EP was concerned.[33] The EU's ability to act is governed in particular by qualified majority voting in Council with parallel co-decision with the EP. "In this area, our aims for the IGC were not achieved", Pöttering observed.[34] Pöttering said that the IGC method of negotiating demonstrably gives unsatisfactory results, suggesting that new methods of amending the EU treaties must be found and referring to the work of the Convention on the Charter on Fundamental Rights as a possible method for future treaty revisions. Martens wrote of "a disaster at Nice" and "a second rate agreement" (Martens 2008: 167).

Speaking in a debate in the EP with the President of Council, Jacques Chirac, and the President of the Commission, Romano Prodi, on the outcome of the European Summit of Nice, the Chairman of the EPP Group,

33 EPP Group Archives, D.5.21, Activity report, Yearbook 2000, p. 129.
34 Ibid.

Pöttering, made a critical evaluation of the outcome.[35] "Our final view on Nice will depend on the inclusion of Parliament in the post Nice process", declared Pöttering.

For the EPP, party and group, the outcome of the IGC was disappointing. For one, the EP powers were not enhanced far enough. The Charter of Fundamental Rights was proclaimed, but as yet had no legal force. On the positive side, the role of the Commission President was strengthened and majority decision-making was introduced in certain additional areas. There was a rebalancing of votes, which represented a power shift towards Germany. Provision was also made for possible 'enhanced co-operation' among countries to pursue greater integration in certain areas in the framework of the EU institutions. Moreover, the Nice Treaty provided a legal basis for the European political parties. However, the treaty adopted in Nice in December 2000 largely failed to meet the demands of the EPP, group and party, including in light of the agenda of institutional reform with a view to enlargement. While there was a move to more majority voting in some areas, it was deemed insufficient. The Christian Democrats in the EPP Group were dissatisfied; for them, the new treaty simply did not go far enough.

The influence of the EP in the discussions and outcomes is difficult to assess, but seemingly less than in the previous IGC. However, MEPs were able to shape the debate through their public appearances. Because they report frequently to the EP and the media, the MEPs are an important source of public information on discussions (Dinan and Vanhoonacker 2000: 8). Neuhold (2006: 354) observes that the EP went into the IGC "with elaborate demands ranging from the constitutionalisation of the Union to altering the procedure for the future revision of the Treaties by introducing a power of co-decision for the Council and the EP". It asked for ambitious institutional reforms, where for example QMV and co-decision should become the 'normal' legislative procedure. When set against the high expectations, the outcome was a failure. It also demonstrated the limits of party politics in EU treaty reform.

While Parliament as a whole did not specifically endorse the Nice Treaty, it did not call for its rejection. Instead, Corbett et al. (2016: 443) note, "it took advantage of the highly critical mood surrounding IGCs as a working method, with complex details settled late at night by tired heads of government, to call for the next reform to be prepared using different procedures". Among the institutional actors, the EP – building on its in-

35 EPP Group Archives, D.5.21, Activity report, Yearbook 2000, p. 130.

creased powers and growing importance – was highly critical of the outcome of the IGC as well as of its 'negotiation modi', that is to say of the intergovernmental method (Neuhold 2006: 364; also Best et al. 2000). It therefore demanded that the IGC in 2004 would be based on a more transparent process, through a convention. Laursen (2012b: 216) concludes: "The dissatisfaction with the way the Nice Treaty negotiations were handled was a major factor in the subsequent decision to have the next reform prepared through a Convention".

The Nice Treaty was in force between February 2003 and December 2009 when the Lisbon Treaty took effect. In between there were renewed attempts to further constitutionalise the EU. The next section will explore that approach further, again paying particular attention to the EPP Group and its role in treaty reform.

### *The EPP Group and the Constitutional Treaty (2004)*

In an Annex to the Nice Treaty (Declaration on the future of the EU, 23), it was envisaged to look into the competences of the Union, possibly in a constitution or a proposed catalogue of competences to establish the hierarchy between the Union and its Member States. A priority now was to strengthen the democratic legitimacy of the Union. The Declaration on the future of the EU only mentioned broad debate, but the EP took the initiative by pressing for a new way to prepare the institutional reforms. The model had already been tested in the preparation of the Charter of Fundamental Rights endorsed at the time of the Nice summit, and it was called a Convention.

The initiative for a constitutional convention to prepare the next IGC and the next treaty, bringing together representative of governments, national parliaments and the EP – a big difference from the narrow intergovernmental nature of the IGCs – gained wide support in the EP. This new round of treaty negotiations would clarify the institutional architecture of the Union. For those who wished the EU to evolve into something much closer to a federal state, this presented an opportunity to push the EU along the path of constitutional reform.

The EPP political family was one of the most powerful engines for this process. According to Klaus Welle, former Secretary-General of the EPP and EPP Group, the EPP was the first European political party to have asked for a convention (Interview Welle, 3.12.2002). The EPP Congress in Berlin on 11-13 January 2001 adopted a new basic document – "A Union of Values" – and established a number of permanent working committees.[36] The EPP Congress called for a convention in preparation of the next IGC with the involvement of parliamentarians. This method for preparing constitutional reform was advocated by the EPP and its parliamentary group, which were in sync on this matter. In the post-Nice context, they took the view that it was time for change in the way in which the EU engages in constitution-building.

The EPP Group tabled a resolution at the EPP Congress in Berlin aimed at providing clear perspectives to overcome the shortcomings of the Treaty (Fontaine 2009: 391). In his memoirs, Pöttering (2016: 205-206), who had succeeded Martens as Chair of the EPP Group in 1999 and shared his vision of a federal Europe, renders the 'post-Nice process' and the opportunity presented by the EPP Congress in Berlin in January 2001: "I was determined that the EPP section of the group should submit a resolution on which congress would then take a vote. ... So I asked our Secretary-General, Klaus Welle, the person best qualified for the job, to produce a draft text" (Pöttering 2016: 206). They managed to secure backing from the group for the draft resolution, which was then submitted to the party in time for the Congress. In his Congress speech, Pöttering called for a Convention as a method to prepare the next treaty. The EPP came out in favour of this new method for revising treaties (Pöttering 2016: 206-208).

At the end of the year, the EPP set out its goals in the document "A Constitution for a Europe that works", which was drafted by the Party and the Group and presented to the Political Bureau of the EPP on 6 December 2001 (Fontaine 2009: 396). As shown by Corbett et al. (2016: 445), during the second half of 2001, the Belgian Presidency worked closely with the EP's Committee on Constitutional Affairs, and especially an informal group of its leading members, including Méndez de Vigo, in drafting the text approved by the Laeken European Council (14-15 December 2001) and known as the Laeken Declaration. It called for a Convention on the Future of Europe in order "to pave the way for the next Intergovernmental Conference as broadly and openly as possible".[37]

The European Council appointed former French President Valéry Giscard d'Estaing (who had joined the EPP Group during his term as MEP in 1991) as Chairman of the Convention and former Italian and Belgian Prime Ministers Giuliano Amato and Jean-Luc Dehaene as Vice-Chairmen. In addition to its Chairman and two Vice-Chairmen, the Convention was composed of 15 representatives of the heads of state or government of the

36 EPP Group Archives, D.5.22, Activity report, Yearbook 2001, p. 77.

37 Laeken Declaration, https://www.consilium.europa.eu/media/20950/68827.pdf

Member States (one from each Member State), 13 representatives of the heads of state or government of the candidate states (one per candidate state), 30 representatives of the national parliaments of the Member States (two from each Member State), 26 representatives of the national parliaments of the candidate states (two from each candidate state), 16 members of the EP and 2 representatives of the European Commission. The EP's representatives were led by Íñigo Méndez de Vigo, with Socialist Klaus Hänsch and Liberal Andrew Duff as his deputies. The most influential organ of the Convention was the Praesidium, which had the role of lending impetus to the Convention, by preparing draft agendas for plenary sessions and overseeing its activities and organisation. It consisted of the Convention Chairman and Vice-Chairmen and nine members drawn from the Convention: the representatives of all the governments holding the Presidency of the Union during the Convention (Spain, Denmark and Greece), two national parliament representatives, two EP representatives (Hänsch and Méndez de Vigo) and two Commission representatives.

The inauguration of the Convention took place on 28 February 2002 in the EP building in Brussels.[38] The objective of the EPP Group, as set out by its Chairman Pöttering, was to have a draft Constitution produced by the middle of 2003 and the final text in the form of a new treaty or possibly even a European Constitution adopted at the end of 2003, following a short IGC.[39] The EPP Group was well-represented, with six out of 16 members within the EP delegation, led by Méndez de Vigo who served on the 12-member Praesidium of the Convention. In sheer numbers, the EPP accounted for 30% (including deputies) of the delegates (*conventionnels*) to the Convention and were therefore obviously a very influential force (Fontaine 2009: 397, drawing on Lamassoure 2004: 309).

Especially significant was the contribution brought by Brok and Méndez de Vigo, who were sometimes seen as rivals or competitors (Norman 2003: 52). Together with Maij-Weggen, Méndez de Vigo was one of the EPP Group members who had taken part in the Convention working out the Charter of Fundamental Rights. They carried with them their experience and lessons from one convention to another. Méndez de Vigo chaired the Working Group on national parliaments. A significant contribution was also made by French MEP and former minister Alain Lamassoure, who chaired the Working Group on external action.

38 The website of the European Convention is still accessible: http://european-convention.europa.eu

39 EPP Group Archives, D.5.23, Activity report, Yearbook 2002, p. 10.

At the outset, representatives of the EPP Group in the Convention met in order to articulate and co-ordinate their work. Brok was appointed to co-ordinate the team at the Convention. Germans involved in the co-ordination of Convention matters within the EPP also included Pöttering and Martin Kamp, a senior political group official (see further below), as well as Klaus Welle and Christian Kremer, Deputy Secretary-General of the EPP and also from the Christian Democratic Union (CDU). Its former leader Wolfgang Schäuble likewise contributed to the preparation of documents, in particular ahead of the EPP Congress in October 2002. Martin Selmayr, then at Bertelmann's Brussels office, attended meetings of the EPP Convention Group.

The European Convention took place from February 2002 to June 2003. During this period, members of the Convention met as political families or groupings. Research shows that party politics did matter in this particular context, not least in the networking among politicians within and around the political groupings at the Convention (e.g. Shaw 2002; Johansson 2003; Norman 2003; Van Hecke 2012).

These political groupings met before each meeting of the Convention to prepare for work at the plenary and they also put forward draft constitutions. Apart from these monthly meetings, the political families also convened for discussions outside Brussels. The EPP political family was organised as the EPP Convention Group, which brought together some 70 members. As lead co-ordinator, Brok played an important role, alongside the special co-ordinators who were appointed for the respective Working Groups in the Convention.

The EPP, party and group, seems to have been particularly active in bringing together Convention members, both in Brussels and during Study Days and seminars held in Roquebrune-Cap-Martin and Frascati in 2002, and in Petersberg near Bonn, Palma de Mallorca and Brussels in 2003.[40] These meetings were instrumental in advancing a meeting of minds within the EPP Convention Group, as well as for discussing issues

---

40 The seminar in Roquebrune (on 27 and 28 June 2002) was a joint arrangement between the EPP, the EPP Group and Konrad Adenauer Foundation. Among the participants were, from the Convention Praesidium, Valéry Giscard d'Estaing, Jean-Luc Dehaene, Ana de Palacio, Michel Barnier, John Bruton, Íñigo Méndez de Vigo; other MEPs including Elmar Brok and Alain Lamassoure also took part. Commission President Romano Prodi, Commissioner Mario Monti and former German Chancellor Helmut Kohl were also invited. The goal of the meeting, according to an internal document of the EPP Group, was to "bring together for the first time the EPP Convention group members in order to create a general

in detail and elaborating on the priorities of its actions, such as safeguarding the Community method, implementing co-decision and QMV (double majority) as a general rule, integrating the Charter on Fundamental Rights, enhancing the subsidiarity principle – especially through the enhanced involvement of national parliaments and regions with legislative powers, establishing a clear delimitation of the competencies of the Union, safeguarding the role of Churches and religious communities and taking a decisive step towards a common foreign policy for the European Union.[41]

Within the Parliament, too, EPP Group representatives continued to play an influential role. Lamassoure was Rapporteur of an important report on the delimitation of competencies between the EU and the Member States (European Parliament 2002a). This report was adopted in the Committee on Constitutional Affairs in April 2002 and was approved by the Parliament in May. The report and resolution called for a Constitution of the Union, and sought to clarify which powers lie with the EU, which remain with Member States and which are shared between the Union and Member States. The report was sent to the Convention on the Future of Europe as the Parliament's submission.

In September 2002, the EPP Convention Group proposed the first draft text for a Constitution of the EU. This text was open for amendment and intended to 'kick off' the discussion on the Convention's resolution. The draft was based on the outcome of the Study Days of the EPP Convention Group held in late June in Roquebrune. Brok stated in a press conference in Strasbourg: "Only along political lines can we bridge institutional differences of opinion between the national parliaments, the Commission, the Council and the European Parliament. This is the most important objective of our political group and this is why we want to produce a draft text as soon as possible".[42]

In the interval between the EPP Group Convention meeting in June and the next one in November, the EPP Congress in Estoril on 18 October adopted the document "A Constitution for a Strong Europe"; the Convention Praesidium and its Chairman, Giscard d'Estaing, on 28 October pre-

EPP consensus on the general process of constitutionalisation". I would like to thank Beatrice Scarascia Mugnozza, who was present at the Convention as support for the EPP delegation, for having let me consult this and other documents in her private archive.

41 Beatrice Scarascia Mugnozza private archives, Priorities for the EPP Convention Group in final stage of the Convention. Study Days of the EPP Convention Group in Palma de Mallorca, 18-05-2003.

42 EPP Group Archives, D.5.23, Activity report, Yearbook 2002, p. 292.

sented the preliminary draft Constitutional Treaty. The timing speaks for itself.[43]

The draft constitution adopted by the Congress held in Estoril noted that the EPP within the Convention worked for a federal constitution, and the EPP also emphasised the connection between the Convention and the upcoming IGC.[44] It was a joint text drafted by the EPP Group and Party, with the significant contribution of Wilfred Martens and Wolfgang Schäuble (Fontaine 2009: 397; Pöttering 2006: 116). Three members of the EPP Group at the Convention were responsible for reporting to the Congress on various issues; the three 'big guns' Brok, Lamassoure and Méndez de Vigo. The EPP document finally agreed at its Estoril congress served as a basis for the EPP Convention members and was meant to set the agenda for the whole Convention (Van Hecke 2002: 844). According to Jansen and Van Hecke (2011: 130), the ideas articulated in the Congress document "were a key precondition for the unity of the representatives at the EPP Convention Group, led by MEP Brok, and they became a driving force in the body charged with writing a European Constitution".

In 2003, the EPP political family met on several occasions and in different forms – most notably through the EPP convention Group – in order to co-ordinate its efforts and maximise its impact on the Convention.[45]

The European Convention proceedings concluded on 18 July 2003 after 17 months and approved by 'consensus' the final Draft Treaty establishing a Constitution for Europe. Parts I and II of the text were adopted on 13 June 2003 and submitted by the President of the Convention, Giscard d'Estaing, to the European Council, which met in Thessaloniki on 20 June 2003. Parts III and IV (dealing with the policies and the functioning of the Union and the general and final provisions) were subject to further work, which was completed on 13 July 2003. The full text of the European Constitution, in its four parts, was submitted to the President of the European Council in Rome on 18 July 2003.

What are the key observations of the Convention experience? What was the role of party politics and, in particular, of the EPP Group? Clearly, the Convention was a more friendly environment for party politics than the

43 A draft text was sent to the EPP Group for comments as early as March 2002, as we learn from a letter sent from EPP President Wilfried Martens to the Group and to national parties (the document is in Beatrice Scarascia Mugnozza's private archives).

44 EPP Group Archives, N.1.1.8, EPP Party, "A Constitution for a Strong Europe", Adopted at the EPP Congress, Estoril, 18 October 2002.

45 EPP Group Archives, D.5.24, Activity report, Yearbook 2003, p. 297 and p. 366.

IGCs, where governments negotiate and are more in control. The main players in the IGCs represent governments, at the highest level the heads of state or government in the European Council, the traditional stronghold of inter-state negotiation. Whilst the European Council is not alien to party politicisation, it constitutes the institution probably most resistant to it (Tallberg and Johansson 2008). It is more likely to act in the name of national interest. The Convention reinforced the trend of growing party politicisation in the EU. Convention outcomes were shaped by transnational party mobilisation. Decision outcomes in the subsequent IGC to a large extent reflected this pattern. Form is important for content – and so are resources.

It is clear that the partisan dimension played an important role throughout the Convention, not least when it reached its final stages. In the words of Norman (2003: 324-325): "The big political families (and especially the well-organised centre-right European People's Party and centrist Liberals) were crucial in the Convention's final weeks. They established bridges between MEPs and national parliamentarians. The party frameworks fostered links that became quite close". The leaders of the political families in the Convention wanted the Convention to be a success, with Brok among the "passionate integrationists" (Norman 2003: 325). Norman further observes that they were "using the political families as a conduit for transferring know-how and back-up resources from the well-organised and well-endowed European parliamentarians to their like-minded but less well-resourced colleagues from national capitals".

What was the role of the EPP Group in the European Convention? To what extent did the EPP Convention Group act as one? On balance, the EPP political family was relatively united, which allowed them to assert themselves on the final outcome of the Convention. As Lamassoure testifies:

> The EPP managed to teamwork in a Convention Group bringing together the Convention members from all institutions, but also the prominent figures of the EPP Party. Quarterly gatherings were organized, President Giscard d'Estaing and Helmut Kohl were invited to take part to them. … EPP was probably the best organized and most influential political family during the Convention. EPP was probably the best organized and most influential political family during the Convention.[46]

46 Personal letter to the author, dated 15 April 2019. Lamassoure further notes: "I don't remember tensions among outstanding members, the friendly rivalry be-

Lamassoure (2004: 308) observes that the EPP set the tone, with particular reference to its Estoril Congress and document adopted on 18 October 2002, and to Martens and Schäuble and to Brok, Méndez de Vigo and Lamassoure himself as Rapporteurs.

In recalling his role as group leader of the EPP delegation, "perhaps the most influential position I ever had", bringing the EPP together, Brok also judged the Convention experience positively, claiming that this method "should be followed" (Interview Brok, 23.03.2018). It is now in the Lisbon Treaty.

Yet it was not always clear what the status of a particular intervention was and whom a single member – in this case also of the Convention – like Brok represented. The draft for a constitution put forward by Brok in September 2002, for instance, was presented to the Praesidium as an individual discussion paper in the Convention. Anyway, as Norman (2003: 67) notes, Brok's strategy "paid off in the very effective way the EPP would later marshal its troops behind specific positions in the detailed discussions on the draft articles for the constitutional treaty".

Méndez de Vigo describes the constitutional Convention as "a kind of alliance between parliamentarians", as "a fantastic experience" of politics and personalities (Interview Méndez de Vigo, 23.11.2018). The EP delegation seized this opportunity. They worked for the Convention to be a much more ambitious exercise than previous instances of treaty reform preparations.

Martin Kamp, at the time Head of Unit for Legal and Institutional Affairs and administratively responsible for several committees, including the Committee on Constitutional Affairs (AFCO), held principal responsibility for the Convention in the EPP Group, reporting directly to EPP Group Chairman Pöttering and serving as his adviser on the European Convention. According to Martin Kamp, the EPP Convention Group "created an atmosphere of a community" (Interview Kamp, 16.12.2019). Kamp was later a member of the EP negotiating team for the 2003-2004 IGC, and became Secretary-General of the EPP Group in 2007.

Beatrice Scarascia Mugnozza, from 1982 to 2007 in charge of the EPP Group within the Committee on Constitutional Affairs and AFCO adviser, served as an administrator for the EPP Group delegation at the European Convention 2002-2003. Working in the EPP Convention team at that

---

tween Inigo and Elmar did not express significant differences on the substance. If you compare the original memo adopted by EPP and the final text, you will be struck by the similarities". See also Lamassoure 2004.

time, she said they were "very committed" to trying to find a way forward at "a very important moment" (Interview Scarascia Mugnozza, 17.12.2019).

These accounts of people directly involved in work related to the European Convention add a sociological-anthropological element of the political atmosphere of co-operation in the context of, notably, the constitutional Convention, thereby capturing this informal social-political dimension of the networks. The preparatory meetings allowed individuals to get together in an informal setting for deliberations and also contributed to the substantive continuity of various documents.

At the beginning, there were some different views on institutional issues amongst the EPP MEPs and the national parliamentarians, the EPP members of the Commission and the heads of EPP governments and their representatives. Thanks to a mutual understanding and the logistics and drafting capacities of the advising EPP organisation, these frictions could be overcome in a consensual and very pro-European way. A consensus was reached over time as a result of discussion.

The narrative suggests that the EPP Group was the real powerhouse, providing the infrastructure, the personnel and other resources, although not necessarily financial ones. This helps explain the effectiveness of the EPP Group in the Convention. At the same time, as in the Convention as a whole, there was a hierarchy and some obviously had more power than others.

Taken together, the gulf between national and European parliamentarians was absolutely vast. Undoubtedly, the EP was at an advantage given that it was the venue of the Convention. The EP "was playing at home", writes Priestley (2008: 37), and "it exercised a decisive influence on the resulting draft Treaty, even in areas which were not of its direct concern". With the Convention on the Future of Europe, the EP "finally gained an official role in constitutional agenda-setting" (Christiansen and Reh 2009: 168). Likewise, Beach (2007: 2012) notes the significance of the EP and its representatives, as well as the partisan dimension towards the end of the Convention. Contacts also facilitated the cross-party consensus reached on the final Draft Treaty establishing a Constitution for Europe in June and July 2003.

The outcome was largely in line with the requests of the EPP Group. For example, the three pillars of the Treaty of Maastricht would be dissolved and co-decision would become the normal legislative procedure in the EU, which would have a legal personality. In its 2004 Yearbook, the EPP Group, emphasising its numerical strength and role, noted that the conclusions of the Convention included "a large number of the Group's priorities for the new constitutional treaty", such as: a clear statement of the values and objectives of the EU; the incorporation of the Charter of Fundamental Rights as an integral component of the treaty; the further development of the Common Foreign and Security Policy and Common Security and Defence Policy (CSDP), including the appointment of a European foreign minister; the establishment of QMV in the Council and codecision between the Council and the Parliament as the normal legislative methods; greater involvement of national parliaments, with an early warning mechanism to identify issues where subsidiarity would apply.[47]

In Rome on 18 July 2003, Giscard submitted the complete draft Constitution elaborated by the Convention to the President-in-Office of the Council, Silvio Berlusconi, who would open the IGC. It was launched on 4 October 2003 in Rome and would be conducted by the heads of state or government, assisted by the Ministers for Foreign Affairs. The EP's representatives – first Hänsch with Méndez de Vigo, then Hänsch with Brok – were no longer observers but full members, and were there from beginning to end at all ministerial meetings (Priestley 2008: 37). The EP President, Pat Cox, participated in the summits of the heads of state and governments.

At their Summit held in Meise on 15 October 2003 and the one held in Paris on 4 December 2003, the EPP leaders discussed the IGC. However, the December 2003 European Council failed to reach an agreement on a Constitution. The subsequent Irish Presidency had until June 2004 to finish the work on a new treaty. In the meantime, the EPP continued to mobilise its networks.

At the Study Days of the Group in Vienna on 23-24 March 2004, one theme was "Making the EU work: Towards an agreement on the institutional reforms".[48] Brok reported on recent developments in relation to the adoption of the draft EU constitution and expressed his opinion regarding the latest proposals, concluding that the acceptance of a new constitution would be essential for the efficient work of the EU 25 and expressing his hope that consensus could be achieved on a new constitution in the near future.[49] The meeting of the EPP Summit in Athens on 19 February 2004, held in preparation for the European Council meeting in March, focused on the EU Constitution and looked into a draft, with a view to reaching a

47 EPP Group Archives, D.5.25, Activity report, Yearbook 2004, pp. 54-55.
48 EPP Group Archives, D.5.25, Activity report, Yearbook 2004, p. 110.
49 EPP Group Archives, D.5.25, Activity report, Yearbook 2004, p. 115.

common position. The next EPP Summit meetings were held in Meise on 25 March and 16-17 June.

Eventually, after the 2004 European elections (during which it was barely mentioned), the new Treaty was adopted by the Brussels European Council (17 and 18 June 2004), despite the tense atmosphere among its members. The Treaty Establishing a Constitution for Europe, or the Constitutional Treaty, was signed in Rome on 29 October 2004.

The heads of state and government managed to resolve the final outstanding issues –notably the QMV system in the Council and the composition of the European Commission – and adopt a final text. A comparative analysis of its main features shows that the new Treaty was largely similar to the outcome of the Convention. The 2003-2004 IGC, which approved the Constitutional Treaty "did not fundamentally modify the essential features of the draft issued from the Convention" (Piris 2010: 19). It left the draft constitution drawn up by the Convention largely intact (Christiansen and Reh 2009: 255). The substantive continuity between the drafts attests to the impact of the Convention and its members.

The Constitution was divided into four parts, and explicitly discarded the system of 'pillars'. As regards competences and the limits of Union competences, rather than setting out a catalogue, the Constitution laid down just the essential principles. The Constitution provided for a strengthening of the role of the EP and more extensive use of the co-decision procedure, which should be elevated to an 'ordinary legislative procedure'; the right to submit proposals for an amendment of the Constitution; budgetary powers which it shares equally with the Council on all Union expenditure; enhanced functions of political control, in particular, the EP will elect the Commission President on a proposal by the European Council. The Convention method, as Brok hoped, will become the standard forum for drawing up recommendations to be submitted to the IGC. In the context of the Union's CFSP, the EP will have a general right to be informed and consulted (see Gagatek in Chapter 4 of this book).

The EPP Group concluded that the outcome of the IGC, representing the culmination of all the work put in since the Laeken declaration on the future of Europe, merits a warm welcome by the EP, and in particular by the EPP Group and its representatives in the IGC, Méndez de Vigo and Brok: "The final text of the Constitution clearly reflects the ideas set out in the EPP's manifesto adopted in Estoril in 2002. Most of the Praesidium that coordinated the work of the Convention were EPP-ED members, and its outcome was a testament to their active participation."[50]

Like all EU treaties, the European Constitution, or Treaty Establishing a Constitution for Europe, as it was formally called, had to be ratified by all Member States before it could come into force. To this end, the EPP, party and group, again reached out to national parliamentary groups. Likewise, the EPP continued to mobilise its leaders. In 2005, the EPP Summit convened in Meise, Belgium, in March, June and December.[51] On the first occasion, Brok was invited. The Chairman of the EPP Group took part, and among the heads of government, German Chancellor Angela Merkel continued to attend and thereby show her commitment. The EPP had clearly been successful at securing the participation of its heads of government in pre-European Council meetings.

The European Constitution was approved by the EP in January 2005, and by referendums in Spain, Luxembourg and, as the basis for its accession, Romania. 2005, though, saw negative outcomes in referendums in France and the Netherlands, two founding Member States. These negative results sent shock waves throughout the EU. At the Brussels European Council in June, the question of what to do with the ratification process of the Constitutional Treaty was discussed. It was decided that a period of reflection would take place before further agreement on how to proceed. A return to the matter in 2006 was agreed. For its part, the EPP Group, its leadership and most of its members, pushed for the EU to move forward on the Constitution.[52]

### *The EPP Group and the Lisbon Treaty (2007)*

Following the failed ratification in France and the Netherlands, nothing much happened during the period from the European Council in June 2005 and the one a year later (Piris 2010: 24). During the Finnish Presidency in the second half of 2006, little was achieved on the matter. The process of treaty reform was revived in June 2007 during the German Presidency, when the European Council of 21 to 23 June 2007 adopted a detailed mandate for a subsequent IGC under the Portuguese Presidency. The Member States agreed to abandon the idea of replacing the previous

---

50 EPP Group Archives, D.5.25, Activity report, Yearbook 2004, p. 158.
51 EPP Group Archives, D.5.26, Activity report, Yearbook 2005, p. 325.
52 EPP Group Archives, D.5.26, Activity report, Yearbook 2005, pp. 10-11.

treaties with a new constitution, and instead decided to amend the existing treaties.

In the meantime, a coalition of pro-Constitutional Treaty governments had started taking shape, backed by a number of MEPs and prominent politicians in the Member States (Ziller 2012: 250). These initiatives tried to revive the Constitutional Treaty of 2004. The EP reports on treaty reform were discussed, mainly in the Committee on Constitutional Affairs. There, Riccardo Ventre (EPP/IT) was one of the three Vice-Chairmen, while Méndez de Vigo served as Co-ordinator for the EPP Group members in the Committee. Thanks to his experience as a member of both conventions and his key role in the European Convention, Méndez de Vigo would play an important role in the ongoing constitutional talks, as would Elmar Brok from his post of EP representative in the IGC. Brok continued to be at the centre of events. Parliament sent a clear message that it must take full part in debate on the future of the EU. This message was voiced by EPP Group Chairman Pöttering in a debate in June 2006 on the upcoming EU summit.[53]

Throughout this period (2005-2007), the EPP network continued to co-ordinate its positions and pushed for a renewed effort, aiming for the EU to have a Constitution in place by 2009. The EPP Group, which after the 2004 European elections was still the EP's largest group (see Bardi in Chapter 5 of this book), held Study Days in Rome (29-30 March 2006) in connection with the EPP Congress, where delegates voted overwhelmingly to continue ratifying the Constitution and adopted a new document; new impetus should be given by the European Council in the first half of 2007 at the latest.[54] The EPP Summit of heads of state and government also continued to meet in preparation for the next European Council. In recent years, the EPP Summit had played an important role in co-ordinating the positions of EPP member governments, notably on the EU Constitution. The European Council meeting in June 2006 gave support for retaining the substance of the Constitutional Treaty and for a time frame for finding a solution before the 2009 European elections.

The EPP Group sought to push the constitutional process forwards: "By the end of 2006 it was time to move on to the next stage, namely the transition from reflection to action".[55] This step was taken under the German

53 EPP Group Archives, D.5.27, Activity report, Yearbook 2006, p. 309.
54 EPP Group Archives, N.1, EPP Party, "For a Europe of the Citizens: Priorities for a Better Future ("Rome Manifesto")", 2006, p. 16.
55 EPP Group Archives, D.5.28, Activity report, Yearbook 2007, p. 229.

Presidency, which began in January 2007, with Chancellor Angela Merkel as President-in-Office of the European Council. At that time, Pöttering was elected EP President, following Spanish Socialist Josep Borrell, and Joseph Daul took on the position of EPP Group Chairman. They met with Merkel in Strasbourg on 17 January 2007.[56] The EPP Group strongly welcomed the German Chancellor's presentation of the Council Presidency's work programme.[57] Daul mainly welcomed the Presidency's goal of finding common ground in order to get the EU Constitution back on track

In 2007, five EPP Summit meetings were held (EPP 2007). One was an extraordinary and enlarged Summit on 24 March in Berlin, where the EPP organised a special event with over 60 participants hosted by Chancellor Merkel – President of the European Council – and chaired by EPP President Wilfried Martens. Not only the EPP family, but also the European leaders gathered in Berlin on 24-25 March 2007, to celebrate the 50$^{th}$ anniversary of the signature of the Treaties of Rome. On that occasion, they adopted the Berlin Declaration: "this short but powerful text", Piris (2010: 29) observes, "was very important and was actually a decisive turning point". Angela Merkel (2010: xv) noted that the celebrations on 25 March 2007 to mark the 50$^{th}$ anniversary of the signing of the Treaties of Rome 'were a significant driver' of the new treaty, since the European heads of state or government, in signing the Berlin Declaration, committed themselves to a set of shared values, tasks and structures within the EU as well as to placing the EU 'on a renewed common basis.' However, Merkel continues: "Converting this commitment into a mandate for an Intergovernmental Conference was by no means easy".

In May 2007, the EP also pressed to overcome the deadlock through a report, authored by Elmar Brok and Enrique Barón Crespo, on the roadmap for the EU's constitutional process (European Parliament 2007d). On 4 June 2007, the Amato Group, a group of high-level European politicians unofficially working on rewriting the Treaty establishing a Constitution for Europe, released a draft text after 10 months of work. Íñigo Méndez de Vigo, Jean-Luc Dehaene and Michel Barnier – like Amato former members of the European Convention Praesidium – were also part of the small Working Group which in 2006-2007 prepared the draft of a new, simplified treaty.

Finally, the mandate for the IGC was adopted by the European Council meeting in Brussels on 21-23 June 2007, with the intention being that the

56 EPP Group Archives, D.5.27, Activity report, Yearbook 2006, p. 393.
57 EPP Group Archives, D.5.28, Activity report, Yearbook 2007, p. 254.

negotiations would culminate in a new treaty before the end of the year. W was to become the Lisbon Treaty was thus negotiated using the traditional IGC method; that is, through negotiations mainly between governmental representatives using unanimous decision-making.

The IGC formally opened on 23 July 2007. The EP participated in the IGC with three representatives: Brok, Hänsch and Duff. However, as we have seen, the negotiations started in early 2007. The heads of state and government were centrally involved, including through their key aides (Sherpas) for EU and foreign affairs. The negotiators met at Lisbon on 18 October 2007 and agreed on the remaining amendments and additions to the texts and gave their final political agreement on what would become the Lisbon Treaty.

With the IGC entering its final phase and before the European Council meeting in Lisbon, the EPP held an extraordinary Summit on 18 October in the presence of Merkel, Daul and others, including Barroso and Pöttering.[58] The EPP leaders, including heads of state and government, called for a final agreement on the new EU Treaty and "gave a decisive backing to reach a deal on the pending points in order to conclude the agreement on the Reform Treaty launched under the German Presidency of the EU" (EPP 2007: 19). "The Reform Treaty provides the instruments that we need in order for Europe to move forward", EPP President Martens said.

The signing of the new treaty in Lisbon on 13 December 2007 was welcomed by the EPP Group Chairman, Joseph Daul, for extending QMV and granting new powers to the EP, "making co-decision the rule in almost all areas of legislation".[59] The EPP Summit in Meise on 13 December 2007 celebrated the historical day of the signing of the Lisbon Treaty, but also of the proclamation of the Charter of Fundamental Rights (a day earlier in Brussels), which was a longstanding goal of the Group.[60]

Widely considered a less ambitious successor to a failed EU Constitution, the 2004 Treaty establishing a Constitution for Europe, or Constitutional Treaty, and the Lisbon Treaty are substantively similar (e.g. Christiansen and Reh 2009; Laursen 2016a; Piris 2010; Ziller 2012). Despite the differences, some of which are purely symbolic, the content is much the same.

Once the new Treaty finally took effect on 1 December 2009, Chairman Daul drew attention to the role of the EPP Group, saying it "was instru-

58 EPP Group Archives, D.5.28, Activity report, Yearbook 2007, p. 340.
59 EPP Group Archives, D.5.28, Activity report, Yearbook 2007, p. 9.
60 EPP Group Archives, D.5.28, Activity report, Yearbook 2007, pp. 95 and 101.

mental in bringing the Lisbon Treaty into force. This Treaty will make Europe both more efficient and more democratic".[61]

The EPP, group and party, contributed to breaking the deadlock and to moving on with the constitutional process. While concessions were made and the Treaty was not a proper constitution, there were important achievements. Notably, the EP had been further empowered. Co-decision, now called the 'ordinary legislative procedure', became the standard mode for the making of EU laws. QMV and co-decision were extended to 40 new policy areas. In line with recent IGCs, note de Ruiter and Neuhold (2016: 115), "the EP has come out of the negotiations on the Lisbon Treaty as a winner insofar as co-decision was extended into a vast array of policy fields". Moreover, the convention method was now laid down in the Treaty for future revisions (Corbett et al. 2016: 451). There was a clearer link between EP elections and the composition of the Commission, which would inevitably become more partisan in character. Tendencies toward parliamentarism strengthened the partisan dimension of EU politics. These changes, together with the constitutional regulation of Europarties, encouraged closer policy co-ordination between Europarties and their respective parliamentary groups.

With the entry into force of the new treaty, the EU was now likely to become something very different from what it had been. Yet, there was a substantive continuity and a developing constitutional order that can be traced back to the Treaty of Maastricht and partly also to the SEA. On that note, the story ends. The conclusion below discusses the main findings and implications of the study, and the role and effect of transnational partisanship in European constitutional politics.

## *Conclusion*

This chapter set out to explore how the EPP Group sought to influence, either directly or indirectly, the constitutionalisation of the EU through the course and outcome of the negotiations leading to the adoption of the successive treaties over the past three decades, from the 1980s onward. How important was the EPP Group in the end?

Drawing on previous evidence and on new sources, this account sheds light on many aspects of constitutional engineering and institutional design in the EU during the period from the 1980s until the 2000s: the mak-

61 EPP Group Archives, D.5.30, Activity report, Yearbook 2009, p. 10.

ing of the Single European Act and the Treaties of Maastricht, Amsterdam, Nice and Lisbon. These treaty revisions have their own kind of dynamic. Whereas the existing literature shows the influence of Europarties, particularly the EPP, less has been written on the influence of EP political groups in this connection on treaty negotiations. Through its systematic analysis of the influence of the EPP Group and the treaties aiming to create an EU constitution over the past four decades, this chapter therefore makes a valuable addition to the existing literature. In the narrative of this chapter, the EPP Group mostly comes out as an influential player, even if not a unitary actor, and on closer examination seems a more formidable force than previous research has accounted for. Over and above this fact, there is the European Council of Heads of State and Government. In all, the strategic importance of party networks within and around the European Council facilitated negotiations and decision-making, providing an alternative or supplementary channel for influence.

The chapter thus asserts that the EPP Group and its members held extensive influence in the continuing process of treaty reform and European integration, and provides more evidence of the partisan dimension of constitutional politics at European level. But whereas the members and the EPP Group in many ways influenced successive treaties, notably through the EPP and its party networks, its influence is also largely conditional on support from governments.

It remains difficult to estimate the influence of the group as a collective. Inevitably, there will be power asymmetries in a group such as this (as Bardi analyses in greater detail in Chapter 5 of this book). There is no escaping the fact that individual MEPs are not equally influential and that some national delegations carry more political weight than others.

The EP gained an increase of legislative powers from the SEA to the Lisbon Treaty. The successive rounds of constitutional reform extended the powers of the EP. The Maastricht and Amsterdam Treaties in particular gave the EP a lot more power than was widely realised at the time. A change took place – and that change, that fundamental change explored in this chapter, had consequences. There were profound consequences for interinstitutional relations, with effects on the power balance between the institutions. When comparing the EP's involvement in constitutional politics over time, we can conclude that it has become more centrally involved and obviously has made a real difference.

EPP (Group) elites clearly played a role in shaping the institutional environment of the EU. Their motivation may be ideational, in the sense of being rooted in their principles, or it may be interest-based, insofar as it entails a desire to alter the institutional setting for their own ends. In any event, they contributed to the political and institutional environment in which they themselves exist.

The informal dimensions of European integration have likewise played out, as argued when introducing this chapter. The significance of the informal in European integration warrants further research. Informal relationships may allow transnational actors to play a more prominent role. Transnational partisanship is one dimension. It offers informal ways of exerting influence, or at least trying to wield influence. That is one reason why European integration has moved forward.

In conclusion, the EPP, group and party, which seemed very much in sync in this study, has retained considerable influence; it developed a sense of its own importance and learned in the process that it can have a major influence and push the process forwards by mobilising its own networks and channels of influence. Though we may argue over the extent, its impact has been undeniable. At this point, the analytic narrative comes to an end.

# Chapter 3 Co-Shaping the Internal Market: The EPP Group and EU Internal Policies

*Carine Germond*

## *Introduction*

The internal policies of the European Union (EU) are listed under part III of the 2007 Treaty of Lisbon and normally have a strong regulatory or redistributive character. They are also a core feature of the European internal market – known also as the European single market. The integration of the economies and public policies of the Member States and the creation of an EU-wide economy and market, in which goods, persons, capital and services would move freely, were among the chief objectives of the Rome Treaty establishing the European Economic Community (EEC) in 1957, the forerunner of the present-day EU. The internal market encompasses all EU Member States and was extended in 1992, with exceptions, to the members of the European Economic Area (EEA). Accordingly, internal policies – for which EU institutions have either an exclusive competence or a shared competence with Member States – have a direct impact not only on the governments of EU/EEA Member States, but also on the everyday life of European citizens. They have thus been of prime interest for the European Parliament (EP), as the democratically elected and accountable body of the EU, and the political groups active within it.

The chapter focuses on four macro internal policies of strategic importance – agriculture, economic and monetary policy, social policy and environmental policy – that occupy a prominent place among the set of existing domestic policies, in terms of the EU's budget, administration, legislative, judicial and public policy action. These policies epitomise the delicate and continuous balancing act between economic liberalisation, which has been a trademark of integration within the European Communities (EC)/EU, and social policy measures intended to moderate the impact of such liberalisation. As a result, they are particularly relevant for the European People's Party (EPP) Group within Parliament.

Despite the centrality of the internal market for the European project and its importance as a driver for further integration, surprisingly, very little is known about the involvement of the EPP Group in the EU's internal policies. Research on the EP has tended to focus on the general development and functioning of the EP, political behaviour and elections, internal party politics and voting practices, organisation and cohesion with a strong emphasis on the party system and interinstitutional bargaining between the EP, the Commission and the Council (e.g. Hix, Raunio and Scully 2003). Up until the 2000s, the relative marginality of the EP in the politics of the European Union and many internal policy areas, as well as the limitations imparted to its interactions with other EU institutions, explains this oversight to a large extent. It does not, however, account for the lack of more recent studies on the legislative empowerment of EP and in-depth examination of how the EP and the political groups within it have used these new powers to influence legislation in those internal policies in which it has gained new competences.

Accordingly, the EP's contribution to the EU as a political system and to the wider institutional framework needs to be reassessed in light of not only its hard-won legislative empowerment, but also its new-fangled role as a "theatre of engagement" (Ripoll Servent 2018: 1), an arena where different ideological and national views on a wide array of topical EU political and social problems are brought together, debated and confronted. From 1979, the EPP Group[1] actively participated in and contributed to these debates, based on its own vision of the European project and shared Christian democratic values. It used its position, human resources and political influence within Parliament to steer the process of European integration. The succession of crises that have crippled the EU for over a decade and the impact of these crises on internal policies and European citizens make such a study particularly topical.

This chapter sets out to explore the role and contribution of the EPP Group in co-shaping the evolution of four internal policies of the European Union since the first election of the EP in 1979. Policy-relevant examples spanning roughly several decades of European integration serve to contrast the influence exerted by the EPP Group pre- and post-Lisbon. In considering both historical and contemporary policy developments, the chapter explores three interconnected questions. First, it examines how and to what extent the partisan preferences, ambitions and positions of the EPP Group in these select internal policies have evolved over the last 30-40 years. Second, it casts light on how the EPP Group pursued its policy goals

1 For simplicity, the chapter uses the abbreviation EPP Group, even for the period (1999-2009) during which the Group was called the European People's Party and European Democrats (EPP-ED).

and positions but also on the internal, external or institutional constraints that affected its action. Finally, the chapter investigates the Group's shifting role and influence within each of the selected internal policies.

The first three sections contextualise the institutional and policy frameworks that determined the EPP Group's ability to shape internal policies and legislation. The first section briefly sketches the history of the EP's legislative empowerment since its first direct election in 1979. Over the years, Parliament successfully managed to carve out a place for itself in the political system of the EU thanks to its own activism and treaty reforms. The gradual increase of its powers has transformed an initially weak consultative assembly into a powerful institution with the power to co-enact legislation in most internal policies. The second section maps out the most important developments in the four internal policies under study, namely the Common Agricultural Policy (CAP), Economic and Monetary Union (EMU) and social and environment policies, up to the present-day. Because the EP is primarily a committee-based parliament, the third section focuses on comitology and casts fresh light on the depth and breadth of the EPP Group's involvement in the committees responsible for debating agricultural, economic and monetary, social and environmental policy matters.

The subsequent four sections focus on the EPP Group's role in shaping each of the four policy domains under study. The fourth section explores the EPP Group's contribution to reforming the CAP. With the extension of the Ordinary Legislative Procedure (OLP) to agriculture, the EP gained new scrutinising powers in this policy area. What consequences this has had for the EPP Group's ability to influence agricultural policy, pre- and post-2007 is examined through the lens of two key milestones of CAP reform: the 1992 MacSharry reform and the negotiation of the latest reform that was agreed in 2013. The fifth section assesses the influence of the EPP Group on shaping important EMU legislation by discussing the negotiations of the Treaty of Maastricht and the debates on the strengthening of fiscal and monetary integration during the economic and financial crisis that hit Europe in the late 2000s (Euro-crisis). The sixth section scrutinises the EPP Group's action to address the social aspects and consequences of European integration and its influence on social regulation. The Group's contribution to making law on labour markets and social inclusion – two crucial vehicles of social policy – is illustrated through the European Employment and the Lisbon Strategies. The last section explores the EPP's role in framing crucial environmental legislation. Environmental conservation was an early concern for Christian Democrats, whose efforts to protect biodiversity and promote an economically friendly environment and climate policy durably shaped what has now become a key EU internal policy.

### *From 'talking shop' to empowered co-legislator: The role of the EP in internal policies*

A strong proponent of further integration, the EP has constantly pushed for a broadening of its competences in internal policies. The institution was long deemed to be not much more than a mere 'talking shop', a relatively powerless institution with limited influence over policy- and law-making. Yet, through self-initiated supranational activism (Roos and Howard 2017), it has become an effective player in co-shaping legislation that covers almost all sectors and policies affected by European integration.

#### Agricultural policy

Historically, decision-making in the CAP was characterised by the Commission as the initiator of agricultural legislation, inter-governmental bargaining in the Council – until 2007 the main decision-maker – and close links between institutions and farming interests (Greer and Hind 2017). Agriculture was thus a policy area where the EP was institutionally weak. Yet, the question of Parliament's actual influence is a matter of intense debate among scholars. Some argued that the EP was a marginal player (Grant 1997: 175-176) due to its limited capacity to affect the agriculture budget and its consultative role, and that it repeatedly failed to obtain a voice in the agriculture policy process (Peterson and Bomberg 1999: 135). Conversely, others asserted that the EP was not simply "a rubber-stamp" endorsing Commission proposals or "an antechamber to the Council of Ministers mirroring the national compromises and alliances struck by agriculture ministers" (Roederer-Rynning 2003: 114).

In effect, the consultation procedure, one of the oldest decision-making procedures, applied to the CAP until 2007. It gave the EP only a consultative role, which entailed being consulted by the Commission and the Council, but both could ignore its amendments. The EP's budgetary powers, including the right to reject the budget – a power it used on several occasions – and to amend it within certain limits and approve the annual accounts, were the main tools that Members of the European Parliament (MEPs) had at their disposal. These budgetary powers were, however, rather limited in practice. The EP could only amend the non-compulsory expenditures but not the compulsory expenditures, which consisted almost entirely of agriculture. Nevertheless, the politicisation of the EC budget, of which the CAP was the largest item, as well as budgetary discipline, became important fixtures of the EP's limited arsenal to influence agricultural policy-making. The budgetary crises that drove most of the agricultural policy adjustments in the 1970s and 1980s allowed Parliament to wield indirect influence. The consultation procedure also allowed Parliament to apply pressure on the Commission and Council through its non-binding recommendations. The expanding scope of agricultural policy into related policy areas, such as the environment, food safety and regional development, where co-decision applied earlier, provided Parliament with additional opportunities to influence the actual content of the CAP beyond its legislative competences.

The 2007 Treaty of Lisbon changed the rules under which agricultural policy is now made. The Treaty on the Functioning of the European Union (TFEU) introduced formal and legislative changes to the agricultural chapter of the EC Treaty, including the renumbering of the provisions in force and the recognition of shared competence between the Union and the Member States. Co-decision replaced the former consultation procedure and was recognised as the ordinary legislative procedure for the CAP. Also, the Treaty of Lisbon simplified the procedure for the adoption of the annual budget through the elimination of the distinction between compulsory expenditure, under which category agricultural expenditures formally fell, and non-compulsory expenditure, and thus assigned to the EP a real role as co-legislator on all budgetary expenditures. For the first time, the EP gained a veto right on CAP legislation, as its consent is required for a proposal to be adopted and is on an equal institutional footing with the Council. Moreover, under co-decision, the EP has a say on legislation relating to the common organisation of agricultural markets, the largest share of the CAP budget under Pillar I, and other provisions necessary for the pursuit of the objectives of the CAP. The decision to give Parliament legislative competences in agricultural matters marks a significant step in the parliamentarisation of the CAP (Roederer-Rynning 2012).

In addition to the interinstitutional decision-making procedures, informal politics have always been an important feature of agricultural policy-making in the EU. Informal influence has been often exerted by transnational networks, relying on the well-established corporatist policy arrangements that were prevalent in Member States like France (Keeler 1987; Culpepper 1993; Roederer-Rynning 2002), Germany (Andrlik 1981; Patel 2009) and the UK (Cox, Lowe and Winter 1986, 1987). A key characteristic of these close relations between government and organised interests was the high degree of co-operation among these groups for steering and framing public policy. In particular, the close ties between state institutions like national agriculture ministries and farm interest groups, with which the vast majority of MEPs involved in the EP's Agriculture Committee were or had been associated, have allowed the EP to exert an influence on the CAP beyond its actual legislative competences.

### Economic and Monetary Union

Although the origins of EMU can be traced back to the early stages of the EC, it only took centre stage with the relaunch of European integration in the 1980s (Dyson and Featherstone 1999). The EP was an early advocate of greater co-ordination of monetary policies (Chang 2009: 20). Given the institutional constraints imparted to its legislative activity, Parliament originally had few possibilities to influence the Council and the Commission regarding the broad orientations of the Community's economic and fiscal policies, even though its budgetary powers provided a kind of leverage at a time when, against the backdrop of low growth, high unemployment levels and enlargement, the budgetary question dominated much of the Community debates in the 1970s and 1980s. In introducing the new procedure of co-operation for all matters related to the single market programme, the Single European Act (SEA) expanded the EP's prerogatives on legislation related to economic matters and bore testimony to its influence in shaping the idea of the single market (Warlouzet 2020). The resulting closer co-operation with the Council and the Commission moreover increased the importance of the work of the parliamentary committees.

The EP had a very limited role in the institutional design of the EMU. It was not only excluded from its creation, since the key decisions were taken by the Member States, but the EP was a marginal player in the administration of the EMU, too (Fabbrini 2016). The 1992 Treaty of Maastricht, however, provided for Parliament's stronger, though constrained, involvement in EMU through consultation, which applied for instance to the implementation of the excessive deficit procedure – including the provisions that led to the adoption of the Stability and Growth Pact (SGP) – or to membership of the single currency. In addition, the treaty granted the EP some supervisory powers in the field of economic or monetary policies. With the TFEU, which substantially boosted the EP's role in EMU, Parliament co-legislates on the design of the rules for budgetary surveillance and the specific provisions for Eurozone members. In a policy field traditionally dominated by the Member States, the EP had, for the first time, the power to co-shape key aspects of EMU.

The Euro-crisis put these newly acquired powers to the test. The financial and sovereign debt crisis laid bare the mismatch between monetary integration and economic and fiscal integration. EU decision-makers responded with a concerted effort to strengthen the Union's fiscal surveillance and reform EMU's imperfect economic governance, with the creation of several new instruments, to improve budgetary surveillance, co-ordination and convergence in the Eurozone (Laffan and Schlosser 2017; O'Keeffe et al. 2016). However, many of the new instruments that were created, e.g. the European Stability Mechanism (ESM), are not dependent on the EU budget, thus depriving the EP of one of its most effective control and scrutiny powers.

The role played by the EP in recent EMU reform is disputed. It has been argued that it wielded those newly acquired legislative powers with a significant impact on the fiscal reform of the Eurozone (Fasone 2014; Laffan and Schlosser 2016), especially during the negotiations of the Six-Pack, a new treaty on stability, co-ordination and governance, and the Two-Pack (Fabbrini 2013). The EP also used several strategies to extend its power beyond the formal powers given to it by the Treaty of Lisbon, such as acquiescing to substantive decisions only under the condition that it was given more institutional power in another arena, forming alliances with national actors in order to influence Member States' decisions, and mobilising public opinion (Héritier 2017). For others, however, the crisis did not fundamentally alter the longstanding logic and practice of the EU's parliamentarisation (Rittberger 2014). The EP's role thus remains largely consultative and it holds no authority or sanctioning powers against the European Central Bank (ECB) (Chang 2009: 83). Nor was the EP very successful in pushing through its preferences, particularly on economic issues (Bressanelli and Chelotti 2016; O'Keeffe et al. 2016). Accordingly, the EP's limited influence on EMU reform owes much to the continued predominance of Member States in policy areas that encompass vital features of state powers. Accordingly, the EP could only act within the confines set by Member States (Bressanelli 2018).

The increased role of the EP in EMU affairs has been the result of a twofold trend. First, as in other internal policies, it was the result of the EP's institutional activism and circumstances. Second, the recent advances in EMU have underscored the important function of Parliament in buttressing the EU's claim to democratic legitimacy. Chang (2009: 83) notes that the EP played a key role in increasing public awareness of the ECB's policies and pressuring it to justify its action, thereby promoting greater transparency and accountability and, incidentally, bolstering its own claim to democratic legitimacy and accountability.

## Social policy

Despite a longstanding, purely consultative and supervisory role, the EP was a keen supporter of developing the EU's action in the field of employment and social policy. MEPs recognised its political and symbolic salience for European citizens and its potential for profiling Parliament in this emerging field of Community action. In short, it "used a thinly defined policy area in order to strengthen its own thinly defined role in the Community's institutional framework" (Roos 2017: 1057). Social policy thus epitomised the relative success of the institution in imposing itself as a legislative actor, despite the constitutional impediments to its action. The EP was extremely active in commenting Commission proposals in the area of social policy, and supported initiatives taken by social partners in this area in 1988 (Anderson 2015: 63). It used various informal channels, for which there was no treaty provision, to circumvent its limited legislative role and influence related legislation during the formative years of the Community. MEPs maintained close contacts with the Commission, whose staff regularly attended the social committee meetings (Roos 2017: 1067). Occasionally, Council members and permanent representatives also accepted the invitation to EP committee meetings. These informal contacts bore a strong resemblance to a pre-draft consultation, although they did not have any treaty basis.

Introduced in 1986, the co-operation procedure re-balanced the institutional discussion of legislative proposals on social policy matters. A further strengthening of the EP's social policy competences was brought about by the Treaty of Amsterdam, which replaced the co-operation procedure with the co-decision procedure. The move to co-decision was particularly important for the EP considering that social policy applies to most aspects of the internal market, the freedom of movement for workers and education and training. Several of the EP's recommendations, such as the inclusion of the Social Agreement and the insertion of an employment chapter, were taken over in the final treaty text, reflecting the EP's growing influence in treaty reform (see Johansson in Chapter 2 of this book).

The Treaty of Lisbon further enlarged the EP's competences in employment and social affairs. Under co-decision, the Council and Parliament colegislate on measures required to bring about freedom of movement for workers. Competence for employment policy remains in the hands of the

Member States and the EP can only be consulted in the formulation of employment policy guidelines. Majority voting in Parliament and the Council continue to apply to EU legislation pertaining to e.g. the protection of workers' health and safety, working conditions, the information and consultation of workers and equality between men and women in the labour market. Consultation with Parliament is required for legislation on minimum standards on social security and the social protection of workers, representation and the collective defence of the interests of workers and employers. Finally, Parliament is only competent to adopt measures to encourage co-operation between Member States, but falling short of harmonising national laws, in the areas of social exclusion and the modernisation of social protection systems (Schmidt-Drüner 2014: 4-5).

### Environmental policy

The EP was a keen advocate of expanding and improving environmental legislation long before it became a crucial EU policy (Meyer 2011) and worked to increase its competences in this emerging policy area. The growing recognition of the political and societal salience of environmental matters and the transnational dimension of environmental problems, together with the environmental consequences of economic growth, provided Parliament with the legitimacy to advance pro-environment positions and profile itself as an advocate of citizens' concerns. As an increasingly high-profile policy area, environment fitted into the post-1979 elections strategy of enhancing public awareness of the need for more democratic control of Community policies. Thanks to the activities of its Environment Committee, which often acted as a trailblazer, Parliament came to be regarded as an environmental champion (Burns 2005; Judge 1993; Weale et al. 2000: 92).

Most environmental legislation originally fell under the consultation procedure. The EP's powers remained closely circumscribed in this area as in other domestic policies. Own initiative reports and resolutions were among the tools developed by the EP to affirm its informal right of legislative initiative. The Environment Committee proved very adept at using own initiative reports to set the Commission's environmental policy agenda (Judge and Earnshaw 2008: 274). Other informal means, such as conferences and hearings with experts and representatives from other institutions, were routinely used by the committee to shape Commission proposals at an early stage (Judge 1992).

With the insertion of a title on the environment, the SEA recognised environmental policy as an area of legal competence for the EU. The EP played an influential role in securing the incorporation of environmental provisions into the SEA. With the introduction of the co-operation procedure, the SEA gave Parliament an increased say in environmental policy legislation, especially for harmonisation measures, e.g. of environmental standards, which were necessary to the completion of the single market that fell under article 100a and thus had to be adopted under the co-operation procedure. Other environmental policy measures, however, continued to be adopted under the consultation procedure. The EP thus had a twofold interest to persuade the Commission to propose legislation and, when co-operation was used, to secure the Commission's support for its amendments (Burns 2005).

The 1992 Treaty of Maastricht awarded the EP new powers with direct application in environmental policy. It formally recognised the EP's right to initiate legislation, a right that the Environment Committee seized in 1994 to bring forward new environmental legislation. Although the co-decision procedure applied initially only to a limited number of treaty articles, it was gradually extended in the treaty reforms of Amsterdam and Nice to include many areas of environmental policy.

With the Treaty of Lisbon, co-decision applied to all environmental legislation. The success of Green parties in recent elections contributed to the emergence of an informal network encompassing Green MEPs and key lobbyists (Burns 2005: 98). While the EP was influential in developing the EU's environmental agenda, its legislative empowerment under co-decision seems to have transformed its green ambitions towards increased pragmatism (Rasmussen 2012; Burns and Carter 2010b).

### *Developments in internal policies*

The establishment of an open European market based on free but fair competition to promote economic prosperity, and the wide array of internal policies that it affected, has been a powerful driver of political and economic unity in Europe. However, the developments that the internal market set in motion have not been homogeneous across all internal policies.

## Agricultural policy

Since the inception of economic integration in Europe after 1945, two important sectors – agriculture and economic and monetary policy – have stood at its heart. Economic and agricultural integration were the twin objectives of the six founding Member States who signed the Treaty of Rome in 1957. As the most emblematic projects of European Union, they played a crucial role in fuelling the gradual integration of the economies and the establishment of the common market. For Christian democratic parties in EU Member States and their elected representatives in the EP, economic and agricultural integration within the European Communities was paramount. Supporting integration in these areas has been a major objective of the EPP Group since 1979.

Although agriculture no longer occupies the preponderant place it once had in the national economies of EU Member States and today employs only a small share of the active population, it continues to hold a symbolic, political and electoral importance for many political parties. Despite its highly contentious character, the CAP remains a major EU public policy, and its economic impact goes beyond farming, as many industries are closely linked to and depend on agriculture. Moreover, the CAP still accounts for a substantial part of the EU budget and is central to the multi-annual budgetary negotiations.

At the end of the Second World War, the agricultural sector faced several cross-border challenges that demanded a European rather than a purely national solution. Paramount among these challenges were the need for sectoral modernisation, food self-sufficiency, and the need to bring farm incomes and living conditions on a par with those prevalent in other sectors of employment. Yet, agricultural integration proved one of the most controversial projects of early European integration. There was widespread agreement on the necessity and benefits of greater co-operation in the agricultural sector, but little consensus on what it should look like, aim at or how to achieve it. After a failed attempt in the mid-1950s in the form of the so-called Green Pool, and protracted negotiations to balance diverging national interests, the CAP was ultimately born in the 1960s. It was the first fully fledged common policy of the newly established EEC in operation, and has been its most essential project in financial and law-making terms.

The Rome Treaty of 1957 assigned five main objectives to the CAP: to increase agricultural productivity, to ensure a fair standard of living for farmers, to stabilise markets, to assure the availability of food supplies and to ensure that those supplies reached consumers at reasonable prices. Despite multiple treaty revisions in the last three decades, these objectives have remained largely intact. The CAP was organised around three core principles. First, market unity posited the creation of a single internal market for agricultural commodities that could be traded unhindered by trade barriers across Community boundaries. Second, a Community preference entailed that Member States were encouraged to give preference to consumption of agricultural goods from within the EU over those from outside, through a system of import levies and export refunds. Agricultural prices, generally set above world market prices, were linked to farm incomes and reviewed annually. Financial solidarity ensured that the costs of the CAP were to be financed out of common coffers and redistributed to farmers in the Member States in the form of subsidies and income support.

In levelling the playing field with a set of rules and mechanisms regulating production, trade and the processing of agricultural products in the EU, combined with welfare provisions for farmers, the CAP had mostly Europeanised the domestic interventionist and protectionist policies of the EEC Member States. It had moreover enshrined the idea of agrarian exceptionalism, which postulated that farming demands distinctive, preferential policies because it is an economic activity unlike any other. This notion relied on two core ideas: first, that farmers have special interests that normal market arrangements cannot accommodate and, second, that agriculture contributes to broader interests and goals. Both justified the protection and state assistance of the sector, at Member State and EU levels.

Agricultural protectionism was part of the post-war consensus on the welfare state, full employment and state involvement in securing economic growth for all. Supporting farmers was vital for obtaining their adhesion to parliamentary democracy and neutralising potential discontent from a section of the electorate that had been traditionally volatile and in which residual attraction for authoritarian and anti-democratic politics was not uncommon after 1945. Parties with strong electoral support from the farming sector, especially Christian democratic parties, were thus keen to secure such support for their constituencies (Girvin and Griffith: xxxvi). This was crucial to preserve social peace and alleviate the consequences of economic, structural and demographic change in the agricultural sector.

The support mechanisms established under the CAP soon produced unintended problems, including the inflation of agricultural expenditures, large surplus production for key commodities and trade distortion. These problems were compounded by the enlargement of the Community and international trade negotiations. Reforms were thus initiated to address these flaws.

The reforms of the 1970s-1980s introduced new instruments, like the co-responsibility levy, quotas for milk and sugar and budgetary ceilings, but they failed to solve the CAP problems. Since the 1990s, successive reforms set out to adapt the CAP to new challenges and make it more market-oriented. The MacSharry reform (1992) introduced corrective measures to restrict production and budgetary expenditures. It decoupled price policy and farm income support through direct payments to farmers that were not linked with production, and changed the method of support from market-based intervention purchases to direct producer payments. The Agenda 2000 (1999) saw a further reduction in market and price support mechanisms and a greater attention paid to rural development and the environment, for instance with the introduction of the cross-compliance principle, which linked aid to farmers to respect for environmental, animal welfare and food quality standards. Agenda 2000 thus acknowledged the emergence of environment and rural development as new priorities. The Fischler reform (2003) formalised the Single Farm Payment (SFP) as a policy tool and the cross-compliance principle. The main innovation of the SFP was the creation of two separate pillars. Pillar I encompasses mainly market support measures and is fully financed from EU resources; Pillar II supports farmers' initiatives and multi-annual rural development measures and is co-financed by the Member States. The Health Check of 2008 further simplified and streamlined the CAP. It abolished all production-based payments, simplified the cross-compliance principle and transferred a greater amount of money to the rural development fund.

In 2010, the European Commission initiated a new review of the CAP. Its goal was to redesign the policy instruments to make it more efficient, simple and coherent with other policy objectives. Also, rather than revising only parts of the CAP, the reform intended to overhaul the entire policy. Adopted in 2013, this new reform introduced a new architecture of direct payments and strengthened rural development. In June 2018, the European Commission launched a new debate on reforming the CAP for the period after 2020.

For a long time, the CAP has been the EEC's only common policy. By the 1980s, however, the CAP came increasingly under pressure from a combination of endogenous and exogenous factors. The reforms it underwent have radically transformed the CAP and its policy objectives, rules and organisational structures. While the process was inhibited initially by the corporatist nature of the sector's governance, the influence of the national and European farmers organisations on national governments and European institutions, vested interests in Member States and the increasing heterogeneity of agricultural structures resulting from enlargement ultimately provided a decisive stimulus for reform. Crucially, the Treaty of Lisbon put an end to the long-time semi-autonomous and special character of the CAP as a policy field and introduced a shared competence between the EU and the Member States. The new role of Parliament as a co-legislator recognises the wider social and societal implications of EU agricultural policymaking.

### Economic and Monetary Union

EMU impacts on a wider range of internal policies, from the single market to competition policy, employment, labour and cohesion policies, most of which are aimed at the convergence of EU Member States' economies. After various early attempts at economic and monetary co-ordination with mixed results, EMU took its eventual shape in the 1990s and experienced severe turmoil in the last 10 years.

The co-ordination of economic policies and monetary co-operation within the Community was initiated in the late 1970s. The 1970 Werner report proposed parallel progress in economic and monetary union, but its proposals were a compromise between two opposed approaches: the German position, for which economic convergence was an essential foundation of monetary union, and the French position, for which monetary co-operation was a means of bringing closer together the Community economies. The collapse of Bretton Woods in 1971 and the ensuing monetary instability severely undermined Europeans' ambitions for EMU. The Six set up an exchange rate system, the 'snake in the tunnel' – in allusion to the upper and lower margins within which European currencies could trade – in order to limit fluctuations between European currencies. Yet, several currencies left the snake and, in some cases, re-joined it. By the end of the 1970s, the snake had become a virtual D-Mark zone with only a few currencies left in it.

After the two oil shocks of 1973 and 1979, economic stagflation and budgetary constraints brought to light the urgent need to achieve a sustainable stabilisation of European economies. In 1979, the EEC thus introduced the European Exchange Rate Mechanisms (ERM) that were based on the European Currency Unit (ECU), the forerunner of the Euro, whose value was determined as a weighted average of all participating currencies. Part of the European Monetary System (EMS), the ERM intended to reduce exchange rate variability and foster monetary stability in Europe. It also provided a tool to bring discipline into weaker economic policies, often forcing a choice for domestic rigour with substantial consequences on economic growth and employment. The experience of the snake and the ERM moved the focus onto the primacy of price stability in economic policy, the necessary management of inflation, the credibility of policy and the independence of central banks. In other words, German ordo-liberal ideas of the pre-eminence of long-term economic stabilisation were gaining critical ground over designs for short-term fiscal or monetary integration (Dyson 2012: 456).

The Delors report of 1989 unveiled a three-stage plan for the achievement of EMU; but the fall of the Berlin Wall and the prospect of enlargement to the Central and Eastern European states gave EMU a pivotal impetus. The 1992 Treaty of Maastricht took up the idea initially proposed by Delors in 1989 of a three-stage realisation of EMU, with a clear timetable for each stage over a period of roughly ten years. It established rules for ensuring the proper functioning of the single currency and for members willing to join it. These rules included specific convergence criteria, which set limits for inflation, public debt, interest and exchange rates, and safeguards to protect price stability in the single currency area. The single monetary policy was to be managed by an independent ECB, a new supranational institution, whose main goal was to pursue price stability in the Eurozone area. In spite of these developments, other important macroeconomic instruments, e.g. fiscal and economic policies on which effective EU-level monetary policy depended, remained in the hands of the Member States. The 1997 Stability and Growth Pact further tightened the rules on fiscal deficit and public debt to safeguard sounder budgetary policies by Member States and improve policy co-ordination.

Since the 1990s, EMU had been characterised by a fundamental dichotomy: a limited process of Europeanisation of domestic fiscal policies and a high degree of Europeanisation of monetary policy. This inherent weakness of the Eurozone's economic governance was laid bare in 2008 when the financial and sovereign debt crisis struck. The crisis not only tested the resilience of the EU's financial institutions, but also the very survival of the Euro when Greece nearly defaulted on its sovereign debt. The so-called Euro-crisis led to the creation of a new intergovernmental body, the European Financial Stability Fund (EFSF) – renamed as the European Stability Mechanism (ESM) in 2012 – to provide financial assistance and better safeguard macroeconomic stability in the Eurozone.

Since its inception in the 1970s, EMU has been a gradual process to develop and strengthen economic governance in the Eurozone. Beyond monetary policy and the recently created financial assistance mechanism, the transfer of formal competences to the EU has remained limited, and economic policy co-ordination is still very much a prerogative of the Member

States in the European Council and the Eurogroup. This has constrained the ability of European institutions, including the EP and its political groups, to influence EMU debates and governance up to today.

## Social policy

Social policy is normally used to characterise a broad variety of redistributive policy measures ranging from social welfare, working conditions, health, vocational training and education to collective bargaining and right of association and equality of (social) rights. Along with regional policy, social policy has been instrumental to channel solidarity in the EC/EU. Due to its cross-sectoral character, it affects many internal policy areas. In spite of this fact, compared to other policies such as the CAP or EMU, social policy occupied a more marginal position in European integration.

Federalists regarded it as a crucial policy area for the implementation of the goal of an 'ever closer union' as stated in the founding treaties. The establishment of a Community-wide social policy was a necessary step in order to ensure social protection and welfare for Member States' citizens and workers across the Community. However, national governments were reluctant to relinquish national sovereignty in this area (Varsori 2010). As a result, the Rome treaty of 1957 did not include specific provisions (Falkner 1998; Anderson 2015: 55).

At the same time, the negotiators of the Rome Treaty recognised that social policy measures would be necessary to facilitate labour mobility within the common market, channel resources, mitigate the impact of economic integration and offset the most significant social consequences that the implementation of the common market would have on the labour force. They also acknowledged the difficulty in integrating, or even harmonising, national social policy regimes with very different historical traditions, underpinning beliefs and existing structures. With the expansion of the welfare state, which offered protection against a wide range of social risks, guaranteed income redistribution and social cohesion, and the period of economic growth and high employment that almost all Western European countries experienced until the 1970s, there was no pressing need to Europeanise social policy and delegate national competences to EU institutions. It thus remained a matter of domestic rather than EU policy.

Institutional activism laid the ground for a social policy enacted by the Union. Early on, the European Commission had been a keen advocate of closer co-operation between members states and promoted the harmonisation of key social policy measures such as social security and working conditions, labour law, unionising and collective bargaining. Likewise, the judicial activism of the European Court of Justice (ECJ) was influential in fleshing out social policy legislation. The context, marked by economic crisis, low growth rates, growing unemployment and budget and state deficits, was also conducive to action in the field of social policy; the first Social Action Programme was adopted in January 1974.

In comparison, the 1980s were a period of relative stagnation for social policy, although there was a strong confluence of factors in favour of consolidating the social dimension of European integration. France had elected a socialist President in 1981 and Jacques Delors, a member of the French Socialist party, was appointed Commission President in 1982. Both were strong advocates of strengthening the social policy dimension of integration. National trade unions and the European Trade Union Confederation (ETUC) also lobbied strongly in favour of a more social Europe, especially against the backdrop of the negotiations of the SEA. In spite of this, the treaty contained only limited innovations in the field of social policy (Anderson 2015: 61), although the concept of a European Social Model was introduced.

The plans for monetary and economic union further fuelled debates about the need to expand EU competences in social policy. With the Treaty of Maastricht, the promotion of a high level of employment and social protection was officially introduced as one of the tasks conferred on the European Community Union. The Amsterdam Treaty expanded the EU's role to other areas of social policy, including issues pertaining to employment and social protection. Endowing the EU with competences in employment policy appeared necessary as part of the efforts to bring the union closer to citizens and their immediate preoccupations, at a time when unemployment remained crucially high in most Member States, but also to alleviate the social consequences of EMU. At the same time, the EU's role was limited to the co-ordination of national employment policies.

Launched in 2000 and revised several times throughout the decade, the Lisbon Strategy aimed at strengthening the EU's social agenda in the field of employment and social inclusion. The Nice, Constitutional and Lisbon Treaties allowed further progress in consolidating the social dimension of European integration. The TFEU emphasises the EU's social objectives, including full employment and solidarity. The economic crisis that struck Europe in the late 2000s, the drastic austerity measures that were taken in its wake and, more generally, its social toll on European societies have reopened the debate about a European social policy. Accordingly, one of the main priority areas of the Europe 2020 Strategy has been to promote inclusive growth, that is a high-employment economy that delivers social and territorial cohesion. However, the recent strengthening of the Union's economic governance may also curtail Member States' social policy leeway, which is likely to be subordinated to strict budgetary and debt thresholds, thus upholding the conundrum of balancing social and economic policies.

Until the present day, the Europeanisation of social policy has remained more limited than in other internal or external policy areas. This was partly due to the original design of the Rome Treaty dispositions, which relied heavily on the ordo-liberal and, in hindsight, naive assumption that market integration and competition would bring about the convergence of national social policies. The development of social policy has been marked by a gradual expansion of social provisions in EU treaties, even though much of the policy-making process in social matters continues to rely on a delicate compromise between Member States autonomy and Union competence. The increasing awareness that economic integration could not solve all the social problems in the EU also brought into focus the need to develop a social dimension of EMU, not least as a means to ensure the continued support of EU citizens for the European project.

## Environmental policy

Environmental policy gained treaty recognition only in 1986 with the adoption of the SEA, but the attention of European institutions towards issues of environmental protection dates back at least to the early 1970s, when the concerns with growing environmental degradation became matters of public concern (Kaiser and Meyer 2017). Following the general international trend of initiating environmental legislation, the Commission published the first European Environmental Action Programme (EAP) in 1973. It defined important general principles, like the 'polluters pay', which provided a general policy framework for the EU's environmental policy. These principles have since been expanded to include sustainable development and the precautionary principle. The Commission has since adopted seven EAPs, with the seventh due to end in 2020.

In addition to addressing growing transnational environmental problems, a major driving force behind the development of a European environmental policy in the 1970s was the concern that common market trade could be obstructed by different environmental policy strategies and standards (Heinelt 2018[2]). The result was an issue-linkage between environmental and market objectives. At the same time, the informal status of EC environmental policy, at least until the SEA, limited the Commission's and EP's opportunity to resort to legislations. While in some cases they were successful in implementing pieces of legislation, such as in the case of the 1979 directive on the protection of birds and their habitat (see Kaiser in Chapter 1 of this book and infra), one powerful ally was often found in the European Court of Justice, which could confirm the legitimacy of environmental norms in the absence of explicit reference in the Treaties, and implement policy measures.

Environmental lobby groups have also been capable of influencing environmental legislation, though sometimes with conflicting or divergent interests. Environmental non-governmental organisations (NGOs), for instance, act both as pressure groups and as a source of information on the implementation of the environmental *acquis* in Member States. Business interest groups also provide EU institutions with expert advice and opinion, and usually have more specific interests, which are easier to relate to particular Commission proposals (Kingston et al. 2017).

Since the early 1970s, EU legislation has encompassed many aspects of environment policy, i.e. the treatment of waste, air, soil and water pollution and the protection of natural resources and of endangered species. Moreover, preserving and improving the quality of the environment and the sustainable management of global natural resources in order to ensure sustainable development is one of the objectives of the EU's external action. Accordingly, the current EAP (2013-2020) stresses the EU's global role in promoting sustainable development and lists three major goals of the EU's environmental policy: to protect, conserve and enhance the EU's natural capital, to turn the EU into a resource-efficient, green and competitive low-carbon economy, and to safeguard EU citizens from environment-related pressures and risks.

The ambitious goals set by the EU's environmental policy should be measured against the Euro-crisis. The impacts of the crisis have been distributed unevenly across policy sectors, but environmental policy was among the most negatively impacted, with some examples of active dismantling. While this may represent a setback for progressive environmental legislation, it nevertheless demonstrates the resilience of EU environmental policy in the event of an economic shock of such proportions (Burns et al. 2015).

### *The EPP Group in the EP's committees*

Sectoral EP committees have existed since the institution was first established as the Common Assembly of the ECSC in 1952, and their number expanded after 1979 to reflect developments in parliamentary powers, the extension of the EU's competences and the ever-widening reach of European integration, as well as the increased size of the EP. Although they originally had limited functions, these committees have been essential to the effective co-ordination of the legislative work in internal policies. Their primary roles have been to scrutinise, prepare and debate legislation and to provide the technical means and expertise for the EP to exert its role. They thus have a crucial function in the process of shaping policy and interacting with other institutions (Neuhold 2001). They came to form the "legislative backbone" of the institution (Westlake 1994: 191) and the place where political groups can wield real influence (Corbett, Jacobs and Neville 2016).

Four parliamentary committees of a different nature are relevant here: the Committee on Agriculture and Rural Development (AGRI), the Committee on Economic and Monetary Affairs (ECON), the Committee on Employment and Social Affairs (EMPL) and the Committee of Environment, Public Health and Food Safety (ENVI).[2] The first three are among the oldest committees, despite slight changes in their responsibilities over time. Co-decision raised the stakes of legislation discussed in these committees and gave political groups a real possibility to co-shape the EU's legislative output. Committee composition is usually representative of the size of the different political groups and the respective weighting of the political forces in presence (Meny 2009: 141). Because EU issues are often technical and complex, policy expertise has been an important criterion for MEP assignment to specific committees and the establishment of close ties with societal and policy-relevant groups who provide such expertise. Accordingly, it is important to examine the EPP Group's representation in these committees over time, which has been an important factor in its ability to influence internal policy developments.

Table 3.1 (see the Appendix) and Figure 3.1 illustrate the historical trajectory of membership in the AGRI, ECON, EMPL and ENVI from the first to the last legislature of the EP. Table 3.1 contrasts the composition of the four committees for the Christian Democrats (EPP), the Socialists (S&D), the Liberal Group (ALDE) and the Greens, the four major political forces in presence.[3] The table shows a relatively equal, and jointly domi-

2 For simplicity here, we have used the committees' current designations and acronyms.

3 These abbreviations are used for the sake of clarity, and include previous denominations/acronyms (e.g. PES, ELDR).

nant, representation of EPP and S&D political group members in AGRI, ECON, EMPL and ENVI, albeit with slight variations in member numbers that have been alternately in favour of the EPP and the S&D. Figure 3.1 helps visualise the somewhat contrasted evolution of the EPP membership in each committee since 1979. Notwithstanding occasional variations, EPP membership in the AGRI, ECON and ENVI steadily increased up until the seventh legislature and then show a marked decrease since across all committees. The EMPL Committee displays a much more jagged line, with significant variations across time.

*Figure 3.1 The evolution of EPP membership in the AGRI, ECON, EMPL and ENVI Standing Committees in comparison, by EP term**

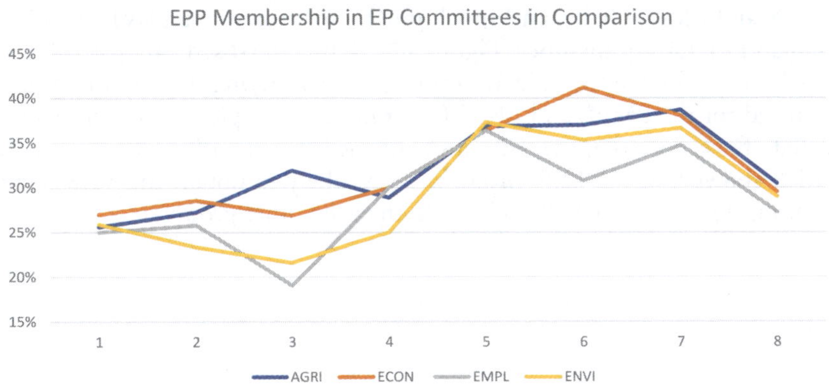


*** EP Terms in this and all other figures and tables are as follows: 1. 1979–1984; 2. 1984–1989; 3. 1989–1994; 4. 1994–1999; 5. 1999–2004; 6. 2004–2009; 7. 2009–2014; 8. 2014–2019;. Depending on layout, they will be listed also in numerical order (1–8) or by beginning of term date (1979–2014)*

Committee Chairs play an important role in the work of the committees and Parliament. They are formally elected by committee members, but their appointment is normally agreed beforehand among the political group leaders (for criteria on the attribution to political groups of EP institutional positions, see also Bardi in Chapter 5 of this book). Committee Chairs are more likely to get reports than members who are not Chairs. Expertise in the jurisdiction of the committee is also an important factor for the selection of the Chair and the Rapporteurs. The political skills and experience of the Chair and the Rapporteurs and the ability of these individuals to dominate their committee, e.g. through their long-lasting chairmanship, to maintain close contacts with relevant policy networks and close consultation with the Commission, have been crucial factors for enhancing the EP's influence on policy.

Figures 3.2 and 3.3 provide an overview of the distribution of the committee chairmanships and vice-chairmanships between the four major parties over time. Given the importance of agriculture and the available farm expertise among EPP members, the Chair of AGRI was more often occupied by an EPP member than by members of other political groups between 1979 and 2019 (Figure 3.2). Interestingly, the Greens won the chairmanship of AGRI in 1999. This was due to the stronger interest of the EPP in obtaining the chairmanship of ENVI rather than retaining that of AGRI, as a result of both policy-making changes and the increasing political salience of environment policy (Roederer-Rynning 2003: 122). The ECON and EMPL chairmanship fell much more often to an S&D member than an EPP Group member (Figure 3.2). While the discrepancy is still relatively small for the ECON Committee, it is to varying degrees more pronounced for the EMPL and ENVI Committees. This picture is slightly corrected if we consider the allocation of vice-chairmanships (Figure 3.3), which shows that the EPP Group is more likely to obtain the Vice-Chair positions for ECON, ENVI and EMPL than the other groups.

4 Figure 3.2 takes into account the fact that committee Chairs often change in the second half of the term.

*Figure 3.2 Chairmanship of AGRI, ECON, EMPL and ENVI Standing Committees, 1979–2019*[4]

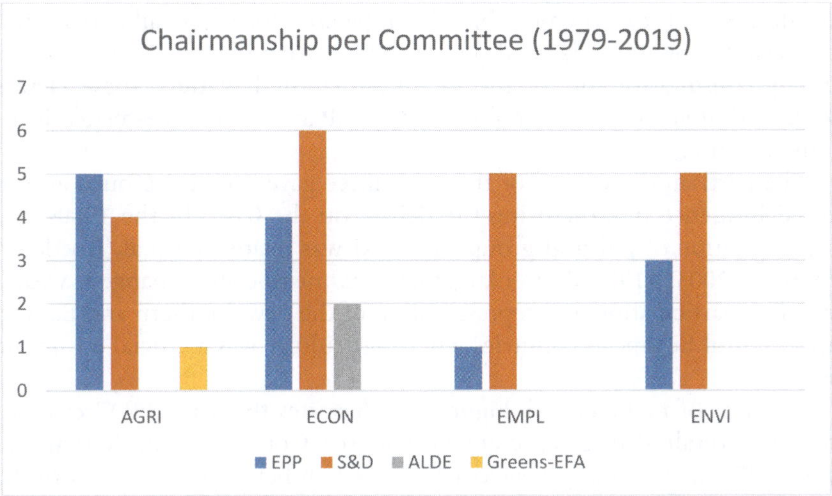


*Figure 3.3 Vice-Chairmanship of AGRI, ECON and EMPL Standing Committees, 1979–2019*

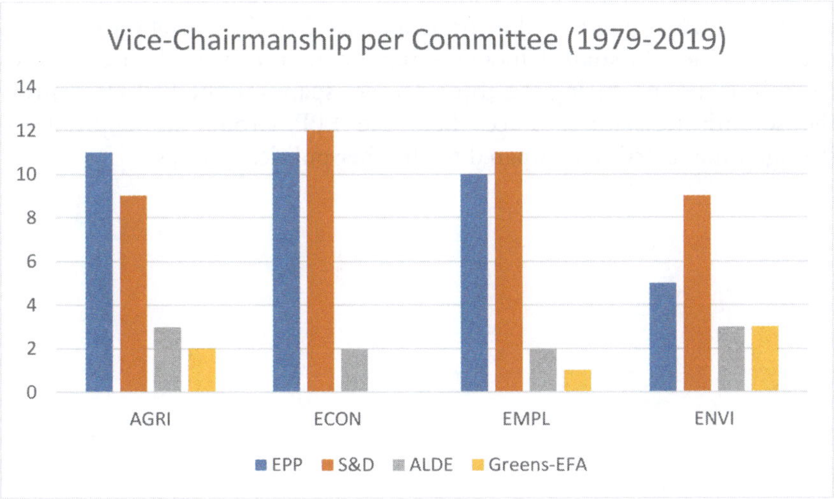

The extension of co-decision to agriculture increased the political salience of the AGRI Committee, the key parliamentary discussion forum for farm politics. In the formative years of the CAP, it was the largest parliamentary committee and it now enjoys broad competence for nearly all agricultural matters. Although its size and political clout stood in stark contrast to the purely consultative role of the EP in agricultural matters, these factors were indicative of the importance of the CAP and agriculture-related legislative activities.

The partisan dimension of the committee gave political groups an unequal influence in structuring the debate on the CAP. In the 1980s, the representation of political groups in AGRI was relatively equal (Roederer-Rynning 2003: 119). With enlargement, its membership changed, with a stronger participation and representation of the new Southern and Eastern and Central European countries where agriculture was a crucial economic sector.

In terms of membership, Figure 3.4 illustrates that the EPP Group has had an overall strong representation in the Committee on Agriculture since 1979, with roughly 25% to 40% of its members. This reflects both the importance of the sector for the Group and the composition of the overall Parliament after elections. During the first four legislatures (1979-1999), the EPP made up a quarter to a third of the committee members (Table 3.1 in the Appendix). With the exceptions of the first and fourth legislatures, the EPP Group has been the dominant political group in the AGRI Committee and has strengthened its presence in AGRI. Figure 3.4 shows, moreover, that the Christian democratic representation in AGRI increased by roughly 15 points during the three decades spanning the first elections to the seventh legislature. Since then, the EPP Group has enjoyed the strongest membership compared to all other political groups.

*Figure 3.4 Political group membership in the AGRI Standing Committee, 1979–2019*

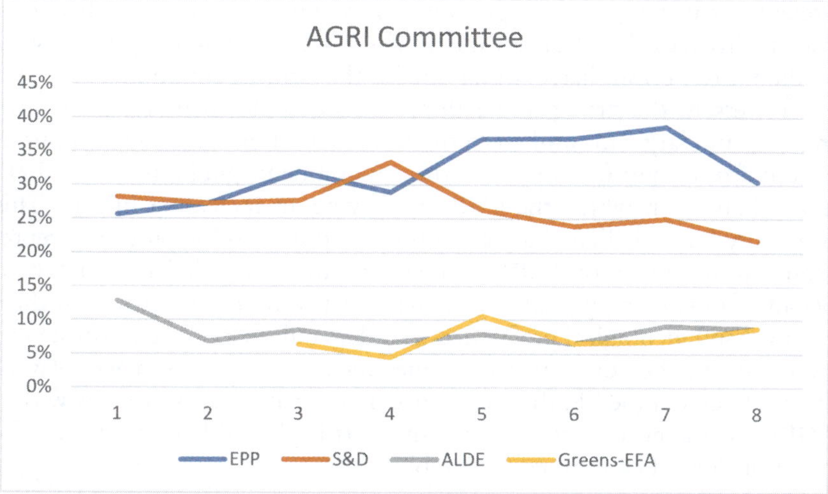


AGRI was crucial for the organisation and structuring of agricultural concerns in the EP. It served primarily as a relay of farm interests insofar as it was chiefly the 'rural' quality of represented constituencies – not their substantive or ideological positions on farming – which brought MEPs together. A key feature of AGRI has been the historical pervasiveness of specialised interests and the strong representation of farmers within it. In the mid-1980s, 10% of the MEPs who specialised in agriculture had direct links with the farmers interests, not to mention MEPs who had networks in rural constituencies (Sidjanski 1984). The committee included several ex-presidents of farmers' unions such as Sir Henry Plumb and Michel Debatisse (Plumb 2001: 14), many of whom had links to Christian democratic or affiliated parties. The business and personal ties between AGRI MEPs and the farming sector or the agricultural industry remain strong to the present day (Greenpeace 2018: 7).

Nevertheless, this farming expertise was of vital importance for ensuring that AGRI was an adequate forum for discussing often technical agricultural matters. The shared background and expertise in farming were a warrant for cohesion, standing and power. The specialised knowledge and expertise of AGRI's members were particularly valuable when the EP enjoyed few legislative, mostly consultative powers: committee expertise gave Parliament a key informational advantage and improved its bargaining position vis-à-vis the Council. The selection of MEPs to AGRI was thus driven in part by the need for expertise and the desire from political groups to appoint policy specialists to the committee. Given the electoral preferences of farmers for right and centre-right parties, the EPP Group had in this regard a clear advantage vis-à-vis other political groups, who could not rely on similarly strong links to the farming community.

Conversely, the strong connections of many AGRI members with farming – by and large not limited to the EPP – has often eclipsed the input of experts from other fields such as the environment, public health and climate change, on which the CAP was having an increasing impact. This proximity both facilitated access to the committee to lobbyists and represented an incentive for AGRI members to provide legislative advocacy on behalf of organised agricultural interests that were in line with both their political and ideological preferences and demands from their constituency. Even though the committee continues today to be the primary relay of farm interests in the EP, the emergence of alternative farm interests within AGRI and the growth of non-farm interests in the EP have weakened the political clout of established farm lobbies.

The informal organisation of EP committees has allowed highly influential committee members to exercise informal quality control over technically deficient or overtly biased information (Marshall 2010). Prominent Christian Democrats with a farming background, such as Isidor Früh, Michel Debatisse or Teun Tolman, could thus exercise considerable influence over the outcome of the committee process, and by implication the final legislative outcome. Over the years, these EPP members regularly contributed as Chairmen, Vice-Chairmen and Rapporteurs. These positions came with prestige and influence, especially at critical junctures of the CAP, when the committee was examining reform proposals.

The powers and competences that the EP had (or rather did not have) have constrained its ability to play a role in the debate on the reform of the CAP and influence the actual changes that the policy underwent since the early 1990s. If anything, the EP was rather conspicuous by its absence in the debate on CAP reform until the early 2010s, when the Commission announced a new reform of the policy. At the same time, the EP's agricultural committee has also been notorious for its conservatism in farm affairs. This conservative attitude was to a large extent rooted in the traditionally close and strong agricultural ties of the committee's members, whether from the national political scene, the academic world, the agro-food industry, farm unions or the farming community itself. AGRI thus had a reputation for being "a conservative forum welded to the defence of vested interests" (Roederer-Rynning 2010: 199). These links were and have become ever more important channels for national and European farm organisations to exert influence on the CAP reform debate. Expertise, but also the close relationship with national farmer unions and COPA-COGECA (the main EU-level farm interest organisations in Brussels) and links to national parliament and governments, especially national ministries, were both powerful, formal and informal, ways to articulate and advance farming interests, that by and large were in favour of preserving the agricultural status quo (e.g. Germond 2013).

The Committee for Economic and Monetary Affairs (ECON) was established in 1973 against the backdrop of the first initiatives for monetary and economic integration.[5] ECON's core competences are the economic and monetary policies of the Union, the functioning of EMU and the European monetary and financial system and other connected issue areas. Since its creation, ECON has actively participated to the legislative process and has consistently figured among the most heavily involved in the co-decision procedure (Whitaker 2011: 33). During and after the Euro-crisis, ECON played a pivotal role in the scrutiny and adoption of legislation responding to the crisis.

Figure 3.5 shows the evolution of the membership of EPP MEPs in the ECON Committee over the last 40 years. While throughout the first four legislatures, EPP Group members in ECON comprised between 25% and 30% of the Committee, their numbers increased by 10 points during the fifth and sixth legislature, up to over 40%. Since then, the number of ECON EPP members has decreased gradually to hover around 30%.

5 HAEU, PE0 20440, Commission économique et monétaire, Réunion constitutive du 13 mars 1973.

*Figure 3.5 Political Group membership in the ECON Standing Committee, 1979–2019*

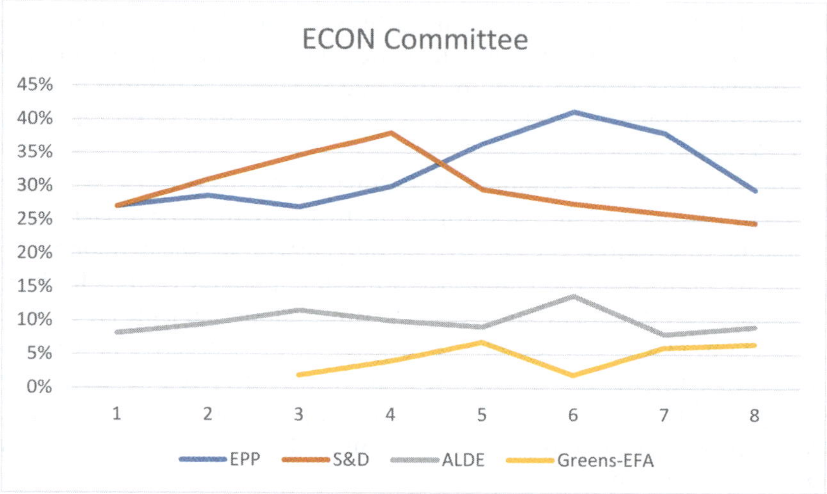


Traditionally, informal politics, networking and lobbying have been important elements of the relationship of ECON members with corporate interests. Due to its competence areas, ECON has been particularly subject to lobbying by business interests to guarantee a friendly regulatory environment for corporate activities within the EU. The increase of the EP's legislative powers in the economic and monetary areas has led to enhanced interest in ECON from business lobbies. One of these lobbies is the European Round Table of Industrialists (ERT), which was instrumental in setting the agenda for the single market programme (Green Cowles 1994) and was used by industrialists to develop informal networks with policy and law makers.

While the EP has traditionally had a reputation for being more open to diffuse interests, ECON has become an important target for lobbyists. MEPs in ECON are said to give due deference to industry and corporate interests (e.g. Kurtzer and Cooper 2013). In fact, it is not uncommon for representatives of business interests to attend the ECON Committee meetings and participate in expert hearings (Bouwen 2004: 482, 484). EU-level associations tend to have better access to ECON than national associations, although the latter enjoy access mostly through MEPs, who often retain their national mandate in addition to their European one. MEPs' active participation in national party politics and their involvement in their country's social life provide multiple opportunities for them to interact with national public and private interests, articulate those preferences during the Committee's debates and influence the amendments and reports submitted by the Committee (Bouwen 2004: 492).

The EP's Social Affairs Committee (EMPL) is among the oldest, most prestigious and salient EP committees; the EPP Group has been involved in it since the creation of the ECSC Common Assembly.[6] The EMPL Committee is mainly responsible for employment policies and all aspects of social policy, working conditions, vocational training and the free movement of workers and pensioners.

The broad trajectory of EPP membership (Figure 3.6) shows a contrasted evolution. For the first 10-15 years after the first direct EP election, EMPL was largely dominated by the S&D, whose MEPs represented between 30%-40% of the Committee members. This predominance can be partly explained by the ideological importance of social matters for social democratic parties and partly by the stronger representation of the Socialist Group in the EP for the first four terms. This had a direct effect on the committee composition and on the distribution of institutional positions (see Bardi in Chapter 5 of this book). From the 1990s, however, the number of EPP MEPs in EMPL increased substantially to settle at around 30%-35%, at a level that was consistent with the growth of the Group's elected members. This increase also reflected the growing electoral salience of social policy issues for the Group at a time when many EU Member States experienced a downturn in economic activity and recession, but also the increased salience of social policy to accompany the process of EMU. Similarly, in the AGRI and ECON Committees (Figures 3.4 and 3.5), the EPP saw its membership decline relatively sharply as of the seventh legislature, possibly as a result of the increased competition of other political groups.

EMPL has drawn upon the technical and expert input and support provided by interest groups representing the social partners involved in collective bargaining, for instance the employers and trade unions and the ETUC. MEPs depend on this expert knowledge to critically assess the technical details of the Commission's proposals, while they also need political information on public opinion and support (Rasmussen 2015: 370). The need for technical and industry-specific expertise is arguably greater for committees dealing with predominantly regulatory issues, while committees dealing with less technical and more political matters, such as EMPL,

6 HAEU, AC 157, Commission des Affaires sociales, Réunion du 12 Janvier 1953.

are likely to be more interested in political information about constituency opinion and support. The MEPs' own occupational expertise in social policy matters has also been an important attribute for the staffing of information-driven committees like EMPL (Yordanova 2013).

*Figure 3.6 Political Group membership in the EMPL Standing Committee, 1979–2019*

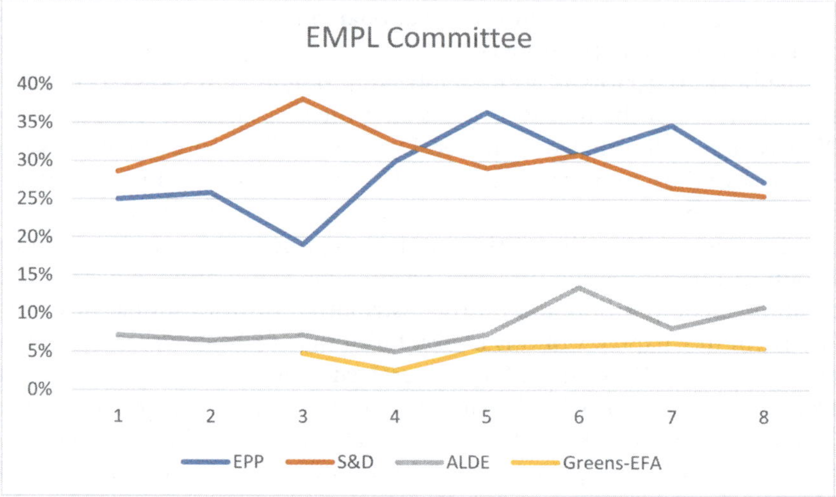


This reliance on interest-driven expertise and information is not uncommon, but EMPL is a particularly interest- and information-driven committee (Yordanova 2009). This proximity has fostered informal contacts and networking between EMPL Committee members and the social partners, and especially labour unions. The mobilisation of these transnational policy networks facilitated the articulation of social concerns from different interests, but they also strengthened the corporatist features of the policy community (Falkner 1998).

The Committee for the Environment, Public Health and Food Safety (ENVI) is the second largest committee within the EP and one of the most powerful, as its deals with more co-decision legislation than any other committee (Burns 2005: 89). Since its inception, it has been successful at shaping the EU's policy agenda and using its legislative powers to amend policy proposals (Burns and Carter 2010). Established in 1972, the parliamentary Committee on Public Health and Social Affairs (renamed Committee on Public Health and the Environment in 1973) has been responsible for debating and drafting environmental and other related legislation. Although the policy areas covered by ENVI have changed over time, to include public health and consumer protection and food safety in the 1990s, ENVI has been characterised by a remarkable continuity in its commitment to environmental goals, regardless of the political affiliation of its leadership and fluctuations in membership.

As shown in Figure 3.7, the S&D was the dominant group in ENVI during the first four legislatures. In 1999, the EPP became the largest political group within Parliament, a fact that is also reflected in the composition of ENVI from the fifth legislature onward. Initial fears that this would compromise the EP's environmentally progressive stance were soon discarded as the EPP Group realised it needed the support of other groups to secure the adoption of its own amendments. Thus, compromise and consensus remained the norm in ENVI.

*Figure 3.7 Political group membership in the ENVI Standing Committee, 1979–2019*

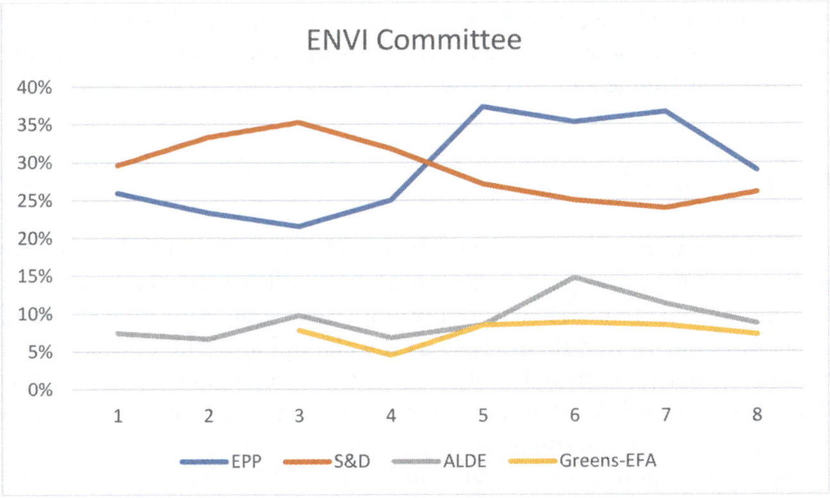


The continuity at the head of ENVI between 1979 and 2007, with three Chairs – two of whom were EPP Group members[7] – explains both the

7 Ken Collins (S&D) was Chair for 15 years (1979-1984, 1989-1999) and sat between as a deputy Chair between these periods (1984-1989). Caroline Jackson (EPP) suc-

committee's remarkable capacity for using the increase of the EP's legislative influence and formal powers during that period to enhance its own ability to initiate and co-shape environmental legislation (Judge 1992; Bomberg and Burns 1999) and for establishing its reputation as an environmental pioneer. The special interest and expertise of the Chairs and Rapporteurs has been key to establishing and perpetuating ENVI's reputation of environmental entrepreneurship (Delreux and Happaerts 2012: 75).

Having to legislate over often highly technical matter unavoidably places great strain upon the ENVI Committee and its personnel. Due to the committee's limited in-house expertise, it often needs to rely on external sources of expertise and information from Commission official and lobbyists. To eschew the problem of partiality, the committee regularly invites independent experts from EU agencies and research institutes to offer their advice on issues falling within the committee's expanding competences. Over the years, the Environment Committee thus developed an intricate web of informal contacts with a variety of actors, from DG Environment officials and policy experts to NGOs and interest groups. ENVI MEPs are entwined in a process of negotiations and trade-offs where information is traded between and amongst EC institutions and other policy actors such as national governments, trade associations or non-governmental organisations (Judge and Earnshaw 2008: 269).

### *The EPP Group and the CAP*

Christian Democrats viewed the CAP as a strategic pillar of European integration and a sectoral policy with an impact well beyond the frontiers of the agricultural sector. They were not only early supporters of agricultural integration but viewed themselves as "the champion of the European agriculture."[8] They participated in the negotiations that would ultimately lead to the creation of CAP (Fontaine 2009: 77-84), in which they saw a means to offer protection to farmers, an important electoral constituency.

Agricultural policy was a vital issue for the EPP, not only for electoral-political reasons – where Christian democratic parties relied on the rural electorate – but also for cultural-ideological reasons. Historically, the ties between the EPP political group and the agricultural community were

ceeded him after his retirement in 1999 and held the position until 2004. Karl Heinz-Florenz (EPP) took over in 2004 and held the chairmanship until 2007.

8 EPP Group Archives, D.5.12, Activity Report, Yearbook 1990-1991, p. 63.

close. Most of the EPP members sitting in AGRI had a close association with agriculture and farming, either through their origins or previous professional activities. Several, like Michel Debatisse and Hans August Lücker, had occupied leading positions in national farmers unions and government. Debatisse had chaired the main French national farm union, the Fédération national des syndicats d'exploitants agricoles (FNSEA), and Lücker had been a long-time agriculture minister under Konrad Adenauer (see Kaiser in Chapter 1 of this book). Others, like Henry Plumb, a British conservative MEP who, although not a Christian Democrat, joined the EPP-ED Group after 1992, was a former President of the British National Farmers Union and COPA-COGECA. Plumb presided over the Agriculture Committee between 1979 and 1982 and was elected EP President in 1987, with the backing of the EPP Group. These men and a handful of women formed a close-knit network: they had known each other and worked together in various professional capacities prior to and after joining the EP.

From the 1960s onward, the high price levels – originally designed to secure food supplies and support farm income – and the guaranteed purchase of agricultural products generated costly surpluses for several food staples. These agricultural surpluses had to be disposed of, stockpiled or dumped on world markets at heavily reduced prices. The rising costs of the price policy and market support – the two core CAP mechanisms – contributed to such a dramatic increase in agricultural expenditure that the Community was virtually on the verge of bankruptcy by the mid-1980s. As a welfare policy designed to help the farming sector in the EEC Member States adapt to the socio-economic transformations of the post-war era (Knudsen 2009), the CAP had failed to remedy enduring farm income problems. Small farmers still struggled to make a living out of their land despite the policy's costly support mechanisms. Moreover, with the rise of environmental awareness in Western European societies, the environmental impact of the type of intensive agriculture supported by CAP subsidies came under scrutiny from public opinion and environmental activists. These developments gave CAP critics a powerful argument to advocate a radical change in the policy's principles and mechanisms.

Reforming the CAP presented a genuine quandary for the EPP Group. The Group recognised the need to tackle the problem of rising expenditures. Faced with Member States' refusal to pay more into the budget beyond the agreed ceiling, a revision of the policy appeared inevitable, if only to preserve its main achievements and allow the development of other redistributive policies, such as social and regional policies, that were aligned with the Christian democratic ideals and values of solidarity. However, its close links with the countryside and the electoral power of farmers meant that the Group could not support a fundamental change that would bring about a strong reduction in the level of protection and intervention guarantees or weaken the CAP subsidy system. To solve this conundrum, the EPP Group favoured making the CAP less costly and supported measures aimed at limited expenditures but did not challenge the policy's fundamental principles (Fontaine 2009: 199).

The Group thus initially supported early reform attempts, such as a co-responsibility levy on surplus production, but in large part because their limited scope was acceptable for its rural electoral. For the most part, Christian Democrats were less interested in forcing a more efficient farming sector than in preserving farmers as an electoral reservoir (Hendrick 1991). The continued reliance of many national Christian democratic parties on the farm vote, especially in countries like France and Germany that had traditionally followed more protectionist agricultural policies, placed them in a precarious position with regard to agricultural reform. The impact that farmers could have on election outcomes could be substantial, as the Christian Democratic Union (CDU) and its Bavarian sister party, the Christian Social Union (CSU), experienced in May 1984 when the party suffered a substantial drop in votes (over 35%) during the Rhineland-Palatinate elections (Hendrick 1988: 86), only a few months after the introduction of the quota system for milk. Under these circumstances, the EPP had little appetite for drastic reforms. The EPP Group's cautious support of the co-responsibility levy also relied on the fact that it did not call into question the key tenets of the CAP, namely the protection and the guaranteed support price. The 1981 Plumb report is exemplary of this line of thinking among conservative MEPs.[9] It also embodied the vested interests that many Christian Democrat MEPs had in preserving the agricultural status quo.

Torn between the interests of its farming electorate and the continued rise in agricultural spending, the EPP Group eventually endorsed the budget stabilisers and the resulting price reductions.[10] The stabilisers were adopted in 1988 by the Council of Ministers as part of a reform package and an agreement on the Community budget, despite heavy pressures at the national level against it and electoral losses for Kohl's government, which held the Council's rotating Presidency (Patterson 1993: 10-12). Yet,

9 HAEU, PE1-17293, Rapport fait au nom de la Commission de l'agriculture sur les améliorations pouvant être apportées à la PAC, 27 mai 1981.

10 ACDP, 09-001-1095/2, Proposition de résolution (no date).

the Group vehemently argued against any further price reduction when the Commission proposed lower prices the following year "since there was no need and it would only reduce farm incomes".[11] Preventing the loss of farm income was among the chief concerns of the EPP Group.[12]

At the same time, the Group had few other options but to acknowledge the need to tackle the structural problems of surpluses. But this could only be achieved in co-operation with farmers, with the aim of safeguarding the family farm as a predominant form of European farming and a fundamental socio-cultural institution in the European countryside. This stance was not only consistent with a Christian democratic vision of family farming (see Kaiser in Chapter 1 of this book) but it also chimed with that of the main national and European farm organisations (Germond 2015).

By the early 1990s, the prospect of enlargement to the Central and Eastern European countries, pressures for liberalisation by the EU's trading partners in international negotiations on agriculture during the General Agreement on Tariffs and Trade (GATT Uruguay Round), enduring problems related to overproduction, budgetary costs and environmental degradation and an entrepreneurial European Commission created favourable conditions for a more radical approach to reforming the CAP. In December 1990, Agriculture Commissioner Ray MacSharry announced that the Commission would present revolutionary changes. His announcement was met with some scepticism, with farmers staging a demonstration in Brussels on 3 December 1990 to coincide with a ministerial-level GATT meeting taking place in the Belgian capital. This demonstration prompted an EP resolution to support a revision of the CAP in line with the objective of giving farmers an income comparable to that of other workers.[13] Outlined broadly in a reflection paper in February 1991 (Commission 1991a), MacSharry's proposals were subsequently fleshed out in the Commission's official proposals presented in July 1991 (Commission 1991b). Their chief novelty was to introduce corrective measures to restrict production and budgetary expenditures.

---

11 ACDP, 09-001-1095/2, Leitlinie der EVP-Fraktion zur Agrarpreisdebatte 1989/1990, Brussels, 1. Februar 1989. [Author's translation from German].

12 ACDP, 09-001-1095/2, Motion for resolution tabled by Mr. McCartin on behalf of the EPP Group, Brussels, 2 March 1988; Textvorschlag zum Agrarteil des Programms der Kommission für 1988, 2. Februar 1988; Motion for a resolution on budgetary problems in 1986, the EPP (no date); Resolution by the EPP Group for the EPP conference in the Hague in April 1986 (no date).

13 ACDP, 09-001-1095/2, Proposta di risoluzione (no date).

More importantly, MacSharry's proposals went beyond the incremental changes that had characterised earlier reforms and attempted to change the policy's paradigm (Garzon 2006). The key measures aimed to decouple price policy and farm income support through direct payments to farmers that were not linked with production but would help compensate any loss of income, and to change the method of support from market-based intervention purchases to direct producer payments. The Commission's main objective was to sever the connection between price and income support to reduce surplus production and improve the economic rationality of the CAP whilst preserving the gist of the CAP as a welfare policy. Also, the direct payments were less trade-distorting than the existing price support mechanisms and therefore likely to alleviate trade conflicts with the EU's main trading partners within the GATT negotiations.

The Commission proposals were extensively discussed within the EPP Group and Agricultural Committee sittings and expert hearings[14] (Fouilleux 1996: 17). With Reinhold Bocklet, a Bavarian member of the EPP Group who was appointed Rapporteur in April 1991 and tasked with drawing up the report on the Commission's proposals on the future development of the CAP, the EPP Group could play a role in co-shaping the debate within the EP on the MacSharry reform.

The family farm, both as an ideational frame and policy paradigm, remained central to the Christian democratic thinking on European agriculture during the discussion of the proposals.[15] In October 1991, the EPP Group held a Study Day in Sirmione, on the shores of Lake Garda, to discuss the future of agricultural policy. The meeting took place against the backdrop of various farm demonstrations in Member States. The debates highlighted clear reservations against a reform of the CAP. In fact, the MacSharry proposals went against the grain of key tenets of the Christian-democratic philosophy behind agricultural policy. The direct payments disconnected part of farmers' income from their ordinary activity of producing foodstuff. This was hardly compatible with the entrepreneurial and commercial skills generally associated with farming as an economic and producing activity. In addition to that, farmers were asked to stop farming their land and set aside part of it instead. EP Rapporteur Bocklet advised against such a complete disconnect between price and income. In his view, the result would only be that "some farmers would produce food while the state would be forced to pay others who … would merely play at being

14 See e.g. HAEU, PE3-19360, Minutes of the hearing 27-28 June 1991.
15 EPP Group Archives, D.5.12, Activity Report, Yearbook 1990-1991.

farmers. In the long run ... this would not be compatible with our Christian-Democrat view of humanity".[16] Similar reservations were voiced about the direct income support scheme. Because it smacked of assistance, it was suggested to make the direct payments part of a performance, such as landscape maintenance or nature management. Beyond this principled reservation, the shift to income support based on price to income support based on compensatory payments that would compensate farmers for the resulting drop in income in full up to a certain ceiling and partially thereafter seemed too prone to be sacrificed in the short or long term to budget-saving measures.[17]

The debates at Sirmione and in AGRI demonstrated the attachment of the EPP Group to supporting CAP reform to the extent that it maintained the protection and support of (viable) family farms, through, for example, the maintenance of a degree of external protection and compensation for income loss. In a nutshell, the EPP Group's position was "no CAP reform without the farmers".[18]

The need for family farmers to draw their income from their land and their 'multifunctional' roles within agriculture also featured heavily in the draft and final reports presented by Bocklet to the Committee on Agriculture in the autumn of 1991. The report stressed that "any reform of the Common Agricultural Policy must ensure that farmers' spirit of enterprise is respected and that they are not turned into perpetual aid recipients [and] should recognise the multiple roles of farmers as cultivators, stewards of the environment and dynamic agents of rural life".[19] Framing the debate through resorting to such a commonly accepted and widely propagated understanding of the family farmer as a combined independent entrepreneur, manager, investor and manual labourer served to justify the maintenance of the CAP as a welfare policy (Germond 2015). This understanding, however, concealed the fundamental and long-standing discrepancy between the narrative of supporting and protecting family farms,

---

16 EPP Group Archives, C.1.30, Study Days in Sirmione 2-4 October 1991, p. 57.

17 HAEU, PE3-22183, Draft report on the Commission communication to the Council on the Common Agricultural Policy, 9 October 1991.

18 EPP Group Archives, D.5.13, Activity Report, Yearbook 1991-1992, p. 49.

19 HAEU, PE3-22183, Report of the Committee on Agriculture, Fisheries and Rural Development on the development and future of the Common Agricultural Policy, Part A, 28 November 1991.

which had been a core feature of the CAP policy discourse since 1958,[20] and the actual practice of subsidising large-scale farms and food companies and farms that profited the most from the support mechanisms instituted by the CAP.

Unsurprisingly, the report also criticised the scale of the proposed price cuts, the intended reduction in external protection and the planned income transfers that would exceed what was politically, economically and socially defensible. In short, the Agriculture Committee report took a conservative position on the MacSharry reform. The draft report drawn up by Bocklet was even more critical. Though it recognised an evident need for reforming the CAP, the proposals, if measured against the objectives that the Commission had set out in its reflection paper – to preserve the environment, traditional landscapes and a model of agriculture based on the family – would merit severe criticisms.[21]

After 1992, CAP reform remained high on the political agenda of the European Commission and the policy underwent a series of successive reforms that radically transformed it. The latest reform was initiated in 2010 by the European Commission. For the first time, the EP and the Committee on Agriculture took part in the negotiation on CAP reform legislation and the modernisation of the EU farming sector, a process which ran parallel with discussions on the EU's multiannual budget.

Throughout 2011, AGRI was at the forefront of the discussion of the Commission proposals thanks to the co-decision role of the EP. This new role came with expectations that Parliament could move the CAP reform debate beyond the national interest and budgetary disputes that had been a characteristic of prior reforms. In particular, the MEPs responsible for amending the Commission's legislative proposals were expected to support the calls for a more targeted, sustainable and resource-efficient policy (Swinnen and Knops 2012: 1). Yet the ability of the EP to flex its newly acquired legislative muscles was constrained in various respects. Interinstitutional working practices are notoriously difficult to change, and the new CAP reform was the very first test for the new, re-balanced relationship between the Commission, the Council and the EP. In addition, despite the expertise of AGRI members, the EP had to catch up on these decades of

20 See Résolution finale de la conférence agricole des Etats membres de la CEE, Stresa, 12 July 1958, on https://www.cvce.eu/obj/resolution_finale_de_la_conference_agricole_des_etats_membres_de_la_cee_stresa_12_juillet_1958-fr-441-fa14a-624a-42fb-997f-b7d0a2aa0471.html.

21 HAEU, PE3-22183, Draft report on the Commission communication to the Council on the Common Agricultural Policy, 9 October 1991.

capacity-building and experience in reforming one of the most technical policies (Swinnen and Kops: 2). The sheer scale and scope of CAP legislation posed a real challenge in terms of resources and the Committee's ability to draw up comprehensive legislative amendment to the Commission's proposals (Greer and Hind 2012).

Moreover, the hopes that AGRI – with its new legislative powers – would become a more attractive forum for non-farm interests, were rapidly frustrated. The Committee's close ties with the farming community remained an obstacle: "Out of the 44 COMAGRI full members, most of them are former agricultural ministers or secretaries of state, agricultural advisors, farmers' unionists, members of farming associations, doctors in agricultural studies or farmers themselves" (Swinnen and Knops 2012: 2-3). The internal distribution of functions, with the chairmanship going to S&D MEP Paolo de Castro and a large majority of key rapporteurships allocated to EPP MEPs, clearly favoured the EPP Group. Whilst the Chair and report allocation reflected the political weight of both groups in the EP, it illustrated the enduring stranglehold of farm interests. It placed EPP Group members in a privileged position to secure the right to author the EP's position on key pieces of draft legislation and other major reports, to obtain a larger number of rapporteurships than other political groups and therefore wield influence on the content of CAP legislation.[22] It also mirrored the strategic priority that the EPP Group continued to give to agriculture.

Before and after the debate on CAP reform was launched in April, the EP was a very vocal actor. In July 2010, the EP had adopted a report that set out its initial outline position on the Commission legislative proposals on the future of European farming (European Parliament 2010a). The most significant (own-initiative) report was authored by the EPP Group's Co-ordinator in AGRI, Albert Dess, a German EPP and CSU member. The Dess report presented Parliament's official response to the Commission Communication on the CAP towards 2020, which had been made public in November 2010 (European Commission 2010), and outlined three possible options, among which the moderately reformist scenario (option 2) was clearly the Commission's favourite. While the July report demonstrated a broad level of consensus on agricultural reform, even among the different political groups of the EP, the first draft of the Dess report raised heavy criticisms (Swinnen and Knops 2012: 3).

22 EPP Group Archives, D.5.32, Activity Report, Yearbook 2011, p. 15.

After tough but successful negotiations led by Dess to ensure that the EPP Group's priorities were maintained, the amended version of the report (European Parliament 2011a) was ultimately brought more in line with the original EP position[23], although it kept key EPP tenets such the need to simplify the CAP and reduce bureaucracy for farmers and administrative authorities.[24] The report backed several key points. It argued for the maintenance of a strong CAP, built on two pillars, and an unchanged budget. It defended decoupled direct payments (and coupled for certain situations) in pillar 1 but supported a fairer distribution. The strong emphasis placed by the Rapporteur on the need to simplify the CAP and reduce red tape for farmers was reflected in the adopted report. Small farms should benefit from a specific aid scheme. Regarding the proposed introduction of a 'greening component' into the CAP, the most controversial element of the draft Dess report, the compromise reached in the report supported additional environmental measures across the Member States. Lastly, it stressed that adequately funded rural development measures under the second pillar should principally benefit farmers, and emphasised the importance of supporting young farmers. Several of the report's key points echoed pressures from COPA-COGECA against any reduction in support and the introduction of measures that would increase production costs and hinder production. Securing the adoption of the Dess Report at the plenary session in June 2011 was considered a major political success for the EPP Group and particularly for the EPP Members in AGRI.[25] However, the EPP Group made it clear that the Parliament's final agreement on the reformed CAP was conditional on an accord on the next financial framework for the EU, which had to provide adequate funding for the policy.[26]

In addition to the EP debates at committee and plenary levels, the prospects of the reform of the CAP were intensely debated internally by the EPP Group within its bureau and dedicated Working Group on Budget and Structural Policies and during Study Days in 2011. At the Study Days in Palermo (May 2011) and Marseilles (December 2011), the EPP Group collectively reaffirmed its support for a reformed CAP that would dispose of a sufficient (and stable) budget, have a major environmental

23 Over 1200 amendments were tabled at committee level but the number was eventually reduced to 85 compromise amendments. EPP Group archives, D.5.32, Activity Report, Yearbook 2011, p. 255.

24 EPP Group Archives, B.1.3. AGRI Plenary Notes JUN 2011, The CAP towards 2020: Meeting the food, natural resources and territorial challenges of the future.

25 EPP Group Archives, D.5.32, Activity Report, Yearbook 2011, p. 254.

26 Ibid., p. 257.

component, and be able to tackle the challenges of feeding the human population, keeping food prices relatively stable and at levels that were remunerative for producers and affordable for consumers.[27]

In October 2011, the Commission presented a set of legislative proposals. The proposals were received with reservations by MEPs (European Parliament 2011b). EPP Group members were subsequently allocated key reports. Michel Dantin was appointed Rapporteur for the Single Common Market Organisation, a giant package covering the internal rules for all the production sectors, and Giovanni La Via authored the report on the Horizontal and Financial Regulation that was crucial for farmers. Both reports concerned two of the four main regulations that were to make up the CAP after 2013. Mairead McGuinness and Elisabeth Köstinger were the EPP Group's Shadow Rapporteurs for the Direct Payments and Rural Development regulations. Key features of the EPP Group's stance remained the improvement of the environmental performance of the CAP and the simplification of its administrative procedures in order to enable farmers to make a sustainable living and to ensure the viability of the European agricultural sector. The EPP Group's emphasis on the need for a strong budget to preserve the multifunctional role of European agriculture was a thinly veiled reference to Parliament's budgetary powers and its ability to reject the Union's budget should it be deemed insufficient.[28]

The debate on the proposals and reports led to a record number of amendments tabled by MEPs over summer and winter 2012. In line with the EPP Group, the Agriculture Committee made it clear that the final vote on the reform would only be held when the EU's long-term budget for 2014-2020 was agreed. In March 2013, MEPs approved the final form of the post-2013 common agricultural policy but rejected the budget, pressuring for AGRI's position to be considered. During the summer, interinstitutional negotiations on the budget reached a compromise, thus paving the way for a final agreement on a reformed CAP.

The last reform of the CAP was the first opportunity for the EP to exert its new co-decision powers and Parliament was eager to make an impact. The process was heavily influenced by Rapporteurs, as the key members of AGRI, who often defended interests such as those of the conservative Member States and agricultural lobbies (Lovec and Erjavec 2015). In this context, EPP Group members and Rapporteurs were influential in toning

27 EPP Group Archives, C.1.49, Study Days in Palermo, 4-6 May 2011; EPP Group Archives, C.1.50, Study Days in Marseilles, 7-8 December 2011.

28 EPP Group Archives, D.5.33, Activity Report, Yearbook 2012, p. 97.

down the most radical of the Commission's proposals and enforcing a relatively conservatist EP position. The strength of the Group also relied on its greater ideological cohesion in CAP reform votes compared to other Groups (Roederer-Rynning 2003; Cicchi 2016: 82-86). While the decreasing relevance of the farm vote made it easier for the EPP Group to endorse CAP reform, the Group continues to be a valuable relay of farm interest within Parliament, not least thanks to its strong representation in AGRI.

### *The EPP Group and Economic and Monetary Union (EMU)*

The EPP Group was an early advocate of economic and monetary integration. EPP programmes supported the creation of a European common market based on social-market economic principles, with free-market rules and redistributive mechanisms (Warlouzet 2020). The economic and monetary turmoil that the EC experienced in the 1970s reinforced the group's belief that EMU was necessary to ensure renewed economic growth without inflation and to combat unemployment. The EPP Group strongly advocated in favour of the creation of a single market through the removal of all barriers to trade. Monetary union and, ultimately, a single currency were considered inevitable consequences of the deepening of economic integration, to avoid any distortion of competition through the manipulation of exchange rates.

EPP Group members were closely involved in the debates on monetary integration prior to and after the SEA. With Fernand Herman, a Christian Democrat MEP, the EPP was well-represented in the Dooge Committee that had been set up after the 1984 Fontainebleau Summit to prepare what would become the SEA (see Johansson in Chapter 2 of this book). In 1984, Karl von Wogau, a long-time advocate of the suppression of internal borders and trade barriers,[29] worked on plans to strengthen monetary integration with representatives from the Bundesbank and Pierre Werner, the author of the eponymous 1979 report (Warlouzet 2020). Von Wogau, who was then serving on ECON, was also actively involved in the Kangaroo Group, which he had co-founded in 1979 and chaired, and drafted in this

29 See e.g. ACDP, 09-001-223/1, Campaign for Europe without borders. April 1982.

twofold capacity influential reports on the completion of the internal market.[30]

The Kangaroo Group had started as an informal gathering of MEPs; but it soon evolved into a cross-political group with members of the European institutions, business and academic representatives. Similarly to the European Round Table for Industry (ERT), whose agency and influence on economic integration has been well-studied (e.g. Green Cowles 1995; Apeldoorn 2002), the Kangaroo Group had an extensive business membership. Within Parliament, it was an influential promotion board for the EP's initiatives on further economic integration and helped to spread the EMU gospel across political parties. Externally, it was instrumental in reaching out to business groups to promote the single market programme (Warlouzet 2020).

The strong support of Christian Democrats for economic and monetary integration was also visible in the reports and resolutions of the EP, many of which were presented in the name of the Group, which contributed to defining and realising the single market programme. For instance, in spring 1989, the Franz Report, authored by EPP MEP Otmar Franz, spelled out measures to be taken in order to achieve economic and monetary union.[31] Influenced by German ordo-liberal ideas, the report recommended the adoption of the ECU as a common currency that would be issued by a European central bank and be used in parallel with national currencies. The report also suggested that the EP would be able to present its view at ECB meetings, though it would not have formal control powers. The resolution attached to the report explicitly stressed the link between the establishment of the single market and European monetary union and the need for a monetary institution whose primary tasks, broadly modelled after the German Bundesbank, would be price stability, growth and employment.[32]

The 1985 Schengen Agreement, signed by five of the ten Member States of the EEC, and the SEA of 1986 (in force in 1987) made it possible for goods, people, capital and services to move freely across and within the Community and established an internal market without internal borders. The implementation of the four freedoms was not only vital for the full

---

30 HAEU, PE1-17655, Rapport sur la communication de la Commission des Communautés européennes au Conseil sur le programme 1982 pour la réalisation de l'union douanière, 4 octobre 1982.

31 HAEU, PE2-18864, Report by Otmar Franz on the process of European monetary integration, 22 March 1989.

32 HAEU, PE2-18864, Resolution, 14 April 1989.

implementation of the single market, but also gave a new impetus to monetary integration, which appeared a logical step for economic and political reasons. For Christian Democrats, the ultimate goals of EMU went beyond laying the groundwork for an efficiently run economy and greater monetary and political solidarity. They also emphasised its social dimension and its contribution to fostering economic, social and regional cohesion within the Communities (Fontaine 2009: 91). A way to reconcile the market and the social aspects was to Europeanise the social market economy, a term that was enshrined in the Treaty of Lisbon and EU discourse (Kaiser 2013).

At Maastricht, concrete shape was given to EMU and political union. Signed on 7 February 1992, the treaty, whose provisions on economic and monetary integration were intensely debated when the Euro-crisis broke out, had far-reaching implications for the EU. After intensive negotiations (Geary, Germond and Patel 2013), the Treaty laid the foundations on which EMU still rests today, despite the adjustments introduced in the wake of the 2010s Eurozone crisis, and gave birth to the Euro, the EU's single currency. The EPP Group was especially active in the run-up to the negotiations of the Treaty, both within and outside Parliament (see Johansson in Chapter 2 of this book).

As long-standing and vocal proponents of further integration, Christian Democrats acknowledged the limitations of the SEA and the need for a quantitative leap forward that should not be limited to the economic realm. Greater economic integration would only be possible if the EU was given a stronger political dimension and decision-making processes were made more democratic. The latter was a thinly veiled appeal for the EP (and the national parliaments) to play a more important role in this process (Fontaine 2009: 299). This greater involvement of parliamentary bodies was exemplified by the convocation of *Assises* in Rome in November 1990, with representatives from the EP and national parliaments. The idea of convening *Assises* originated in the Martin I report, which recommended that a conference of Parliamentarians should be held before each ICG to discuss treaty revisions.[33] In preparation for the Rome *Assises*, the EPP Group organised several meetings. The Group met over the summer of 1990 for a week of discussion. The manifesto that was adopted at the end of the meeting reaffirmed the Group's commitment to a federal Europe (Fontaine 2009: 300). The EPP Group also organised a congress in Dublin,

33 HAEU, PE3-22010, Rapport sur la Conférence intergouvernementale dans le cadre de la stratégie du Parlement européen pour l'Union européenne, 14 mars 1990.

just a few days before the official start of the Rome *Assises*. At Rome, Christian Democrats were thus able to present a united front and ensure that the final declaration reflected their federalist positions and emphasised the eventual goal of a federal style constitution, political and monetary union and greater democratic legitimacy with a genuine co-legislator role for the EP.

The broader Christian democratic transnational network was an important channel for securing the Group's influence. At the time, six of the 12 governments were led by Christian Democrats and Christian Democrats chaired the IGC. Several party summits that were organised between summer 1991 and winter 1992 allowed the six heads of state or government, the EPP party leaders and the Chair of the Group, Egon Klepsch, to hold regular talks throughout the negotiations that would inform negotiations in the ICG (Fontaine 2009: 302-303) There was, moreover, close co-operation between the EPP party and the Group based on shared objectives to push through Christian democratic ideational preferences.

The EPP Group also contributed to shaping the EP's position on and the process of EMU through several key reports. Building on the 1989 report by Otmar Franz on monetary integration, the EP adopted a resolution setting out the basic objectives and framework for EMU. Adopted in May 1990, the report by Fernand Herman on EMU described how the future monetary system, with a single European currency and an independent ECB, should operate, and listed the tasks and objectives of the monetary institutions to be created (European Parliament 1989b). In a subsequent report, drawn up in preparation for the ICG on EMU, Herman set out the necessary amendments and additions to the EC to place national jurisdiction into a framework in keeping with the internal market in the field of monetary, economic and budgetary policy.[34]

The eventual text of the Treaty of Maastricht incorporated many of the EPP Group's positions, among which the most important were the timetable set for EMU, extended co-decision powers for the EP and an independent ECB. Another success for the EPP Group was the inclusion of the subsidiarity principle, which was an integral part of a Christian vision of Europe (see Kaiser in Chapter 1 of this book). Not all goals were achieved, but the negotiating process of the Treaty bore witness to the EPP Group's ability to co-shape a decisive moment in EMU's history. With the

34 EPP Group archives, D.5.11, Activity report, Yearbook 1989-1990, pp. 110-111, 116-117.

appointment of Wim Duisenberg as the President of the new ECB, the EPP Group, which had supported his candidacy, scored another success.

With the introduction of the Euro on 1 January 2002, EMU became real for millions of EU citizens. The single currency was a strong identity-building symbol that relied upon a vision and a political commitment supported by the EPP Group (Fontaine 2009: 433). The economic and financial problems that shook the entire global financial system in 2008-2009 were the Euro's first major test.

Christian Democrats were in a good position to contribute to devising solutions to the financial crisis. Several Christian democratic personalities occupied key positions during the crisis. Jean-Claude Juncker was the first permanent head of the Eurogroup (2005-2013) before he succeeded José Manuel Barroso as President of the European Commission. Moreover, in French President Nicholas Sarkozy and German Chancellor Angela Merkel, the EPP had two influential personalities with significant weight in EMU negotiations. These contacts were invaluable at the height of the monetary turbulence in 2008, during which it was mainly Christian Democrats who "piloted the European plane" (Fontaine 2009: 445).

Traditional core elements of the Christian democratic political philosophy framed the EPP Group's broad position on the responses to the economic and financial crisis. In line with its traditional pro-European stance, the EPP Group argued in favour of a more united Europe and insisted that the reform of the international financial architecture should foster better accountability and transparency, keep intact the integrity of the internal market and improve the co-ordination of economic policies.[35] The road to economic recovery should be based on solidarity and the social market economy, which Christian Democrats viewed as the best way to overcome this crisis and return to sustainable growth.[36] In a nutshell, "the future of Europe's peoples and nations is a community of responsibility and solidarity, united in the social market economy."[37] As a result, the Group emphasised the need to promote growth, employment and social cohesion as a fundamental part of the solutions to the crisis.

All political groups in the EP broadly agreed that reforming the EMU was vital to remedy the flaws in the Euro area's architecture. It was neces-

35 EPP Group Archives, C.1.47.B, Study Days in Athens, 28-30 June 2009, Conclusions, 02/07/2009.

36 EPP Group Archives, C.1.47.C, Study Days in Bonn, 8-9 December 2009, Conclusions, 9/12/2009.

37 EPP Group Archives, C.1.52, Study Days in Bucharest, 17-18 October 2012, Dossier Theme I, p. 5.

sary to address the EMU's lack of a common fiscal capacity to protect against financial shocks and structural imbalances, which the economic and financial crisis had so blatantly exposed, and to improve the Eurozone's governance. Yet there were substantial differences about how to respond to the crisis, with some defending ordoliberal solutions based on intergovernmental fiscal discipline and others defending Keynesian counterframes supporting increased supranational fiscal solidarity (Warren 2018: 640).

The negotiations of the two legislative packages to strengthen the Stability and Growth Pact, known as the Six-Pack and the Two-Pack, triggered ideological debates within the EP regarding the distributive implications of fiscal and economic policies. Negotiated under the OLP, both legislative packages reshaped the EU's economic and monetary governance. They also exposed very different conceptions of economic policymaking. Whereas the Christian Democrats, the Conservatives and the Liberals presented themselves as the guardians of fiscal discipline, the Social Democrats and the Greens strongly emphasised growth, public investment and social cohesion. The ordoliberal credos of the EPP Group came to the fore in several reports presented by EPP members. Due to their larger number in the EP, the EPP-ALDE alliance was influential in shaping the EP position, although it was not immune to occasional disagreements.

The EPP Group addressed the Euro area debt crisis by taking an approach that combined sustainable economic policies with fiscal discipline. In the Group's opinion, the outbreak of the crisis had highlighted the ineffectiveness of the control mechanisms that existed at European level, especially in the absence of a central European government with strong economic and fiscal powers. The urgent reform of these mechanisms should thus rest on the two pillars of fiscal stability and structural reforms for growth. In line with the EPP Group's stance of sound monetary and fiscal policy, the first task of restoring fiscal stability should take precedence.[38]

As the largest group in the European Parliament, the EPP took the lead in formulating Parliament's contribution to EMU reform. The predominance of Christian Democrats in several Member States' governments allowed for frequent informal consultations between representatives of all three EU institutions and effective co-ordination in trilogue negotiations. Informal meetings between ministers, EU Commissioners and EPP Group representatives before ECOFIN meetings helped prepare the tactics for the subsequent discussions at the official negotiations (Djankov 2014). This

38 EPP Group Archives, D.5.31, Activity Report, Yearbook 2010, pp. 209-210.

close co-operation between Christian Democrats in the EP and in government made it possible for EPP members to apply pressure to national leaders to take their views into account. Conversely, it also allowed national governments to put pressure on the EPP Group to bring legislation closer to preferences expressed in the Council and the European Council. With the new powers granted by the TFEU, the European Parliament was able to act as a full co-legislator in the adoption of the Six-Pack and Two-Pack secondary legislative acts and was afforded limited participation in the negotiation of an overlapping intergovernmental treaty on a 'fiscal compact' (Warren 2018: 633). The EPP Group was instrumental in shaping crucial parts of the Six-Pack, the so-called preventive and corrective arms of the SGP. EPP ECON members Corien Wortmann-Kool and Diogo Feio were the Rapporteurs on these matters. The Rapporteurs involved in the Six-Pack negotiations often met formally during the drafting period to co-ordinate their positions, and continued to do so in the run-up to the votes in the committee and plenary.[39] One of the most recognisable successes of the EP was the application of Reverse Qualified Majority Voting (RQMV) to most decisions taken under the Excessive Deficit Procedure.[40] This was strongly supported by the EPP Group, both in the Wortmann-Kool report and in the final stage of the trilogue negotiations.[41]

Similarly, the EPP Group was at the forefront of the process of financial regulatory reform in the EP. This was a far less divisive issue that had more to do with institutional design than with policy trade-offs (O'Keeffe 2014). EPP MEPs Werner Langen, Sari Essayah, Othmar Karas and Burkhard Balz acted as Rapporteurs for the EP Regulations on derivatives, payment services, capital requirements and insurance respectively.[42]

The EPP Group also welcomed the Fiscal Compact, which as an intergovernmental Treaty was drafted without a substantive contribution from the EP. The Fiscal Compact was in line with its main objective of enhancing fiscal discipline among the Eurozone members. In fact, the Group claimed that the core elements were proposed by the EP during the Six-Pack negotiations and underlined that the two measures were complementary and had the same rationale (Wortmann-Kool and Willemen 2013: 496). Due to its intergovernmental character, the Fiscal Compact remains

39 EPP Group archives, D.5.32, Activity Report, Yearbook 2011, p. 215.

40 According to RQMV, a Commission recommendation is deemed to be adopted unless the Council decides by qualified majority to reject the recommendation within a given deadline.

41 EPP Group Archives, Stratégie politique, Plenary Notes, June II 2011.

42 EPP Group Archives, D.5.33, Activity Report, Yearbook 2012, p. 82.

outside the EU's legal framework and legislative process. Even so, the EPP Group attempted to include as many elements of the Fiscal Compact as possible into the Six-Pack and the Two-Pack, to enshrine them in EU law and make them enforceable by EU institutions.

The negotiations on the Two-Pack showed that the positions defended by the EPP Group were more in line with those of the Council and the Commission than with those of other groups in the EP. This exemplifies the cohesion of Christian Democrats, not least thanks to the regular exchanges of views organised between parliamentarians and national leaders. Interestingly, the EPP Group's views were not just divergent from those of the Socialists, but also, this time, from the Liberals, with which the EPP had allied on previous occasions (EPP Group 2013).

EPP MEP Jean-Paul Gauzès was responsible for drafting the first regulation on strengthening the economic and budgetary surveillance of Eurozone Member States experiencing or threatened with serious financial difficulties (European Parliament 2012). In his report, he introduced elements for an orderly default scenario, thus allowing a Member State to restructure their debt and regain access to the capital markets. He also advocated in favour of the introduction of RQMV to increase the automatic nature of decisions by shifting weight from the Council to the Commission. After long negotiations in the ECON committee, in the EP and in the trilogues, a compromise was reached on all major issues. The final texts of the Regulation broadly reflected the view of the EP and were welcomed as a satisfactory outcome by all the political groups. The rights to information of the EP were strengthened, while the use of RQMV in the SGP was further extended, as requested in the Gauzès report. More generally, the EP was able to strengthen the 'social side' of enhanced economic and budgetary surveillance, as an integral part of the traditional Christian democratic defence of the social market economy model.

Even so, the commitment of the EP to promoting the reform of European economic governance and its successful attempt to amend the draft regulations did not mean that the EP was able to reinforce its position in the new institutional framework. On the contrary, it was left in a weak position compared to the Commission and the Council (Fasone 2014). The increased use of summitry and the continued importance of the Council reinforced the intergovernmental rather than the supranational character of EMU decision-making, despite the extension of OLP.

The EPP Group played a leading role in EMU reform, by capitalising on its role as a majority group at the time. Likewise, through formal and informal channels, it established an effective convergence with the Council, where there was a dominant representation of EPP members, and the

Commission. It was therefore able to ease the negotiation process leading to the SGP reform. More generally, the EPP Group's efforts to reinforce the role of Parliament ran parallel to those of the EP to confer increased democratic legitimacy onto an ever deeply integrated single currency area and thereby strengthen its own role in EMU (Rittberger 2014).

### *The EPP Group and social policy*

As part of a broader set of solidarity policies, social policy has a symbolic importance for the EPP Group due to its unique resonance with traditional Christian ideals and beliefs. Solidarity, responsibility, respect and social justice are core values underpinning the Christian democratic philosophy and the Group's vision of the organisation of society and the economy in Europe.[43] These goals came to the fore in the Group's electoral platform for the first elections in 1979.[44]

Since the early days of the Communities, Christian Democrats have promoted a social policy agenda and important social objectives (Fontaine 2009: 113). They saw their role as a "social goad."[45] They envisioned a social market economy that would combine capitalist economic efficiency with social justice and solidarity. An efficient social policy was thus key to the just redistribution of the wealth created to those in need or left behind. Conversely, without a flourishing economy, social progress was not possible (Fontaine 2005: 115). For the EPP, the European social model, based on social welfare protection and economic competitiveness, was the foundation of the social market economy. Social requirements were thus essential elements in the formulation and implementation of EU policies.

The importance of social policy for the EPP Group can also be attributed to the links that existed between several of its members and trade unions and employers' associations with ties to Christian Democracy. These ties between the EPP and social partners were kept active through regular meetings and discussions (Fontaine 2005: 119), over time forming a stable network. Moreover, these contacts were invaluable in the context of the social dialogue promoted by the EP. Social partners were encour-

---

43 EPP Group Archives, Stratégie politique, Position Papers, EPP Group position paper: A Modern Social Europe, 2016.

44 EPP Group Archives, N.1, EPP Party, Electoral platform, February 1979.

45 EPP Group Archives, A.1.22, PVS du Groupe, Minutes WG Politique sociale, Procès-verbal de la réunion constitutive du group de travail "Politique sociale", Réunion du 12 décembre 1974, Luxembourg, 18 décembre 1974.

aged to articulate their views and positions to EMPL, which had gradually become the major body concerned with employment in the EC/EU, before it drew up any reports on proposals affecting them and their constituencies. In this way, they could wield substantial influence on the EMPL committee's and EP's positions on social legislation for the EU.

Although social policy encompasses a broad range of different, albeit linked, areas – social security insurance, employment, vocational training and education, health and social inclusion – employment and social cohesion have been at the top of the EPP Group's agenda due to their centrality in the development of well-functioning economies, labour markets and societies. Employment and social cohesion were core social policy elements that combined economic and social policy goals. The establishment of a Europe of economic and social progress and full employment is a key objective for the Group.[46]

The EU has long been active in regulating certain aspects of employment policy (Anderson 2015: 112). The emergence and maintenance of a high level of unemployment as well as demographic changes that put social systems increasingly under pressure undermined the assumption that economic integration would automatically bring about an expansion of employment. With the implementation of the European international market and EMU, the focus of social policy shifted more and more to the question of effectively tackling unemployment. Introduced in 1997, the European Employment Strategy (EES) was a response to the many concerns raised by the completion of the internal market and its impact on the employment of EU workers.

The road towards the EES begun in Essen with the European Council of December 1994, during which Member States confirmed the EU's commitment to the promotion of employment and agreed on implementing measures at a national level in five key areas: vocational training; flexible organisation of work and working time; efficiency of labour market institutions; active labour market policies; and the promotion of access to the world of work for specific target groups (young people, long-term unemployed and women) (Goetschy 1999). The co-ordination of national employment policies was institutionalised by the Treaty of Amsterdam, where employment was given a specific title and became a top political priority.

The employment chapter was one of the most difficult issues for the EPP in the IGC, since Christian democratic governments were divided on the matter (Tallberg and Johansson 2008). A compromise was reached

46 EPP Group Archives, N.1, EPP Party, Electoral platform, February 1979.

when Chancellor Kohl gave the go-ahead to an agreement on the issue. As a result, the EPP supported the employment chapter, while at the same time emphasising the application of the principle of subsidiarity. For Christian Democrats, specific employment policies were essentially a matter for the national or regional level, while the EU should frame, co-ordinate and guide such policies, bringing forward new ideas and initiatives.

The Group then focused on leading the process of implementation of the treaty's guidelines, which were to be discussed at the Luxembourg European Council in November 1997. The EP was asked to prepare a contribution for the extraordinary summit. The EMPL committee thus drafted a report, authored by S&D MEP Wim van Velzen as Rapporteur, which was discussed and approved at the plenary session in October (European Parliament 1997b). The EPP Group did not identify with all the proposals set out in the van Velzen report, and was able to pass substantial amendments concerning co-ordination between economic and employment policies, the individuals' right to continuing training, and the transition from passive measures to active employment measures.

Concomitantly, the EPP also drew up its own employment guidelines. The document was drafted by an ad hoc Working Group, with the participation of the Group's representatives, most notably Dutch MEP Bartho Pronk.[47] The guidelines emphasised the need to act with determination and without delay, since unemployment had reached an intolerable level, becoming the greatest social and economic challenge facing Europe in the late 1990s. The answer was not to be found in "miracle solutions", but in social dialogue involving business and trade unions, with active contributions from national and European institutions, in order to combine competitiveness and social justice. The EPP congress in Toulouse adopted the recommendations on an effective employment policy, and these guidelines were then used by Jean-Claude Juncker, Luxembourg's Prime Minister and then Council President, as a basis for the Luxembourg Employment Guidelines that were adopted subsequently at the Luxembourg summit.[48]

The summit launched a co-ordinated strategy for national employment policies, thereby implementing the process envisaged in the Employment Title before the Treaty of Amsterdam had been ratified. The so-called Luxembourg process provided concrete content for the European Employ-

---

47 EPP Group Archives, A.1.45-2, minutes of EMPL committee, 29 October 1997 and 5 November 1997; EPP Group Archives, C.8.56 Employment: a European Strategy - Documentation, July 1997.

48 EPP Group Archives, D.5.19, Activity Report, Yearbook 1997-1998, p. 87.

ment Strategy, which was to be implemented by Member States through National Action Plans (later known the National Reform Programmes) that set out the policy responses to the key macroeconomic, microeconomic and employment policy priorities, with the involvement of the social partners.

The objectives set in Luxembourg were in line with the EPP Group's positions, but the implementation process was by no means straightforward. The Group emphasised that the harmonisation of employment legislation would not be possible and effective without the completion of the single market and the introduction of the single currency. Despite the progress made towards freedom of movement for goods and services, there was still a great deal to be done to create a single market, with its beneficial effects for growth and the labour market.[49] Economic and social policies were presented as two sides of the same coin.

From 1997 to 2002, the Guidelines rested on the four pillars of entrepreneurship, employability, adaptability and equal opportunities. In 2003, the four-pillar structure was replaced by three main objectives: full employment, improving quality and productivity at work, and strengthening social cohesion and inclusion. The latter two had been an objective of EU policy since the 1970s (Anderson 2015: 197) but became a major priority for the EU in the new millennium.

At an extraordinary meeting of the European Council in March 2000 in Lisbon, the heads of state or government defined a new strategic objective to bolster employment, economic reform and social cohesion. Confronted with the dramatic effects of globalisation – both economic and social – as well as the challenges arising from an increasingly knowledge-driven economy and Europe's ageing population, the Council's new strategy, which became known as the Lisbon Strategy, aimed at laying the ground for the transition to a knowledge-based economy and society. It set out to step up efforts at structural reforms, completing the internal market and modernising the European social model to better fight social exclusion and support growth.

In short, the Lisbon Strategy was a 10-year action and development plan for the EU and proved influential in framing the EU's social agendas for the first decade of the 21st century (Hantrais 2008: 20). The Lisbon agenda supported the modernisation of the European social model by shifting the emphasis from protecting the rights of those already employed to actively creating employment and fighting unemployment, a recurrent problem

49 Ibid., p. 88.

since the 1970s. (Anderson 2015: 70) Simultaneously, however, it became a "catch-all phrase", an overarching narrative for the reconfiguration of the European economy and the reform of its welfare states. (Copeland and Papadimitriou 2012: 1)

Many of the measures agreed at Lisbon relied on intergovernmental decision-making, based on co-ordination and benchmarking among Member States, often limiting the EP's role to that of a bystander. The EP, though, had two main opportunities to influence the implementation of the strategy. First, some of the measures required Community legislation, and Parliament could play a key part in those areas for which it was co-legislating with the Council. Second, since the Lisbon Strategy consisted of a set of political ambitions rather than a specific European policy or programme based on a legal framework, and therefore required a complex political coordination and management mechanism – the so-called open method of coordination (OMC) – the EP could frame the debate about the strategy's development and implementation.

While the Lisbon Strategy was debated, Parliament insisted that employment and social considerations should play a role in the design of growth strategies for the EU and Member States, confirming its – and the EPP Group's – traditional commitment to bringing together economic and social policy measures. It asserted that a high level of social protection should be central to the Lisbon Strategy and deemed it unacceptable that people could live in poverty or in a position of social exclusion (Schulz 2019).

After the launch of the strategy, the EP expressed doubts on the Member States' ability to deliver the Lisbon commitments and stressed its right to be involved in any follow-ups. Moreover, it warned against setting too many targets and underlined the need for more wide-spread consultation with interested parties, including applicant countries from central and Eastern Europe (European Parliament 2009b). This position was identical to that of the EPP Group. In March 2001, EPP Group Chair Hans-Gert Pöttering had stressed that the Lisbon Strategy was an important political objective, but should not be used by Member States to push national responsibility for the economic and social reforms onto the EU. Pöttering also demanded that the Lisbon strategy should be extended to the wider EU so that the countries that were negotiating their accession could start introducing the economic and social policy instruments into their national policy objectives.[50]

50 EPP Group Archives, D.5.22, Activity Report, Yearbook 2001, pp. 212-213.

In 2004, the European Council and the Commission decided on a mid-term review of the Lisbon process and appointed former Dutch Prime Minister Wim Kok to lead a group of experts with the objective of reviewing it. Presented in November 2004, the Kok report concluded that little progress had been made over the first five years and recommended to refocus the agenda on growth and employment. It also underlined the need for real ownership by the Member States of the reforms needed. The EPP political family agreed with the report's conclusion. A document approved by the EPP Congress in preparation of the Spring Council demanded to "speed up all structural reforms necessary to regain a high level of competitiveness, and to increase growth and employment". The Group further noted that "four years later, the Lisbon goals seem to be almost out of reach. Though some individual Member States' development and competitiveness have improved substantially, Europe is lacking growth, competitiveness and economic dynamics" (CORDIS 2004).

Following the recommendations of the Kok report, the Barroso Commission proposed in 2005 to restart the Lisbon Strategy and focus the European Union's efforts on two principal tasks: delivering growth and creating more, better employment opportunities (Bongard and Torres 2012). The Commission's proposal was unanimously welcomed by the EPP Group. It was supported in a resolution drawn up under the leadership of EPP MEP Klaus-Heiner Lehne, who was co-Rapporteur together with PES MEP Robert Goebbels, and adopted by the EP in March 2005.[51] In December 2004, the EP had also set up the Lisbon Strategy Co-ordination Group with a view to creating a forum for discussion, action and inter-institutional dialogue and facilitating collaboration and co-ordination with national parliaments. To this end, regular meetings – the Joint Parliamentary Meetings – were scheduled between the EP and national parliaments, usually before Council meetings. The Co-ordination Group was made up of 33 representatives from the different political groups representing the 10 EP Committees most concerned by the Lisbon Strategy and was chaired by Joseph Daul, then President of the Conference of Committee Chairs, a prominent EPP personality and later Chair of the Group.

The EPP's influence on the Co-ordination Group was strengthened by the presence of several other EPP members in leadership positions, such as Marianne Thyssen, who was both Vice-Chair of the EPP Group and Co-ordinator of the Lisbon Strategy Group. In her view, better co-ordination and a clear differentiation in the areas of responsibility between the differ-

51 EPP Group Archives, D.5.26, Activity Report, Yearbook 2005, p. 187.

ent actors involved in the implementation of the agenda were necessary to make the strategy work.[52] The need for "the Lisbon Process to develop from a political manifesto to a controllable and reviewable action programme for the whole European Union and all its Member States"[53] was further emphasised by Othmar Karas, the other person responsible for the Lisbon strategy within the Group. The synergy between the Commission and the Parliament was thus supported by the EPP network (CORDIS 2005).

Despite some degree of progress, the 2008 global financial and economic crisis was a major impediment to the implementation of the revised Lisbon strategy. The effectiveness of the Lisbon instruments in fostering reforms relevant for growth and employment was mixed at best. (Bongard and Torres 2012; Copeland and Papadimitriou 2012; European Commission 2010). As a result, the Lisbon strategy gave way to Europe 2020, a new programme broadly modelled on the Lisbon agenda to target employment, education and the fight against poverty and social exclusion, among other issues. The new programme had a stronger governance structure, but still relied on soft governance instruments. Its adoption in 2010 coincided with the metamorphosis of the economic and financial crisis into a sovereign debt crisis, whose resolution called for enhanced economic coordination that went beyond the new strategy.

The EPP Group supported the revised Lisbon strategy, which at least until 2008 seemed to deliver good results despite an increasingly difficult social and economic climate.[54] The Group organised regular meetings, at least once per year, with national parliamentarians belonging to the same political family to prepare the Joint Parliamentary Meetings. This was an opportunity to co-ordinate strategies and elaborate common positions and maximise the resources and influence of the EPP network. At the 2008 EPP meeting, Thyssen highlighted that "today, perhaps for the first time, we can see that the new approach is bearing fruit".[55] The impact of the economic crisis between 2008-2010, though, made results much more difficult

52 EPP Group Archives, D.1.2005.2-0011, Press release: EPP-ED Group backs new Commission plans for Lisbon Strategy. Marianne Thyssen MEP.

53 EPP Group Archives, D.1.2006.1-0085, Press release: Lisbon Strategy: EPP-ED Group calls for setting priorities, not writing a telephone book. Marianne Thyssen, Othmar Karas and Klaus-Heiner Lehne MEPs.

54 EPP Group Archives, C.1.44.C, Study Days on Social Policy in times of Globalisation, 9 February 2006.

55 EPP Group Archives, B.3.2.7, Relations with National Parliaments, 4th Joint Parliamentary Meeting on the Lisbon Strategy.

to achieve, and disappointment with the underperformance of the Lisbon strategy surfaced. Exemplarily, the conclusions of the meeting of the EPP Group Bureau held in Budapest in March 2010 stated that "the goals set by the Lisbon Strategy were the right ones, but they were too many. There was uncertainty in terms of political priorities and ... the major stakeholders had different understandings of these goals. We were lacking benchmarking, ownership and communication ability in the process".[56] The Group therefore focused its efforts on the new Europe 2020 strategy, which was expected to provide a comprehensive framework for action and was aligned with social market economy principles.

### *The EPP Group and environmental policy*

The European Parliament and the ENVI Committee played a major role in promoting public awareness of the importance of environmental conservation, particularly the protection of biodiversity and climate policy. Even before the 1979 elections, Christian Democrats had actively engaged in promoting and shaping the emerging environmental policy. This was partly out of genuine concerns for the planet as a complex ecological system, partly out of political motives in order to profile the EP as a real parliamentary body tackling issues of concern for European citizens, and partly for electoral reasons against the backdrop of a rise in environmental activism and political ecology and growing societal interests spurred by major environmental incidents. Faith also accounted for the interest of Christian Democrats in environmental protection. As God's creation, nature ought to be protected from exploitation by mankind. The EPP Group thus lobbied to raise awareness that mankind is "responsible for preserving creation. Only those who declare their faith in environmental protection as a means of sustaining existence and protecting future generations can rightly claim that their technology is a technology for mankind. The commitment to a Christian view of mankind means shaping the future in a way that respects creation. This body of values underlying our environmental policy must be given in future greater prominence".[57]

This early green activism of members of the EPP is best illustrated by leading figures such as Hans Richarts, Hans Edgar Jahn, both MEPs, and Jacob Boersma, a Christian democratic Labour unionist. These men were

56 EPP Group Archives, D.5.31, Activity Report, Yearbook 2010, p. 244.
57 EPP Group Archives, D.5.11, Activity report, Yearbook 1989-1990, p. 195.

instrumental in putting on and moving up the European agenda major environmental issues like water and air pollution and the protection of wildlife and birds, and establishing rules that paved the way for the EU's present-day nature and biodiversity conservancy policy (Meyer 2010, 2011, 2014). In framing environmental problems as critical transboundary problems that required European concerted action, these Christian Democrats were influential agents in the discursive construction of the environment as a problem for European institutions, and especially the EP, to deal with. They were supranational activists who presented themselves as advocates of citizens' growing ecological awareness. In invoking not only ecological and moral but also economic arguments and the need for harmonisation as grounds for environmental action, they moreover contributed to linking environmental issues to the common market.

The latter had long-lasting consequences for the Group, which came to view respect for the environment as one of the benefits that citizens could derive from the existence of the internal market (Fontaine 209: 447). For the EPP, nature conservation was not incompatible with economic prosperity. On the contrary, the Group set out "to incorporate the protection and restoration of the environment into the market economy system".[58] Just as it had sought to reconcile the market economy and solidarity, free enterprise and social justice in the concept of the social market economy, its objective was to reconcile economics and ecology in the concept of sustainable development, which Christian Democrats were the first to use.[59] With its idea of an environmentally friendly and sustainable market economy, the EPP Group wanted to protect the environment without threatening economic growth, aiming to influence all areas of legislation, whether environmental, economic, energy, transport, regional or agricultural policies.[60] As EPP MEP Eija-Riitta Korhola quipped during a Study Day in 2008: "On climate issues, we are not the Group of watermelon policies – green on the outside but with a red heart. We are the Group that strives to balance the climate agenda with business, promotes market mechanisms

58 EPP Group Archives, N.1, EPP Party, EPP Basic Programme Athens 1992.

59 EPP Group Archives, C.1.43.A, Study Days in Vienna, 23-24 March 2004, European People's Party Action Programme 2004-2009, p. 27.

60 EPP Group Archives, C.1.43.A, Study Days in Vienna, 23-24 March 2004, Priorities of the EPP-ED Group for 2004-2009. A contribution of ideas to policy formation, p. 3.

with an eye on employment."[61] The Group thus considered environmental policy to be an integral part of the economic and social process.[62]

The origins of the Natura 2000 network of protected areas for wildlife, nowadays a centrepiece of the EU's nature policy, can be traced back to the Birds and Habitats Directives (respectively 1979 and 1992); two directives generally regarded as the most advanced and effective regional conservation instruments (Trouwborst 2011: 69). Jahn, who had worked extensively on the issue of bird protection and acted as a Rapporteur for the ENVI Committee, had been a vocal advocate of preserving birds and their habitat and influential in bringing about the 1979 Birds Directive (Meyer 2010, 2014; see also Kaiser in Chapter 1 of this book).

Proposed by the European Commission in 1987, the Habitat Directive (Council 1992) was a response to the steady deterioration of European natural habitats and the worrying decline of wild species on the one hand, and mounting pressures from the EP (Jackson 2018) to adopt a definitive legal instrument for nature and biodiversity conservation on the other. A central and ambitious element of the directive was to establish an ecological network under the name of Natura 2000 to protect the unique European natural heritage and conserve Europe's most valuable and threatened wild fauna and flora and habitats (Jackson 2018: 2). Natura 2000 would provide a streamlined legal framework encompassing both the earlier Bird and Habitat directives.

While Christian democratic personalities had been at the vanguard of conservationist efforts in the 1970s, the role of environmental promoter was taken up in the 1980s and 1990s by new people such as Stanley Johnson (European Democrats) and Hemmo Muntingh, a Dutch MEP from the S&D Group. In autumn 1988, the EP published three reports penned by Muntingh on the Birds Directive and three other international environmental conventions,[63] which together threw significant weight behind the Habitats Directive proposal (Jackson 2018: 133-134). The reports called on the Commission and the Member States to step up efforts towards the implementation of the Bird Directive and other existing conventions and to draw up a legal instrument that would protect all species of fauna and flora and their habitats. In autumn 1989 and 1990, Muntingh drafted two additional reports on the Commission's Habitats Directive proposal.[64] De-

---

61 EPP Group Archives, C.1.46, Study Days in Paris, 2-4 July 2008, p. 43.

62 EPP Group Archives, C.1.27, Study Days in Palermo, 4-5 September 1988, p. 116.

63 Respectively the Bern, Bonn and Washington Conventions.

64 HAEU, PE3-21735.

veloped in consultation with nature conservation organisations and co-ordinated with the main environmental lobby group, the European Environmental Bureau (EEB) (Jackson 2018: 167-165), these reports suggested amendments to both the text of the directive and the annexes.

The apparent lack of EPP Group members reporting activity on the Habitat Directive may appear surprising given the prior engagement of Christian Democrats in the Birds directive. The overall weaker representation of the EPP Group in the ENVI committee during the first three legislatures of the elected EP (Figures 3.1 and 3.7) does not alone provide a sufficient explanation. By the late 1980s, the environmental focus of the EPP Group members within ENVI had shifted to subjects that were particularly connected to the realisation of the internal market, such as consumer protection and food safety, rather than purely environmental ones. However, this is not to say that ecological considerations were not important or had fallen down the agenda. Several reports penned by EPP MEPs and addressing air and water/sea pollution matters demonstrate the continued interest of the Group in environmental issues. Moreover, at the request of the EP, it arranged an Environmental Protection Day during the Group's Study Days in Palermo in September 1988 to discuss various issues pertaining to broadly conceived environmental policy.[65] The Group continued to advocate in favour of sustainable policies and to support consistent environmental protection on the basis of strict rules throughout the EU.[66]

However, for the EPP Group, environmental protection could not be envisaged as separate from the realisation of the internal market, of which it should become one of the crucial features.[67] In fact, the Community's environmental policy was considered to be "one of the most important frameworks for completion of the internal market" whose "goal [wa]s not the internal market as such but the creation of an internal market with a high level of environmental protection".[68] This change reflected first the growing issue linkage between environmental and market objectives, as environmental policy moved from the margins of the single market project to become a central element of the internal market and economic policy. Second, it reflected the increasing impact of environmental legislation on internal market regulations and the competitiveness of industry. Finally, it also chimed with the EPP Group's overall industry-friendly

65 EPP Group Archives, D.5.9, Activity report, Yearbook 1987-1988, p. 199; EPP Group Archives, C.1.27, Study Days in Palermo, 5-9 September 1988.

66 EPP Group Archives, C.1.43, Study Days in Vienna, 23-24 March 2004.

67 EPP Group Archives, D.5.10, Activity report, Yearbook 1988-1989, p. 211.

68 EPP Group Archives, D.5.11, Activity report, Yearbook 1989-1990, p. 193.

stance. In legislative terms, it meant that the co-operation procedure applied to environmental legislation geared towards the internal market, which, however limited, still gave the EP a greater say than the consultation procedure.[69] But the Group was also a strong supporter of the closer integration of environmental policy into other common policies, from the CAP to industry, employment and development.

If nature conservation and the preservation of biodiversity had taken centre stage during the formative years of environmental policy, the focus gradually shifted to climate change by the 2000s in light of the ever more conspicuous and disruptive effects of global warming. The EU committed itself to a leading and international agenda setter role in relation to climate change policies. To that effect, it has been advocating a drastic reduction in greenhouse gas emissions and an increase in renewable and sustainable energies in the EU's overall energy consumption. The EP has historically had little leeway to shape the EU's climate change policy. However, it did send delegations to international conferences such as the regular Conferences of Parties (COP) meetings on climate change in which the members of the EPP Group participated. It also regularly issued reports and resolutions, but its impact remained limited (Burns, Carter 2011: 58).

The introduction of co-decision gave Parliament an opportunity to go beyond its traditional symbolic environmental leadership both by pushing the use of particular policy instruments to deliver climate change emission reductions, chief among them the EU's Emission Trading Scheme (ETS) directives and the climate and energy package, and establishing in 2007 a new institutional forum, the Temporary Committee on Climate Change (CLIM), to look into all possible ways and means to reduce greenhouse gas emissions (Burns, Carter 2011: 60). Although the CLIM had little legislative power, it provided an alternative venue for the EP to express its preferences for climate change and exert leadership (Burns 2016). With 21 members out of a total of 60 and roughly the same number of deputies, the EPP had a strong contingent in CLIM,[70] although it did not obtain either the Presidency or Vice-Presidency of the committee. Under co-decision, the EP could amend the content of legislative proposals and contribute to strengthening the EU's environmental standards and its international leading role in the fight against climate change.

---

69 EPP Group Archives, C.1.27, Study Days in Palermo, pp. 135-137.

70 EPP Group Archives, Confidential, Presidence, 2007, Chrono 2007 September, Temporary Committee on Climate Change.

Within Parliament, the EPP Group played an active and leading part in these developments. The environment and, in particular, climate change remained major priorities for the Group. It thus voiced its support for the reduction of greenhouse gas emissions and the emergence of a low-carbon economy, notably by supporting the adoption of various pieces of legislation on fuels and biofuels, fuel-efficient engines and gas emissions, and for the EU to become a world leader in the fight against climate change.[71] Two members of the Group were instrumental in promoting significant political decisions through the positions they held, which also mirrored the broader stance of the Group on those issues.

In 2009, Karl-Heinz Florenz, who acted as Rapporteur for the CLIM, produced a crucial report on the future policy of the European Union on climate change. Entitled "2050: The future begins today – Recommendations for the EU's future integrated policy on climate change" (European Parliament 2009a), the report made ambitious recommendations for the actions necessary to combat climate change. It called for a review of whether the EU's commitment to cut temperatures by 2°C would be enough to avoid dangerous climate change and demanded a 25-40% reduction of greenhouse gas emissions by 2020 and 8% by 2050.

Another important EPP Group member to play a role in the policy process was the ENVI Rapporteur Avril Doyle, who prepared several compromise amendments for the revision of the Directive on the ETS (European Parliament 2008). Like Florenz, Doyle sat in CLIM. The revised ETS directive was part of a set of crucial pieces of legislation to be adopted in the run-up to the next round of COP meetings in Copenhagen. Rather than allocating the reports via the usual bidding system within the Environment Committee, the reports were divided between the political groups on the grounds that this important package required co-operation across the groups, to provide the opportunity for all groups to contribute actively to what was regarded as one of the most important packages of legislation to be adopted in the 2004-2009 legislature (Burns 2013: 995). The close co-operation between Doyle and Chris Davies (ALDE) was instrumental in promoting a stronger linkage between the ETS and Carbon Capture Storage policies (Boasson, Wettestad 2014: 409).

For the EPP Group, combating climate change and other major environmental threats did not necessarily need to have a negative impact on the economy. On the contrary, they believed that it should promote oppor-

71 EPP Group Archives, C.1.43, Study Days in Vienna, 23-24 March 2004, European People's Party Action Programme 2004-2009, p. 27.

tunities for the development of ecological innovation and create jobs with significant benefits for society, industry and citizens.[72]

*Conclusion*

The story of the EPP Group's contribution to the process of European integration has been intrinsically linked to that of the EP's legislative empowerment since 1979. Before and after its first election by direct universal suffrage, Parliament fought hard to expand the scope of its institutional powers and acquire new law-making competences, to buttress its political legitimacy as the only democratically accountable EU institution to become a co-legislator in its own right. The institutional activism of MEPs, including that of EPP Group members, as well as the seminal role played by the EP's standing committees in debating and reporting on legislation, even when their opinions hardly mattered, have been instrumental in the rise of Parliament over time.

The extension of the EP's prerogatives has been particularly significative in the realm of internal policies, in which the institutional balance of powers traditionally favoured the Commission and the Council. Yet, the ability of the EPP Group to provide legislative input was also affected by internal development in each of the four policy areas under study. Certain policies, such as agriculture and EMU, were key to the completion of the internal market; others, like social policy, have been more peripheral to European integration, while environment policy has seen its importance grow dramatically in the last few decades. Critical policy junctures, including reforms, treaty revisions or major crises, have offered the political groups inside Parliament opportunities to weigh in on the broad policy orientations. Economic, social and environmental policies were also crucial for the EPP's core programmatic objective of completing the internal market.

As one of the leading political groups in Parliament over the last eight legislatures, the EPP has been in a privileged position to secure strong representation in parliamentary committees. This includes committees like AGRI, which mattered most for partisan or electoral reasons, or ECON, EMPL and ENVI, which were important for ideological reasons. If the strength of membership is a tell-tale indicator of influence, the EPP has been very successful at obtaining key positions such as the chairmanships, vice-chairmanships and (main or shadow) rapporteurships, too. These in-

72 EPP Group Archives, C.1.28, Study Days in Athens 29 June-2 July 2009, p. 55.

fluential functions made it possible for EPP MEPs to impact the practical parliamentary work of the committee. They were well-placed to inform and frame the discussions in the EP committees and plenary in accordance with the group's preferences and ultimately to shape Parliament's position on key economic, social and environmental issues. They also validated the expertise and political and networking skills of EPP Group members.

This study of the EPP Group's agency in select EU internal policies brings to light the enduringly strong pro-European stance of the EPP Group, which was a powerful driver of the Group's action in the EP and of its contribution to co-shaping crucial internal policy areas. The influence the EPP Group exerted on the socio-economic orientations of the EU were twofold: intellectual and ideational as well as ideological. First, the EPP Group's intellectual and ideational contribution was made possible by the specialised knowledge of the internal policy areas that its members possessed, either as a result of their own personal and/or professional background and professional experience within and outside Parliament.

Second, many of the ideological preferences of the EPP Groups are reflected in the four selected internal policies. For instance, key tenets of the Christian democratic thinking on agricultural policy, such as the preservation of the main protectionist features of the policy, and the Christian democratic vision of family farming, have largely survived the various reforms that the CAP has undergone in the last three decades. The family farm as an ideational frame remains central to the discourse of a multifunctional agriculture. The EPP Group's ordo-liberal ideas for a sound economic, monetary and fiscal policy and its support for a social market economy are broadly reflected in the form and institutions given to EMU in the 1990s and have influenced the recent reform of EMU governance. Also consistent with Christian democratic values was the emphasis on and efforts towards strengthening the social dimension of EU financial and budgetary governance. The same holds true for the EPP's commitment to a qualified social interventionism designed to combat social injustice and promote social solidarity within the EU as a necessary corollary to a functioning free-market economy, which echoed the Christian tenets of solidarity and social justice. Coined by Christian Democrats, the concept of a social market economy best encapsulates this idea of a moderate free-market economy balanced with adequate social policy measures that is prevalent in today's EU. Another ideational legacy can be found in the idea of an environmentally friendly market economy that was promoted by the Group to bring together economics and ecology in the concept of sustainable development. This study of four policy areas thus exemplifies how and to what extent the EPP Group was able to apply Christian principles to the formulation of public policies in the EP and steer legislative debates accordingly.

The formation of transnational networks alongside political lines and shared interests, values and beliefs with a broad range of state and societal actors is moreover crucial to understanding the role and contribution of the EPP Group within the elected Parliament. These networks built on the long-standing transnational ties that had existed between Christian Democrats before the Second World War (see Kaiser in Chapter 1 of this book) but its members were also united by their pro-European commitment, the promotion of peace, subsidiarity, anti-communism and the promotion of a social market economy. The mobilisation of transnational Christian democratic networks was key for the EPP Group to increase the EP's profile and wield influence beyond the limited confines of the institution's legislative competences.

Those transnational networks came in various shapes and forms. In the CAP and social policy, close-knit networks and policy communities involving MEPs, farm and labour unions and government emerged and were crucial for connecting the EPP Group with relevant constituencies and policy-makers. In agriculture, a single-minded policy community (Daubjerg 1999) was influential for allowing only relatively moderate reforms and preserving the agricultural status quo as well as the path-dependent character of CAP reforms (e.g. Kay 2003). These networks also facilitated the articulation and mediation of societal interests and their incorporation into the position of the EPP Group in the EP and in other institutional forums, such as Intergovernmental Conferences (IGCs). In EMU, the Kangaroo Group networked and lobbied state and non-state actors in favour of the single market. In social policy, EPP Group members drew upon ties with social partners, e.g. trade unionists, with links to Christian Democracy and their oft strong representation in bodies like the Lisbon Strategy Group.

Moreover, the EPP Group could draw upon the wider Christian democratic political family and party members in national governments and parliaments. Regular contact between EPP Group members, and especially the Group's president, the Euro-party and fellow Christian Democrats holding offices in the governments or parliaments of the Member States, were important channels of influence in internal policy areas, especially those with a strong intergovernmental dimension. The wider Christian democratic network thus facilitated the elaboration and co-ordination of joint strategies and the maximisation of its resources and impact. It further allowed the Group to exert influence beyond the institutional confines of the EP. This is particularly clear in the case of EMU, where the group could use party summits and direct contacts with political leaders to inform debates and negotiations in the IGCs.

More generally, the Christian democratic transnational networks cast fresh light on the ubiquity of the formal and informal channels used by the EPP Group as well as its protean ties with a large variety of policy-relevant, societal and state actors. Both have been a vital element of its capacity to contribute to and shape internal policies since 1979.

There are also some striking differences in the EPP Group's activity in these internal policies. Electoral considerations have been a predominant feature of the EPP Group's stance vis-à-vis agricultural reform and account at least partly for the early interest of Christian democratic personalities in environmental protection. However, they played a largely marginal role in EMU and social policy, in which ideological considerations were particularly significant.

Coalition formation was also more important in certain committees than in others. Co-operation with similar-minded groups, such as the Conservatives or the Liberals, was at times necessary to push through important legislative elements. For instance, in ECON, the EPP-Conservative-ALDE alliance was key to ensure the maintenance of the primacy of fiscal discipline over measures supporting growth, employment and social cohesion that were championed by the Socialist and Green political groups. In ENVI, the co-operation between the EPP and ALDE Rapporteurs was instrumental to better embed Carbon Capture Storage into the revised European Emissions Trading Systems, thus providing the EU with legislative tools to achieve its emissions reduction objectives.

Two aspects that have been only superficially addressed in this chapter, due to methodological choices and the archival material available, deserve further scholarly attention in the future. First, Group cohesion is likely to have varied across committees and over time. The existing scholarship tends to argue in favour of political groups being generally cohesive entities, with differences emerging over time in specific groups and particular policy areas and committees. Studies have shown that national divisions tend to be more relevant in some committees than in others (Roederer-Rynning 2003; Whitaker 2011; Cicchi 2016). Further qualitative and quantitative research of voting data, especially an analysis of roll-call votes, may be able to shed light on the extent to which these four committees and policy areas stand out in this regard. Second, such a longitudinal study of the EPP Group in the EP raises the question of the impact of institutional change on voting behaviour and internal committee work. The introduction of co-decision in 2007 and the elevation of the EP to a co-legislator role has strengthened the role of certain standing committees and altered voting participation, coalition building and group cohesion. This applies to AGRI (Schwartz 2018) but remains to be examined for the three other sectoral committees studied in this chapter.

*APPENDIX*

*Table 3.1 Composition of the AGRI, ECON, EMPL and ENVI Standing Committees, by political group and EP term*[73]

| EPP Full Members (C= Chair) | | | | |
|---|---|---|---|---|
| | AGRI | ECON | EMPL | ENVI |
| 1. 1979–1984 | 10 | 10 | 7 (C) | 7 |
| 2. 1984–1989 | 12 (C) | 12 | 8 | 7 |
| 3. 1989–1994 | 15 | 14 | 8 | 11 |
| 4. 1994–1999 | 13 | 15 (C) | 12 | 11 |
| 5. 1999–2004 | 14 | 16 | 20 | 22 (C) |
| 6. 2004–2009 | 17 (C) | 21 | 16 | 24 (C) |
| 7. 2009–2014 | 17 | 19 | 17 | 26 |
| 8. 2014–2019 | 14 (C) | 18 | 15 | 20 (C) |

| | EPP Members % | | | |
|---|---|---|---|---|
| | AGRI | ECON | EMPL | ENVI |
| 1. 1979–1984 | 26 % | 27 % | 25 % | 26 % |
| 2. 1984–1989 | 27 % | 29 % | 26 % | 23 % |
| 3. 1989–1994 | 32 % | 27 % | 19 % | 22 % |
| 4. 1994–1999 | 29 % | 30 % | 30 % | 25 % |
| 5. 1999–2004 | 37 % | 36 % | 36 % | 37 % |
| 6. 2004–2009 | 37 % | 41 % | 31 % | 35 % |
| 7. 2009–2014 | 39 % | 38 % | 35 % | 37 % |
| 8. 2014–2019 | 30 % | 30 % | 27 % | 29 % |

73 All tables and figures listed in this chapter were compiled by Jacopo Cellini based on documents from the EPP Group archives. Since the composition of each committee often changes mid-term, with some members swapping committee duties in the course of the legislature, the tables and figures only take into account the original composition of the committee (i.e. the committee members appointed at the start of the legislature), which also reflected electoral results.

| | S&D Full Members (C= Chair) | | | |
|---|---|---|---|---|
| | AGRI | ECON | EMPL | ENVI |
| 1. 1979–1984 | 11 | 10 (C) | 8 | 8 (C) |
| 2. 1984–1989 | 12 | 13 (C) | 10 | 9 (C) |
| 3. 1989–1994 | 13 (C) | 18 | 16 (C) | 18 (C) |
| 4. 1994–1999 | 15 | 19 | 13 (C) | 14 (C) |
| 5. 1999–2004 | 10 | 13 (C) | 16 (C) | 16 |
| 6. 2004–2009 | 11 | 14 (C) | 16 (C) | 17 |
| 7. 2009–2014 | 11 (C) | 13 | 13 (C) | 17 (C) |
| 8. 2014–2019 | 10 | 15 (C) | 14 | 18 |

| | S&D Members % | | | |
|---|---|---|---|---|
| | AGRI | ECON | EMPL | ENVI |
| 1. 1979–1984 | 28 % | 27 % | 29 % | 30 % |
| 2. 1984–1989 | 27 % | 31 % | 32 % | 33 % |
| 3. 1989–1994 | 28 % | 35 % | 38 % | 35 % |
| 4. 1994–1999 | 33 % | 38 % | 33 % | 32 % |
| 5. 1999–2004 | 26 % | 30 % | 29 % | 27 % |
| 6. 2004–2009 | 24 % | 27 % | 31 % | 25 % |
| 7. 2009–2014 | 25 % | 26 % | 27 % | 24 % |
| 8. 2014–2019 | 22 % | 25 % | 25 % | 26 % |

| | ALDE Full Members (C = Chair) | | | |
|---|---|---|---|---|
| | AGRI | ECON | EMPL | ENVI |
| 1. 1979–1984 | 5 | 3 | 2 | 2 |
| 2. 1984–1989 | 3 | 4 | 2 | 2 |
| 3. 1989–1994 | 4 | 6 (C) | 3 | 5 |
| 4. 1994–1999 | 3 | 5 | 2 | 3 |
| 5. 1999–2004 | 3 | 4 | 4 | 5 |
| 6. 2004–2009 | 3 | 7 | 7 | 10 |
| 7. 2009–2014 | 4 | 4 (C) | 4 | 8 |
| 8. 2014–2019 | 4 | 5 | 6 | 6 |

| | **ALDE Members %** | | | |
|---|---|---|---|---|
| | AGRI | ECON | EMPL | ENVI |
| 1. 1979–1984 | 13 % | 8 % | 7 % | 7 % |
| 2. 1984–1989 | 7 % | 10 % | 6 % | 7 % |
| 3. 1989–1994 | 9 % | 12 % | 7 % | 10 % |
| 4. 1994–1999 | 7 % | 10 % | 5 % | 7 % |
| 5. 1999–2004 | 8 % | 9 % | 7 % | 8 % |
| 6. 2004–2009 | 7 % | 14 % | 13 % | 15 % |
| 7. 2009–2014 | 9 % | 8 % | 8 % | 11 % |
| 8. 2014–2019 | 9 % | 8 % | 11 % | 9 % |

| | **Greens-EFA Full Members (C = Chair)** | | | |
|---|---|---|---|---|
| | AGRI | ECON | EMPL | ENVI |
| 1. 1979–1984 | | | | |
| 2. 1984–1989 | | | | |
| 3. 1989–1994 | 3 | 1 | 2 | 4 |
| 4. 1994–1999 | 2 | 2 | 1 | 2 |
| 5. 1999–2004 | 4 (C) | 3 | 3 | 5 |
| 6. 2004–2009 | 3 | 1 | 3 | 6 |
| 7. 2009–2014 | 3 | 3 | 3 | 6 |
| 8. 2014–2019 | 4 | 4 | 3 | 5 |

| | **Greens-EFA Members %** | | | |
|---|---|---|---|---|
| | AGRI | ECON | EMPL | ENVI |
| 1. 1979–1984 | | | | |
| 2. 1984–1989 | | | | |
| 3. 1989–1994 | 6 % | 2 % | 5 % | 8 % |
| 4. 1994–1999 | 4 % | 4 % | 3 % | 5 % |
| 5. 1999–2004 | 11 % | 7 % | 5 % | 8 % |
| 6. 2004–2009 | 7 % | 2 % | 6 % | 9 % |
| 7. 2009–2014 | 7 % | 6 % | 6 % | 8 % |
| 8. 2014–2019 | 9 % | 7 % | 5 % | 7 % |

# Chapter 4 Values, Strategies, Actions: The EPP Group and EU External Relations[1]

*Wojciech Gagatek*

Making the EU a global player has remained one of the top priorities of the EPP Group[2] since the 1990s. An ambitious Common Foreign and Security Policy (CFSP) (including an enhanced EU defence policy); a firm conviction that a free trade area is an opportunity, rather than a danger; a development policy that helps eradicate the root causes of poverty while safeguarding peace and human dignity, are today high on the Group's agenda. The post-2004 enlargements have increased the EU's geopolitical and economic power, enabling it to exert an influence on world affairs, whereas the changes introduced by the Treaty of Lisbon have further extended the Parliament's role in shaping and scrutinising these policies, including by making the officials both in the Commission and in the Council more accountable. Consequently, the political groups, and the European People's Party (EPP) being the largest one, have also received better instruments for exerting their influence on EU external policies.

And yet the role of the political groups in shaping external policies is an under-researched area of study. Given the typically intergovernmental nature of most, if not all, of these external policies, scholars have tended more to investigate the role of other EU institutions, such as the Council or the Commission, than the European Parliament (EP). If, on the other hand, they do acknowledge the role of the latter, then they usually take its final position as a point of reference, thus diminishing the role and possible impact of the political groups. However, given the growing role and ambitions of the EPP Group, the improved standing of the Parliament since the Treaty of Lisbon entered into force (in 2009), and the growing

1 I would like to thank Lorenzo Cicchi and Angela Romano from the EUI for their insightful comments on the earlier version of this chapter. As always, all errors are entirely my own.

2 For simplicity the chapter uses the abbreviation EPP Group, even for the period (1999-2009) in which the Group was called the European People's Party and European Democrats (EPP-ED).

salience of some EU external policies (particularly trade), a new research agenda should include the role of the political groups, too.

This chapter encompasses a broad area of EU external policies, which is defined in relation to Part V of the Treaty on the Functioning of the European Union (TFEU). These primarily include Common Foreign and Security Policy (CFSP), Common Security and Defence Policy (CSDP), development policy, Common Commercial Policy (external trade), and EU enlargement. In some cases, such as Common Commercial Policy, the EU has the exclusive competence, and the role of the Parliament, as in the case of the rejection of the Anti-Counterfeiting Trade Agreement (ACTA) by the EP in 2012, might prove to be fundamental. In other cases, an intergovernmental mode of co-operation prevails, in which the EU supplements, rather than creates, policies, and the role of the EP is even less visible.

Three interrelated questions will guide this analysis: 1. What values, positions and goals has the EPP Group presented regarding external policies and how it formulated them? 2. How has the Group tried to achieve these goals? 3. What impact and influence did the Group gain? Apart from secondary sources and academic literature, the primary sources will include the EPP Group policy positions; debates, proposals, resolutions, amendments and votes in the EP plenary and in the relevant parliamentary committees (AFET, INTA, DEVE)[3]; and interviews with the key personalities involved in relevant policy fields (e.g. Group's committee Coordinators) from the EPP Group (see the Appendix for a detailed list). The time span will mostly cover the period after 2004, and it does so for the following reasons. First, while the 2004 and subsequent EU enlargements have extended the geopolitical and economic position of the EU in world affairs, many observers feared the integration of MEPs from new states would create unsolvable tensions, making EU institutions, and the EP in particular, unable to work in an effective manner. Is this really the case? How well have the new MEPs been integrated into the EPP Group and how has their arrival influenced its priorities? Second, while the role of the EP in this field has been always rather complementary to that of the Council and the Commission, the Treaty of Lisbon's entry into force has made it possible for the Parliament to increasingly accentuate its presence and position in the entire field. This was possible thanks to the strengthening of the EP's consultative powers in CFSP, the insertion of human rights clauses into in-

3 AFET – Committee on Foreign Affairs; INTA – Committee on International Trade; DEVE – Committee on Development.

ternational agreements, and finally, the reinforcement of Parliament's role in the conclusion of these agreements. In short, it seems reasonable to concentrate on the period after 2004 and refer to the previous developments only when necessary.

This chapter will be structured as follows. First, it will present the nature of EU external relations from the point of view of party politics in the European Parliament, showing the instruments of influence that the European Parliament possesses, and subsequently, reminding the reader about the key events in EU external relations that have taken place since 2004. Next it will cover the overall priorities of the EPP Group, the way they were formulated, the degree of internal cohesion and the nature of party competition in the EP in the field of external relations. Finally, it will close with a detailed look at the enlargement process through the perspective of the deepening vs. widening debate and in particular by offering a case study of Turkey.

Before analysing the case of the EPP Group, it is necessary to first address the issue of the role and instruments of influence that the European Parliament possesses in the field of EU external relations. This analysis is a precondition to assessing the impact that political groups such as the EPP can exert.

### *The role of the European Parliament in EU external relations*

The Treaty of Lisbon has created some new powers in the field of external relations for the whole EU vis-à-vis the Member States. Some of them will be reviewed below. In most cases, this development has also meant the EP's role has become stronger. Still, the picture that emerges here is quite varied. That is why a clear distinction should be drawn between the scope of the EU's competence and the Parliament's prerogatives in different policy fields within EU external relations.

Beginning with foreign affairs and security policy, the Treaty of Lisbon extended the EP's powers of scrutiny over CFSP, CSDP and a newly created post of the EU's High Representative for Foreign Affairs and Security Policy, who is also the Vice-President of the European Commission (hereafter HR/VP). Nevertheless, from a formal point of view, that role is still rather complementary, not to say secondary, to that of other EU institutions. That usually means that the Parliament has the right to be consulted and informed, for example, about the HR/VP's decisions and activities of and the views of the EP shall be "duly taken into consideration" by the HR/VP (Article 36 of the Treaty on the European Union, TEU) or that the

Parliament can hold the responsible commissioners accountable. This point can be further extended in two directions. First, from a normative point of view, the question remains whether the EP should be involved in external relations and if so, how (Lord 2011; Sjursen 2011; Wagner 2006). Both foreign and trade policies of the EU have been designed as intergovernmental spheres of activity (regardless of the changes introduced in the Treaty of Lisbon). During the work of the European Convention, the Member States resisted granting the EP a greater role in external relations (Norman 2003). Additionally, in comparison with internal EU policies, there is much less law-making involved. This field is also quite often kept secret due to the general nature of diplomatic relationships or trade negotiations (Eriksen 2011; Lord 2008). In this context, it is important to observe that, at a national level, external relations have traditionally belonged to the domain of governments, with a much smaller role for parliaments and weak instruments of parliamentary accountability (Hänggi 2004; Raunio and Wagner 2017). In other words, parliaments of all kinds do not play first fiddle in external relations, although they have important budgetary and scrutinizing functions, and no major international treaty can be ratified without their consent (Hill 2003). If that is so, why should the engagement of the EP be required? As the history of inter-institutional relations between the EP and other institutions has shown, it was through constant reference to democratic principles such as legitimacy, the need to increase the role of the only directly elected EU institution as the EP is, the genuine interests of citizens in foreign policy and human rights, the need for responsibility, transparency and accountability, overall, the entire narrative resulting from the 2001 Laeken declaration, that the Parliament managed to achieve a greater role to that formally stipulated in the Treaty (Rosén 2015b). For this reason, scholars interpret the EP's role in foreign policy as a product of an inter-institutional battle with the Commission and Member States, with the EP considering itself as "the conscience of other EU institutions" (Bickerton 2011: 69), and its participation in this field as a means to reduce the EU's democratic deficit. In short, as Servent put it, the Parliament has creatively extended its right to be consulted into a right to be involved (Servent 2014). This is the case regarding CSFP, CSDP, development policy and human rights promotion.

The most visible example of this phenomenon is the negotiations over the establishment of the European External Action Service (EEAS), which took place in 2010 (Raube 2012; Rosén 2015b; Wisniewski 2013). There were no formal rules specifying that the EP should play an important role. Article 27 para. 3 of the TEU, as modified by the Treaty of Lisbon, indicated that "The organisation and functioning of the European External Action Service shall be established by a decision of the Council. The Council shall act on a proposal from the High Representative after consulting the European Parliament and after obtaining the consent of the Commission". The legal term consultation denotes that the EP has to be heard, but its opinion is non-binding. However, through the changes introduced by the Treaty of Lisbon, the Parliament now co-decides with the Council on the EU budget, and precisely because of this, the EP assertively conditioned its agreement on the EU budget on receiving more formal and informal rights as far as scrutiny of the EEAS is concerned (Raube 2012). Even before the announcement of the first proposals from the HR/VP and the Member States, the Parliament adopted a report drafted by Elmar Brok (European Parliament 2009c). The report hinted that the Parliament would not accept a secondary role in the process of establishing the EEAS, but wished to be placed on equal footing with the Council. That is why it argued that setting up the EEAS "requires a solution based on consensus" between all actors listed in the above Treaty article. Furthermore, it added that "given the budgetary consequences, an early and substantive dialogue with Parliament is essential for the effective start-up of the EEAS and to ensure that it receives the necessary financial resources" (European Parliament 2009c). In various subsequent reports and resolutions jointly drafted by Elmar Brok (EPP) and Guy Verhofstadt (ALDE), while emphasising that the EP's concerns about the EEAS stem from the wish to "provide it with political legitimacy", the EP revealed its detailed concerns over the EEAS' institutional positioning, structure and "democratic accountability". The EP saw the EEAS as a supranational body, integrated in or closely related to the Commission in administrative, organisational and budgetary aspects, but otherwise remaining an autonomous body assisting the HR/VP while accountable to the EP in political and budgetary terms. In particular, the EEAS budget should be a part of the EU general budget, thus guaranteeing the EP's veto powers. Its staff should be independent, geographically and gender-balanced and "full budgetary transparency" of the EEAS operation should be guaranteed (Brok and Verhofstadt 2010). Additionally, the EP demanded, among other things, the possibility of holding EU foreign policy representatives accountable; the right to decide on the nature of appointments within the EEAS; the possibility of organising public hearings of high-ranked EU representatives to third countries before their appointment; access to diplomatic documents; various consultation mechanisms with the HR/VP; and overall, through those changes it wanted to establish "strengthened consultation mechanisms regarding Council decision-making on the Common Foreign and Security Policy" (Brok and Verhofstadt 2010). While the final set-up of the EEAS was a compromise where all parties involved in the negotiations, including the EP, had to drop some of its proposals, it is fair to say that the EP achieved much more than it could hope for given the consultation procedure specified in the above Treaty article, namely the EP gained recognition as an important player by other EU institutions and the HR/VP specifically (Erkelens and Blockmans 2012; Wisniewski 2013). Similar cases concern, for example, civilian missions (but not military ones) that are run within the CSDP, or stabilisation programmes in various parts of the world, which also need the Parliament's approval as far as their budget is concerned. In other words, sometimes the EP's role in external policies is strengthened by its much greater formal powers in internal policies, something that the literature refers to as issue linkage (Farrell and Héritier 2003). Generally speaking, while Member States agreed that EU external relations, including foreign policy, must be sensitive to the issue of democratic legitimacy, most literature would concur that "the role of the Parliament in CFSP/CSDP is hardly that of decision maker" (Raube, 2014, p. 138). This perspective is shared by the practitioners in the EPP Group (Interviews Salafranca, 10.10.2018; Saryusz-Wolski, 4.09.2018; Kalniete, 10.10.2018).

The EP enjoys greater powers regarding development policy, but in this case not due to changes introduced by the Treaty of Lisbon, but through provisions introduced in earlier treaties. The most important difference with the CFSP or CSDP is that the EP co-decides together with the Council on adapting "the measures necessary for the implementation of development cooperation policy" (Article 209 para 1 of the TFEU). This includes, for example, the voice over the programming and implementation of this policy, which, as with the case of foreign policy, relates to its overall powers concerning the EU budget (Verschaeve and Delputte 2015). The Treaty of Lisbon states that the EU's development policy and that of the Member States complement and reinforce each other. What the Treaty of Lisbon did change, however, was to reduce the number of aims of EU development policy to a single one, namely the eradication of poverty (Article 208 TFEU).

The EP's role seems to be even greater within trade policy. First, the EU has exclusive competence over this policy area, which means that the Member States cannot act alone in this field (i.e. have their own trade agreements with third countries). In other words, the role of the EU has always been much greater in trade policy than in any other field belonging to EU external relations. At the same time, up until the Treaty of Lisbon, the EP played a marginal role here and could only count on informal consultations (Van den Putte et al. 2015). The Treaty of Lisbon has significantly extended Parliament's legislative powers in trade policy by subjecting it to the co-decision procedure (the Ordinary Legislative Procedure, OLP), where the EP stands on equal footing with the Council. This increased role is also visible in the practice (not in formal rules) of drawing up international agreements, whereby the Parliament is involved from the early stages of negotiations up to their conclusion (Kleimann 2011; Niemann 2013). Nevertheless, it is the Commission that sets the agenda and negotiates international agreements, whereas the Council specifies the negotiating mandate, monitors the Commission's performance and ratifies the agreement (by a qualified majority). It is important to highlight that until the Treaty of Lisbon, and even soon after its adoption, the Council would not accept a greater formal role for the EP in this field, citing national sovereignty as the main reason for its objections, and additionally arguing that parliamentary involvement might reduce the necessary margin of manoeuvre and flexibility in international trade negotiations, thus impeding the EU's bargaining position vis-a-vis its partners (Rosén 2015b; Woolcock 2018).

Another case concerns the role of the EP as far as consent to international agreements is concerned. Since the Treaty of Lisbon, the EP has given its consent to a range of international agreements, comprising all agreements with important budgetary implications and all agreements where the ordinary legislative procedure applies (Corbett 2012). However, the Parliament can only accept or reject the whole agreement, which means it is not involved in negotiations. Nevertheless, it is the threat of rejecting or delaying the consent that increases the EP's overall role. This was the case when the EP refused to give its consent to international agreements with Syria and Morocco due to concerns over human rights protection; or with regard the so-called SWIFT agreement, signed with the USA and concerning banking data transfer via the SWIFT network. By rejecting this agreement (though it gave its consent soon after), the Parliament sent a message to the Commission and the Council to take its opinions more seriously.

Finally, with regard to enlargement, the EP has both formal and informal mechanisms to express its position. From the formal point of view, Article 49 of the TEU indicates that the accession treaty must receive the EP's consent. The Commission must inform the Parliament on the course of negotiations (in the form of country reports). On its turn, the EP presents its opinions by adopting annual resolutions on the progress made by each candidate or potential candidate country. From an informal point of view, the EP uses the means of parliamentary diplomacy to foster links with parliaments and party groups in the candidate countries.

Overall, we see a mixed picture as far as formal competences are concerned. Treaty rules provide for a different role for the EU versus the Member States, and for the EP versus other institutions. In foreign affairs policy domain (CFSP, CSDP, HR/VP), these competences are rather weak; in development policy, the EU shares a competence to act with the Member States, and the EP gets co-decision instruments; and last but not least, in trade policy we see an unusually strong role for the EU as far as EU external relations are concerned (given the exclusive competence), and the role of the EP has become much stronger since the Treaty of Lisbon. However, in all cases it is very important to bear in mind the practice of applying these competences and the effective role of the EP irrespective of formal rules.

Regardless of the legal basis and its formally defined role, the EP is pursuing its own role by the means of parliamentary diplomacy with many countries and regions of the world (Stavridis and Irrera 2015). This includes maintaining active relationships with parliaments and parliamentarians in other countries, permanent or more flexible inter-parliamentary delegations, and rhetorical diplomacy (resolutions, reports, statements, urgency debates, etc.) (Fiott 2015). MEPs often go on fact-finding missions to other countries, for example, as election observers, and in reverse the Parliament receives foreign guests including heads of states.

The European Parliament is very active in human rights promotion. The main instruments that are used are value-oriented resolutions, declarations and public hearings. The EP's Annual Report on the EU's policy in the field of human rights serves as a benchmark against which the EP priorities are defined. Perhaps the most well-known element of the EP's human rights promotion is the Sakharov Prize for Freedom of Thought that the Parliament has awarded to individuals and organisations since 1988. Although symbolic in nature, it serves as an important tool of help, recognition and publicity for the laureates, and a source of persuasion on the oppressing regimes. This issue will be covered again in the subsequent section of this chapter.

It must be borne in mind that in its parliamentary diplomacy the EP and its political groups are not constrained in the same way as national parliamentarians, particularly those from the governing party. This usually results in much stronger opinions on various issues than the Commission or the Council can afford due to the limits of regular diplomacy. For example, the EP caused serious diplomatic consequences for the EU's relations with Turkey when it recognized the Armenian genocide on several occasions and asked Turkey to do the same. By establishing relations with foreign and international actors, the EP again tries to challenge the monopoly of other institutions in foreign policy making, or even "to portray itself as an actor without which decisions cannot be made" (Jančić 2016: 121). For all its activities, the EP is frequently recognized in the literature as a norm entrepreneur for the EU's human rights policy (Balfour 2013).

One further point worth developing here concerns the role of the parliamentary committees. The fact that, formally speaking, the EP has the least powers regarding foreign policy within the EU's external relations does not mean that members are not interested in this policy, quite the contrary.[4] The most obvious and basic fact is that the EP Committee on Foreign Affairs (AFET) is commonly perceived as the most prestigious EP committee, with 74 members in the legislative term 2014-2019. In contrast, in the same EP mandate, membership of the Committee on Development (DEVE) amounted to 28 members. Simply put, its members do not perceive membership of the DEVE committee as prestigious (Interviews Preda, 10.10.2018; Kaczmarek, 8.09.2019, Engel, 5.02.2019).

The key condition of influence relates to the question of membership figures in parliamentary committees. Table 4.1 below show the partisan composition of INTA, DEVE and AFET from 2004 to 2019 for EPP, Socialists and Democrats (S&D) and Alliance of Liberals and Democrats for Europe (ALDE).[5] A clear trend is that over the years the rate of EPP domination in these committees has dropped quite considerably, which also reflects the overall changes in the composition of the EP.

*Table 4.1 Composition of AFET, DEVE, INTA by political group and EP term*

AFET

| | **2004–2009** | **2009–2014** | **2014–2019** |
|---|---|---|---|
| **EPP** | 36.47 % | 34.62 % | 28.38 % |
| **S&D** | 27.06 % | 24.36 % | 24.32 % |
| **ALDE** | 14.12 % | 10.26 % | 10.81 % |
| *N* | 85 | 78 | 74 |

4 Note that the number of members in each committee is not permanently fixed, but reflects the preferences of MEPs. The agreement between the Groups at the beginning of each term indicates how many members each committee will have.

5 These abbreviations are used for the sake of clarity, and include previous denominations/acronyms (e.g. PES, ELDR).

DEVE

| | 2004–2009 | 2009–2014 | 2014–2019 |
|---|---|---|---|
| **EPP** | 38.24 % | 36.67 % | 30.00 % |
| **S&D** | 23.53 % | 30.00 % | 26.67 % |
| **ALDE** | 8.82 % | 10.00 % | 10.00 % |
| *N* | 34 | 30 | 30 |

INTA

| | 2004–2009 | 2009–2014 | 2014–2019 |
|---|---|---|---|
| **EPP** | 45.16 % | 32.26 % | 31.71 % |
| **S&D** | 25.81 % | 25.81 % | 19.51 % |
| **ALDE** | 3.23 % | 9.68 % | 9.76 % |
| *N* | 31 | 31 | 41 |

*Source: official data from the European Parliament website.*

The role of the committees seems to be of crucial importance for the result of EP's action. Major decisions are formulated within parliamentary committees even before the plenary session. If, as is usually the case, committee decisions are the result of a wide coalition of major parties, then later the EP plenary adopts them with overwhelming majorities (Bressanelli 2014). On the other hand, if major political groups oppose each other, then intra-group cohesion decreases (Bowler and McElroy 2015). Furthermore, committees hold various EU institutions accountable, such as the Commission. For that reason, ensuring effective mechanisms of policy co-ordination within and between various EP committees is one of the key conditions of political groups' success.

Apart from committee Chair, the most important role is played by the Rapporteur. There is a complex auctioning mechanism that helps to allocate rapporteurships to political groups based on the perceived importance of a report and the size of each group. When a political group receives a rapporteurship, it must designate its own member to prepare the report. Usually this is the responsibility of the group's Coordinator in a committee, and mostly depends on the size of the national delegation in the group. These reports are either legislative or non-legislative, the latter being adapted by the Parliament on its own initiative (Kaeding 2005; Yordanova 2013).

The question that arises quite obviously at this point concerns the role of political groups in building the EP's priorities, positions and defining the overall role. The few studies that do show the role of the EP in external relations usually focus on the CFSP and trade (Baja 2015; Rosen and Rabe 2018; Rosen 2017; Barba and Harran, 2005; Eulalie and McNaughton 2008; Diedrich 2004; Brown 2013; Rejewski 2013; Richardson 2012). At the same time, nothing or very little is written on the role of the political groups. An even more troubling case is EU development policy. As Delpute and Verschaeve observe, most studies on EU development policy largely ignore the existence of the EP, and, to an even greater extent, the political groups, while at the same time studies on the EP ignore development policy (Verschaeve and Delputte 2015). However, it is not only in the field of external relations; the role of political groups in the EU decision-making process seems to be largely understudied on the whole (Fiott 2015). A recent publication edited by Stavridis and Irrea (2015) has made visible progress in understanding the role of the EP in international relations, but the role of the groups or partisan divisions is still very much understudied.

There is yet another problem that stems from reviewing studies related to EU legislative politics and their application to the field of external relations. Most of these studies would take the formal, that is Treaty-defined, role of the Parliament as a point of reference (König, 2008; Selck and Steunenberg 2004; Tsebelis et al. 2001). In light of the analysis so far, this applies to external relations only to a limited extent. For example, formal powers of the EP in relation to foreign policy have barely changed since the Maastricht Treaty (Wessels and Bopp 2008), yet, as illustrated above, there is no doubt the current EP plays a bigger role there. On the other hand, studies analysing the international role of the EP largely focus on the question of democratic control of other institutions by the Parliament as such, while ignoring the question of partisan divisions. The issue of the 'impact' of the EP and its groups is further complicated by a lack of tangible results in terms of legislation, and overall, their effectiveness in this field (Hix et al. 2007). In order to win concessions from other institutions, the EP must show unity and hence gather support from across the political spectrum (Kreppel 2002). That was clearly the case with negotiation over the EEAS, in which the EP was united and the key personalities that represented it (Elmar Brok from the EPP, Guy Verhofstadt from ALDE and Roberto Gualtieri from S&D) had a strong mandate from the majority. Generally speaking, there is still quite a limited research that aims to explain the Parliament's increasing influence in the field of external relations (despite some notable exceptions such as Herranz-Surrallés 2014; Rosén 2015a), let alone its own groups, which makes this research both interesting and demanding at the same time.

*Developments in EU external relations since 2004: an overview*

The key and most important event, or series of events, was without doubt the EU enlargement. Ten new states joined the EU in 2004, two in 2007, and the most recent one (Croatia) in 2013. The EPP Group, like the whole Parliament, consistently supported the EU enlargement process. Over the years, various EP reports on the Commission's enlargement strategy were drafted by Elmar Brok MEP, a former long-standing Chair of the AFET Committee in the EP (European Parliament 2000d; European Parliament 2002). Not only has the enlargement led to a new situation within the EU, and in the EP in particular (see below), but it has also resulted in several consequences beyond this. The EU now borders new countries in Central and Eastern Europe such as Ukraine, Belarus, and Moldova, and, last but not least, Russia. An important question has emerged as to how to build relationship with these countries, given that some of them present ambitions for EU membership. For this reason, the EU initiated the European Neighbourhood Policy (launched in 2004), making it possible to intensify its relations with countries such as Ukraine, Moldova or Armenia, although not offering prospects for EU membership (Bicchi and Lavenex 2015). At the same time, this region is a source of international tension and geopolitical rivalry not only through Russian aggression of Georgia (2008) and Ukraine (2014), but also due to internal issues taking place within these countries (such as the Orange Revolution in the Ukraine in 2004-2005). In all these cases, the Parliament, and the EPP Group in particular, have taken a very proactive attitude to showing its impact and strengthening pro-European and pro-democratic tendencies in this region. As far as Russia is concerned, the Group and the Parliament increasingly criticised this country not only for its lack of progress in democratisation, or its militaristic attitude, but also for directly interfering in domestic affairs of EU Member States, such as through attempts to influence the electoral process. This stance is clearly visible in various reports and policy papers that the Group has adopted since 2004 (European Parliament 2015c), or that the Group has supported overwhelmingly, such as the Malmstrom report on EU-Russia relations from 2005.[6] A long-standing problem is the dependency of many European states on Russian oil or gas, to which the EU, and the EPP Group, tries to respond by focusing on external aspects of

6 EPP Group Archives, Strategie politique, Position Papers, 2017, EPP Group position paper on Russia.

energy security, such as in an EP 2007 resolution drafted by Jacek Saryusz-Wolski MEP (European Parliament 2007a).

Other countries, particularly in the Western Balkans, are knocking on the EU's door, hoping for accession. The Group supports their ambition on the condition of fulfilling certain political and economic criteria (EU conditionality) and provided the EU has enough absorption capacity. One particularly difficult case concerns Turkish membership of the EU, a candidate country since 1999. This issue has long divided the EPP Group, with some delegations (including the British Conservatives until 2009) advocating Turkish membership if it continued its democratic path; and others opposing it, such as the French and German delegations, who argued for a special type of privileged association with this country but excluding EU membership. However, in the last few years, Turkey has reversed its democratic process, which has led to the closure of its prospects for EU membership for the time being, a matter on which the EPP Groups seems to be united at this moment. This case will be dealt with extensively in the last section of this chapter.

Certainly, in the same way as the EU is not only focused on Central and Eastern Europe, the EP develops positions and maintains relationships all over the world, both far away from Europe and a little bit closer to its borders. The EPP Group has traditionally been very active in fostering relationships with Latin America. Regarding the former, at the initiative of Jose Ignazio Salafranca Sanchez-Neyra, a former long-standing Spanish member of the Group and its Coordinator in the AFET, a parliamentary assembly comprising South American parliamentarians and MEPs called EUROLAT was created in 2006. Similar examples of this kind of parliamentary co-operation embrace the ACP countries (the ACP-EU Joint Parliamentary Assembly), the Euro-Mediterranean Parliamentary Assembly (EMPA), or Eastern European countries in the form of EURONEST. Transformations in Northern Africa, commonly labelled as the Arab Spring, which led to a change of power in countries like Tunisia, Egypt and Syria, caused fundamental consequences for the EU as well by leading to the massive influx of immigrants and refugees coming to Europe from these and other countries. Finally, the Middle East peace process has always stood in the close interest of the Parliament and the Group. In particular, the Group has always advocated the establishment of a democratic and peaceful Palestinian State, with Jerusalem as a shared capital[7] (EPP Group

7 EPP Group Archives, D.1.2009.4-0012, Press release 2009, Nuovo Governo israeliano/New Israeli Government. Vito Bonsignore MEP.

2009a), although inconsistencies between its delegations became visible a few times.

The EU and its Member States together account for about 60% of global aid for development. This EU policy has been closely linked to the United Nations' initiatives and goals such as the UN Millennium Development Goals (2000-2015) or the Sustainable Development Goals (2015-2030). The most important of these are the eradication of extreme poverty and hunger, the achievement of universal primary education, the reduction of child mortality or the combat of AIDS, malaria and other diseases. The 2000 UN document set a target of 0.7% of gross national income that each developed state (including EU Member States) should spend on development aid. Some authors argue that rather than being an optional extension, development policy is a fundamental pillar of European integration (Holland 2002; Carbone 2007). Since 2001, the operational goals of EU development policy have been closely linked to security issues, and since 2015 to migration, which currently seems to be the most important political factor driving this policy. In its resolution, the Parliament argued that this might put at risk the autonomy of development policy, as it subordinates it to migration management (European Parliament 2017a). However, the biggest challenge for the EU is that the development policies of the individual Member States are not integrated enough into its own policy in this field, and that from the horizontal point of view, development policy is not sufficiently integrated with other EU policies such as trade, agriculture or migration. Additionally, there is a huge gap between the rhetoric behind development policy and the reality of its actual delivery (Bengtsson and Elgström 2012). The same conclusion is shared by key practitioners representing the EPP Group in the DEVE Committee both at present or in the past, such as Filip Kaczmarek, Frank Engel or Cristian Preda (Interviews Kaczmarek, 8.09.2018; Engel, 5.02.2019; Preda, 10.10.2018).

While the dynamics of trade policy mostly relate to market liberalisation and the enhancement of economic welfare, they also serve to achieve a much wider set of foreign policy goals *sensu largo*, thus having a geopolitical significance (Young and Peterson, 2015). In building up its relationship with developing countries (which intensified in 1990s), the EU tries to include various additional conditions in trade agreements to influence the domestic politics of these countries, such as human rights protection or free elections. Overall, for the last few years, the EU has been carrying out its policy of trade liberalisation through signing bilateral free trade agreements (FTA) in addition to the multilateral approach within the World Trade Organization framework (particularly under the Doha round). Recently, the EU has signed or concluded negotiations over several

FTAs with large economies such as South Korea (2010), Japan (2017) and Canada (2017). However, the most salient case was the agreement negotiated with the US called the Transatlantic Trade and Investment Partnership (TTIP), which raised enormous levels of interest all over Europe. The EPP Group has always prioritised the benefits of liberalising world trade, and at the same time emphasised its priority to maintain a very close relationship with the US, stressing the commitments of both parties to the democratic values such as freedom, democracy and human rights.[8] At the same time, the US has been frequently criticised, such as in a recent report drafted by Elmar Brok (European Parliament 2018), for something that the Parliament described as unilateralism, due to the lack of US ratification of such treaties as the Kyoto Protocol on reducing greenhouse emissions, the treaty establishing the International Criminal Court, or a recent withdrawal from the Paris Agreement by the Trump administration.

In all spheres of the EP's and EPP Group's activities and policies, there is fundamental concern over human right issues and their violation. They have always believed that the EU could promote human rights more effectively around the world, criticising the Council for some of its steps leading to the blocking or rejection of proposals on human rights. The EPP Group proposed funding a financial instrument called the European Instrument for Democracy and Human Rights (EIDHR). Linking the field of human rights and security, the EP embraced the term human security in its resolutions. The EPP Group contributed to the nomination of Sakharov Prize candidates such as Oswaldo Paya (2002), the United Nations (2003), the Belarusian Association of Journalists (2004), Ladies in White (2005), Aleksandr Milinkevich (2006), Salih Mahmoud Osman (2007), Memorial (2009), Guilhermo Farinas (2010), Malala Yousafzai (2013), Democratic opposition in Venezuela (2017) and Oleg Sentsov (2018).

Certainly, while it is not possible to review all initiatives and events in this period, the selection above seems to point to the Group's main priorities.

8 EPP Group Archives, F.6.1. Priorities of the EPP-ED Group for 2004-2009 — A contribution of ideas to policy formation; EPP Group Archives, C.8.100, Ten priorities for the EPP Group 2009-2014: Putting people at the heart of Europe.

*The process of formulating EPP Group positions in EU external relations*

One of the most striking phenomena concerning the functioning of the political groups in the European Parliament is how they manage to build internal compromises and what means they employ to achieve this. Their multinational membership poses great difficulties in finding the middle ground, acceptable to the maximum possible number of MEPs. Furthermore, the biggest political groups face further troubles, inter alia, from their prima facie diverse ideological character. In contrast to national politics, the political groups in the EP do not have much of a say in candidate selection for the EP elections, and the lack of government and opposition dynamics, which in national politics normally ensure a relatively united stance from parliamentary groups, poses further challenges to ensuring group unity in the EP. On the other hand, the fact that most policy divisions between the groups concern socio-economic and ideological, rather than national or even pro/anti European, lines, is a positive factor for ensuring group internal cohesion (Hix et al. 2007; McElroy and Benoit 2012; Schmitt and Thomassen 2009). Furthermore, the sheer number and scale of the EP's legislative activities mean that no single MEP can follow all policy fields, and for this reason it is most convenient for them to follow the group line (Ringe 2010). For all these reasons, it is commonly agreed that what becomes the most important incentive to be cohesive and united is the policy impact that membership in political groups, and in the EPP as the biggest group in particular, offers to national political parties and individual MEPs alike.

The detailed presentation of the Group structure does not seem to be necessary here. Instead a few points require particular attention. First, the Group's internal decision-making process and the relationships between its organs suggest that significant decentralisation and a division of responsibility are the defining features of the Group's functioning. The existing literature has already established, inter alia, that in all major political groups there is always an attempt to look for compromise. Outvoting is the last resort, and even a national delegation that is defeated in its course has the right to vote against the party line in exceptional circumstances when critical national interests are concerned, though it should inform its group of such an intention (Hix and Lord 1997). These observations were common to all the people interviewed for this research.

Second, most of the work on policy issues is done within parliamentary committees. If there is an agreement of Group members within a certain committee, then that matter will not even appear on the agenda of other Group bodies, including the Plenary Assembly (other than for the fact that the Plenary Assembly will probably be informed about an agreement within a parliamentary committee or the Working Group). In other words, it is unusual for the Plenary Assembly to discuss each policy issue even if the rules grant it such a right.

There is a widely shared belief that any problems should be solved as soon as possible and at the lowest possible level. Therefore, before a matter appears on the agenda of the Plenary Assembly (Group meeting), other responsible bodies must do their bit. If there is no agreement over a policy issue in the committee Working Group, then the matter becomes an issue for a standing Working Group such as the Working Group on Foreign Affairs. It is responsible for such areas as foreign affairs, security and defence, human rights, international trade, etc. Once more the Group members present in a working group attempt to reach a compromise (this time in the presence of other Working Group members from other committees and the Group Vice-Chair). Only if this effort does not lead to an agreement, is the matter sent further up, namely to the Plenary Assembly. In other words, Group members seem to share the belief that problem-solving should be held at the lowest possible level, though it is inevitable for some unresolved matters to move further up the ladder.

Group MEPs and officials explain that Coordinators are not appointed but elected by the Group members on the same committee. Juan Salafranca points out that Group Coordinators are elected not because they come from the biggest delegations, but because their colleagues on the committee respect them as being a good, effective person to be the Coordinator (Interview Salafranca, 9.07.2018). Others add that Coordinators "have always reflected the strongest characters of the group in the committees", but also point out that there are very different models of co-ordinating Group parliamentary work within the committees, that is that some Coordinators will be really 'co-ordinating', and others might be pushing hard to put certain issues on the agenda (Interviews Kaczmarek, 8.09.2018; Preda, 10.10.2018; Salafranca, 10.10.2018; Kalniete, 10.10.2018; Kamp, 3.10.2019). MEPs who have been sitting on a certain committee for a long time have greater chances of being elected, and those who were Coordinators in the previous legislature are quite likely to be re-elected.

Coordinators divide the files between Group members within each parliamentary committee, set the agenda in the relevant fields of the Group, but also of the parliamentary committees for the next 6-9 months in co-ordination with the Chair or Vice-Chair representing the Group within individual parliamentary committees. Overall, their role is both directed at organising group work internally, and negotiating with other groups.

As regards the situation concerning the nationality of Coordinators before and after the 2004/2007 EU enlargement, the 1999 European elections gave the EPP Group the largest number of MEPs since the establishment of direct elections in 1979. With 233 elected MEPs, the EPP had a safe majority over the Socialists' 181. The five largest national delegations (German, British, Italian, Spanish and French) amounted to 73.9% of the overall size of the Group (173 out of 233 seats). A few national delegations monopolised the positions of Group Coordinators on parliamentary committees. Most notably, out of 18 Coordinators in total, the German and Spanish delegations had both four Coordinators, while three Coordinators were British. The third biggest national delegation, the Italian delegation, with 34 MEPs, did not, in contrast, have any Coordinators on the parliamentary committees or even one deputy Coordinator. Conversely, the small Austrian delegation with seven MEPs had two Coordinators. This proportion looks even larger when it comes to comparing the number of deputy Coordinators by national delegation. The German delegation had ten deputy Coordinators, the British five and the Spanish four, out of 21 in total. After the 2014 EP elections, out of 18 Coordinators in total, Germany had 6, Spain, Poland, and the Netherlands 2 each, and a few others one Coordinator. Apart from a huge domination of the German representation (even though the overall proportion of the German delegation dropped from 22.64 to 15% of the total Group membership), again, there was not a single Italian member either as the Coordinator or deputy Coordinator, even though the Italian delegation amounted to 17 members (out of 221 members in total). Overall, some national delegations in the EPP are disproportionally over- or under-represented.

The question arises as to how the process of formulating EPP Group positions is designed? It seems fair to observe that this process depends at least on two interrelated group of factors: one related to the organisation and functioning of the European Parliament, and another to policy development without a direct link to legislative work. The first one is defined by the rules of parliamentary work. The key source of power is to be appointed as a Rapporteur for a legislative or non-legislative work package. While Rapporteurs should in principle draft a resolution which reflects the majority view in the Parliament, they still can drive the report onto the road they desire or choose points upon which the report will focus. Research has tested conditions under which the role of the Rapporteur is particularly important, and this concerns cases of early legislative agreements under the ordinary legislative procedure and under the consultation procedure (Costello and Thomson 2010). If the Group is unable to appoint its member as a Rapporteur, then it nominates a shadow Rapporteur from its own ranks to prepare the Group's position and negotiate with the Rapporteur in co-operation with the Group Coordinators in the relevant committee. Both Rapporteurs, shadow Rapporteurs and Coordinators report to the Working Group, and subsequently the Chair of the Working Group to the Group Presidency. An informal role played by the key personalities in the field of EU external relations cannot be underestimated. Each month the Chair of the Working Group on Foreign Affairs, and three Coordinators from AFET, DEVE and INTA meet in Strasbourg for lunch to discuss and make decisions on the most important elements of parliamentary work (Interview Saryusz-Wolski, 4.09.2018).

The basic framework on which the Group's legislative and non-legislative activities are built is the set of general priorities adopted every five years. These priorities reflect the input of each of the five Working Groups tasked with different policy areas. However, the most important novelty that marked the recent era are position papers, which are much more detailed than the general EPP Group priorities. When Manfred Weber became the Chair of the Group in 2014, he took a decision that a position paper should be prepared concerning the main subject of every Group Bureau meeting (Interview Kalniete, 10.10.2018). These papers are adopted in two readings, with a final adoption taking place during the Group meeting in Strasbourg. The interviewees commonly noted that these papers play an important role, not only in specifying concrete positions which can be presented to the public, but also because they organise the work within the committees by specifying the positions as well as the red lines the Group would not accept (Interviews McAllister, 10.10.2018; Kalniete, 10.10.2018; Preda, 10.10.2018).

The Group and its most important members in the field of EU external relations are systematically targeted by foreign embassies or parliamentarians from third countries. Examples are quite numerous, and they range from foreign diplomats and politicians calling to withdraw or lighten up the so-called urgencies (resolutions adopted every month on the most urgent cases of human rights violation in the world) to numerous meetings between foreign diplomats and selected MEPs (Interview Salafranca, 9.07.2018). Without much doubt, the members dealing with trade are systematically lobbied by various groups, and they treat this as a natural phenomenon (Interviews Fjellner, 16.01.2019; Quisthoudt-Rowohl, 29.11.2018). In the field of development policy, lobbying is less visible, although MEPs have regular contact with NGOs, who often contact MEPs to present their opinions, suggestions or even draft amendments to various policy documents (Interviews Preda, 10.10.2018; Kaczmarek, 8.09.2019).

Finally, one interesting finding concerns the relationship with the members of the European Commission. Apart from the standard routes of contacts between the EP and the European Commission, an important informal exchange channel exists along the lines of party families. This is particularly typical for bilateral contact between commissioners on the one side and Rapporteurs and group Coordinators on the other. All of them have working relationships with commissioners. According to some interviews, this relationship is much more fruitful if the commissioner and an MEP belong to the same party family (Interviews Preda, 10.10.2018; Kaczmarek, 8.09.2018, Saryusz-Wolski, 4.09.2018, Salafranca, 10.10.2018). This is related to a much wider problem of partisan co-operation across various institutions. A particular role in this regard is played by the extra parliamentary EPP, which is a political party at European level that facilitates this kind of contact by organising EPP sectoral Working Groups, to which it invites national MPs, MEPs, commissioners and national ministers if they belong to the EPP. Martin Kamp recalls that a particular effort to improve the co-operation between the Group and extra parliamentary party organisation took place once former Group President Joseph Daul became party President, and could understand the two types of party organisation (Interview Kamp, 3.10.2019). Nonetheless, the evidence regarding whether this co-operation matters is mixed, with some members acknowledging a role of the extra parliamentary party (Interviews McAllister, 10.10.2018; Saryusz-Wolski, 4.09.2018; Salafranca, 10.10.2018), and others being much more sceptical about it (Interviews Preda, 10.10.2018; Engel, 5.02,2019, Wenta, 25.09.2018; Fjellner, 16.01.2019; Kaczmarek, 8.09.2018).

### *EPP Group cohesion in matters related to the EU external relations*

Party positioning is a complex research exercise with different methods having their pros and cons (see Marks et al. 2007 for details). Scholars use various sources from party manifestos, speeches in parliament, attitudes of parliamentarians, and finish with their voting records. Here the EPP Group's internal unity will be analysed on three levels: the attitudes of national party leadership, the attitudes of MEPs themselves and the voting records in the EP plenary.

National party leadership

An overall picture of the political spectrum of the EPP Group can be shown by data on selected policy positions of national political parties belonging to the EPP Group from the Euandi 2014 dataset (Garzia et al. 2017). Euandi was a voting advice application created for the 2014 EP elections, and its dataset included policy positions of 242 parties from the EU-28. Thirty policy positions were coded on an ordinal, 5-point Likert scale ranging from completely agree to completely disagree. For our purposes, we have extracted the positions of EPP member parties, and selected two statements from the dataset relating to foreign affairs and security and defence policy. The result has shown a very high level of coherence between attitudes of EPP member parties on these two questions.

*Figure 4.1 EPP parties' positions on EU's defence and security policy (as of 2014)*

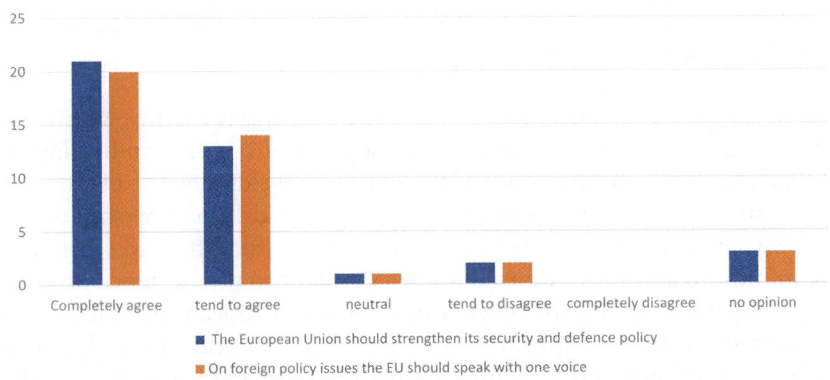


*Source: euandi dataset* http://euiresdata.eui.eu/xmlui/handle/123456789/23

A second group of policy attitudes will be extracted from the well-respected Chapel Hill Expert Survey, and the 2014 data release (Polk et al. 2017). Experts were asked to code policy positions of the party leadership in 2014 on a 7-point scale[9]. Based on this dataset, we can estimate party general attitudes toward the EU, EU foreign policy in general and Turkish membership (the last issue will be discussed in further sections).

9 1 = Strongly opposed, 2 = Opposed, 3 = Somewhat opposed, 4 = Neutral, 5 = Somewhat in favour, 6 = In favour, 7 = Strongly in favour.

Table 4.2 presents the mean position of EPP member parties on the variables measuring overall orientation of party leadership concerning EU integration, on EU foreign and security policy and on EU enlargement to Turkey.

*Table 4.2 Descriptive statistics on the selected policy positions of the EPP Group member parties*

| | Position on the development of European integration in general | Position toward the development of EU foreign policy | Position toward Turkish membership in the EU |
|---|---|---|---|
| Mean | 6.0785 | 5.862 | 3.9221 |
| Median | 6.4 | 6.0 | 4.0 |
| Std. Deviation | .91527 | .78672 | 1.04357 |
| Minimum | 2.71 | 3.0 | 1.73 |
| Maximum | 7.0 | 6.89 | 5.61 |

*Source: Chapel Hill Expert Survey*

The first variable measures the overall attitude towards the EU. While the mean values for all three variables are not that surprising, indicating in general a positive attitude towards the EU, the development of EU foreign policy and a much less enthusiastic stance on Turkish membership of the EU, what matters here from our perspective are the differences between the minimum and maximum values, which point to the existence of some sceptical parties as far as the overall position on European integration and EU foreign policy is concerned. For this reason, in order to analyse this problem in greater depth, Figure 4.2 below is a scatter chart setting the variable measuring overall support for European integration against the variable measuring party position on EU foreign and security policy.

*Figure 4.2 Scatterplot: the overall position toward European integration by the position toward EU foreign and security policy*

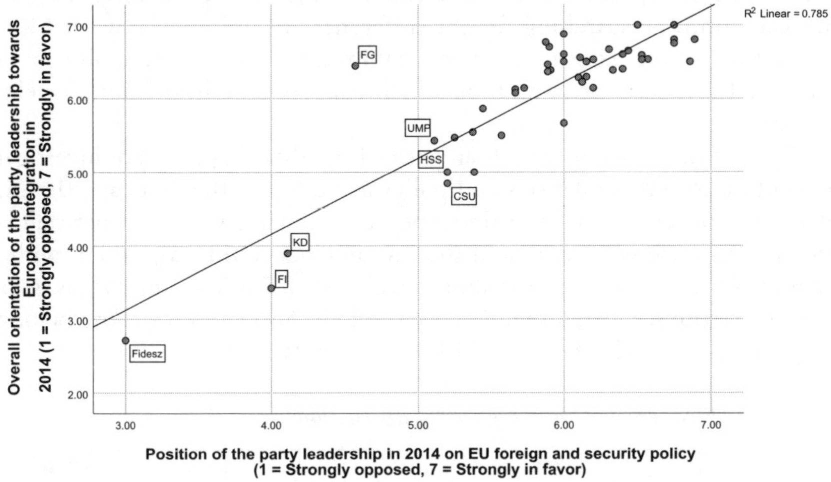


*Source: Chapel Hill Expert Survey*

The result indicates a strong positive linear relationship between the views on the EU in general and on development of its foreign and security policy. In other words, focusing on the EPP Group member parties, the more supportive the stance toward the EU in general, the more enthusiastic the opinion concerning the development of EU foreign policy. The outliers in this case are the Hungarian Fidesz (2.71), the Italian Forza Italia (3.41) and the Swedish Christian Democrats (KD) (3.90), which are responsible for the attribution of the small minimum values mentioned above. Without them, the minimum value for the variable measuring the overall position on the EU would be 4.85 (CSU).

## MEP survey data

This section is based on the 2015 European Parliament Research Group (EPRG) Survey, which was released in 2016 (Whitaker et al. 2016).[10] In the 2016 release, there were 37 respondents from the INTA and AFET commit-

10 Previous versions of the questionnaire did not discriminate respondents by committee membership, so they cannot be used here.

tees, 15 of whom were from the EPP and 8 from the S&D. Given the figures concerning committee composition cited above, these numbers are relatively low, but still worthy of deeper investigation, particularly because we can continue searching for the differences of opinion between MEPs belonging to the external relations committees and all remaining ones. The total response rate was 30%, which is acceptable in this kind of elite survey.

Two set of questions which are crucial for this chapter were investigated: voting recommendations and policy attitudes. In the first case, the survey question concerned the frequency of receiving voting recommendations from various sources, and the respondents could order them with a score from 1 (never) to 5 (for almost every vote). Table 4.3 below gives the average responses for all members of the EPP, S&D and for those belonging to committees in the field of EU external relations.

*Table 4.3 Frequency of receiving voting instructions*

| | **National party** | **Political group in the EP** | **National delegation** | **EP Committee** | **EU Commission** | **National government** |
|---|---|---|---|---|---|---|
| EPP General | 2.02 | 4.17 | 3.83 | 2.94 | 1.74 | 2.38 |
| S&D General | 2.02 | 4.30 | 3.57 | 2.80 | 1.64 | 2.07 |
| Ext rel gen. | 1.73 | 3.80 | 3.47 | 3.33 | 2.33 | 2.33 |

*Source: The 2015 European Parliament Research Group Survey*

Table 4.4 offers a more focused look at the within-group differences between members and non-members of the AFET, DEVE and INTA.

*Table 4.4 Frequency of receiving voting instructions (II)*

| | **National party** | **Political group in the EP** | **National delegation** | **EP Committee** | **EU Commission** | **National government** |
|---|---|---|---|---|---|---|
| EPP without EXT REL | 2.10 | 4.23 | 3.93 | 2.83 | 1.60 | 2.38 |
| EPP in EXT REL | 1.73 | 3.80 | 3.47 | 3.33 | 2.33 | 2.33 |
| S&D without EXT REL | 1.89 | 4.21 | 3.50 | 2.79 | 1.62 | 2.00 |
| S&D in EXT REL | 2.71 | 4.75 | 3.88 | 2.88 | 1.71 | 2.43 |

*Source: The 2015 European Parliament Research Group Survey*

Concerning attitudes about concrete policy proposals in the EPRG survey, out of five questions focusing on the field of EU external relations, three concerned TTIP, one EU foreign policy as a counterweight to the US, and one the relationship with Russia.[11]

Figure 4.3 reports the average scores for the following categories of respondents: EPP members from non-external relations committees, S&D members from non-external relations committees, EPP members from external relations committees, S&D members from external relations committees, and all respondents belonging to external relations committees.

*Figure 4.3 Policy attitudes on five topics of the EU External Relations*

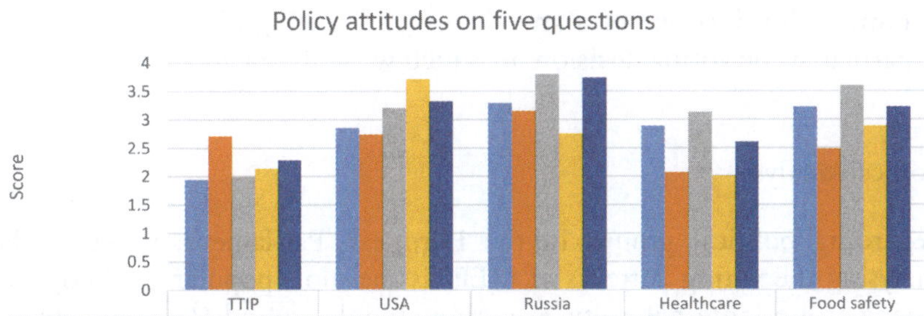


| | TTIP | USA | Russia | Healthcare | Food safety |
|---|---|---|---|---|---|
| EPP non EXT REL | 1.94 | 2.86 | 3.29 | 2.89 | 3.22 |
| S&D non EXT REL | 2.71 | 2.74 | 3.15 | 2.06 | 2.48 |
| EPP EXT REL | 2 | 3.21 | 3.8 | 3.13 | 3.6 |
| S&D EXT REL | 2.13 | 3.71 | 2.75 | 2 | 2.88 |
| EXT REL all | 2.28 | 3.32 | 3.74 | 2.61 | 3.22 |

*Source: The 2015 European Parliament Research Group Survey*

A few points can be made. First, the sharpest differences between EPP and S&D members not belonging to external relations committees are observed for the question of the TTIP, including its health care and food safety elements. However, differences concerning responses to the issue of EU foreign policy as a counterweight to the United States, and even more interesting, on the relationship with Russia are minimal. At the second level,

11 These questions were: The Transatlantic Trade and Investment Partnership (TTIP) will be beneficial for my country; EU foreign policy should develop as a counterweight to the United States; The EU should develop closer political ties with Russia despite concerns about democracy and human rights in that country; The TTIP should exclude healthcare; The TTIP should exclude food safety regulation. Respondents could give a score: 1 – strongly agree, 2 – agree, 3 – neither agree nor disagree, 4 – disagree, and 5 – strongly disagree.

we can assess the differences in the same political group depending on whether an MEP does or does not belong to an external relations committee. For the EPP Group, these differences are either non-existent or minimal for the general question on the TTIP, USA, health care, and somewhat greater for other questions. As far as the S&D Group is concerned, members of external relations committees are more positive regarding the TTIP, whereas at the same time much less positive concerning the question whether EU foreign policy should develop as a counterweight to the United States. Finally, when the members of external relations committees are concerned, we observe the largest, and quite significant, differences on the issues of Russia and health care and food safety issues in the TTIP. However, it should be borne in mind that personal attitudes of members is an important, but just one of many, factors influencing his or her decisions, in particular the voting decision, to which we will now move.

## Roll-call analysis

Regarding political groups in the European Parliament, it seems that analysing the voting patterns of MEPs is the most popular method of assessing groups' internal unity, even though only around 1/3 of all votes are recorded (the so-called roll-call votes), and despite the fact that there are certain methodological controversies surrounding them (Cicchi 2016). Despite the multinational composition of the major groups, different national sensitivities, priorities, viewpoints, etc., the analysis of roll-call votes has shown that major political groups have proven to achieve surprisingly high levels of cohesion, which oscillate between 80 to 90%. In other words, in 80 to 90% of the roll-call votes, MEPs present a united front. What is also striking is that the arrival of new members of the EP after the 2004/2007 enlargement did not affect the voting cohesion of the main political groups in the EP (except during a short initial period), as over time, new members started to behave quite similarly as far as loyalty or disloyalty to the group line is concerned (Bowler and McElroy 2015; Lindstädt et al. 2012). At the same time, over the years, the cohesion of the EP as a whole has gone down, which means that the policy positions presented in the EP became more heterogeneous. Scholars investigate the scope and reasons for disloyalty, offering a number of explanations, from those emphasising the salience of national issues impacting on voting behaviour (Costello and Thomson 2016; Klüver and Spoon 2015), to the proximity of various events, such as national or European elections (Koop et al. 2018).

For the purposes of this analysis, while still using the roll-call data, we want to check how coherent the EPP Group MEPs from AFET, DEVE and INTA are, and secondly, how members of the same committee vote in the plenary in relation to the EPP line.[12] This type of analysis will further allow us to see the distance (in percentages) to members of other political groups. All data in Table 4.5 is based on plenary roll-call votes from July 2014 to the end of January 2019 and was obtained from the EPP Group secretariat.

*Table 4.5 The level of agreement between the EPP Group line and members (in percentages) in relation to the EPP Group line*

| Commitee/ Group | NI | ENF | EFDD | ECR | EPP | S&D | ALDE | Greens/ EFA | GUE/ NGL |
|---|---|---|---|---|---|---|---|---|---|
| DEVE | 40.6 % | 31.4 % | 52.6 % | 81.2 % | 94.7 % | 73.0 % | 77.5 % | 56.9 % | 36.4 % |
| AFET | 36.1 % | 21.8 % | 28.2 % | 75.1 % | 96.3 % | 79.5 % | 84.2 % | 64.2 % | 31.0 % |
| INTA | 61.6 % | 30.7 % | 38.1 % | 91.0 % | 98.2 % | 86.0 % | 95.1 % | 52.3 % | 40.1 % |

*Source: EPP Group secretariat.*
*NI: Non-Inscrits; ENF: Europe of Nations and Freedom; EFDD: Europe of Freedom and Direct Democracy; ECR: European Conservatives and Reformists; EPP: European People's Party; S&D: Groupf of the Progressive Alliance of Socialists & Democrats in the European Parliament; ALDE: Alliance of Liberals and Democrats for Europe; Greens-EFA: Greens – European Free Alliance; GUE/NGL: European United Left – Nordic Green Left.*

What we see in the case of AFET, DEVE and INTA EPP MEPs is that the clear majority of them follow the Group line in plenary votes. These figures range from 94.7% in the case of DEVE members to 98.2% in the case of INTA members. In other words, in this regard, we do not observe any variance between these policy fields. This is not that surprising because

12 There are different methods of calculating voting cohesion. One of the most popular methods is the Agreement Index used by Hix et. al (2007), which estimates the degree to which MEPs vote together, considering votes in favour, against and abstentions, regardless of the voting recommendation issued by the political group. It ranges from 0 to 100. For example, if the voting recommendation of the hypothetical group composed of 100 members was to vote in favour, and all 100 members abstained, then according to Agreement Index the cohesion level would be 100. The measure we use here is used by the EPP Group itself and is different from the Agreement Index: the point of reference is the type of voting recommendation as specified by the decision of the group meeting. So, if the group line is, for example, to vote in favour, but all members of the group abstain, then in our measure the score would be 0, whereas for the Agreement Index it would be 100.

usually MEPs from the relevant parliamentary committees have the key voice over deciding the Group line.

The next important question concerns the distance from the EPP Group line to the members of other political groups. These figures give further evidence of the patterns of coalition building within the 8th EP term, but generally speaking they do fall within already established patterns known from the previous terms. This picture varies depending on the committee. In plenary votes involving the portfolio of INTA, we see quite a high level of agreement between four major political groups (EPP, ALDE, ECR and S&D). MEPs from the Greens/EFA Group agree with the EPP line in 52.3% of cases, whereas the remaining three groups (GUE/NGL, EFDD and ENF) agree with the EPP line in only 30-40% of cases. These coalition patterns are much less typical in the plenary votes falling to the portfolio of AFET or DEVE, where the distances presented by the four largest groups from the EPP line are much greater. In the plenary votes on AFET issues, the closest group to the EPP is ALDE (84% of agreement), and the farthest is ENF (21%). In plenary votes concerning the portfolio of DEVE, the closest group is ECR (81% of agreement), and the farthest is ENF (31.4%).

The problem with the overall roll-call figures is that while, generally speaking. they offer a good overview of groups' cohesiveness, they put some very important and some rather non-important issues into the same basket. In the 2014-2019 legislature, for instance, the portfolios of AFET, DEVE and INTA amounted to more than 1200 votes. For this reason, while widely consulting advisors in the EP, five of the most important votes for each of the three committees have been identified. The main criteria for selection were the high level of political controversy, the relatively high level of public interest, and the strategic importance of selected portfolios for the EU. The list of these votes is provided in the footnote.[13] Obviously, this selection can be criticised from a number of perspectives, but

13 INTA votes: A8-0009/2017 – EU-Canada Comprehensive Economic and Trade Agreement – approbation; A8-0175/2015 – Negotiations for the TTIP – Resolution; A8-0366/2018 – EU-Japan Economic Partnership Agreement – Approbation; B8-0607/2016 – China's market economy status – Resolution; A8-0236/2017 – Protection against dumped and subsidised imports from countries not members of the EU – Amendment 22.
AFET votes: A8-0194/2015 – Report on the review of the European neighbourhood Policy – Resolution; A8-0290/2016 – EU strategic communication to counteract propaganda against it by third countries – Resolution; A8-0316/2016 – European Defence Union – Resolution; A8-0045/2017 – Addressing Refugee and Migrant Movements: The Role of the EU External Action – Resolution;

these cases clearly stand out among the huge number of ordinary, routine votes. A few observations are suggested by this data.

First of all, the majority of these votes concerned resolutions, which are not a part of a legislative process. This illustrates yet again the non-legislative nature of parliamentary activities in the field of external relations. Second, not all these votes concern the texts for the final drafts, but rather amendments. In many cases, it is the vote on amendments that conditions whether certain groups will support the final text of the resolutions. Understanding their importance requires qualitative judgement and analysis, but it is commonplace knowledge in the EP that quite often political groups condition the general support for a given vote on accepting one or more key amendments. Third, even without detailed analysis of the press content and public opinion, it is evident that all five of the most important votes from INTA clearly overshadowed anything discussed in AFET, let alone DEVE (see further sections). This yet again confirms a very interesting development whereby trade issues, while being a matter reserved for specialists and big business until the year 2010, moved to the centre of political and public attention thanks to the importance of TTIP. Some of these votes will be recalled in the sections below, starting with the question of political conflict in the field of EU external relations.

### *The nature of political competition in EU external Relations*

For many years, political science literature was concerned with a question whether the European Parliament is a 'normal' parliament, and in this context, what 'normal' means. For some scholars, a negative answer to this question was related to the assumption that EP groups are not competitive and the EP, as such, is too consensual (Dinan 1999); or if they do compete,

---

DEVE votes: A8-0334/2017 – The EU-Africa Strategy: a boost for development – Resolution; A8-0338/2018 – Digitalisation for development: reducing poverty through technology – Resolution; B8-0390/2017 – The new European Consensus on Development – our world, our dignity, our future – Resolution; A8-0170/2017 – Report on the proposal for a regulation of the European Parliament and of the Council on the European Fund for Sustainable Development (EFSD) and establishing the EFSD Guarantee and the EFSD Guarantee Fund - Amendment 106; A8-0261/2017 – Decision to enter into negotiations pursuant to Rule 69c: Report on the proposal for a regulation of the European Parliament and of the Council amending Regulation (EU) No 230/2014 of the European Parliament and of the Council of 11 March 2014 establishing an instrument contributing to stability and peace.

then not along the Left-Right axis, but rather based on the national divisions (Moravcsik 1998). Around the early 2000s, a new wave of scholarship emerged, based on the analysis of the roll-call votes, showing that the Left-Right dimension is in fact the main predictor of the voting patterns in the EP (Hix et al. 2006). In the context of EU external relations, the crucial question that arises quite obviously is what could Left-Right politics mean in this policy field? So far this issue has been unexplored in academic literature (Kerremans and Reykers 2015).

## Foreign policy

Foreign policy is a special case with regard to political competition for at least two reasons. First, in many parliaments in the world, in what we would call 'normal' parliaments, parties do not compete that much in matters related to foreign policy. There is an informal agreement that, in order to safeguard major geopolitical and existential priorities in foreign policy, parties should stay united in the name of the national interest (Hill, 2003). Furthermore, except for major crises such as military intervention, foreign policy issues do not play that important a role in electoral competition and in elections in general. This logic could also be relevant to the European Parliament. However, what we must bear in mind is the specific inter-institutional context in which the EP operates (see previous sections), but also the fact that there is an informal coalition in legislative committees between the EPP and S&D (sometimes joined by other groups). Nevertheless, the MEPs Cristian Preda and Jose Ignacio Salafranca pointed out that precisely because there is not much, if any, legislation in AFET, political groups would want to highlight political differences along the Left-Right dimension. "We often have compromises in AFET and agree on major issues. But if we disagree, and decide to highlight our differences, we do not lose anything in terms of legislation" (Interview Preda, 10.10.2018). There is no doubt, however, that if there is a disagreement within both AFET and the plenary, as previous sections have shown, most likely opponents will be found in GUE/NGL, Greens and Eurosceptic parties.

Political competition is reflected on a number of levels. First, the legislative process could be traced in order to establish the degree of success. However, given the conditions of EP politics explained above, in particular referring to coalition politics, most of the time wide coalition building is necessary, which then results in the division of eventual success or defeat. Nevertheless, David McAllister provides a long list of examples of salient topics where the EPP Group managed to make its mark, including CFSP,

CSDP, Russia, Ukraine, Turkey, North Korea or migration. Second, a lot depends on the division of positions of influence within the committee, and the allocation of rapporteurships, over which political groups compete. David McAllister argues that, in the 2014-2019 term, the EPP Group "succeeded in getting by far the most important reports" in AFET, such as the reports on the relationship with the US, Russia, Serbia (which David McAllister treats as the most valuable report for any group due to the importance of Serbia in the Western Balkans), and Ukraine (the same logic used as in the case of Serbia, this time referring to Eastern Neighbourhood countries). By definition, a source of influence comes from the chairmanship of the committee, including the rapporteurship on what McAllister believes is the most important AFET report, namely on the implementation of the CFSP (Interview McAllister, 10.10.2018).

This keeps the question open as to what a Left or Right position would mean in foreign policy. A few examples can be provided to illustrate this case. The first observation instantly visible to anyone starting to analyse the role of the EP in foreign policy is that there is a geographic specialisation of MEPs, in other words, that they specialise in and concentrate on different parts of the world. Usually, this stems from geographical, cultural, linguistic or political proximity to the third countries. Typically, Spanish MEPs would focus on Latin America, those from Central and Eastern Europe on Russia, Belarus and Ukraine, the Italians on North Africa, the French on their former colonies, etc. This is visible, for example, both as far as various discussions in parliamentary committees are concerned.

All MEPs treat this as a natural phenomenon, although Jose Ignacio Salafranca tried to limit this specialisation in some cases so that a greater sense of issue ownership is created across the group. Nevertheless, an important question emerges about the consequences of this situation. For example, would Spanish MEPs stay united on the policies towards Latin American countries regardless of their political affinity? The evidence is quite mixed in this regard. In the Cuban case, EPP Spanish members and S&D Spanish members differ quite significantly precisely due to their different attitude toward the Cuban regime. This is a part of a wider, longstanding difference between the S&D and EPP on that question. For example, in 2015 an S&D delegation led by the group leader Gianni Pittella paid a visit to the Cuban parliament and government, supporting the strengthening of political and economic ties between the EU and Cuba (Euractiv 2016). The EPP, on the other hand, has always been much more reserved towards the Cuban regime, emphasising that EPP support depends on protecting human rights (EPP Group 2017d). The case of Russia is different because neither the Russian President nor his party are associated with any political families in Europe. There is, however, quite a visible difference as far as some examples of votes in the EP prove. This seems to be primarily related to an important role that MEPs from Central and Eastern Europe play in the EPP Group (Interview Brok, 10.12.2018; Salafranca, 9.07.2018; Kalniete, 10.10.2018). In the case of the vote on EU strategic communication to counteract anti-EU propaganda by third parties, which was clearly targeted at Russian influence without naming it, this partisan division between the EPP and S&D saw the light. Furthermore, EPP Group MEPs point out an unusually positive attitude toward Russia from various Eurosceptic and nationalist circles in the EP. This point has been also observed in the literature, whereby far-right parties, which usually present quite hawkish stances, soften their attitudes in this regard as Russian foreign security threats increase, which was the case for Russian action in Ukraine and the Crimea (Ishiyama et al. 2018). Overall, this phenomenon provides an opportunity to highlight partisan Left-Right divisions as far as relationships with third countries are concerned, and Russia is just one of many examples. The newly established contacts between Israel and some far-right European parties are particularly striking, which both sides use for their own strategic purposes (Pardo and Gordon 2018).

*Figure 4.4 Vote on EU strategic communication to counteract anti-EU propaganda by third parties (14 October 2016, (2016/2030(INI))*

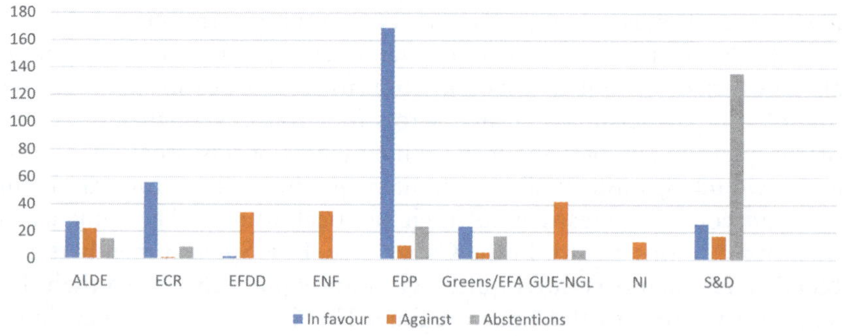


However, in some cases, there is an interesting phenomenon that if the party in government in a third country is somewhat related to one of the political groups in the EP (for example, being a sister party, or associated member of the political parties at the EU level), this then influences its attitude. To offer a few examples, the EPP members interviewed for this research (Interviews Saryusz-Wolski, 4.09.2018; Brok, 10.12.2018) confirmed that the EPP was particularly active in the release of the former Ukrainian Prime Minister Julia Timoshenko from prison, also because her party and she herself were EPP observer members. More recent examples concern an attitude of political groups towards the government in Moldova (with S&D members defending the leftist government in this country).

*Figure 4.5 Vote on European Parliament resolution on the human rights situation in Cuba (15 November 2018, 2018/2926(RSP))*

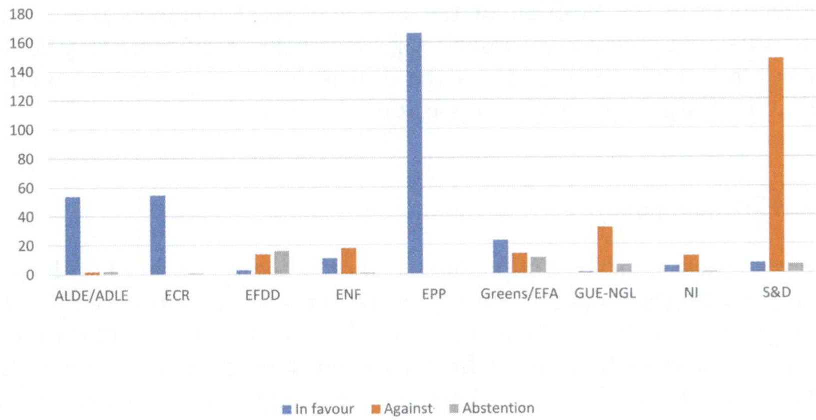


Nevertheless, one of the biggest difficulties in politicising this field relates to the long-standing problem of a lack of government and opposition dynamics in the EU (Gagatek 2009; Mair 2007). In this context, it is worth remembering that, both in 2009 and in 2014, there was an informal agreement to divide the major positions of influence in the EU between political families. As such, the EPP candidate became the President of the European Council and of the European Commission, whereas the PES proposed a candidate for the position of HR/VP. One could therefore ask whether the fact that both Catherine Ashton and Federica Mogherini were linked to the PES matters when it comes to shaping the relationship with political groups in the EP. In other words, did we observe a different approach by socialist MEPs to Catherine Ashton and Federica Mogherini in terms of their common political background? This question is quite difficult to answer due to the nature of relationships between the EP (and its AFET committee) and other EU institutions. Many cases, such as the dispute over the formation of the EEAS, have shown that the EP had to stay united vis-à-vis other institutions if it wanted to have an impact. Second, while Catherine Ashton was rather reluctant to engage with the EP and coordinate her activities with AFET from the very beginning of her mandate, Federica Mogherini showed quite a different attitude. Still, both received similar types of criticism relating to the lack of activism and a more passive stance than the EP expected. However, Cristian Preda points out that in his opinion quite often the EPP members were much more favourable toward Mogherini than the S&D members on such cases as the Middle East, or the relationship with Latin America, whereas Elmar Brok argues that "we are definitely much politer than the Socialists". Overall, while some differences in the position of the EPP and S&D members toward the HR/VP could probably be observed, it nevertheless seems that they do not play a major role, which shows the difficulties of organising EP politics based on the government and opposition dynamics.

## Development policy

Development policy is a different case, mostly because within DEVE there is a prevailing atmosphere of compromise and agreement between the major groups, which are united in their calls that the EU should do much more for development aid. Filip Kaczmarek even goes on to argue that there are so few differences between the groups that they deliberately search to identify some (Interview Kaczmarek, 8.09.2018). On major lines, this consensus also extends itself to the Commission and the Council, which was revealed during the work on the adoption of the European Consensus for Development of 2006, a joint declaration of the Council, the EP and the Commission[14]. In 2011, the EP adopted a report by Filip Kaczmarek MEP on how to maximise the impact of EU development policy (European Parliament 2011c). Among the key postulates were that development policy should be oriented towards effects and concrete results much more so than in the past; and that much greater co-ordination between the EU's and its Member States' development policies is necessary. These points also seem to gather universal support among the mainstream, pro-European political forces.

In its various policy documents, such as the position paper on the development policy adopted in 2015, the EPP Group would usually call for addressing "the root causes of poverty instead of treating the symptoms" and

14 OJ C 46/1, 24.2.2006.

framing it as "people-centred and rights-based".[15] Frank Engel adds that it should be results-oriented, most importantly in creating economic development in the targeted countries, at the same time "autonomising" them "in order to reach the point where development co-operation will no longer be needed" (Interview Engel, 5.02.2019). In an earlier document adopted in 2008, entitled "EPP-ED Development Chapter: 100 points for a better world", not only did the EPP present its own priorities, but also attempted to show aspects that distinguish it from other political groups. Those priorities that the EPP believed were (and still are) widely shared across the political spectrum concerned solidarity and human dignity as the cornerstones of development policy, accountability and transparency both within the EU but even more importantly in the countries receiving development aid, and good governance and effective administration as the key factors conditioning an effective use of aid from the EU. However, there were three major points that the EPP Group itself believed distinguished it from other groups. The first concerned its objective of encouraging "the enterprising spirit, including creating property ownership for the dispossessed". The second was about what the document calls "responsibility taking" on the part of the targeted countries. "Economic development is best achieved in a climate that encourages enterprising spirit and innovation and emphasises personal responsibility and initiative". The final and most visible difference concerned the protection of life and the desire to "work towards protecting life across the developing world".[16] Indeed, when studying various proposals for amendments to EP policy documents, or by analysing the debates in the DEVE committee or in the plenary, one reaches a quick conclusion that when political conflict emerges, it seems to be mostly about values such as abortion, sexual rights, and freedom of religion, rather than any concrete proposals for policy action, such as means to ensure access to drinking water. In the vast majority of resolutions concerning all parts of the world, in particular African and Asian countries, and observing not only the plenary votes but also various amendments put forward by the groups, the leftist groups would normally propose such topics and phrases as gender equality, sexual and reproductive health and rights, etc. The EPP is either fully opposed or at least does not understand why in various resolutions and development aid programmes such ethical

15 EPP Group Archives, C.8.162, EU Development Policy: Our world, our future, our dignity.

16 EPP Group Archives, C.8.98, EPP-ED Development Charter. 100 points for a better world.

and moral values should be highlighted to such a strong extent. This conclusion is quickly reached by analysing the content of the debates in the EPP Working Group on Foreign Affairs from 2010 to 2018, during which the EPP always took a stance to vote against the notion of sexual reproductive rights. Group representatives such as Filip Kaczmarek argue that this concept used by leftists in fact aims mostly at promoting the right to abortion in the targeted countries, which goes against the ethical position of the EPP Group, even if it must be acknowledged that the Group itself is becoming much more heterogeneous on these issues, too (Interview Kaczmarek, 8.09.2018). This is reflected in the fact that more recently there is no group whip on these matters and members can vote freely.[17]

## Human rights

Human rights promotion has become the main concern of EU external action. It is present in all spheres of action of EU external relations. EU policy in this regard faces a fundamental challenge between a norm-driven and interest-driven approach, or between idealism and realism. This division has its origins in a wider split between EU Member States, with some preferring the latter approach and others the former. The standard line of criticism is to point out that as far as human rights promotion is concerned, the EU is hard on weak states, and soft on strong states, or in other words, that it emphasises the human rights issue when it is cost-free, but forgets about it when it might bear some consequences (Kissack 2015).

Similar arguments have been voiced in the past against the European Parliament, despite the fact that the EP perceives itself as the main promoter of human rights of all EU institutions. And while there is a high level of consensus among the political groups about the goals, different sensitivities are clearly identifiable. Scholars observe that the highest level of activism in proposing various legislative and non-legislative proposals for human rights protection, often radical in its tone, came from the leftist political groups, namely GUE-NGL and Greens/EFA (Feliu and Serra 2015). The EPP representatives (Interviews Grzyb, 25.09.2018; Salafranca, 9.07.2018; Engel, 5.02.2019) criticise their proposals on the grounds of the fact that the vast majority of these parties do not and will not govern in their own

---

17 EPP Group Archives, B.1.4, Minutes of the Working Group on Foreign Affairs, 5.09.2017; EPP Group Archives, B.1.4, Minutes of the Working Group on Foreign Affairs, 5.12.2017; EPP Group Archives, B.1.4, Minutes of the Working Group on Foreign Affairs, 26.06.2018.

countries, which is completely different for most of the EPP member parties. The collective experience of governing brings a bit more of caution in building diplomatic relationships, including through the means of parliamentary diplomacy, which is alien to the majority of parties in GUE-NGL and in Greens/EFA. As Juan Salafranca puts it: we are principled about apparent violations of human rights in the world, but sometimes we consider the need to keep the best intergovernmental relations. Martin Kamp goes in the same direction when he argues that there is certain geopolitical thinking typical for the Group that conditions its repertoire of actions in this field. Along these lines, Elmar Brok (Interview 10.12.2018) criticises the instruments of the urgency resolutions which are overused by the radical groups in the EP and which interfere in the long-term building and maintenance of diplomatic relationships by the EU. Some other Left-Right divisions are also visible, and the above cited practitioners identify two areas as the key examples. The first is the attitude toward Russia, which the Socialists are traditionally less reluctant to disapprove of; and on the opposite side there is the case of the US, this time with the EPP less willing to criticise due to its treatment of this country as the EU's natural ally. The second case concerns Palestine and Israel, where the Socialists are more favourable toward the former, and the EPP toward the latter. Furthermore, a less radical attitude of the EPP stems from a different vision of linking external relations (in particular with regard to trade) with human rights promotion. Instead of sanctioning, EPP members argue that incentives would work much better than sanctions in helping developing countries not only to strengthen their economies, but also the quality of democracy and the rule of law (Interview Quisthoudt-Rowohl, 29.11.2018). However, all the interviewees argue that overall human rights promotion is mostly not about Left-Right divisions.

The most symbolic type of competition takes place in the way in which the Sakharov Prize for Freedom of Thought is awarded. The prize is named after a Russian scientist and dissident Andriej Sakharov and has been awarded to either individuals or organisations since 1988. The motion for resolution establishing the prize was submitted by the liberal group in 1984 and supported by all major groups except the Communists and the Regionalists. In explaining their opposition to the proposal for the establishment of this prize, apart from arguing that "this prize would therefore aggravate the Cold War and the ideological conflict between East and West", opponents also objected to the idea of awarding the prize based on parliamentary majority, rather than by an independent jury (European Parliament 1985a). Nonetheless, the proposal received overwhelming support.

Each year, major political groups or at least 40 MEPs nominate their candidates for this prize. Out of this list, the joint meeting of AFET, DEVE and DROI (an AFET sub-committee on human rights) assesses the candidates, whereas AFET and DEVE members shortlists three candidates, with the final decision about the awardee taken by the Conference of Presidents of the European Parliament (EP President plus the political groups' chairmen). Given that the Conference of Presidents decides by holding a vote, and that none of the groups have an overwhelming majority, coalition building is typical if one group wants the award for its own candidate.

By reading the minutes of the EPP Presidency and of the Working Group on Foreign Affairs, as well as listening to the key MEPs involved, it seems evident that the EPP Group treats it very seriously. In all cases every effort is made to ensure the EPP candidate gets the final nomination. However, most of the time, candidacies are supported by members of different political groups, so ultimately it is difficult to ascertain which group can claim the success. In some cases there is a wide coalition in favour of one candidate (such as in 1991, 1999, 2001, 2007, 2011, 2013), in others the divisions are much wider (such as in 1994, 2010) (Vaniomäki and Deschamps 2018). Since 2004, we observe a much greater number of awards for dissidents from former Soviet states such as Ukraine, Belarus or Russia (the Belarusian Association of Journalists, Aliaksandr Milinkevich, Memorial, Oleg Sentsov), proposed by MEPs from Central and Eastern European countries. Quite often the partisan lines are cross-cut along national lines. For example, in the campaign in favour of the candidacy of Oleg Sentsov, Sandra Kalniete encouraged EPP members to convince members from Central and Eastern European countries from other political groups to vote in favour of the Sentsov candidacy (personal observation).

## Trade policy

In trade policy, bearing in mind the previous analysis concerning the different legal basis and the nature of legislative activities in matters belonging to EU external relations, the Left-Right division is most apparent, where both in the EU and in the Member States, and with some degree of simplification, the Left means protectionism and the Right means free-market trade (Jančić 2017). In the EP, if we analyse the voting records, then the most free-market oriented group is the ECR, followed by the EPP (except for some French, Italian and Greek members), and ALDE. S&D seems to be divided into two halves, which was particularly visible in the 2014-2019 EP term. On the opposite side stand the Communists and

Green parties, with Eurosceptic members also mostly against the free market approach. At the same time however, an East and West divide becomes evident, with MEPs from Central and Eastern Europe being much more positive towards free trade than those from the West (which is mostly related to the position of French and Italian parties) (Frantescu 2016). Nevertheless, despite internal divisions, in the key vote on the continuation of TTIP negotiations, as well as the conclusion of an agreement with Canada, the EPP managed to stay united, whereas S&D was divided to quite a considerable extent. Similar pictures emerge from analysing parliamentary debates (Roederer-Rynning 2017).

*Figure 4.6 Vote on European Parliament resolution of 8 July 2015 containing the European Parliament's recommendations to the European Commission on the negotiations for the Transatlantic Trade and Investment Partnership (TTIP) (2014/2228(INI))*

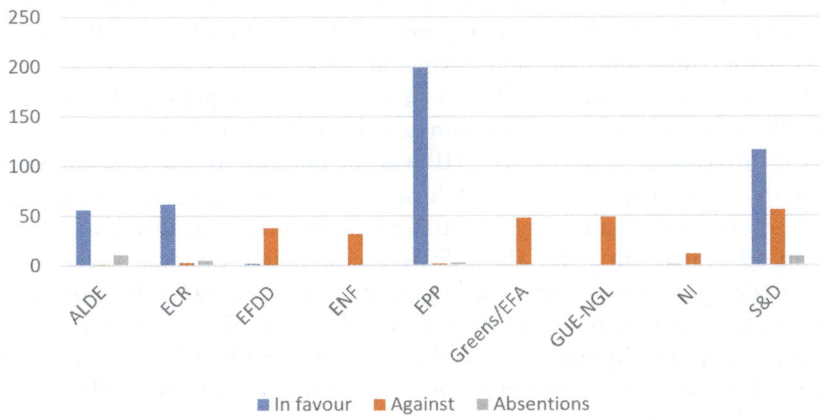


In its position on international trade, the Group presented a number of economic benefits from free trade and globalisation for both the EU and the world.[18] They mostly focus on the reduction of poverty, unemployment and on general economic growth, and refer to all signed agreements, in particular with Canada. The support for "a deep, comprehensive and mutually beneficial" TTIP is not only rooted in economic considerations,

18 EPP Group Archives, Strategie politique, Position Papers, 2015, EPP Group position paper on International Trade.

but also stems from the belief in the necessity of a strong transatlantic cooperation. Today, rather than focusing on removing obstacles, trade agreements promote and manage deep integration, not only focusing on markets, but also investments, financial services, competition policy, public procurement, intellectual rights, etc. For the EPP, the main obstacles hindering transatlantic trade lie in the existence of non-tariff barriers, such as different regulatory standards in Europe and the US. Here the EPP sees the greatest benefits of TTIP. At the same time, some sectors of the economy should be kept protected, proportionate EU trade defence instruments should be introduced, and in all cases special care should be paid to data protection. Responding to one of the main criticisms concerning the confidentiality of the TTIP negotiations, the EPP Group stated: "We want transparency and openness at all stages of the negotiations, but defend confidentiality where necessary to reach the best negotiating results". Godelieve Quisthoudt-Rowohl compares it to a poker game, asking whether players show their cards to one another. "Why do the negotiators have to show their red lines?" She also believes that the executive and the European Parliament have different roles to play, and the EP must understand it is not a negotiator (Interview Quisthoudt-Rowohl, 29.11.2018).

Due to space limitations, it is not possible to fully present the content and the process of trade negotiations on the TTIP. However, the most politically divisive element of the TTIP was the question of the Investor-State Dispute Settlement system (ISDS), which will be discussed in greater depth. It is a system allowing investors to sue governments directly in front of an arbitral tribunal for the infringement of international investment and trade agreements. From the beginning, the American side demanded that such a system was a part of the TTIP, which was also a default position of the European Commission. In the first vote on the TTIP in the EP in May 2013, even before the negotiations started, 78% of those who voted were in favour (460 in favour, with 105 against, and 28 abstaining), and at that time the EP did not even mention the ISDS (European Parliament 2013a, 2013b). However, public criticism of this proposal emerged rapidly soon after and with huge intensity. It was organised by a broad group of civil society organisations, which argued that the ISDS is a danger to democracy and sovereignty (Siles-Brügge 2017). More than three million signatures were collected against the TTIP in the framework of the European Citizens' Initiative. These developments led to a new political situation (Gheyle and De Ville 2019). Namely, the leftist political groups in the European Parliament, traditionally linked to these protesting civil society organisations, demanded to exclude ISDS provisions from the TTIP and instead protect investors through standard means of legal disputes existing in the EU and in the US. In 2015, the Rapporteur for the TTIP in INTA, a German social democrat Bernd Lange supported a proposal that investor rights can be protected without including the ISDS provision into the TTIP, through "a state-to-state dispute settlement system and the use of national courts" (European Parliament 2015a). Still, this proposal did not fully satisfy the Greens and the Communists, and they voted against it in the INTA Committee (28 votes in favour, 13 against, with no abstentions). This clearly represented the success of the EPP+ALDE+ECR coalition, although many of the opponents' amendments were carried out. Subsequently, a compromise amendment was put forward to replace the ISDS with a new system based on publicly appointed, independent professional judges and which included an appellate mechanism. Before the final vote, the Socialists hardened their stance arguing that they would not accept any kind of private arbitration (Vincenti 2015). The EP resolution finally adopted (61% of MEPs in favour, see fig. 4.6 above) called for a new, public arbitration system to replace the previously proposed extra-judicial ISDS (European Parliament 2015b), which later led the Commission to propose an alternative adjudicating system along these lines. This phrasing was supported by EPP, ALDE and ECR Groups, whereas the alternative amendments rejecting the ISDS provision in part or in whole were not carried out (European Parliament 2015d).

In its position paper, the EPP Group argued for a "modernised, transparent and impartial ISDS mechanism that would strike a balance between, on the one hand, ensuring legal certainty and the applicability of international treaties, and on the other hand, preserving the democratic legislative prerogatives of signatory sides" (EPP Group 2015a). Regarding the EPP's position on the ISDS, its Coordinator in INTA, a German MEP David Caspary argued that the new, reformed dispute settlement system "should not undermine the effectiveness of the ongoing system which ensures a good protection of our investors worldwide".[19] Regarding the 2015 EP draft resolution, despite the internal divide within the S&D, the support of at least some of its delegations was necessary to reach the majority. The EPP Group had three major objectives. First, to keep the text as short as possible in order to give a strong message of support; second, to make the text more positive, focus on listing economic benefits, and in particular, to avoid setting any new red lines; and third, to avoid the phrase proposed by the Socialists "without the use of ISDS private arbitration", the

19 EPP Group Archives, B.1.4, Minutes of the Working Group on Foreign Affairs, 21.04.2015.

meaning of which was explained above.[20] In the whole process, the EPP strongly supported the European Commission, and the then Commissioner for Trade, Cecilia Malmström attended the meeting of the EPP Working Group on Foreign Affairs in April 2015, thanking the Group for the support (EPP Group 2015d).

The EPP appointed Godelieve Quisthoudt-Rowohl as a shadow Rapporteur for the Lange report. In her opinion, the reason why the EPP managed to shape the TTIP resolution was that because, contrary to the Socialists, it stood united. That unity was carefully established during the preparatory work on the above cited position paper on international trade, which preceded the 2015 TTIP vote. This exercise helped to understand different sensitivities within the Group. Still, like in the EPP position paper, Quisthoudt-Rowohl identifies the biggest challenge for the EPP Group, which is to have a better communication strategy about the benefits of free trade to ordinary citizens, since "we are not populists and it means that our messages are balanced and more difficult to 'sell'" (Interview Quisthoudt-Rowohl, 29.11.2018). Christofer Fjellner MEP adds yet another explanation for this unity, namely the fact that having "very ideologically driven opponents" is a uniting factor for the EPP Group. Nevertheless, apart from the direction of trade policy, in which the EPP is unequivocally in favour of free trade, Fjellner identifies another difference relating to strategy. In his opinion, too often the Left focuses on everything but trade, while the EPP is mostly concerned with trade policy in a narrow sense. As an example, he cites the case of the free trade agreement with Morocco, in which the main preoccupation of the Left was not matters directly related to trade, but the status of the Western Sahara, which, as Fjellner admits, is an important issue, but it should not stand as the main focus (Interview Fjellner, 16.01.2019). This characteristic is similar to that typical of development policy, illustrated in the previous sections.

### *The role of the EPP Group in the process of EU enlargement: deepening vs. widening*

Since the 1990s, enlargement has been portrayed as one of the most important instruments of the EU's external relations (Hill 2002). First, by more than doubling its membership since the 1990s, and in particular, its mar-

20 EPP Group Archives, B.1.4, Minutes of the Working Group on Foreign Affairs, 02.06.2015.

ket and economic magnitude, the EU has risen up to one of the most important economic players in the world, able to increasingly affect the state of the international trade. Second, by offering prospects for membership to countries from Central and Eastern Europe, through its conditionality, the EU stimulated internal democratisation in these countries and the overall consolidation of liberal democracy (Johansson-Nogues 2015). In short, EU enlargement was perceived both as an instrument of stability and security-building in Europe and as a tool for further foreign policy influence and for the development of the EU's status in the world.

Despite acknowledging all the positive effects of subsequent enlargements, the question that appeared quite prominently on the agenda from the very beginning of the first membership bids was whether enlargement does not in fact negatively affect the prospects for further deepening of European integration, the latter understood to mean increasing the scope of the EU's authority. This debate has been commonly referred to as deepening vs. widening, and it has been present both in academic and political circles. Since the 1990s, many scholars have tended to argue that these two goals (deepening and widening) are incompatible and there is always a trade-off (see Laurent and Maresceau 1998). Accordingly, the EU can no longer integrate politically when it accepts more and more new members, particularly from countries from Central and Eastern Europe, commonly portrayed as both politically and even more so economically distant. However, other scholars such as Kelemen et al. argued relatively recently that in EU history expectations of an enlargement (widening) often stimulated institutional changes that in the long run led to deepening, in other words that deepening and widening could go hand in hand (Kelemen et al. 2014).

Similar kinds of concerns also characterised the EPP Group (see also Bardi in Chapter 5 of this book). The memoirs of Pascal Fontaine, Wilfried Martens and Hans-Gert Pöttering provide us with a detailed view on this topic. Throughout the 1990s, the leadership of the EPP Group had a clear stance of fully accepting membership applications but, at the same time, arguing that deepening must precede widening, and above all that widening cannot take place at the expense of deepening. Referring to the debate on the Treaty of Maastricht, the then Group leader Leo Tindemans said succinctly: "No expansion until we have a constitution for Europe" (cited in Fontaine 2009: 313). From this moment onwards, the Group consistently called for the necessity to prepare for subsequent enlargements by first making the institutional changes enabling the bigger EU to function effectively. That was a baseline argument of the whole Parliament in the 1990s. For the EPP, this set of reforms meant a federal structure based on the principles of solidarity and subsidiarity, with a constitution and a set of democratic institutions. One of the key demands was the introduction of Qualified Majority Voting (QMV) in the Council in a greater number of cases to avoid legislative clinches and the strengthening of the European Parliament. However, the final result in the form of the Maastricht Treaty was not totally satisfactory for the Group in political and institutional terms, namely that it did not go as far as the EPP Group wanted. This dissatisfaction was so strong that some EPP members even demanded postponing the enlargement until the necessary institutional reforms were implemented. In the internal vote held in the Group in 1994 concerning the decision on the approval of the accession agreements with Austria, Sweden and Finland, 77 members voted in favour and 23 against, the latter group protesting against the widening without what they thought must be the necessary deepening (Fontaine 2009). With this experience, while fully supporting the bid for EU membership from Central and Eastern European countries, the Group and the EP as a whole strongly advocated various institutional reforms in anticipation of this big-bang enlargement, which finally took place in 2004/2007. These proposals went along similar lines as mentioned above, pointing to the overall deepening of political and economic integration, and in particular to the strengthening of the EP's role. Neither the Treaty of Amsterdam and especially the Treaty of Nice satisfied the EP and the EPP Group, and the overall feeling was that the EU was not ready for enlargement from an institutional point of view (Martens 2008; Pöttering 2016). Yet the Group decided to support the Treaty of Nice arguing that it was better to have some, even imperfect, basis for the enlargement than not to have it at all (Fontaine 2009; see also Johansson in Chapter 2 of this book). Overall, the whole process shows that while the prospect of enlargement fuelled institutional debate, the overall result in the form of the Treaties of Amsterdam and Nice was far from satisfactory for the EPP Group. At the same time, rejecting the 2004/2007 enlargement in protest of the insufficient progress in political integration would be inconceivable for political and geopolitical reasons. Simply put, the value of the enlargement per se outweighed the concerns over the lack of institutional progress, thus making the widening possible without the expected deepening. Currently the Group advocates both widening and deepening at the same time, which for the former means creating a European perspective for the Western Balkans, and for the latter the call for an institutional conference (Interview Kamp, 3.10.2019).

Various debates and conflict concerning enlargement were traditionally held along national lines, rather than being a case for a Left-Right struggle. In these frameworks, some Member States traditionally favoured the narrative 'deepening first, enlargement (if at all) later'; whereas for others the enlargement was a tool for diluting the prospects of further political integration. The enlargement of 2004/2007 coincided with opening the accession negotiations with Turkey and Croatia, which took place in 2005, and opening prospects for membership to other Western Balkan states. Below the focus will be on one major case that best brings into fore the EPP intraparty divides, and the role it played in parliamentary and party-political activities, namely the case of Turkey.

### Turkish membership in the EU

The prospect of EU membership for Turkey has always created tensions. Turkey submitted an accession application in 1987. However, the EU did not agree to opening the accession negotiations, citing the low level of development and a very large population as the main reasons for the rejection, in addition to various issues concerning the rule of law, the right of minorities and the Cypriot problem. It was not until 1999 that Turkey received official candidate status, and in 2005 it opened accession negotiations. However, progress was very slow due to the Cyprus problem and the internal political instability in Turkey itself. Since the failed coup d'état in 2016, Turkey has left the road to EU accession, and the EP has called to freeze all accessions negotiations until Turkey stops repression. Nevertheless, common interests concerning the problem of migration and fights against terrorism keep both parts together (Türkeş-Kılıç 2019).

Political divisions and disputes on the question of Turkish membership related mostly to the position of national political parties, resulting from overall public opinion trends towards this issue, and included economic, ideological and in particular, cultural and identity-based considerations (de Vreese et al. 2008). Countries such as Italy, Spain, UK were in favour of Turkish membership and on the other side of the spectrum were France and Germany, among others, who proposed and promoted the concept of privileged partnership, that is extended economic and political co-operation without structural integration in EU institutions, i.e. the right to vote. Such a scheme was criticised for not offering much more than what Turkey enjoyed already, and hence was unattractive to Turkish political elites and society (Türkeş-Kılıç 2019). This position seems to be commonly attributed to the EPP Group, despite the variety of opinions on this matter within the Group itself. The developments in Turkey after 2016 concerning the massive repressions after the failed coup d'état have made the Group, and the EP as a whole, more united than ever in the opinion that

Turkish membership of the EU is unlikely in the near future (Interviews McAllister, 10.10.2018; Kalniete, 10.10.2018). However, that was not the case throughout the entire period since the early 2000s.

According to the Chapel Hill Expert Survey of 2014, as regards the positioning of EPP Group' national member parties, a clear split is observable, in which about 50% of EPP member parties are more in favour, and about 50% less in favour of Turkish membership of the EU. The median position is 'neutral', but the range of attitudes is quite high.

*Figure 4.7 Histogram illustrating the positions of the EPP Group member parties on the question of the EU enlargement to Turkey*

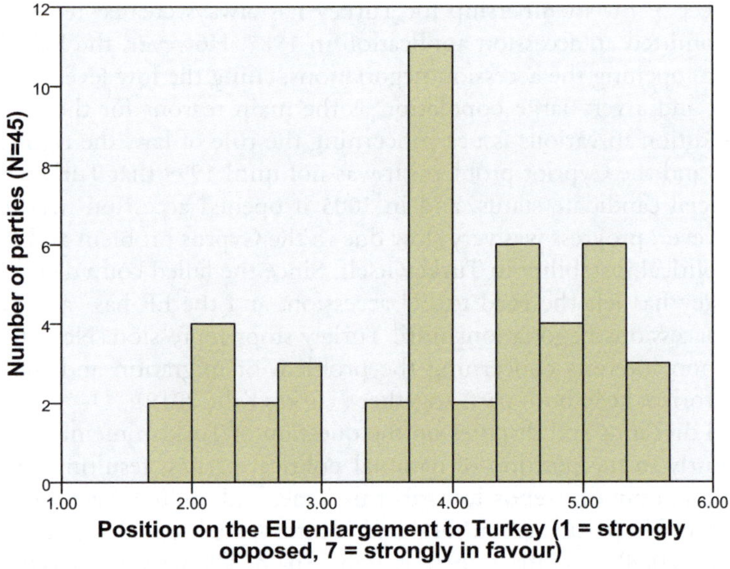


*Source: Chapel Hill Expert Survey (Polk et al. 2017).*

What is more, it seems evident that party attitudes on Turkish membership are not correlated with its overal stance on European integration.

*Figure 4.8 Scatterplot: the overall position toward European integration by the position on the EU membership of Turkey*

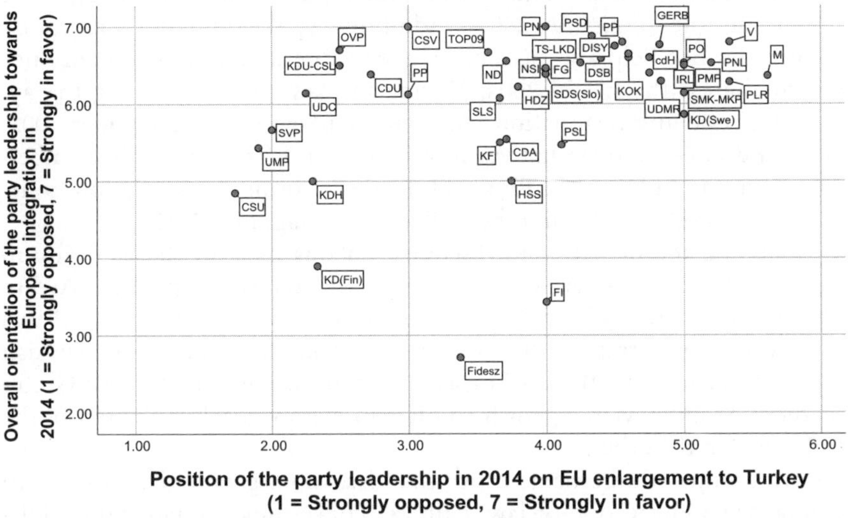


List of Abbreviations: cdH: Centre Démocrate Humaniste (BE); CD&V: Christen-Democratisch en Vlaams (BE); KF: Det Konservative Folksparti (DK); CDU: Christlich Demokratische Union Deutschlands (DE); CSU: Christlich Soziale Union in Bayern (DE); ND: Néa Dimokratía (GR); PP: Partido Popular (ES); UMP: Union pour un Mouvement Populaire (FR); FG: Fine Gael (IE); UDC: Unione di Centro (IT); FI: Forza Italia (IT); SVP: Südtiroler Volkspartei (IT); CDA: Christen- Democratisch Appel (NL); PP: Partido Popular (PT); PSD: Partido Social Democrata (PT); ÖVP: Österreichische Volkspartei (AT); KOK: Kansallinen Kokoomus (FI); KD: Kristillisdemokraatit (FI); M: Moderata Samlingspartiet (SE); KD: Kristdemokraternah (SE); SDS: Sayuz na demokratichnite sili (BG); DSB: Demokrati za Silna Baˇlgarija (BG); GERB: Grazhdani zaevropeysko razvitie na Balgariya (BG); KDU-CSL: K̆resťanská demokratická unie – Ceskoslovenská strana lidová (CZ); TOP09 (CZ); IRL: Erakond Isamaa ja Res Publica Liit (EE); Fidesz: Fidesz—Magyar Polgári Szövetség (HU); V: Vienot¯iba (LV); TS-LKD: Te ̇vyne ̇s sąjunga—Lietuvos krikščionys demokratai (LT); PO: Platforma Obywatelska (PL); PSL: Polskie Stronnictwo Ludowe (PL); PNL: Partidul Naţional Liberal (RO); UDMR: Uniunea Democratˇa Maghiaraˇ din România (RO); PMP: Partidul Mis ̧carea Popularaˇ (RO); PLR: Partidul Liberal Reformator (RO); SMK-MKP: Strana maďarskej komunity-Magyar Közösség Pártja (SK); KDH: Kresťanskodemokratické hnutie (SK); SDS: Slovenska Demokratska Stranka (SL); SLS: Slovenska Ljudska Stranka (SL); NSI: Nova Slovenija-Krščanska Ljudska Stranka (SL); HDZ: Hrvatska Demokratska Zajednica (HR); HSS: Hrvatska Seljačka Stranka (HR); PN: Partit Nazzjonalista (MT); CSV: Chrëschtlech Sozial Vollekspartei (LU); DISY: Dimokratikós Sinagermós (CY).

*Source: Chapell Hill Expert Survey (Polk et al. 2017).*

Pascal Fontaine recalls internal disputes within the Group on this matter since the 1990s, referring to a number of EPP Group study days devoted to this question, in which cultural and human rights issues played the most important role (Fontaine 2009). Additionally, the refusal to recognise Cyprus did not help and became an even more important problem once Cyprus joined the EU in 2004. During the key vote concerning the approval of opening negotiation talks with Turkey on 28 September 2005, S&D and Green representatives in principle supported Turkish membership, whereas ALDE and EPP stood divided, scoring unusually low cohesion rates (ALDE – 48%, and the EPP – 17%) (Braghiroli 2012).

Analysing the debates and discourse on this issue in the EPP Group since 2005, research has come up with the following picture (Aydın-Düzgit, 2012; Türkeş-Kılıç 2019). In the discursive rhetoric, the EPP was divided into two strands. On the one side stood the supporters of Turkish members such as the British Conservatives (until they left the EPP Group in 2009), Scandinavian, Spanish and Italian members, while the rest of the EPP were on the other.

Five groups of arguments drove the discussion: geopolitical, related to democracy and the rule of law, cultural, concerning human rights violations and finally, those pertaining to the potential threat to the integration process. The first emphasised the geostrategic importance of Turkey, its role as a NATO member, and the role it played during the Cold War and in the fight against terrorism, and at the same time presented Turkey as a bridge to the Islamic world. The rejection of Turkish membership would have negative consequences from the point of view of the clash of civilizations (Aydın-Düzgit 2012). On other hand, sceptics within the EPP Group argued that Turkish membership would create a security threat for the EU as it would bring it closer to such difficult spots as Iran, Iraq or Syria. The second line of argument revolved around the criticism of the quality of democracy in Turkey in contrast to European and Western standards, the portrayed clash between European 'individualism' and Turkish 'collectivism', or even to the issue of mentality. This argument was set against a belief that Turkey could change if it received help from the EU. The next type of arguments was related to a threat to European cultural identity. The fourth line, emphasised by the Greek and Greek Cypriot members, portrayed Turkey as a human rights violator. Another argument was to present Turkish membership as a potential threat to the project of European integration, and this argument was particularly vivid from the German and French members. Turkish membership would mean serious economic and financial problems for the EU, and with 80 million inhabitants, Turkey would become the most populated EU Member State, able to im-pose its views and even 'national identity' on the rest of the EU. On the other side, opponents argued that the EU would be able to accommodate Turkey institutionally and financially. What is more, for them, Turkish membership would strengthen their preferred model of European integration of sovereign nation-states, in opposition to a unified political system. Finally, many members argued that once negotiations had started, then the EU would have to keep its word and if all conditions were fulfilled, agree to opening new negotiating chapters, and ultimately, accept Turkey as a member (the pacta sunt servanda argument).

The problems of maintaining parliamentary and partisan relationships can be illustrated by two examples. The first concerns the role of the European Parliament in fostering relationships with Turkish parliamentarians through the work of the EU-Turkish Joint Parliamentary Committee (JPC). It has a long history of fruitful co-operation in parliamentary diplomacy. In principle, this committee should ensure socialisation mechanisms and serve as a forum for the exchange of views. However, this is rarely the case. First, this committee is disproportionately composed of MEPs who are very critical of Turkey from countries such as Greece or Cyprus, who for this reason dominate the entire discussion and set the tone of the meetings. On the other hand, due to sometimes harsh criticism of the Turkish authorities by the EP, in particular relating to the Armenian genocide and the Cyprus problem, Turkish authorities respond by mocking the EP, and accusing it of being biased against Turkey. This atmosphere translates itself to the work of JPC. Both sides were unable to agree on the agenda of these meetings, and the Turkish side tended to postpone them due to domestic political developments. Participants from the EP side interviewed by Gurkan reported a bad atmosphere and a lack of constructive dialogue (Gürkan 2018). Overall, Wódka (2016) argues that the activities of JPC can be only seen negatively, and the results contrary to those intended and expected, in particular through the de-Europeanisation of Turkish political elites.

Similar observations can be drawn from the process of bringing the Justice and Development Party (AKP) to the EPP as an observer member, which took place in 2005. During this time, both the extra- and parliamentary branches of the EPP started the process of contact, the exchange of views and political dialogue with the AKP. Wilfried Martens, the longstanding President of the EPP, recalls this process in his memoirs. On the one hand, direct motivation to invite AKP to the EPP as an observer member was that, according to Martens, European Liberals were desperate to bring AKP into their ranks (Martens 2008). On the other hand, observer membership in the EPP is usually the first step to more advanced types of membership offered to political parties from the acceding countries, and Turkey was soon to receive such a status. Since 2002, the AKP government made some visible progress on the road to democracy, and as such gained enough credibility as a political partner for the EPP. Both sides needed each other: AKP to legitimize its status both internally and externally; and the EPP, to bring into a family a strong political party from a very important political ally. The main question was whether AKP would be able to accept the EPP programme, in particular about its Christian democratic legacy. On the other hand, in the discussion on the Constitutional Treaty, the EPP pressed on inserting clauses confirming the Christian heritage of Europe, and additionally, that Turkey should become a privileged partner, but not a full EU member. This concept has always been rejected by AKP and other Turkish political parties. Finally, the EPP denied AKP full membership status by modifying its rules of procedure that only a party from an EU Member State could become a full EPP member. For all these reasons, in 2013, AKP decided to leave the EPP and instead join the Alliance of European Conservatives and Reformists, AECR (Wódka 2016).

## *Conclusion*

The empirical material gathered in this chapter allows us to come back to the research questions formulated at the beginning of this chapter. The first of them concerned the values, positions and goals of the EPP Group and the way Group formulates these. On major issues of external relations, in foreign policy (for example, the attitude towards Russia or the US) or trade policy (for example, positions towards free trade agreements with the US or Canada), the position of the EPP Group is clearly identifiable and seen as contrary to those presented by other mainstream political groups, in particular the Socialists. One of the explanations stems from the fact that in recent years the EPP member parties were in government more often, which created a sort of collective government experience that is familiar to all members of such governing parties, and which impacts on the policy choices and strategies of political action. The case is different for development policy, in which the consensus is so large that except for one or two issues it is difficult to pinpoint the exact distinguishing features of the EPP programme that would be different to other major groups. These observations should be treated with a necessary caution relating to the assumption that while the roll-call analysis proves a high level of internal unity, these roll-call votes cannot be taken as the sole and only indicator that could serve as the main argument for internal unity. For this reason, in this chapter we have also referred to other sources, enabling national political parties to be positioned over major issues of interest.

An important implication of this chapter is that overall the new members of the EPP Group from Central and Eastern Europe integrated with the parties from the West quite quickly. The common opinion inside the Group is that the way in which the members from the post-2004 countries were integrated and united is one of the EPP's biggest successes. Their distinctive role can be traced on at least two levels. First, somewhat naturally, their geographical and cultural expertise in Eastern Europe meant a much greater interest in this region for the whole Group than in the past. This is reflected in various concerns of these members, their policy proposals (e.g. the external dimension of the energy security) or in symbolic politics (through numerous proposals for candidates for the Sakharov Prize). On other hand, their membership in all political groups has caused another line of division as far as trade is concerned, with the members from Central and Eastern European countries generally speaking being much more positive about the benefits of free trade.

Concerning the process of policy formulation, while some aspects of group work are conditioned by the nature of the European Parliament, there are also some distinctive features. Indeed, this chapter has placed emphasis on the role of the EPP Working Group on Foreign Affairs, and equally as important but hardly noticed by wider audiences, the role of the committee Coordinators. Overall, we see a bottom-up process, in which members of one committee play a pivotal role in setting the agenda of the Group in the fields relating to their area of expertise. Internally within the Group, we see several co-ordinating mechanisms, including formal mechanisms, such as the Working Group on Foreign Affairs, and informal ones, such as lunches of committee Coordinators. Externally, there is a framework of communication and exchange of views with all institutions of the EU and other stakeholders. What matters in this case from a political point of view is an increasing number of cases in which the relationship between the EP vis-à-vis other institutions is organised and carried out in the first, informal phase by the members of the same party family.

How the Group tried to achieve its goals was the second question posed at the beginning of this chapter. Obviously some mechanisms and strategies are typical of all parliaments in the world: formal and informal politics, coalition building, legislative resolutions, etc. Bearing in mind some differences between national parliaments and the European Parliament, this chapter has presented these techniques based on the case of the EPP Group. Through the bottom-up process, the Group puts a lot of trust in its Coordinators and key members within the parliamentary committees, who are given an important source of power. Constant attention is placed on the question of internal unity, which is promoted by early exchanges of views and common discussions and compromise building on EPP position papers and other programmatic documents.

The third question concerned the impact of the EPP Group. The major difficulty in assessing the impact of any political group, in the case of this book on the EPP, is that it could be quite difficult to disentangle the impact of the EP in general and that of its political groups. The reasons are numerous and were presented in this chapter. They include structural factors (no stable majority), institutional ones (the atmosphere of compromise is all-pertaining), strategic ones (the need to unite all the groups to show the unity vis-à-vis other EU institutions and Member States) as well as the nature of EU external relations, which can be characterised in two ways. In normal cases, it is not electorally important, and second, it does not really include law-making in terms of adopting regulations and directives, which would make it easier to identify the impact of each group. This picture fully applies to the cases of foreign affairs and development policy, but it differs in trade policy in the fact that this policy has recently started to matter much more politically and electorally in at least some Member States. Nonetheless, depending on a qualitative judgement of the MEPs interviewed for this research, the impact can be measured by whether a group received an important rapporteurship or whether it succeeded in ensuring committee Chairmanships; in terms of policy impact, measured by the extent to which EPP priorities were carried out in the final version of EP's decisions; and last but not least, by the internal unity which reaches high levels despite the heterogeneous character of the group.

The new legislature of 2019-2024 will need to confront a number of challenges, from which the creation of the membership perspective for the Western Balkans seems to be most pressing and important. The debate on this issue has already started, with some countries such as France demanding to freeze the enlargement process and instead focus on the deepening. The EPP Group has continued to present a view that deepening and widening can go hand in hand, and that proof of the effectiveness of EU foreign policy will be clear from the case of Western Balkans. As far as development policy is concerned, during the 2019 election campaign for the European Parliament, Manfred Weber, the EPP Spitzenkandidat promised that once elected, he would appoint a commissioner for Africa, to boost relationship with the continent and at the same time help control migration. Given that Weber remains the EPP Group leader, we will see to what extent the relationship with Africa will become a priority for the Group. Finally, in trade policy under the Presidency of Donald Trump, any new progress on a EU-US trade agreement is difficult to expect; this topic is likely to remain high on the agenda.

# Chapter 5 The Heart of the Core: The EPP Group in the EU Institutional and Political Framework

*Luciano Bardi*

## *Introduction*

This chapter starts from the notion that the European People's Party (EPP) Group has had and still has a fundamental role in the European Union's (EU) institutional development, in its own right and as the main component in 'public office' of the EPP Party as a whole.[1] This is clearly visible in two very important respects. The first one concerns its role as the most influential, and at times quasi-hegemonic, component of the European Parliament (EP) party system's core. The existence of such a core, which also includes the Socialists and Democrats (S&D) and Alliance of Liberal and Democrats for Europe (ALDE) Groups, has long been accepted as being a strategically crucial asset for the strengthening of the EP's supranational character and internal cohesion. These characteristics have no doubt helped the EP grow in importance following increases in its formal powers and its political leverage vis-à-vis the other EU institutions. Secondly, the EPP Group has consistently been one of the driving forces behind all initiatives intended to extend the role and scope of the EU's institutions as well as of the EU itself. The very notion of the European party system core would be meaningless were it not for the role exercised by the EPP in its construction and maintenance. The understanding between the EPP and the other major groups has no doubt been the engine behind the EP's institutional progress, not only because of the impulse it has imparted to the extension of the powers of the EP, but also because of the system of rules

1 According to Katz and Mair (1993), party organisations present three different components, which they call 'faces': the party on the ground (the membership), the party in central office (the party's central organisation at national level), the party in public office (all party officials in government and/or in elected office). The development and integration of the three faces is necessary for the performance of party functions, especially those pertaining to the connection of citizens to the institutions.

and structures it has created that have permitted the EP's full development as an institutional actor within the EU.

The sheer size of the group and the quality and activism of its leadership have made it one of the main protagonists of fundamental EU advances over the decades, including the Single European Act (conceived and approved at least partially in response to Spinelli's Draft Treaty on the European Union of which the EPP Group was a strong supporter) and the decision to nominate Spitzenkandidaten in the 2014 EP elections. Notably, the outcome of this decision, which was shared by the other more important political groups in the EP, S&D, ALDE (now Renew Europe), the Greens/European Free Alliance (Greens/EFA) and European United Left/Nordic Green Left (GUE/NGL), was the appointment of the EPP's own Jean-Claude Juncker as President of the EU Commission, albeit without the support in Parliament of the last two political groups.[2] Moreover, throughout the important 'season of the treaties' (1987-2007), the EP political groups, and the EPP Group in particular, contributed to the succession of reforms as well as to the expansion of the EU's membership that occurred at the time by 'floating ideas' towards other EU institutions, certainly the Commission, but also the Council of Ministers[3].

This chapter focuses on: a) the role, growth and institutionalisation of EP political groups; b) the trajectory of the EPP's electoral strength in absolute terms and in relation to the other groups, the Socialist one in particular; c) the EPP Group's organisational strength and institutionalisation; d) its role in the institutional development and strengthening of the EP since its first direct elections from a merely consultative body to an institution with full decisional powers; e) its role in building and maintaining for the EP stable and fruitful relations with other main EU institutions, first and foremost the Commission but also the Council.

2 This latter action was deemed to have significant potential implications for the future politicisation of the EU political system, where by politicisation of the EU we mean the ability of the European dimension of politics to enter the mainstream political debate and to create a veritable political cleavage at EU level capable of introducing government/opposition dynamics in the EU party system. However, the appointment of Ursula von der Leyen to the Presidency of the EU Commission in 2019, albeit an EPP exponent herself, can be seen as a setback for this strategy, as she was chosen by the European Council at the detriment of the official EPP *Spitzenkandidat* , Manfred Weber. As such, her nomination was hardly the expression of a majoritarian party coalition within the EP.

3 On the EP's ability to exercise an informal power of political guidance and even legislative initiative, see section 8 below.

In general, the analysis is based on secondary sources, such as scientific articles and monographs, relevant reports commissioned by the EP and other EU institutions as well as publications of the EPP itself. But the most important and original part of the research in this chapter relies essentially on primary sources, including official electoral results, EP composition and membership data, EPP Group internal debates, policy positions, resolutions and declarations, debates, proposals, questions, amendments and votes in parliamentary committees as well as in the EP plenary. For the purpose of mapping the less formal relations between the EPP Group and other EP groups and EU institutions, we have interviewed selected EPP Group members or officials.

### *Political parties and political groups at EU level*

After the EP's first universal suffrage elections were held in 1979, most opinions expressed a positive association between universal suffrage EP elections and Europarty development (see for example: Herman and Lodge 1978; Marquand 1979; Pridham and Pridham 1981). Early approaches to Europarties often started from the simple consideration that elections are necessary for creating democratic systems and political parties, which are essential institutional foundations of democratic systems.

Most authors limited themselves to studying EP political groups (see, for one: Attinà 1990). It could be argued that this is an important limitation as it neglects other relevant party components, such as central and territorial organisational structures, which would correspond at the EU level to the aforementioned faces of party organisations in 'central office' and 'on the ground' (Katz and Mair 1993). The latter in particular are completely absent in the early Europarty literature, not only in empirical analyses, which is hardly a surprise given that such structures were for all practical purposes non-existent (individual membership in European parties is a relatively recent and still scarcely relevant development), but also in more normative works. In this case, the omission is more serious, if, as affirmed in the established tradition of these studies, Europarties should provide a link between European citizens and EU institutions, something that is not possible without party structures 'on the ground'. It was not until Regulations (EC) 2004/2003 and (EC) 1524/2007 defined the role of European political parties and the requirements needed for parties to become eligible to receive funding from the EU that non-EP-based Europarty components acquired relevance and visibility.

The transnational party federations, the structures that were created to co-ordinate party activities outside the EP after the 1979 elections, were undoubtedly very weak institutions in terms of territorial rooting, membership, professionalisation and financial resources (Bardi 1992, 1994). This was even true of the strongest ones, those of the Christian Democrats (EPP) and of the Socialists (PES). Both federations played an important role, above all in working out common positions for intergovernmental conferences. This somewhat overshadowed their increasing internal differences as both displayed decreasing levels of internal homogeneity due to the expansion of the number of national party delegations that followed successive EU enlargements and, more importantly, due to the parallel extension of membership to parties of diverse traditions. This was particularly true of the EPP-ED (European Democrats) which added a large conservative component to its original Christian-Democratic nucleus. The difficult growth of transnational federations and of the current European political parties can be explained by the lack of 'demand for Europe' from the base. Being aware of this, the basic national components of the European political parties find it more profitable to represent their electorates directly through exponents at the European level (ministers) than to strengthen their EU-level organisations. Currently, this is the main obstacle to the rise of Europarties that would be capable of effectively carrying out the representative functions at the European level.

Thus, EP political groups were, and to a large extent still are, the only relevant manifestations of party presence at European level.[4] Not only does focussing on EP political groups allow for the most relevant components of the developing EU party system to be observed, but it also provides a more accurate perspective for monitoring the progress made by European parties in the 40 years since the first direct elections of the EP (Attinà 1990; Raunio 1997; Jacobs et al. 2003).

Positive trends in EP political group consolidation were indeed observed during the EP's first five elected terms, but they seem to have suffered interruptions and even reversals because of less than positive EP elections results (Bardi 2002).[5] The fragmentation of the electoral arena, the very high proportionality of many of the 28/29 electoral laws contributing

4 European political groupings are present in the Committee of the Regions as well, but they are not nearly as important as their EP counterparts.

5 For an update of the last four terms, see Tables 5.1 and 5.2 below.

to this phenomenon[6] and the continuing expansion of the EU all provide possible explanations for these impasses. However, the most negative effects of EP elections can be ascribed to the absolute lack of interest national parties seem to have in giving them an effective European connotation[7]. Thus, EP elections can be very disruptive, especially for the more recent and smaller EP political groups, and hinder party system consolidation.

On balance, however, there is an overall positive trend in EP political group consolidation. With the lingering effects of the latest (from 2004 onwards) accessions and with the rising wave of various brands of Eurosceptic parties as well as, perhaps paradoxically, Brexit, it came as no surprise that in 2019 the party system structuring disturbances normally associated with elections sustained the trend exhibited in the recent past. Some of these, however, could be neutralised, as in the past, in the course of the legislature. On the positive side, momentous changes such as the ones witnessed in 2019 should be associated with a politicisation of the European political system, something which is also necessary for its democratisation.

### *EP elections (1979–2019) and the evolution of the EPP Group*

The last four EP elections were, in their combined effects, unprecedented events in the history of the Europarty system because of the sheer numerical impact of the new Member States' delegations on the existing political groups. Moreover, what can be broadly defined as qualitative differences between the newcomers and the longer established parties from the older Member States were greater than at any time in the past. Both types of differences have had an impact on Europarty development and on that of the EPP Group in particular. Whilst it might be too soon to speculate about the full consequences of the latter, it is possible to empirically study the effects on the former.

Our focus on the EPP Group does not only allow for the evolution of its institutional relevance and role within the framework of the EP to be assessed, but also for the strengthening of the party system at European level as well as its democratic impact on EU institutions to be monitored. The

6 Some texts report the existence of 29 different electoral laws in EP elections up until 2019 because in the UK two different systems were used respectively in Great Britain and in Northern Ireland.

7 This has changed only recently with the rise of sovereignist Eurosceptic parties that have finally put Europe on the EP electoral campaign's agenda, albeit antagonistically.

EPP Group, with those connected to the other two historical transnational federations, the PES and the Liberals (ELDR/ALDE), certainly constitutes the core of the Europarty system. The EPP Group's centrality has deep roots in the history of the EU. Perhaps more importantly given the focus of this study, its fundamental relevance is also evidenced by the party's electoral performance in the forty years of the elected European Parliament.[8]

The fortunes of any political group depend first and foremost on the ability of its national components to be successful in the EP elections that take place as separate competitions in the individual Member States. Other factors, however, have to do with structural variables and institutional/political dynamics that are not related, or are only partially related, to the formal competition to obtain seats at EU level. It can be argued that the evolution of the EPP Group, and, in relation to it, of its counterparts in the EP, has been strongly influenced by three sets of factors deriving from: the 'socialising effect' of EP membership on national party delegations and individual MEPs; the accession and incorporation of new national party delegations following EU enlargements; and strong fluctuations in national seat distributions that result from rule of the game or party system structure changes that have occurred at national level. As such, this last factor must be considered as something different to the normal up and down fluctuations in party delegation size that result from the ordinary adjustments in national electoral trends that do not produce changes in the structure of the party system but only in the relative size of some of the groups.

The first factor is widely recognised has having had an impact on the evolution of EP political groups and of the EU party system throughout the EP's elected history. It is well known that national party delegations and individual MEPs benefit from major political and institutional advantages as well as from better access to material resources if they join a political group, especially a strong one. Even national delegations that exhibit such peculiarities as to make them look like very unlikely coalition partners seek alliances that will allow them to benefit from group membership as soon as they are 'socialised' into the ropes of the EP system. At various points, this has created perhaps unexpected and even awkward associations, such as, in the first elected Parliament, the one between the

8 Even if the share of EP seats belonging to the EPP Group has declined rather sharply in the last three elections, it remains by far the EP party system's strongest political group.

French Gaullists and the Irish Fianna Fail, outflanked by Fine Gael in their bid to join the EPP, and the Group for the Technical Coordination and Defence of Independent Groups and Members, which included extremely diverse members and parties, most notably the Danish Anti-EEC People's Movement and the Italian Radicals. It could also be argued that it was this factor that brought large national parties, such as the British Conservatives and Forza Italia, whose values and ideals overlapped only partially with those of Christian Democracy, into the ranks of the EPP Group.

The importance of the second factor is almost self-explanatory: the size of the EP increased from 410 in 1979 to 751 in 2019, with fluctuations between 1981 (accession of Greece) and 2020 (Brexit).[9] It is more than reasonable to assume that the sheer magnitude of this increase (83%), and even more so that of the number of Member States (MS), which more than trebled (from 9 to 28) between 1979 and 2019, had a strong impact on the political and cultural homogeneity/diversity of the EP and a disruptive effect on the composition and relative size of the political groups when the new national delegations were incorporated. A similar effect, probably not as impactful but certainly less predictable, can come from the third factor listed above: strong fluctuations in the composition of national delegations in the respective EP elections, such as those caused by the transition from plurality to proportional representation (PR) in the UK in 1999 and Italy's earthquake election in 1994, which saw the rise of Forza Italia and the visible decrease of MEPs amenable to the parties of the previously dominant Christian democratic tradition[10].

The graphs in Figure 5.1 aptly illustrate the relevance and force of the EPP in the European Parliament and in relation to the other political groups. Each line traces the evolution of the percentage of seats obtained

---

9 The number of MEPs peaked at 785 in January 2007, after the accession of Bulgaria and Romania, and was reduced to 736 in 2009. In 2014, it was decided that the number of MEPs should be stabilised at 751. Subsequently, a reduction to 705 seats was decided upon because of Brexit, but the UK's failure to find an exit plan in time to avoid holding EP elections in the UK in 2019 voided this decision at least temporarily. The number of EP seats assigned in 2019 was still 751 and was definitively reduced to 705 only after the official completion of Brexit on 31 January 2020. As our general analysis is based on electoral results, all values in tables, charts and indices for the 9th EP term will be those based on the 751-seat distribution after the 2019 elections. However, where appropriate, reference will also be made to post-Brexit values in selected parts of the text.

10 A detailed analysis of the effects of the 1994 elections in Italy is provided below.

by the various groups in the nine universal suffrage elections that have been held so far[11].

*Figure 5.1 Seats percentages for EP political groups by EP term**

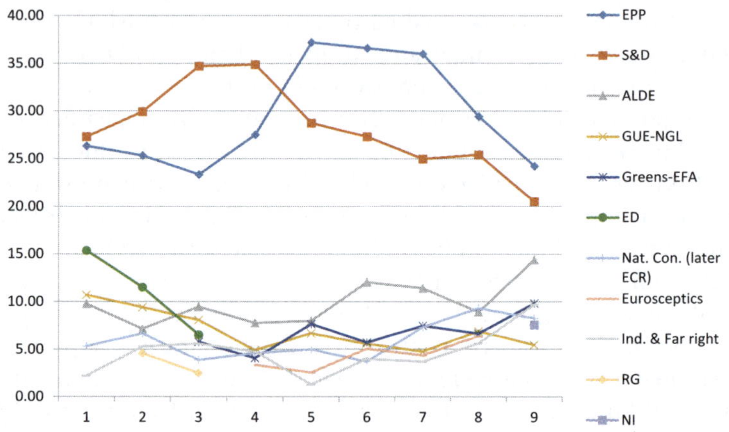


** EP Terms in this and all other figures and tables are as follows: 1. 1979–1984; 2. 1984–1989; 3. 1989–1994; 4. 1994–1999; 5. 1999–2004; 6. 2004–2009; 7. 2009–2014; 8. 2014–2019; 9. 2019–2024. Depending on layout, they will be listed also in numerical order (1–9) or by beginning of term date (1979–2019)*

| Political group | Abbreviation | Notes |
|---|---|---|
| European People's Party | EPP | Includes EPP-ED |
| Socialists and Democrats | S&D | includes previous denominations/acronyms (e.g. PES) |
| Alliance of Liberal and Democrats for Europe | ALDE | includes other denominations/acronyms (e.g. ALDE, Renew) |
| European United Left – Nordic Green Left | GUE-NGL | Includes COMM ALL from first 2 legislatures |
| The Greens European Free Alliance | Greens-EFA | |
| European Democratic Group | ED | from 1992 to 2009 part of EPP-ED |
| National Conservatives | Nat. Cons. | What today is ECR |
| Eurosceptics | | What today is EFDD |
| Independents and Far Right | Ind & Far right | Sometimes presented together, sometimes apart |
| Rainbow group | RG | |

11 Seat and not vote percentages are used here to trace the groups' electoral trajectories over time. Owing to the digressive proportionality with which seats are apportioned to different Member States, the latter are less accurate indicators of a Europarty's strength in the EP.

The EPP's share has been over 25% for most of the EP's elected history, with the highest average of all the political groups at 29.6% (see Table 5.1 below).[12] This fact alone makes the EPP Group historically the most important. But a more in-depth analysis needs to involve observing the evolution of its individual electoral trajectory over time, as well as looking at it in relation to that of the other groups, especially the most relevant ones. As has been mentioned, there is a tendency in the literature to stress the importance of the EP party system's core, represented by the combined size/strength of the EPP, the Socialists and the Liberals. The existence of the core is no doubt an important attribute of the EP and a crucial factor in its institutional development throughout its history. But any analysis of the EP's electoral history needs to focus even more sharply on the relationship and mutual positioning of the EPP and of the Socialists. This is not only because of the much greater size of these two groups in relation to all the others, including the Liberals, but also because of their oscillating fortunes that have seen them alternate in the number one position in the EP.

By contrast, the ALDE Group, the third leg of the core, has remained rather steadily at levels only marginally above or below 10% throughout its history. This has happened despite a rather troubled internal history and numerous changes in its national delegation composition. The group's relative positioning vis-à-vis the two larger ones did not change much in forty years, irrespective of its political importance, at least at times. The impact of the recent transformation of the French party system, however, might have created the conditions for more significant and lasting growth than in the past. For the first time, thanks to the successful bid of Emmanuel Macron's La République En Marche for ALDE membership, albeit making it necessary for the political group to change its name to Renew Europe, the European Liberals have a sizeable French delegation. This has given them their highest showing ever with 14.4% of the seats. This result notwithstanding, the dominant dynamics of the EP political group system is no doubt the relationship between the EPP and the S&D.

12 The exceptions were the 1989 elections, when the EPP got 23.4% of the seats, and the most recent ones in 2019, when it obtained its second worst result ever with 24.2%.

*Table 5.1 EP political groups seat % by EP term**

| EP terms | Political groups | | | | | | | | | |
|---|---|---|---|---|---|---|---|---|---|---|
| | EPP | S&D | ALDE | GUE-NGL | Greens | ED | ECR | EFDD | Ind. & Far Right | RG |
| 1. 1979–1984 | 26.34 | 27.32 | 9.76 | 10.73 | | 15,37 | 5.37 | | 2.19 | |
| 2. 1984–1989 | 25.35 | 29.95 | 7.14 | 9.45 | | 11,52 | 6.68 | | 5.3 | 4.61 |
| 3. 1989–1994 | 23.36 | 34.75 | 9.46 | 8.11 | 5.79 | 6,56 | 3.86 | | 5.6 | 2.51 |
| 4. 1994–1999 | 27.51 | 34.92 | 7.76 | 4.94 | 4.06 | | 4.58 | 3.35 | 4.76 | |
| 5. 1999–2004 | 37.22 | 28.75 | 7.99 | 6.71 | 7.67 | | 4.95 | 2.55 | 1.28 | |
| 6. 2004–2009 | 36.61 | 27.32 | 12.02 | 5.60 | 5.74 | | 3.69 | 5.05 | 3.96 | |
| 7. 2009–2014 | 36.01 | 25.00 | 11.41 | 4.76 | 7.47 | | 7.34 | 4.35 | 3.67 | |
| 8. 2014–2019 | 29.43 | 25.43 | 8.92 | 6.92 | 6.66 | | 9.32 | 6.39 | 5.59 | |
| 9. 2019–2024 | 24.23 | 20.51 | 14.38 | 5.46 | 9.85 | | 8.26 | | 9.72 | |
| Averages | 29.56 | 28.22 | 9.87 | 6.96 | 6.75 | | 6.00 | | 4.67 | |

*Consistently with what we have done for the first 8 elected EP terms, all entries for the 9th one in this and in the following tables and figures, will be based on the 751 seat distribution after the 2019 elections, and not on the 705 seat distribution after Brexit.*

For the first 20 years of the elected EP, the EPP Group was second only to the Socialist one. As positive as this result may appear, it was certainly disappointing for a group that had always been the strongest in the appointed EP from 1953 to 1974. It is true that the EPP's lead had been steadily declining and was reduced to just above 1% in 1974. However, for the group connected to the party responsible for the creation of the European Community (EC) to be overtaken by their Socialist arch-rivals in the first universal suffrage election was a shocking event, as revealed by many Christian democratic MEPs who participated in the first MEP Survey in 1983. The EPP Group was no doubt penalised by the absence in Denmark and in the UK, two of the three countries that joined the EC/EU in 1973, of Christian democratic traditions comparable to the rest of the existing Member States. In the 1979 elections, the EPP obtained no seats in the two countries, as opposed to the Socialists' 22, whereas in the third country, Ireland, both groups obtained the same result (4 seats). This caused a difference that was much greater than that produced by the overall electoral returns (6 seats), which saw the Socialists obtain 113 seats as opposed to the EPP's 107. The 1973 enlargement's effect was thus decisive for the Socialists' successful bid for first place in 1979.[13] In the first EP elections, the impact of the UK's accession on the mutual positioning of the two largest groups in the EP could have been even stronger were it not for the crushing defeat suffered in the UK by Labour at the hands of the Conservatives led by a triumphant Margaret Thatcher.

The difference between the EPP and the Socialists widened significantly in the next ten years marked by the 1984 and 1989 elections, a period during which three new Member States' accessions took place: Greece's, Portugal's and Spain's. In 1984, the Socialists obtained 20 more seats than the EPP, mostly because of a better showing (33 seats, 15 more than in 1979) of Labour in the UK. The accession of Greece's delegations did not produce significant changes in the positioning of the two groups, with the Socialists obtaining 10 seats as opposed to the EPP's 9. In 1989, however, the combined effect of the two Iberian countries joining the EC/EU was very impactful and the difference between the two largest groups in the EP increased to 59 seats when Portugal and Spain brought a combined 35 seats to the Socialists and only 19 to the EPP. At the same time, and for the first

13 This effect of the first accession of new Member States to the EC/EU had already manifested itself in the appointed EP after 1973 in the aforementioned form of a strong reduction in the EPP's lead.

time, Labour won the European elections in the UK, giving the Socialists 46 seats, as opposed to only 1 coming from the UK for the EPP.

The effect of the plurality electoral system used in Great Britain up until 1994 was in this case dramatic.[14] In 1989, Labour, with only 7.1% more of the popular vote than in 1979 (with an intermediate increase of 3.7% in 1984), obtained an increase of 36% in its share of the seats. The reversal in favour of Labour reached its peak in the 1994 elections, the last ones to be held with a plurality system in Great Britain, which were also marked by the increase in the number of EP seats to 567.[15] Labour obtained 62 seats, the largest number ever of any national party delegation, and allowed the Socialists to maintain the lead by 41 seats, even if for the first time a sizeable UK delegation (19 Conservatives) joined the EPP Group, which eventually called itself EPP-ED after the 1999 elections.

The 1994 elections were thus very important because they finally ended the absence of a significant UK delegation in the EPP at least temporarily. This event, certainly of great historical relevance, was somewhat counterbalanced by the disruption, caused at European level as well, by the collapse of most traditional parties, most notably the once mighty Democrazia Cristiana (DC), in the 1994 Italian elections. The void left by the near disappearance of the DC and its allies was at least partially filled by the birth of a new conservative (although ostensibly neo-liberal) party, Forza Italia, led by media tycoon Silvio Berlusconi. The Italian result noticeably reduced the size of the EPP's Italian delegation to only 12 members, from 27 in 1989, making it the fifth largest after having been consistently second only to the German one. According to many analysts, Forza Italia attracted many former DC electors and obtained a whopping 27 seats, the highest number in history for a new party and a number that was enough for it to form its own single-party EP group, Forza Europa[16].

This is probably the most important evidence of the potentially disruptive effect of revolutionary political/electoral developments at national lev-

---

14 A Proportional Representation system with Single Transferable Vote (STV) was used to elect the three MEPs from Northern Ireland. Thus, the analysis on the effects of plurality is only based on results in Great Britain.

15 This was the only increase in the history of the EP that was not caused by the accession of new MS, but rather by the need to readjust the relative size of MS representation in the EP following German reunification and the de-facto creation of the new MS size category.

16 Forza Italia's exploit was surpassed only when the UK Brexit Party, technically a new party despite being related to the UK Independence Party in many ways, returned 29 seats in 2019.

el. Not only did the Italian result deeply affect, in this case negatively, the overall showing of an existing political group, the EPP, but it also altered the EP party system's structure by permitting the formation of a new one. Conversely, the impact of the Italian electoral earthquake of 1994 was moderately positive for the S&D Group, as their ability to attract the 18 MEPs of the ostensibly post-Communist, but in reality Socialist-leaning, Democratic Party of the Left (PDS) more than compensated for the near-disappearance of the Italian Socialist Party (PSI), which obtained 2 seats, and of the Italian Social Democratic Party (PSDI), whose lone representative became part of the NI. In the end, the 1994 Italian presence in the S&D rose to 20 MEPs, up from 14 in 1989, and in total the S&D/EPP swing in the 1994 EP elections in Italy was of 21 seats in favour of the former.

This situation has dramatically changed in the last five elections, when the S&D's share of the seats dropped to under 30% in 1999 and exhibited a negative trend in the next two elections reaching a temporary low of 25% in 2009, rebounding only slightly to 25.4% in 2014 and sinking again to a new low (20.5%) in 2019. All in all, the S&D Group lost more than 14 percentage points in 25 years. During the same period, the evolution of the EPP's share followed a partially different pattern, one that allowed it to overtake the S&D and keep it at a safe distance, despite being marked by a similar declining slope (see Figure 5.1) in the last three terms. The decisive elections were the ones held in 1999, when EPP-ED MEPs were 37.2% of the total, up by almost 10 points from 1994, and the S&D's were only 28.8%. It is indeed in these elections that the EPP-ED obtained its greatest victory ever.[17] Despite a decline that was initially very mild and became rather sharp in 2014, as well as continuing in 2019, the huge advantage obtained in 1999 still permits the EPP to maintain the number one spot in the EP even after the ED split. Three potentially relevant factors were at play in the reshaping of the ratio between the EPP and S&D political groups between 1994 and 1999: the accession of Austria, Finland and Sweden in 1995; the merger of Forza Italia and of the French Rassemblement pour la République (RPR) into the EPP-ED; and the reform of the Great Britain part of the UK electoral system.

What needs to be stressed is that in both cases the changes were not due to electoral dealignment processes but rather the result of selected national

17 The EPP became the first group when it absorbed Forza Europa in June 1998. Our analysis however is based on election cycles and therefore we consider the 1999 election as the relevant one in this case.

political parties changing alliance strategies at European level. The other side of the coin in these cases was the willingness/ability of the European Parties and their EP groups to accept new national delegations, often coming from different ideological, cultural and even value traditions from those of the original party family's core. With the inclusion of Forza Italia and RPR, for example, the EPP-ED's composition shifted rather sharply in the direction of its conservative/moderate secular component that accounted for 126 MEPs as opposed to only 107 that were properly Christian democratic. This trend of course had begun in 1984 with the accession of Greece into the EU and of New Democracy into the EPP, had continued with the inclusion of Spain's Alianza Popular (AP) in 1989 and reached its symbolic peak with the acceptance of the British Conservatives in 1994. The first factor did not have much of an impact, as the three new accession countries brought a combined 19 and 16 seats to the EPP-ED and to the S&D respectively. This small difference was certainly not due to structural differences but rather resulted from normal electoral contingencies, as demonstrated by the fact that in the subsequent 2004 elections the three countries returned an equal number of seats (15) to both groups. Forza Italia's contribution to the EPP-ED was, on the other hand, very significant, as its 22 MEPs decisively contributed to the Italian delegation within the group returning to habitual levels (34 MEPs in total). As the Italian Socialists dropped by one unit, the effect of the 1994 swing was more than compensated for, with 23 seats in favour of the EPP-ED this time. The contribution coming from the two French delegations was also significant: a total of 21 seats, 12 of which came from the RPR and 9 from François Bayrou's Union pour la Démocratie Française.

Finally, the introduction of PR in the UK coincided with Labour's defeat and loss of seats not only at the hands of the Conservatives, but also at those of the Liberal Democrats and of other smaller parties. Whilst the reform might have actually mitigated the net effect of the vote swing in favour of the Conservatives in 1999 (which no doubt would have been greater with plurality), the change created the conditions for the transformation of the UK party system at EU level from a two-party structure to a three-party and eventually four-party one, with the fourth party, the UK Independence Party (UKIP) taking the number one spot in 2014.[18] The disruptive swings between the Conservatives and Labour thus came to an end

18 The criterion for counting the number of parties that determine the definition of a party system's structure is their relevance: See Sartori (1976) for a definition of party system structure and for criteria of party relevance.

and the impact of UK elections on the relationship between the EPP-SD and the S&D was greatly reduced, being limited to normal up and down trends in voting behaviour that were more accurately reflected by PR than plurality in the allocation of seats.

The next four elections marked a maintenance of the EPP's primacy and showed its ability to keep its relative strength more or less constant, including in the post-Brexit 27 Member State EU, despite the objective difficulty for all EP groups to incorporate newcomers from the new accession Member States. Between 1999 and 2014, the number of Member States almost doubled (from 15 to 28) with an overall increase of 125 seats (from 626 to 751) in the EP. The EPP showed a remarkable ability to incorporate national parties and obtain seats in the new accession countries, always outdistancing the S&D by more than 30 seats in the new Member States (10 to 13 of them depending on the election) and obtaining between 33 and 42% of all seats allocated to them in each given election. Despite this undeniable success, the EPP Group declined slightly in 2004 and 2009, hovering between 37 and 36%, but increased its lead on the S&D to 11% due to the latter's drop to 25% (see Table 5.1). Actually, the slight decline in the EPP's share of seats in 2009 has to be considered a huge success as its main cause was the decision by British Conservative leader David Cameron not to have the party's 19 MEPs re-join what in his view had become a too pro-European EPP. This move was part of what turned out to be his ill-fated strategy to defuse the Eurosceptic drive (eventually towards Brexit) in the UK. In most other Member States, EPP parties performed very well and collectively outdistanced the S&D by more than 100 seats, something that had never happened in EP history.

In the 2014 elections, the EPP seat share experienced a more serious drop of about five points but this was not enough for it to lose its primacy despite a disappointing return to below 30% levels and the overall loss of 50 seats (215 vs the 265 obtained in 2009). The main threat to the EPP (and to the other established EP political groups including the S&D, albeit in a more limited measure) came from the rise of the sovereignist and Eurosceptic parties that emerged or regained strength across Europe in recent years and joined the Non-Attached (NI)[19] or the Europe of Freedom and Direct Democracy (EFDD) and Europe of Nation and Freedom (ENF)

19 The acronym conventionally used to indicate non-attached MEPs is the abbreviation of the French Non-Inscrits, probably to avoid confusion with alternative meanings to Non-Attached that NA has in English (Not available, Not applicable).

Groups. The difference to the S&D was reduced to only 30 seats in 2014 and 28 in 2019. However, the gap between the two groups has widened again to 40 (187 to 147) with Brexit owing to the S&D's loss of 10 Labour MEPs and the distribution of the seats assigned to other Member States.

### *The EPP Group in the European party system*

The analysis of electoral trends in the EP, especially that of the EPP Group, has evidenced the political groups' ability to absorb the national party delegations of old and new Member States, as they almost quadrupled (from 54 to 198) between 1979 and 2019. The figures in Table 5.2 clearly show the resilience of political groups, particularly those belonging to the EU party system's core, when facing potentially difficult challenges such as those posed by many successive enlargements. The EPP Group has had MEPs coming from all Member States in four EP terms out of nine, was short by one Member State on three occasions and by two on two, the aforementioned 1979-1984 term, when the group failed to find Member parties in Denmark and in the UK, and the current term.[20] The PES/S&D has been more successful at being present in Member States, reaching an *en plein* six times out of nine. Its failures were respectively due to the difficulties faced by a relatively small party like Labour in relation to the rather disproportional PR system in Ireland, where the PES/S&D got no seats in 1984, and due to the even more serious problems experienced by Socialist parties following the moderate wave that swept most post-Communist Member States in 2004, when the Socialists did not fare very well in general and got no seats in Latvia. The most disappointing result for the S&D came in 2019 when both their weaknesses were at play. In fact, in the current EP they have no seats, once again, in Ireland and in a post-Communist Member State, Czechia, this time.

20 After Brexit, the EPP Group eventually acquired delegations from all remaining MS when the additional seat attributed to Estonia (with the UK the other MS with no EPP representation in the 2019 elections) went to Riho Terras of EPP affiliate party Isaamalit.

*Table 5.2 Number of total Member states represented in the EP political groups by EP term*

| **EP groups** | **EP terms** | | | | | | | | |
|---|---|---|---|---|---|---|---|---|---|
| | **1979** | **1984** | **1989** | **1994** | **1999** | **2004** | **2009** | **2014** | **2019** |
| **EPP** | 7/9 | 9/10 | 12/12 | 12/12 | 15/15 | 25/25 | 26/27 | 27/28 | 26/28 |
| **S&D** | 9/9 | 9/10 | 12/12 | 12/12 | 15/15 | 24/25 | 27/27 | 28/28 | 26/28 |
| **ALDE** | 8/9 | 7/10 | 10/12 | 10/12 | 10/15 | 20/25 | 18/27 | 21/28 | 22/28 |
| **GUE/NGL** | | | 4/12 | 5/12 | 10/15 | 14/25 | 11/27 | 14/28 | 14/28 |
| **Greens-EFA** | | | 7/12 | 7/12 | 12/15 | 13/25 | 14/27 | 17/28 | 16/28 |
| **ECR** | | | | | | | 11/27 | 15/28 | 15/28 |
| **EFDD** | | | | | | | 12/27 | 07/28 | |
| **ENF* ID** | | | | | | | | 8/28 | 9/28 |

*Updated from Bardi (2008) from EP official sources*
**ENF formed in June 2015 by parties that were previously in the NI*

Remarkably, even the ALDE, penalised as they are in some countries by electoral thresholds that they find difficult to pass, are normally present in a majority of the Member States (more than three quarters of them in 2019). Our figures also indicate an overall positive trend towards greater inclusiveness by other groups such as the Greens and the GUE/NGL. Both have grown out of other groups that have a long history in the EP, the Rainbow Group and the Communists, after having gone through countless changes and even dramatic transformations. In general, they include fewer national components than the core transnational federations, but they have been able to attract, at least in the last few EP terms, member parties from at least half of all Member States.

The other two groups that are currently present in the EP have a much shorter history. As has been mentioned, the ECR was created in 2009 when the British Conservatives decided to leave the alliance with the EPP and found partners in 10 other Member States, a number that increased to 15 in 2019. After Brexit, the group continued to fare well as the relative weight of the departing British Conservatives, which had been reduced to a dismal 4 after the 2019 EP elections, had become negligible and was no longer decisive for the survival of the Group. The requirements for forming and maintaining a group have, on the other hand, been an issue for the EFDD and the ENF. Whilst it may be relatively easy for political groups to find 25 MEPs who wish to sit together in the EP, it is more problematic to draw them from at least seven different Member States. Both the EFDD and the ENF, especially the latter whose eventual member parties sat as NI for a year after the 2014 elections, had difficulties meeting the criteria. The EFDD was indeed disbanded after the 2019 elections, when its two main potential components, the UK's Brexit Party (effectively the replacement of the UKIP) and Italy's 5 Star Movement joined the Non-Attached. The ENF evolved into the Identity and Democracy (ID) Group.

Another interesting observation that the data allows concerns what appears to be the growing Europeanisation of EP political groups, as demonstrated by the relatively small size of the largest national delegations, at least within the five major ones. It goes without saying that the greater the distribution of seats across national delegations the more difficult it will be for strong national stands to emerge at the expense of more collegial, ultimately European, positions. Within the EPP Group, the German Christian Democratic Union (CDU)/Christian Social Union (CSU) contingent was always the largest, but its relative size declined from its initial and highest level of about 40% in 1979 to less than 16% in 2019.[21] This has certainly had an impact on the group's internal institutional balance and political orientation, aspects that will be addressed in detail later in a dedicated section in this chapter.

In 2019, the S&D's largest national delegation (the Spanish Socialist Workers' Party, PSOE) consisted of about 13% of the total, with the ALDE's being slightly more than 19% (due to the assertive arrival of the French party En Marche), the GUE/NGL's and the Greens' respectively about 15% (a level reached by four national delegations: France's, Germany's, Greece's and Spain's) and 34% of the two groups' total seats. In the latter case, the fairly high figure is due in part to the presence in the German delegation of four MEPs elected in four party lists other than the Greens who thus constitute 28% of the group. Interestingly, one of these MEPs, Damian Boeselager, was the only exponent of Volt, the self-declared transnational party, to be elected Europe-wide. The overall level of Europeanisation of the five more established EP groups as measured by this indicator appears to be rather reassuring, albeit fluctuating. Conversely, the other two groups' (ECR and ENF/ID) largest national contingents, the Polish and Italian ones respectively, have reached levels that are about 40% of the total, consistently with their sovereignist/Eurosceptic leanings or effective positions.

21 On the internal distribution of seats in the EPP Group between 1979 and 2009, see Fontaine 2009: 593-604.

*Table 5.3 The EPP Group in the Europarty system: indicators by EP term*

| Term | Nr. of EP political groups* | | NI MEPs plus Dominant-Party Political groups % | | S&D, EPP, ALDE Total Seat % | | EPP % of core at beginning of each term |
|---|---|---|---|---|---|---|---|
| 1. 1979–1984 | 8 | 8 | 33.9 | 19.6 | 63.4 | 64.5 | 41.5 |
| 2. 1984–1989 | 9 | 9 | 29.3 | 18.5 | 62.4 | 63.1 | 40.6 |
| 3. 1989–1994 | 11 | 9 | 20.8 | 11.4 | 67.6 | 77.8 | 34.6 |
| 4. 1994–1999 | 10 | 9 | 21.2 | 11.8 | 70.2 | 73.0 | 39.2 |
| 5. 1999–2004 | 9 | 8 | 1.3 | 5.1 | 73.9 | 73.5 | 50.4 |
| 6. 2004–2009 | 8 | 8 | 4.4 | 3.8 | 75.7 | 77.1 | 48.3 |
| 7. 2009–2014 | 8 | 8 | 5.0 | 4.3 | 71.7 | 72.2 | 50.2 |
| 8. 2014–2019 | 8 | 9 | 13.3 | 2.7 | 63.8 | 62.3 | 46.5 |
| 9. 2019- | 8 | - | 7.2 | - | 59.3 | - | 40,8 |

*Source: Luciano Bardi (2014) The evolution of the Europarty system after the 2014 elections of the European Parliament Directorate General for Internal Policies Policy Department C: Citizens' Rights and Constitutional Affairs Committee: Constitutional Affairs Catalogue N. QA-04–14 -943-EN-C- ISBN 978- 92 -823–6175–7 as adapted and updated from (Bardi: 2008).*

*Note: The first figure in each cell refers to the beginning and the second one to the end of the term.*

**NI counted as one group*

Table 5.3 includes values for three measures of the EU party system's institutionalisation. The fourth column pertains to the relative size of the EPP Group within the EU party system core and is not a proper indicator of the party system itself. It is included here as a measure of the EPP's hegemonic potential. The first indicator is the absolute number of EP political groups. Its operationalisation is self-explanatory and the purpose of its inclusion in the table is to give an initial impression of how the system's structure has evolved as well as to provide a yardstick for the assessment of all the other indicators' values. The second indicator is the sum, measured as percentage of the total, of all MEPs in dominant-party political groups or being NI. These scores are included in the table as measures of overall MEP resistance to being Europeanised. By definition, NI MEPs are resistant to being incorporated into groups with a clear ideological/value identity and, generally, with a European orientation. Dominant-party political groups are defined as groups where one national party delegation has at least 50% of the members.[22] The logical assumption in these cases is that the oversized national delegations will act very independently and will ignore or take little notice of the other smaller delegations' positions when they diverge from their own. As such, the Europeanness and collegiality of such groups is at least questionable. Finally, the third indicator, the total of the seat percentages of the three core political groups, is included to permit a direct assessment of the overall Europeanisation and consociational character of the EP party system, given the already underlined pro-European and coalitional propensities of the three EP groups in the core. All cells for all the indicators contain two values:[23] one observed at the beginning of each parliamentary term and one observed at its end. The comparison of the values in the individual cells allows for an assessment of the EP's socialising effect on MEPs and national party delegations during each term.

For a long time, the Europarty system has appeared to be on a path towards consolidation, despite what seems to have been setbacks in the 2014 and 2019 elections. This impression is still supported, but only partially, by the values of at least one of the indicators in Table 5.3. Considering the high number of national parties that obtain representation in the EP, the number of EP political groups has remained remarkably stable, with eight groups having been formed in 2019, as had been the case in 1979.[24] Some fluctuations took place between the second and the fifth EP term, but the number had stabilised at the original eight at the end of the latter.[25] More importantly, the party/EP-Group ratio has risen constantly over the years, reaching a high of about 27:1 in 2019[26], as compared to a low of close to 7:1 in 1979. The EPP has certainly been a champion of attractiveness and inclusiveness, having expanded the size of its national party delegations' membership from 9 in 1979 to 48 in 2019, by a ratio that is higher than the EP's as a whole.

---

22 In the past, these groups were defined as one-party groups (see for example: Bardi 2008). It now appears that 'dominant-party political group' is more accurate.

23 Except for the fifth column where only the beginning of term values are provided.

24 The NI are counted as a group in Table 5.3.

25 A new group, the ENF, which included many of the MEPs that joined the NI after the 2014 elections, was formed in June 2015 to raise the total number to nine. This is still an acceptable number given the number of national parties that have elected representatives in the EP.

26 There about 210 individual party identities (including independents from various Member States) in the current EP. This means that the average party size is 3.6 MEPs.

Thus, the political groups, besides being able to maintain a presence in most Member States, demonstrate an unquestionable capacity to incorporate new parties, irrespective of their provenance and distribution across Member States. This positive trend is confirmed by the other indicators' values only until 2009. The turmoil caused by the 2014 EP election results and confirmed if not enhanced by the 2019 ones in many Member States produced a return to values that are very similar to 1979's, especially for the Europarty system's core. The core had grown, even if not dramatically, from about two thirds, a level it maintained until 1989, to just above three quarters of the EP's total membership between 1994 and 2009, with some ups and downs. The 2014 elections marked a return to the 1979 origins, as the core shrank to less than 64%. Its further shrinkage in 2019 was probably one of the reasons why the procedure for the choice of the most voted *Spitzenkandidat* as the President of the Commission, which is far from being fully institutionalised, was not repeated in 2019, although it was clear that most Member States, notably Germany, were very eager to give the European Council back its primacy in the matter.

As part of this trend, the position of the EPP Group within the EU party system's core has also suffered a setback. In the previous terms, the EPP had always accounted for half or nearly half of all MEPs in the party system's core, making it the veritable driving force behind the EP's Europeanist nucleus. On average, the EPP Group boasted 48.9% of the core MEPs, an increase of almost ten points over the first four EP terms' average (39%). The 2019 results indicated that the EPP Group is now 40.8% of the core and returned it to levels that are very close to its pre-hegemonic phase. However, this result is mostly due to the increase of the ALDE in its new Renew Europe incarnation. The relative size of the EPP Group has even improved vis-à-vis the S&D and its leading role within the EP should continue to be of fundamental importance.

On the positive side, there is a near disappearance of dominant-party political groups, which were made almost impossible to constitute by the criteria for the formation of the EP's political groups, and a significant decline in the combined percentage of the MEPs that belong to dominant-party political groups or are NI since 1979. As positive as this trend may appear, it must be taken with a degree of caution, as it is sometimes counterbalanced by phenomena that are not exactly positive for the EP party system's consolidation. For example, in the eighth EP term the percentage of NI MEPs was reduced significantly from an initial 13.3 to 3.1% following the formation of a new group, the ENF, something that did not in reality reduce the EP party system's fragmentation or (in)stability. In fact, the ENF's transformation into ID and the EFDD's failure to reform in the ninth term had a dual effect: the downsizing, once again, of the party system from 9 to 8 groups, and, at the same time, the increase of the NI to their second highest level (7.2%) since the end of the elected EP's fourth term. The percentage of NI MEPs (3.8%) returned to more habitual levels following Brexit, when 30 British MEPs left the NI and the EP. Their number might be reduced even further in the future should the fourteen members of the Italian Five Star Movement be successful in their attempts to join one of the established political groups.

Finally, a contrast can be observed between post-election values and those registered at the expiration of each term. Generally, all party-system institutionalisation indicators' values are much more positive at the end of each term than at its beginning. As has been mentioned, this is to be taken to indicate a propensity by newly elected MEPs and newly accessed national party delegations not only to be socialised into increasingly accepting the rules of the game in the EP, but also, and more importantly, to become acquainted with and attracted by the material and political advantages to be obtained by playing by those rules (i.e. by making themselves attractive to existing EP groups, ideally strong and influential ones).

Overall, these findings, based on post-election and end-of-term data for the first eight elected EPs confirm the hypotheses suggested by the literature. The hypothesis that institutional and political pressures during the legislature favour inter-group co-operation and eventually foster group integration is indeed consistent with the data. At the same time, the hypothesis that elections can produce very disruptive effects on the Europarty system also appears to be confirmed, as is the one suggesting that 'external' shocks, such as enlargements or political/institutional changes (electoral laws, criteria for the formation of EP groups), can also be very significant. It might appear, however, that the 2004-2009 (as well as the Croatian part of the 2014) elections did not have a measurable negative impact on the Europarty system. The quantitative measurements of the indicators in Table 5.3 were in line with those of previous elections, when EU membership was much lower. It might be too soon, however, to discount the possible qualitative effects of enlargement. All countries involved had to simultaneously convert to democracy, develop free-market economies and pluralist societies, adopt full national sovereignty and meet EU conditionality criteria within a relatively short period of time. From this perspective, Europarties' efforts at pro-actively socialising the political forces of future Member States into the European mainstream had important implications both for themselves and for party institutionalisation as well as party system development in candidate countries. Paradoxically, however, the success that Europarties have demonstrated in attracting most of the new national party delegations might cause further slackening of their identity and cohesiveness. It is still unclear, in fact, whether such efforts have been able to overcome differences in the cultural and value cleavages expressed and articulated in the developing new Member States' parties and party systems. For these may well spill over into broader EU political processes with unpredictable effects on Europarty development.

### *The EPP Group's organisational strength and institutional relevance*

Despite the less than felicitous outcome of the 2014 and 2019 elections, the EPP Group can be considered the most important, electorally and politically, in the 40-year history of the elected European Parliament. Even when it was second, in terms of numerical strength, to the Socialist Group, the EPP was extremely influential, owing to its cohesiveness and almost hegemonic ability to build strategic coalitions as well as ad hoc alliances with the aim of reaching specific objectives.

In the exercise of this role, not only has the EPP Group demonstrated cohesiveness and political strength, but it has also developed a more than significant institutional presence in its own right. The narrative description of the role and positions held by EPP exponents during the first eight elected terms of the EP would be very lengthy. For the sake of synthesis and hopefully also of analytical effectiveness and clarity, we have developed an Institutional Relevance (IR) index.[27] Table A1 in the Appendix includes the list of the relevant institutional positions and the scores that we have attributed to each position or category.[28]

---

27 The purpose of the index is to provide a synthetic measure, comparable across political groups and over time, of the groups' institutional success in the EP or lack thereof. The index is calculated by attributing different weights to different institutional positions in the EP. Such weights are then treated as points to be added together to determine the total score for each group. The index is then obtained by dividing any given group's score by the total of all the scores calculated for all political groups. Each group's index is thus the percentage of the total of all the EP political groups' scores. For the weighting of institutional positions in the EP, see table A1 in the Appendix. For the scores obtained by the political groups in institutional categories, see tables A4-A8 in the Appendix.

28 The scores have been determined by consulting expert academics and practitioners. This method should have permitted us to limit the arbitrariness of our choices. In any event, the data produced in this way can be used for diachronic and comparative analyses even if the absolute values remain arbitrary, especially if we consider that the values calculated are percentages of the total possible scores. As

In any given parliament it would be reasonable to assume that the relative size of a political group would be a decisive factor in its ability to secure important institutional positions and that the largest groups should have the highest IR values, whereas the smaller groups should have the lowest ones. In the EP, this assumption is comforted by the informal understanding amongst the groups that institutional positions are allocated according to an adapted form of the d'Hondt method of seat apportionment widely used in PR electoral systems (Poptcheva 2016). Thus, the number of positions attributed to the groups is proportional to their numerical strength in the EP, with the degree of distortion in favour of the larger groups that is typical of d'Hondt. The d'Hondt method allows for proportional allocation and, to an extent, also qualitatively relevant distribution of the number of institutional positions across the groups. Political considerations and power struggles can come into play to occasionally alter the mathematically determined distribution. In any event, however:

> The d'Hondt method ... not only allows the quantitative distribution of seats, but also their distribution according to an order of precedence, which is of particular importance where, for instance, parliamentary committee chairs and other leadership positions are distributed, enabling political groups to choose the posts of most interest to them according to the order resulting from the d'Hondt calculation. (Poptcheva 2016: 3).

As has been mentioned, the use of this method is not formally adopted in the EP's rules of procedure and

> the proportionality sought with this informal agreement among the political groups has to be confirmed formally in a majority vote for the election of the committee bureaux in the committees' constituent meetings (Rule 204 RoP). As a result, committee Members can still vote down a candidate for the chair or vice-chair from a political group that has been informally 'assigned' the post according to the calculation using the d'Hondt method, and choose another one, from either the same or another political group, during the constituent meeting. This was the case in the constitution of several committees in the ..., eighth, term, with the EFDD group's candidates losing the committee vote against candidates from other groups (Poptcheva 2016: 6).

---

such, they pose no problems for comparison. Tables containing all the IR scores we have calculated can be found in the Appendix.

This could imply that in the end a simple calculation of the number of positions attributed to each group would be a sufficient indicator of its institutional relevance. In fact, thanks to the d'Hondt method, the more important positions are also distributed proportionally, albeit with a precedence for the larger groups. The decisive qualitative difference is thus the attribution of the EP's Presidencies. Given the importance of this position, it was decided that the presidential term would last for only half a legislature, meaning that there have been 17 Presidencies so far in the history of the elected Parliament.[29] Being a monocratic position, the Presidency is the only one that is not subject to the d'Hondt method of allocation. The President is elected with the absolute majority of the votes cast in the EP plenary, a threshold that cannot be reached by any single group. The 'fairness' of the rotation of the groups in this fundamental office is then ensured only through understandings and compromises amongst the groups that are part of the core. It should come as no surprise that 16 Presidencies out of 17 have gone to the EPP (7), to the S&D (6) and to the ALDE (2). The lone non-core EP President, Henry Plumb (ED), elected in the 2nd half of the 2nd term, benefited from criteria that initially considered Member State as well as political group as relevant for the rotation. The decisive factor in his election, however, was a desire on the part of both the EPP and the ED to restore a more positive feeling of mutual trust after the misunderstandings that led to the election of PES/S&D candidate Piet Dankert in 1982 at the expense of Egon Klepsch (Fontaine 2009: 181; see also Wolfram Kaiser in Chapter 1 of this book). Be that as it may, the election of a non-EP-party-core candidate was an exception, never to be repeated in the next eight EP terms.

Figure 5.2 gives a very good initial empirical impression of the relationship between EP group size and institutional relevance, by providing clear evidence that it is a positive one. In statistical terms, this should mean that the two variables present a significant correlation. Figure 5.2 depicts the correlation between them in graph form. The graph very clearly illustrates the existence of a very strong positive relationship, which is also demonstrated by the very high $r^2$ value (approximately.87).[30] The graph also shows the existence of two very visible clusters respectively grouping the values for the two EP groups (S&D and EPP) that were hegemonic, albeit

29 There have been only 16 EP Presidents as Martin Schulz (S&D) served twice in the 7th (2nd half) and 8th (1st half) legislatures.

30 The range of $r^2$ values is 0–1 and.87 indicates a very strong positive relationship between the two variables. In other words, they co-vary, going up or down together at the same time.

*Figure 5.2 Correlation between EP political groups seat percentages and IR values*

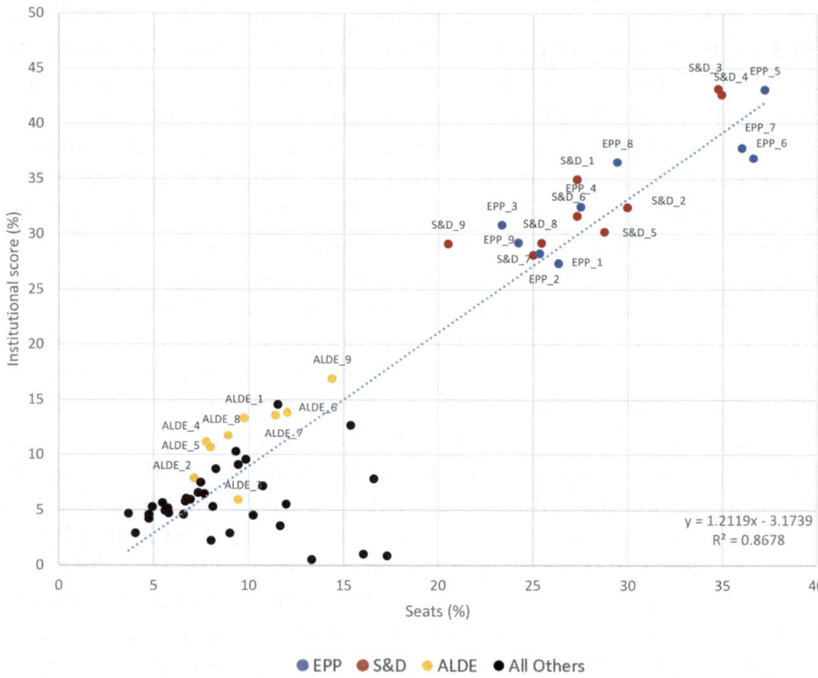


alternatingly, during the eight, prospectively nine, elected EP legislatures and all the other groups. Given its oscillating but generally not very positive fortunes, the ALDE scores cluster with those of the other, smaller groups and not with those of the two major core groups. However, similarly to those of the EPP and of the S&D, the ALDE scores all are situated above the trendline, indicating proportionally higher IR values than seat percentages. Thus, the graph confirms the advantage the three core groups have in the institutional rewards they receive, either for the sheer effects of the d'Hondt method or for the political weight they individually and collectively bring to bear on the allocation of institutional positions. Conversely, the groups belonging to the 'smaller' category are generally underrepresented, although at least some of them benefit from the fact that the NI are totally neglected in the allocation, which allows for some of their scores to be above the trendline as well, albeit at its low end.

*Figure 5.3 Institutional Relevance (IR) Index per legislature: trends for EPP, S&D and ALDE*

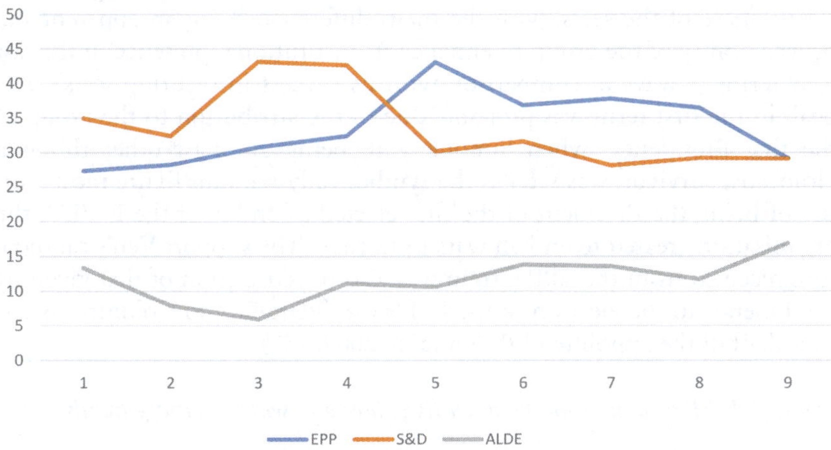


The graph in Figure 5.2 provides a general overview of the relationship between group size and institutional presence. Figure 5.3 allows for a more in-depth analysis of how IR values have evolved over time for the three groups that make up the European party system's core. As could be expected, the three lines follow patterns that are very similar to those that describe the trends in the seat shares of the three groups (see Figure 5.1). Particularly, the EPP Group's IR values are the highest for the last five EP terms and are lower than the S&D's for the first four.[31] This is a very similar pattern to the one observed for the distribution of seats over the nine EP terms. The main difference concerns the absolute level of the IR values, which peak at levels that are above 40% for the S&D and the EPP, as opposed to about 35% (S&D) or slightly above (EPP) for their seat percentage values (see Fig. 1). After the 2019 elections, the IR values for both groups have dropped under 30%, in keeping with the trends, but are still significantly above the levels of their respective seat percentages, especially for the S&D. The near equivalence of the post-2019 election IR values for the two major EP groups is essentially due the election of David Sassoli (S&D) to the EP Presidency. The fork between the two trendlines will widen again at the end of his mandate, in a more or less visible way de-

31 The EPP Group's value for the ninth EP term is very marginal and not visible in the graph (29.21 vs 29.12 for the S&D)

pending on whether an EPP exponent or some other group's exponent is elected.

The ALDE Group's IR index line also follows a very similar pattern as for its share of the seats, with the main difference being an apparent improved ability of the group to enhance its institutional presence in the last four terms (always in comparison with its success in securing seats). The peak in the first term was probably due to the attribution to the group of the first Presidency, when Simone Veil, being amongst other things a Holocaust survivor, was seen as the symbolically relevant figure most worthy of being the President of the first elected assembly of the EC/EU, the organisation created to end all wars in Europe. The support Veil's candidature received from the EPP Group was also in retribution of that given by the Liberals to the election of the EPP's candidate Emilio Colombo as last President of the appointed EP (Fontaine 2009: 157).

*Figure 5.4 EPP: comparison between IR values and seat percentage trends*

Figure 5.4 is intended to provide a detailed view of how trends in the EPP's seat percentage and IR index values have evolved during the eight EP terms in graph form. The most interesting observation afforded by the graph is that the IR values' oscillations are generally more pronounced than those of the seat percentages. As could have been expected from the previous analysis, the seat percentage line is in fact flatter and not just generally lower (with the exception of the 1st and 6th EP term when the two lines are very close or meet) than the line for the IR values. The relation-

ship between the two is not necessarily linear, as the institutional relevance of groups is only partially, albeit predominantly, determined by their electoral strength. It is striking that, after beginning at their lowest level ever,[32] EPP IR values went up for the next four terms, even if their share of the seats actually went down in the 2nd and 3rd EP terms. Even more puzzling is the pattern exhibited by the EPP's IR values in the last four terms, during which the oscillations in IR values caused the line to drop by more than 6 points so that it was very close to the seat percentage line in the 6th EP term. Whilst the relatively low IR score in the 1st EP term can be explained by the attribution of the Presidency to Simone Veil of the ALDE Group and, on other appointments, an unavoidable lack of experience in the brand-new institution, the drop in the 6 th EP term requires a more detailed explanation. It is true that the increase between the 4th and 5th EP terms had been exceptionally high. As such, a decrease in the 6th EP term IR value had to be expected. Moreover, the 2004 elections took place right after the largest enlargement in the history of the Union (ten new Member States). Enlargements should theoretically impact more on the distribution of seats and institutional positions amongst MS and not political groups, especially those that fared relatively well like the EPP. But it is plausible that the concerns caused by what appeared to be legitimate demands for institutional positions coming from so many new Member States' delegations in all political groups were met by the Group with a willingness to accommodate them (Interview Ryngaert, 5.12.2019). Even so, the magnitude of the EPP Group's IR drop appears to be beyond reasonable expectations.

It appears that, in all likelihood, this is one of those cases where the Group's institutional strategy in the EP was co-ordinated within the framework of the EPP's wider approach to the distribution of positions in all EU institutions. It was paramount for the party to have José Manuel Durão Barroso obtain the Presidency of the EU Commission and thereby ensure the Commission's stability. It is reasonable that in order to facilitate a coalition capable of effectively offsetting what appeared to be a serious challenge from the ALDE candidate, Guy Verhofstadt, the EPP Group took a less assertive position on the distribution of institutional positions within the EP for the elected term (Interview Ryngaert, 5.12.2019).

Finally, a closer look at the actual IR and seat percentage values can help to fine tune the analysis of the relationship between the two variables. Ta-

---

32 The low value in the 1st EP term is at least partially due to the EPP's failure to obtain one of the Presidencies during the term.

ble A2 in the Appendix lists the total differences between the three core groups' IR index values and their combined total percentage of seats in the nine EP terms. Given the importance of the Presidency and the weight we have accordingly attributed to it in our index, it is consequential that the sum of the three core groups' IR values is always higher than the sum of their seat percentages irrespective of the proportionality afforded by d'Hondt-based allocations for all other positions. Such differences are always positive by at least 5 percentage points and by more than 10% in five cases, the $1^{st}$, $3^{rd}$, $4^{th}$, $8^{th}$ and $9^{th}$ EP terms, with the $5^{th}$ falling minimally short of that level. The $9^{th}$ EP term is the one with the highest difference (16.11%). Whilst it would be inappropriate to try and identify a trend in such scores, it is definitely significant that they are always positive, indicating an ability of the groups that are stronger and better positioned in the EP to obtain an institutional presence that is greater than they could expect to have in proportion to their electoral performances, as well as beyond the mathematical advantage the d'Hondt method gives the larger groups. The very high increase in the core groups' IR/seat percentage difference scores in the $8^{th}$ EP term (13.69%, almost double that of the $7^{th}$) is particularly significant as it coincided with their biggest collective loss of seats (over 8%) in the elected EP's history. Perhaps even more telling is the fact that the further loss of seats collectively suffered by the three core groups coincided with their highest IR/seat percentage difference ever. In other words, the core EP groups lost almost no institutional positions despite a visible electoral decline. This is suggestive of the hypothesis that the core groups effectively reacted to the rise of Eurosceptic parties and groups by maintaining a united front and voting down would-be recipients of institutional positions from the new groups in the relevant committees' constituent meetings.

Individual group peaks (in terms of IR/seat percentage differences) usually coincide with their acquisition of Presidencies. Being that these rotate, what seems to be more important is the averages of IR/seat percentage differences for the nine EP terms, which are positive for all three core groups. As for the EPP, it is somewhat surprising that it only exhibits the highest difference of the three core groups three times, in the $2^{nd}$, $5^{th}$ and $8^{th}$ EP terms. Even in the $6^{th}$ and $i^{th}$ EP terms, when it greatly outdistanced the S&D in terms of seats, the EPP was unable to do so in terms of IR index values. One possible explanation for this is some form of path dependency that the S&D were able to establish during the first four terms when they were numerically stronger. Be that as it may, the primacy of the EPP should now be consolidated, including in terms of its institutional presence.

### *The EPP Group's internal organisational structuring and inter-delegation balance*

In the 40 years since the EP's first direct elections, the EPP Group has undergone numerous and significant changes not only in terms of its sheer political and institutional relevance, but also in terms of its internal organisation and, even more so, its national party delegations' internal balance and structuring. From a formal viewpoint, the criteria for membership in the group have become more open and, implicitly, more flexible. The Group's 1979 rules of procedure recited that group membership was granted to those MEPs who, "belong[ed] to Christian democratic groups in their national legislative bodies or to a group or party of a similar political outlook".[33] To make no mistake, a complete list of the eligible parties was provided in a footnote. Besides the established CD parties from the six original Member States, the list included Ireland's Fine Gael and, expectedly, no British or Danish parties. Moreover, a rather vague provision was made for other MEPs to become members if they subscribed to the policies of the Christian democratic Group. This formula had been maintained with no change from the last (1975) appointed Parliament's version and was replaced in 1989 by one that reflected the Group's need and desire to incorporate members from Denmark and the UK with fewer difficulties than those encountered in attracting parties from the new Member States (Greece, Portugal and Spain) that joined the EC/EU following their return to democracy (see Kaiser in Chapter 1 of this book). The new membership rules instituted two types of membership: ordinary membership criteria were more or less unchanged (the list of national parties was replaced by a reference to the list of member parties of the European People's Party), whilst allied membership required subscription to the Group's political programme and acceptance of its rules of procedure. For one, this allowed the British Conservatives to join the Group, aptly renamed EPP-ED in 1999, without joining the EPP Party as a transnational party organisation (see Kaiser in Chapter 1 of this book). Overall, the introduction of the allied membership category marked a very important change in the strategy and ideological make-up of the Group. On one hand, the Group's ability to meet its strategic objective to attract members from most, and frequently all, Member States was certainly enhanced (see Table 5.2), although this might have happened anyway as most new member parties joined the EPP Group outright and did not opt for the allied status. On the other hand,

33 EPP Group Archives, E.1.2.5, Rules of the Group, 1979.

the Group's ideological make-up and purity was inevitably altered following the inclusion of non-confessional conservative parties from new (but also old, if one thinks of the replacement of the DC by Forza Italia within the Italian delegation and the Group) Member States.

This political price could not be avoided considering the absence of a Christian democratic tradition similar to that of the EC's six founding Member States in many of the new accession countries. Of the 2004 accession countries' parties, only the Czech Civic Democratic Party joined the ED component of the group. Minor parties from Italy, Spain and Portugal were also part of the ED, but the bulk of its membership was made up by British Conservatives. The importance of the ED component, however, goes beyond its sheer numerical relevance, as through the EPP-ED alliance the principle was established that Christian democratic ideological purity was no longer an absolute requirement for membership in the Group, whose criteria for membership were thus implicitly relaxed, irrespective of the existence of an allied category. Very revealing of this was the transformation of Spain's Alianza Popular into Partido Popular and its parallel switch from the ED to the EPP Group in 1989 (see Kaiser in Chapter 1 of this book).

This important formal change in the rules of procedure regulating EPP Group membership permitted, but also in part reflected, the Group's internal composition and inter-delegation balance. The first elected EPP Group was arguably dominated by the German and Italian delegations who respectively had 40 and 28% of the seats. Belgium and the Netherlands (both with 9%) were distant thirds and even the combined Benelux delegation did not go beyond third place with 21% of the seats. Notably, the German delegation's membership was larger than all the other countries' combined, excluding Italy. At first sight, the situation changed only slightly in 1981 after the accession of Greece, whose national delegation was dominated by the EPP member party New Democracy, which obtained 14 of the country's 24 seats (Fontaine 2009: 593-594). But this change is noteworthy because it marked the beginning of a progressive decline in the relative importance of the two largest national delegations that has continued through the EP's nine terms and has so far reached its nadir in 2014 when the two delegations obtained a combined membership of less than 18% (see Figure 5.5).[34] In 2014, Germany's very primacy came into question

34 The combined score went up again to almost 20% in 2019, but this was only due to a German gain of almost 5 points. The Italian delegation dropped to less than 4%, eighth in size with Bulgaria's and Portugal's.

when its delegation was separated from Poland's by less than 1% of the seats, but the diverging 2019 election results in the two countries restored Germany's advantage.

In any event, the delegation triad that has historically governed the Group consists of the German, Italian and Benelux delegations (see also Kaiser in Chapter 1 of this book), which share a common history in the path towards European integration, coming from a genuine Christian democratic background, and similar supranational proclivities towards the creation of a stable federal union at European level. Such orientations and proclivities were not consistently shared by the sixth founding Member States' delegation, France's. Although, at least initially, the French delegates in the EPP Group were genuine Christian Democrats, their numbers were too low for them to be able to make an impact (in 1979, the French delegation in the EPP Group was the 5$^{th}$ largest, being smaller than the Belgian and Dutch ones). Moreover, some of their positions were influenced by France's half-hearted acceptance of, and even resistance to, strong pro-European initiatives, as dictated by the country's positioning set by General De Gaulle in the 1960s. Ironically, France's role in the EPP Group has increased in more recent years with the accession of more sizeable and less sceptical post-Gaullist components in 1999, not only in terms of numerical relevance (see Figure 5.5), as Joseph Daul's tenure as President of the EPP Group between 2007 and 2014 demonstrates.

Be that as it may, the Italian delegation's drift into numerical irrelevance and the decline of the Benelux delegations, besides the aforementioned alternating fortunes of Germany's delegation, have made the EPP Group's leading party triad a thing of the past. The most evident outcome of these trends is the very high fragmentation of the EPP Group, demonstrated by the growth of the combined size of the smaller countries' delegations, which now account for more than 50% of the total membership of the Group (see Figure 5.5). Although the German delegation remains very influential, exercising its leadership is becoming increasingly difficult.

Considering the previous analysis of the distribution of seats amongst national delegations within the EPP Group as well as what emerges from the literature, the German, Italian and Benelux delegations could have been expected, at least initially, to have prevailed in the acquisition of important institutional positions within the EP, reflecting a rather clear continuity with the established practices in the appointed EP until 1979 (see also Kaiser in Chapter 1 of this book). Whilst this is certainly true in absolute terms, given the sheer size of those delegations, the same does not hold relative to their actual numerical strength. As we have done for political groups, we can calculate institutional relevance indices for the national delegations within the EPP Group, considering the same institutional positions and applying the same weights as for the groups.

*Figure 5.5 The EPP Group's internal balance. National delegations seat percentages 1979–2019*

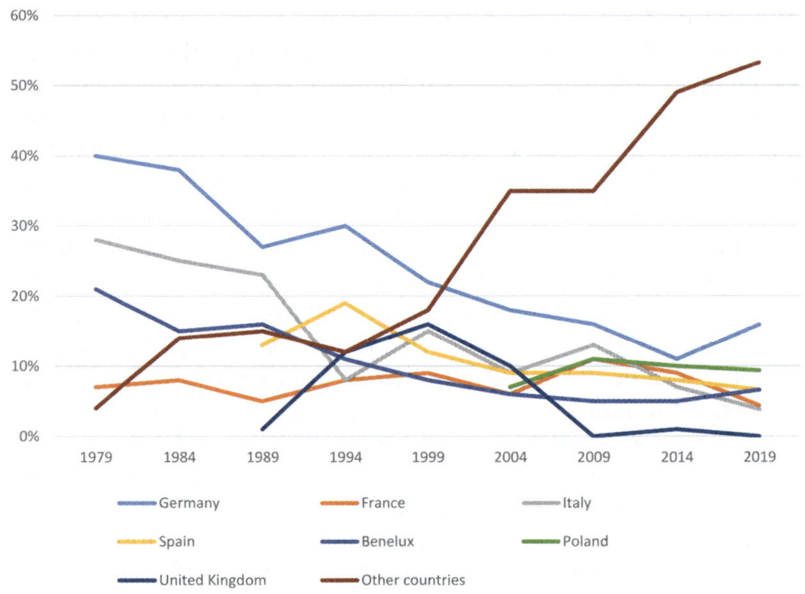


Both Italy and Germany exhibited IR scores that were in line, marginally below and above respectively, with their shares of seats in the EPP Group (see Figures 5.6, 5.7, 5.8). The Benelux combined score was slightly higher than the three delegations' numerical strength (see Figure 5.9), to a large extent because of Luxembourg's over-representation. It would appear then that the early history of the elected EPP Group was characterised by a magnanimous attitude by the largest delegations, as they did not demand retribution beyond their proportional share[35]. This changed somewhat over time, as other large national delegations from Spain, the UK and Poland

35 It appears that avoiding power struggles within the Group was more important than affirming national superiorities, especially in view of the subordinate position (to the PES/S&D) in which the EPP Group found itself after the 1979 election results. The group's strategies at EP level were naturally complicated by the electoral outcome. After having obtained 7 EP Presidencies out of 11 between

joined the group. As the relative size of the German and Italian delegations declined so did their IR scores although not at the same rate (see Figures 5.7 and 5.8). The ratio between the Italian delegation's numerical size and IR index has varied across the nine elected terms of the EP, with the IR score being higher than the seat percentage only four times out of nine. Interestingly, this has happened for all the last four EP terms, and never during the first five.[36] On the contrary, the German delegation's score was higher seven times out of nine, with 1979 and 1984 being the exceptions. Thus, excluding the first two terms, the German IR score was always comfortably higher, in one case (2004) by more than ten points, than the delegation's share of the seats.

*Figure 5.6 Institutional Relevance Index per legislature: trends for the delegations of Germany, Italy, Spain, Poland and UK*

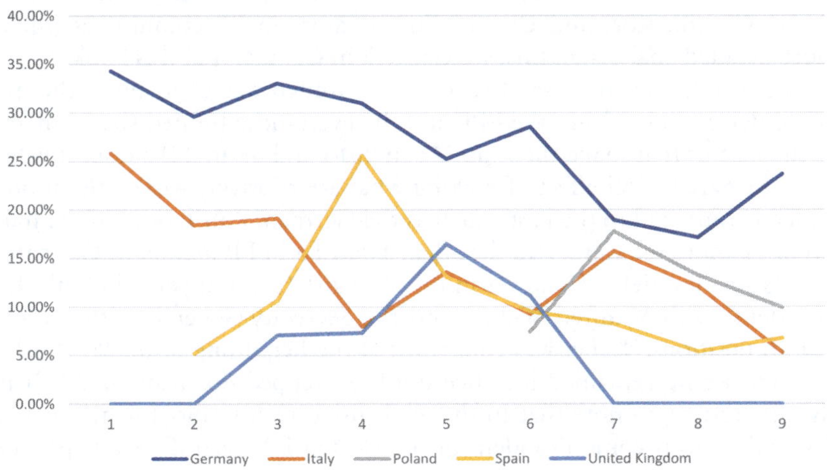


This is no doubt indicative of the German delegation's growing tendency towards the acquisition of a hegemonic role, one that was made more evident by its ability to obtain relevant positions within the EPP Group itself. Arguably, besides the General Assembly, which includes all of the Group's members, there are three important institutional bodies/positions within

1958 and 1979, the EPP failed to have one of its candidates elected during the first term of the elected EP.

36 In the 4th EP term, the Italian delegation's IR score almost coincided with its share of seats.

the EPP Group: the Presidency, the Bureau and the Secretariat. As the Bureau's composition is also influenced by the delegations' size, the analysis here is limited to trends in Presidency elections and Secretariat nominations. In the EP's nine elected terms, there have been 17 Group Chair elections and 8 Secretary-General appointments (see Table A9 in the Appendix).[37] MEPs from the German delegation have prevailed in Chair elections 10 times, obtaining almost 59% of all positions, nearly two and a half times the mean of its share of all the EPP seats (about 24%) over the first eight EP terms. As of 15th May 2020, German exponents had held the Secretary-General position for almost 24 years, also in this case about 59% of the time throughout the whole elected EP's history. Also during this period, only three Secretary-General positions and no Chairmanships have gone to non-founding Member States' delegations. The German delegation's ability to secure institutionally relevant positions is evident also for some that are not included in the calculation of the IR index, such as Group Coordinators and Deputy Coordinators in EP committees (for a more detailed analysis on this, see Gagatek in Chapter 4 of this book).

In general, one could say that the very limited size of many of the national delegations within the EPP and the even more limited size of many of the parties that make them up (52 in 2014 and 48 in 2019 respectively) have the paradoxical effect of making what are relatively weak delegations (at least compared to the past), such as the German, Polish or even the Italian ones, more relevant. With less than 11% of all EPP members, Germany had its smallest delegation ever in the 8$^{th}$ legislature and yet held both the President (with Manfred Weber) and the Secretary-General (with Martin Kamp) positions. Weber was confirmed at the beginning of the 9$^{th}$ legislature and Kamp remained in office until he stepped down in 2020.[38] It is also interesting to note that in the 8$^{th}$ legislature Antonio Tajani was the first Italian to become President of the elected EP, even if he was part of

37 According to the EPP Group's rules of procedure:
(1) The Group Plenary Assembly shall elect the Chair and the ten Vice-Chairs.
(2) The elections shall be held before the beginning of the new legislature.
(3) The term of office of the Group Presidency shall be the same as the effective term of office of the President of Parliament. If this term ends before the end of the legislature, new elections shall be held at least one month before the end of term of office of the President of Parliament.
Given that the President of the Parliament's term is two and a half years, so is that of the EPP Group's Chair.

38 Martin Kamp had also held the office for part of the 6$^{th}$ and all of the 7$^{th}$ legislature. In fact, Kamp was the longest-ever serving Secretary-General, from 1/9/2007 to 30/4/2020.

what was at the time the smallest ever Italian delegation in the EPP Group (with less than 7% of all EPP members).[39]

In any event, given the several enlargements undergone by the EU and because of the EPP Group's consequent increasing fragmentation, all major delegations exhibit downward trends in their IR scores (see Figure 5.6). Even the relative newcomers, such as Spain, the UK (newcomer to the EPP Group) and Poland, follow this pattern despite having experienced important peaks (in the 4th, 5th and 7th EP term respectively). If this could be readily expected, it is interesting to note that national delegations fared differently in terms of their ability to maintain a high institutional profile as their size declined.

*Figure 5.7 Germany: comparison between IR values and seat percentages*

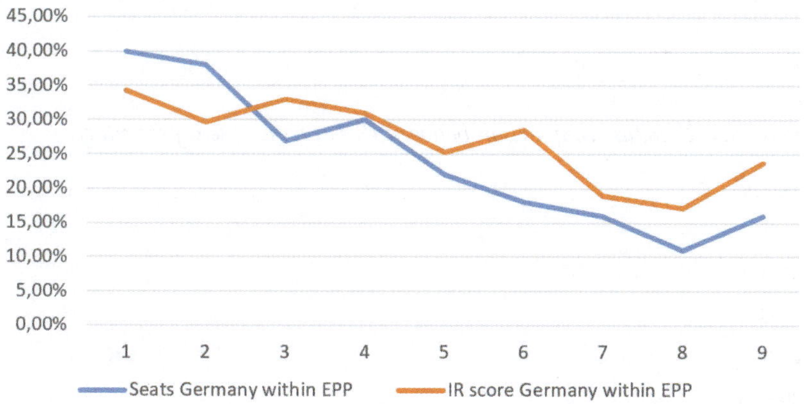


39 In the 9th legislature, the Italian delegation shrank even further to 3.9%.

*Figure 5.8 Italy: comparison between IR values and seat percentages*

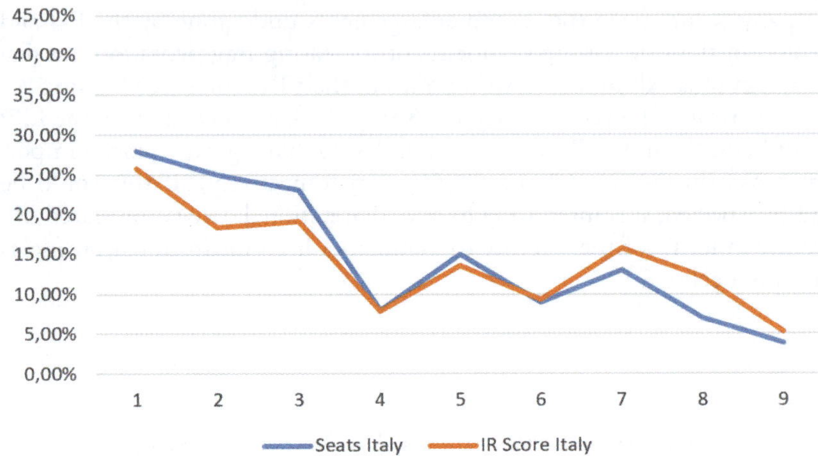


*Figure 5.9 Benelux: comparison between IR values and seat percentages*

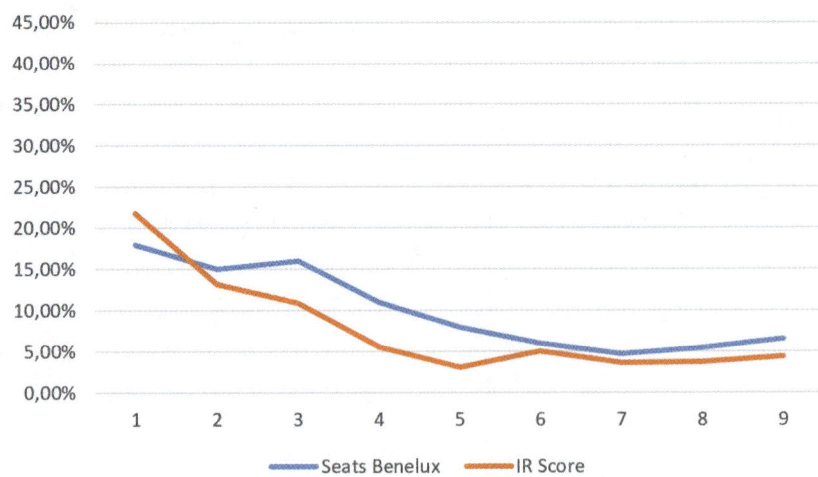

Figure 5.10 France: IR values and seat percentages

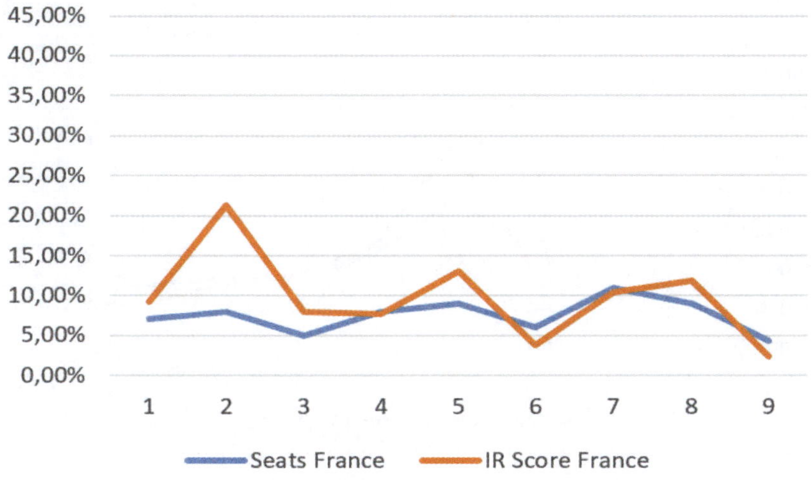


*Figure 5.11 UK: IR values and seat percentages*

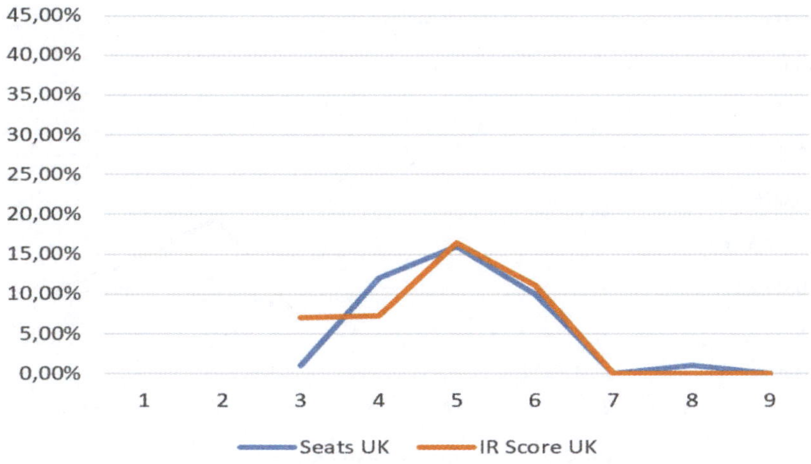

*Figure 5.12 Spain: IR values and seat percentages*

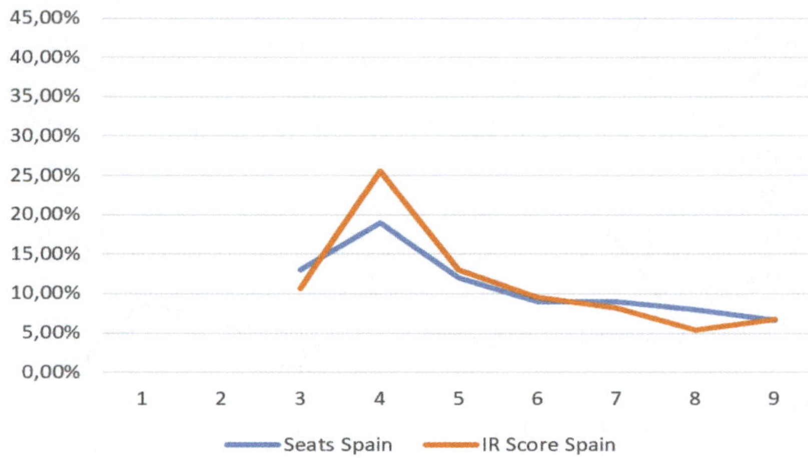


*Figure 5.13 Poland: IR values and seat percentages*

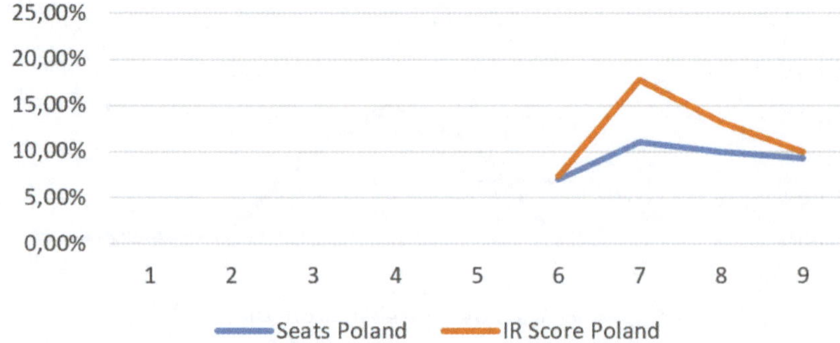

The German delegation's trend is rather interesting (see Figure 5.7). During the first two terms, its IR score was actually lower than its share of the seats. This is consistent with what was said earlier about a magnanimous attitude on the part of the largest delegations. It is plausible that their sheer political influence and strength (see Fontaine 2009 and Kaiser in Chapter 1 of this book) were so overpowering that they were able to compensate the smaller delegations with a good share of institutional positions. This is even more true of the other two main components of the EPP Group's core: the Italian and the Benelux delegations.

Whilst the German delegation started reaping important institutional rewards from the 3rd EP term on, reaching the highest positive IR index/seat percentage differential in the 6th term, the Italian delegation (see Figure 5.8) did not clearly exploit its 'big delegation advantage' until the 7th elected EP term, when it was actually not so big anymore. Although declining in size, the Italian delegation remained politically important and was obviously taking advantage of its remaining influence.

The combined Benelux delegations' trend is even more negative than the Italian delegation's (see Figure 5.9). Their IR/seat percentage differential was never positive throughout the entire history of the elected EP, with best performances in the 6th and 7th EP terms when the two values were almost identical. In this case as well, a generally positive disposition and the inherent loyalty towards Europe derived from being hosts to important EU institutions may have resulted in a sense of fulfilment and in an enhanced sense of institutional responsibility within the Group on the part of MEPs from all three countries. In other words, the overall political advantage of being part of what for most of the period being observed has been the most important group within the EP might have suggested a strategy aimed at maintaining the EPP Group's cohesion and strength by rewarding other, often smaller, delegations.

Contrary to what might have been expected considering the ostensible understanding amongst the German, Italian, and Benelux delegations, all the other larger national delegations display trends that are more positive than the Benelux and Italian ones. France's (see Figure 5.10) IR/seat ratio was positive in 6 terms out of 9 with an important peak in the second term, the UK's was positive in 3 terms out of 6 (see Figure 5.11), Spain's (see Figure 5.12) had one very important peak in the 4th term and Poland's (see Figure 5.13) was always positive, albeit marginally in the 6th and 9th EP terms, also reaching its highest level in the 7th term when it obtained the EP Presidency with Jerzy Buzek.

France's and Spain's peaks coincided with the EP Presidencies of Pierre Pflimlin and José Maria Gil-Robles respectively. France also had another, smaller, peak in the 5th term when Nicole Fontaine was elected EP President. Thus, the French EPP delegation had two Presidencies, as did the German delegation. By contrast, the Italian delegation only had one (Tajani) and the Benelux delegations had none (see Table A10 in the Appendix). Finally, although numerically preponderant, the other 19 national delegations have obtained very meagre institutional rewards (see Table A3 in the Appendix) collectively and, with rare exceptions, individually. Their cumulative IR score/seat share percentage ratios have always been negative and in the forty years of the elected EP they have only obtained three Secretary-General positions (Portugal with Mario David in the 4$^{th}$ term, Denmark with Niels Pedersen in the 6$^{th}$ term and Malta with Simon Busuttil in the 9$^{th}$ term) and no Group Chairs.

It thus appears that the national delegations' troika that has politically governed the EPP Group has relied on the contributions of the other larger Member States' delegations to have an effective institutional presence in the EP. But the most important finding that emerges from this analysis is the undisputed hegemonic role of the German delegation. This is evidenced not only by the success it has had in securing top positions in the Group and in the EP but also in guiding the EPP Group through alternating fortunes.[40] As Figure 5.14 shows, there is no clear relationship between the IR scores of the German delegation and the EPP as a whole. The only observable pattern could be the tendency of the German delegation's score to decline more visibly than the EPP Group's. This would reflect a commendable unwillingness by the delegation to exploit its leadership to secure more coveted posts for itself in the EP than justified by its weight within the Group. This sense of institutional responsibility is consistent with an attitude that privileges the unity of the Group in the pursuit of its overall European strategy.

---

40 The expansion strategy of the EPP Party and Group was set up by Helmut Kohl and Wilfried Martens, with Klaus Welle acting on their behalf. The decision to enlarge the EPP to include non-Christian Democrats was thus taken by the EPP Party leadership and accepted by the EPP Group.

*Figure 5.14 Seats and IR scores. Comparison between the German national delegation and the whole EPP*

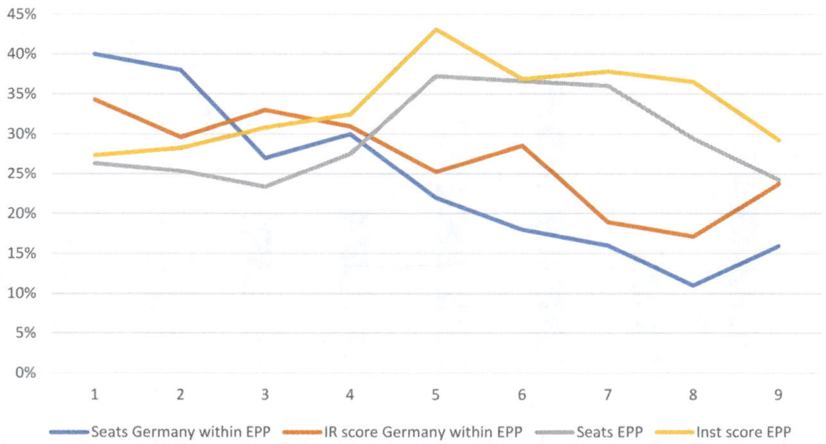


The German delegation's primacy certainly stems from having been the strongest numerically within the EPP Group for all nine terms of the elected Parliament and from representing the strongest and most influential EU Member State. It must be stressed, however, that the acceptance of its predominant role by the other delegations depends also on the recognition of its ability to embody and propel the EPP's European view and ideals. This is also reflected in the greater commitment to building a strong presence and personal political careers in the EP respectively, which the German delegation and individual German MEPs seem to have more than all other nationalities.

*Figure 5.15 Replacement rate* of EPP MEPs*

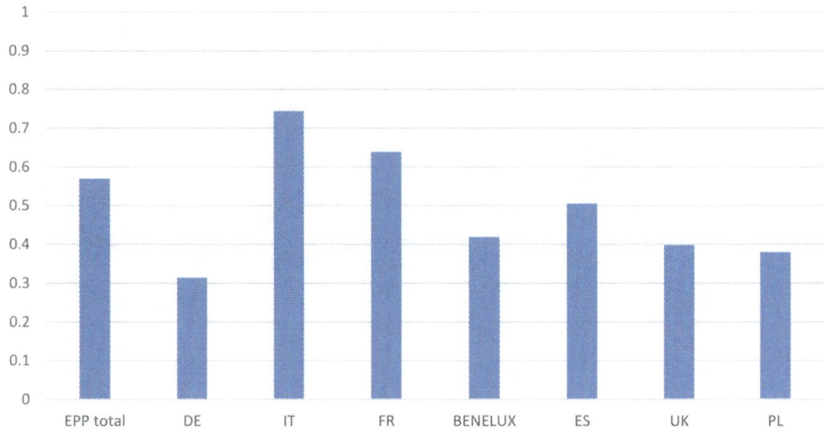


* If replacement rate = 1, all MEPs are replaced at each election; If replacement rate = 0, the same MEPs have stayed in office throughout all elected terms[41]

Figure 5.15 illustrates graphically the EPP's MEP replacement rate by national delegation. The Italian and French delegations display the highest replacement rates. On average, Italian MEPs spend less than six years in the EP and French MEPs slightly less than seven years, which equates to not much more than one term in either case. Conversely, the EP tenure of German MEPs is about 12 years (almost two and a half EP terms). It goes without saying that the greater experience and possibly also the degree of personal respect and consideration towards fellow MEPs within and outside the EPP Group that German EPP MEPs build up over time give them a great advantage over the members of other delegations in their bids to occupy strategic positions.

41 ***Replacement rate calculation:*** (total single MEPs between 1979 and 2019 / total seats won) – (average N of seats at each election / total seats won); ***Examples:*** Germany: (152/340) – [(340/8)/340] = 0.44 – 0.125 = 0.315; Poland: (53/70) – [(70/3)/70] = 0.76 – 0.33 = 0.43.

*The EPP Group's role in the progress and development of the European party system and of political foundations at European level*

The European Union's democratic deficit is at the centre of one of the dominant debates at EU level. It clearly emerges from the literature that one essential prerequisite for overcoming the deficit is an increase in the powers of the European Parliament.[42] In the last fifty years, the powers of the EP have been increased several times. The trajectory that started in 1970 with the Treaty of Luxembourg (see also Wolfram Kaiser's account in Chapter 1 of this book), whereby the EP obtained significant budgetary powers, continued after a rather lengthy interval with the season of the treaties, from the 1987 Single European Act to the Treaty of Lisbon in 2007, and transformed the EP into a veritable co-legislator. The role of the EPP Group in this process was certainly prominent, as reported by Karl Magnus Johansson in Chapter 2 of this book. The increase of the EP's legislative powers, however, is still insufficient, perhaps not in itself, but certainly as a condition for democracy at European level. There is an "other side of the *democratic deficit coin* (emphasis in the original) – at least if democracy is defined as democratic party government – [that] is the absence of real European parties, and of a single European party system" (Bardi, Katz and Mair 2015). Indeed, most contemporary notions of representative democracy are based on the belief that "the political parties created democracy and modern democracy is unthinkable save in terms of the parties" (Schattschneider 2004). More precisely, it is necessary to "evaluate the different implications of transnational parties competing for purely legislative office, on the one hand, and competing for executive office, on the other hand, as might be the case were the Commission President to be directly elected, or were the Commission to be wholly accountable to the Parliament" (Bardi, Katz and Mair 2015). Thus, the development of a democratic system at European level requires the political parties to be organised in a competitive party system in relation to control of the European executive.

This section will examine the EPP Group's positions and actions vis-à-vis the development of European political parties and a European party system. This assessment, in turn, requires a study of the European electoral law and of regulations concerning the status and financing of political par-

42 The expression "democratic deficit" in relation to the European Union was probably used for the first time by David Marquand (1979). Marquand's emphasis was precisely on the need to increase the Parliament's powers.

ties at European level. Moreover, for a genuine transnational party system to develop, specific dynamics of political competition must be created at European level. The discussion of how these dynamics can be created is less straightforward, as some of the necessary innovations would require reforms of the treaties that have been proposed more than once, most notably at the time of the Draft Treaty for European Union initiated by Altiero Spinelli, but have never come close to being enacted.

In the last forty years, the EPP Group has confirmed its awareness of the need to make progress in all these areas for the pursuit of its 'European ambition'. The group's role has naturally been essential, not only because of its sheer size and prominence, in all of them, albeit with different degrees of initiative. But even when Europe-building initiatives have come from different groups, as was the case in a different context with Spinelli's Draft Treaty (Fontaine 2009 and Wolfram Kaiser in Chapter 1 of this book), the EPP Group's role has usually been paramount and certainly essential for the success or at least the progress of the projects.

The EEC Treaty (Article 138) provided "an unequivocal mandate" for the EP "to draw up proposals for elections by direct universal suffrage in accordance with a uniform procedure in all Member States". This might have been the only case in which the EP actually had a right of legislative initiative (Grunert 1992: 487). In light of having a uniform electoral law at European level being considered a fundamental pre-requisite for the development of parties and representative democracy at European level, the electoral law used for the first direct EP elections appeared to be inadequate. And the progressive increase of the EP's powers made the need for a more uniform electoral law than the one used in the first four elections more pressing (Bardi 1990: 525).

The most important distortion the electoral law created in the party system came from the adoption of a plurality system of seat apportionment in Great Britain, as opposed to PR in the other 8 Member States at the time, as well as in Northern Ireland. Although the original law had many other flaws, eliminating the cross-Member State methodological disparity in the apportionment of EP seats was the first and foremost target of would-be reformers of the system. The EPP Group has been at the forefront of the EP's attempts at electoral reform. EPP Group members acted as Rapporteurs in the Political Affairs and later in the Constitutional Affairs Committees on proposals for the reform of the EP's electoral law. Most notably, EPP MEPs Jean Seitlinger and Reinhold Bocklet proposed, amongst other things, the introduction of PR in reports respectively published in 1982 and 1985 (European Parliament 1982b, 1985b). Both attempts were unsuccessful, even if in the latter case a joint inter-committee Political and Legal Affairs

Working Group had elaborated what had appeared to be an acceptable compromise, including for the UK's staunchest opposers of PR. Eventually in 1999, PR was adopted with an Act of the UK Parliament for the first time for the whole of the UK as well. Needless to say, this outcome was welcomed by the EPP Group and decisively supported by its UK component, the British Conservatives.

The debate on the electoral law continued even after this important milestone was reached and became more focused on elements that could enhance the supranational character of the EP-based party system, such as the so-far unsuccessful introduction of transnational lists in the EP. Although the leading figure behind that proposal was British ALDE MEP Andrew Duff, the idea had first appeared in the 2007 report on the composition of the European Parliament drafted by EPP MEP Alain Lamassoure with Adrian Severin (S&D) that "propose[d] ... to study the possibility of electing some Members of the European Parliament on transnational lists; [and] consider[ed] that *this would help to impart a genuine European dimension to the electoral debate, particularly by entrusting a central role to European political parties* (emphasis ours)" (European Parliament 2007b). The EPP repeatedly promoted, supported or at least voted in favour of the introduction of transnational lists. It would thus appear, through the texts elaborated by its Rapporteurs and the votes of its members in committee, that the EPP Group considered transnational lists an innovation that would help the transnationalisation of the EU political system. In the 8th term of the elected EP, however, the EPP Group's support for transnational lists became less explicit and eventually turned into outright opposition. The report by EPP MEP Danuta Maria Hübner and S&D MEP Jo Leinen on the reform of the electoral law of the European Union (European Parliament 2015e) did not mention transnational lists but simply stated that "the reform of Parliament's electoral procedure should aim to enhance the democratic and transnational dimension of the European elections and the democratic legitimacy of the Union decision-making process".

The turnaround was completed with the vote held during the EP's plenary session in February 2018 on the post-Brexit distribution of the European Parliament's seats amongst the remaining 27 Member States that was to become effective with the 9th elected EP term. Table 5.4 illustrates the result of the vote on a specific proposal to remove any reference to transnational lists from the resolution on seat re-apportionment. The proposal was approved with a comfortable majority.

*Table 5.4 Vote against transnational lists by EP political group**

| | **Political Groups** | EPP | S&D | ALDE | GUE-NGL | Greens | ECR | EFDD | NI | Total | % |
|---|---|---|---|---|---|---|---|---|---|---|---|
| **Votes** | | | | | | | | | | | |
| Yes** | | 167 | 39 | 11 | 22 | 12 | 65 | 24 | 11 | 368 | 54,43 |
| No | | 27 | 118 | 54 | 15 | 37 | 3 | 18 | 2 | 274 | 40.53 |
| Absten-tion | | 2 | 19 | 0 | 11 | 0 | 1 | 1 | 0 | 34 | 5,03 |
| Total | | 196 | 176 | 65 | 48 | 49 | 69 | 43 | 13 | 676 | 100 |

*Source: https://www.votewatch.eu/blog/bad-news-for-macron-as-majority-of-policymakers-opposed-transnational-lists-for-ep-elections/
**Yes = Remove transnational lists; No = Introduce transnational lists

The EPP Group's vote against the introduction of transnational lists was decisive for its rejection and represented a very uncharacteristic divergence from the positions of the other two groups in the European party system's core who prevalently voted in favour of the proposal. It is noteworthy that the EPP's vote was the more disciplined than that of the other two core groups, which, conversely, were both predominantly in favour of a transnational constituency. This was no doubt remarkable for the EPP Group given what turned out to be a rather controversial outcome. A satisfactory 85% of EPP MEPs voted according to the Group's line, as opposed to a still high 83% of ALDE and a significantly lower 67% of the S&D. Once again, EPP MEPs' propensity to rally around the flag was confirmed. The only significant defections came from members of the Spanish delegation (all 14 who participated in the vote). The rest of the dissenting EPP MEPs came in small numbers from Austria (2), France (4) and Poland (2) as well as from Belgium, Bulgaria, Italy, Poland and Romania (1 each).

This decision was described on the EPP Group website as being justified by the fact that transnational lists "are neither European nor democratic but rather a centralist and elitist artificial construct" (EPP Group 2018). It was also reported that György Schöpflin, MEP and EPP Group Spokesman in the EP's Constitutional Affairs Committee, stated: "Not only is there no legal base for such an experiment, what we're looking at is yet another elite-driven project in Europe that will only end up making the EU even more remote from the voters than they already are". Alain Lamassoure elaborated on this point when asked why the EPP Group's position on transnational lists had changed in the course of the EP's 8th elected term:

> The main reason for this evolution is the gradual transformation of the EP into a fully-fledged Parliament. As long as its legislative powers were very limited, resorting to transnational lists was deemed as a way to develop a common European spirit. But since the MEPs have been lawmakers, our duty is to bring the decider as close as possible to the citizens. The smallest the constituencies the better. As for me, I would even recommend to opt for single Member constituencies, but no one else is willing to drop proportional representations. Transnational lists would mean to ensure that the citizen has no MEP to deal with his or her personal concerns and that the EP focuses on theoretical debates, irrespective of concrete local situations.

Although this position ostensibly aims to reaffirm a pro-European rationale, it appears to be too weakly argued and superficial (the EP had already been a co-legislator since the Lisbon Treaty and the EPP only changed its position on transnational lists 12 years later). According to most transnational list projects, no elector would have "no MEP to deal with his or her personal concerns" as the vote for transnational lists would be in addition to that for national lists. More importantly, and even more worryingly, there was an evident departure in the traditional EPP's coalition strategy in favour of an understanding with broadly speaking Eurosceptic groups against the other core groups.[43] This position seemed at the time to be even more incongruous in view of the strategic synergy that, according to some, appears to exist between transnational lists and the institutionalisation of the procedure for the election of *Spitzenkandidaten* to the Commission's Presidency, which the EPP was still strongly supporting (see below).

Former EPP Group official Johan Ryngaert provided a different, more tactical/technical explanation (Interview Ryngaert, 3.04.2019). Rather than a complete strategic turnaround, the rejection of transnational lists was due to the awkward and politically complex context of the vote at the time. The proposal was framed in the discussion on the apportionment of the EP's seats to be vacated by the UK as a result of Brexit amongst the remaining 27 Member States. For many of the EPP Group's national delegations, the interests at stake concerned first and foremost the number of

---

43 Schöpflin's choice of words in justifying the negative vote on transnational lists, which he described as an "elite-driven project" was also reminiscent of the Eurosceptic parties' populist rhetoric.

seats their countries would get as a result[44]. As such, they were incompatible with a project that would assign a relevant portion of the seats made available by Brexit to a transnational constituency.

If time should prove that this latter explanation is correct, its mid- to long-term consequences could be less drastic for the EPP's position on transnational lists than those of the Group's 'official story', as its reasons do not stem from an outright opposition to the principle of transnational lists but from contingencies related to the circumstances in which the decision against transnational lists was made. There is a chance that they would no longer apply should the proposal be put forward again in the future.

The European electoral law can include provisions facilitating the development of political parties at European level. The EPP Group, at least until the recent turnaround on transnational lists, has always shown a favourable disposition towards such provisions. The current electoral law does provide an acceptable framework for the development and maintenance of political groups. But political parties are more than just instruments for electoral competition; they are complex organisations that consist of three separate faces.[45] For them to be fully functional, all three faces must be sufficiently well developed and reciprocally integrated. For almost twenty-five years, the only developed face at EU level was the party in 'public office', and, as shown in a previous footnote, only in its parliamentary component. In the last two decades, specific legislation has been introduced that defines the status of political parties at European level and regulates their financing. What is known as the Europarty statute, Regulation (EC) 2004/2003, recognised and formalised the status of an extra-parliamentary component of European political parties, the European 'party in central office', that is. The follow-up Regulation (EC) 1524/2007 in turn started the process whereby a European 'party on the ground' could be created. It introduced European political foundations (PFELs), organised as

44 The seat distribution in the EP before Brexit has always been criticised because the principle of digressive proportionality that regulates it creates visible and, according to some, unacceptable distortions. The re-allocation that was eventually approved, also at the expense of transnational lists, went in the direction of easing such problems.

45 The political groups in the EP are the legislative component of the 'party in public office'. They have always been the most developed face of European political parties. The executive component of the party in 'public office' is still in an embryonic stage, following the European political parties' decision to nominate *Spitzenkandidaten* to the Presidency of the Commission.

entities that are formally affiliated to European political parties, the objectives of which they are expected to support and underpin through their activities, including at national level. This in turn might increase the European awareness of the national member parties on the ground.

According to Dorota Dakowska (2009b), "in a Commission proposal issued in June 2007, European political foundations were defined as 'catalysers of new ideas' and as a means of strengthening 'informed debate on current and future European issues' … Faced with the challenge of communicating increasingly complex common policies to the public, the Commission officials perceived political foundations as a solution with the potential to involve citizens in the process of European integration". Gagatek and Van Hecke (2014: 89), on the other hand, emphasise the role of PFELs in complementing the activities of European political parties and as "a possible factor for a greater politicisation (or more precisely polarisation) of the EU-level party scene". Be that as it may, there seems to be enough evidence that the combined effects of two regulations on the statute and funding of European political parties and European political foundations and their follow-ups (Regulations 1141/2014 and 2018/673) have laid the ground for the development of the other two faces of political parties at European level – 'in central office' and 'on the ground'.

The EPP Group has been the main driving force behind this process, which has spanned over almost two decades. EPP Group members have acted as Rapporteurs or Co-Rapporteurs on several occasions, beginning with Giorgos Dimitrakopoulos who reported on "The amendments to the European Parliament's Rules of Procedure following the adoption of the Regulation governing the statute and the financing of political parties at European level" in the Committee on Constitutional Affairs (European Parliament 2004). More interestingly, the EPP Group's position expressed by Shadow Rapporteur Ursula Schleicher on the report by S&D MEP Jo Leinen on the proposal for a European Parliament and Council regulation on the statute and financing of European political parties (European Parliament 2003) agreed that "a European political party must be an association of citizens or federation of political parties from Member States which contributes at European level to forming and expressing the political will of the citizens of the Union while being represented in the European Parliament". Mrs Schleicher, however, also reported that the EPP Group did not approve of the provision according to which appropriations for funding European political parties should be entered in the budget as Commission expenditure, "as [the Group] has always thought that allotted appropriations should be considered as Parliament expenditure, as stipulated in the Commission proposal".[46] The EPP Group's position was in favour of the Leinen report even if its proposed amendment, which would have arguably strengthened the political character of the parties, was not accepted.

Subsequently, EPP MEP Véronique Mathieu drafted the Opinion of the Committee on Budgetary Control for the Committee on Constitutional Affairs on "The proposal for a European Parliament and Council regulation amending Regulation (EC) No 2004/2003 on the regulations governing political parties at European level and the rules regarding their funding" (European Parliament 2007c) suggesting important amendments to be adopted in the final decision on the establishment of European political foundations. A plenary briefing note by Shadow Rapporteur EPP MEP Jean-Luc Dehaene on a second Leinen Report on European political parties asserted "that during the stage of reflection on the future of the European Union, the role of European political foundations should be considered, in order to complement the work of the European political parties and to see what influence political parties can have on referendums, on European Parliament elections and on the election of the Commission President" and expressed the EPP Group's favourable position.[47] The EPP Group's positive vote on the 2004 and 2007 Regulations was essential for their adoption.

After the initial trial period, it became apparent that the legislation on European political parties and foundations could be fine-tuned. The EPP Group was also very active in the process of revision that culminated with two more Regulations in 2014 and 2018. EPP MEP Marietta Giannakou acted as Rapporteur in an own-initiative procedure on the application of Regulation (EC) No 2004/2003 on the regulations governing political parties at European level and the rules regarding their funding (European Parliament 2011c) and on "The proposal for a regulation of the European Parliament and of the Council on the statute and funding of European political parties and European political foundations" (European Parliament 2013c) both in the Committee on Constitutional Affairs.

An EPP Group press release (EPP Group 2014) commented on the adoption of the Giannakou report by the majority of the European Parliament in Strasbourg: "The statute for European political parties has a political and symbolic role. It increases the visibility, effectiveness and trans-

46 EPP Group Archives, B.1.1.4, SWG 1999-2004, WG D – Constitutional Affairs, plenary note Leinen – political parties.

47 EPP Group Archives B.1.2.4, SWG 2004-2009, WG D – Constitutional Affairs, plenary notes Leinen – political parties.

parency of European political parties. Individuals can become members of European political parties directly and participate in European politics more actively. In short, the Regulation is a tool for increased democratic legitimacy and aims to bridge the gap between national and European political parties." This statement echoed what Rapporteur Marietta Giannakou herself said after the vote: "The adoption of the Regulation is the result of a difficult and time-consuming negotiation process with the Commission and the Council, which lasted over one and a half years. It is a very useful legislative tool at European and national level. It represents a significant step forward in the organisation and functioning of European political parties. At the same time, it stimulates citizens to get involved actively and directly."

Finally, EPP MEP Rainer Wieland was Co-Rapporteur on the proposal for amending the regulation on the statute and funding of European political parties and European political foundations (European Parliament 2017b) in the Committee on Constitutional Affairs and commented: "Our report closes loopholes which until now allowed a European Political Party to be created only for financial reasons. Funding will now be linked to actual voting results at the European level, making European political parties more European." Wieland was supported by his Co-Rapporteur S&D MEP Mercedes Bresso who declared: "We have managed in this report to adapt the current regulation to the latest developments and needs of European politics. By lowering the threshold for distribution of funds, we have enhanced the democratic representation of political parties and foundations, through financing which is truly proportionate to their presence in the Parliament. While doing so, we safeguarded the prerequisites for a diverse and democratic political landscape, respecting the values of the EU and its financial interests" (Stur 2017). These revisions thus appeared to be not only consistent with but also driven by the EPP Group's vision of a more democratic and responsive European political system. Its positive vote on both EP reports and in the plenary was decisive for the adoption of the two regulations (2014 and 2018).

Jointly, parties and foundations potentially possess the organisational characteristics to provide a link between European society and EU institutions. What is still missing is the political dynamics that can transform the formal organisational link into a veritable channel of representation. Since the Treaty of Rome, there has been a widespread belief that the direct election of the European Parliament would lead to the "creation of a European political space in which the practices of democratic party government as found in the Member States would be reproduced at the European level" (Bardi, Katz and Mair 2015). This has not happened as the EU is not sufficiently politicised yet. This shortcoming is seen by many as one of the main causes of the EU's democratic deficit. According to supporters of a federal and democratic EU, direct elections will enhance European democracy only if the Parliament's powers are extended to allow some form of control over the European executive. "If only the Parliament had the power to choose the President of the Commission ... there would be a focus for the construction of real European parties, each either nominating its own Europe-wide candidate for the presidency, or else joining in a coalition with other European parties to support a joint Europe-wide candidate – and from this, with the winning coalition electing its popularly endorsed candidate to head the Commission without requiring the nomination or approval of the Member governments, would follow real Europe-level democracy" (Bardi, Katz and Mair 2015).

Introducing the direct election of the President of the Commission would require a reform of the treaties. The Treaty of Lisbon, following what had been stipulated in the failed Constitutional Treaty before that, only went as far as confirming that the EP elects the President of the Commission and approves the Commission as a college taking into account the outcome of the European elections, as proposed by the European Council. However, it would be too much to assert that the President of the Commission enjoys the 'confidence' of the EP, as the Commission's political programme does not emanate formally from the EP but is only approved, with the nominated candidate, by it. This situation is not bound to change in the short or probably even in the medium term, as the conditions for the drafting and approval of a new treaty, especially one including such radical reforms, do not exist at the moment.

It is true, however, that the EP, although not directly responsible for the elaboration of the Commission's programme, is now much more involved in influencing its political priorities and more active in monitoring its implementation. Much of this progress has been due to the EP's well-known propensity and ability to informally exploit the popular legitimacy it has obtained with universal suffrage elections. As early as 1981, the EP took the initiative of endorsing the incoming Thorn Commission with a vote after the presentation of the college and of the programme. But it was not until the Maastricht Treaty changed the Commission's mandate to five years, to eventually coincide with the EP's, and the EP started voting on the Commission's President's, that an albeit informal parliamentarisation of the relationship between the two institutions began to materialise. The near coincidence of the two institutions' terms is what "later gave the Parliament the leverage for the linkage with the election outcome" (Peñalver García and Priestley 2015: 45). The EPP Group's votes were decisive for the approval of the Jacques Santer Commission and merged with the PES/S&D Group's for the one led by Romano Prodi (Voerman and van der Harst 2015: 282-283). After the approval of the Nice and, even more so, Lisbon Treaties, the EP went beyond the simple approval of the Commission's President and college by exploiting its new powers to delay the approval of programmes (Barroso II and von der Leyen) or cause reshuffles in the composition of the college, most notably by forcing the Italian government to withdraw Rocco Buttiglione's candidature for a position in the first Barroso Commission in response to allegations of the former EPP MEP's discriminatory attitudes towards homosexuals and his views on the ostensibly subordinate position of women within marriage. The decisive discussion within the Committee on Civil Liberties, Justice and Home Affairs (LIBE), in a rare occurrence of serious disagreement between the core political groups, saw a convergence of some ALDE MEPs with PES/S&D and other leftist MEPs which resulted in the EPP's attempt to defend Buttiglione being defeated by a one-vote margin. Although this incident was particularly resounding, it has by no means been isolated. All successive Presidents of the Commission have been forced to withdraw proposed nominees or reassign portfolios to obtain the Parliament's approval.

The European political parties and the EP's political groups also elaborated an innovative interpretation of the aforementioned provision of the Treaty of Lisbon concerning the European Council's prerogative to propose to the EP a candidate for the Presidency of the Commission *taking into account the results of the European Parliament's election*. According to the parties' interpretation, on this basis, they could nominate *Spitzenkandidaten* to lead the parties in European elections.[48] If the Council was to take into account the result of the elections, the argument went, it could not refuse to consider the *Spitzenkandidat* who could muster the support of the highest number of elected MEPs in the new Parliament. As no party can possibly get an absolute majority of seats in the EP, the political groups made it clear that they were willing to rally behind one 'coalition' candidate if it should prove necessary to force the Council's hand. This idea had in reality already been vented in 2002 in the EPP Congress Document "A Constitution for a Strong Europe". Article 47 of the document recited: "A candidate for the President of the European Commission should be proposed to the European Parliament by the European Council in light of the outcome of European elections, and by qualified majority vote. The Euro-

48 EPP Group Archives, EPP Group Presidency Service, A new start for Europe. Appointment of the European Commission 2014–2019, 2014.

pean Parliament should give or withhold its approval by majority vote.. *This would give European political parties the opportunity to present their own candidates in the framework of the campaign for European elections. It would ensure a more personalised election campaign and increase democratic control and support of the European Commission* (emphasis ours)".[49]

This recommendation was never included in the draft Constitutional Treaty and in the Treaty of Lisbon. It was Commission President José Manuel Durão Barroso who re-introduced the *Spitzenkandidaten*[50] idea in his 2012 State of the Union address before the European Parliament in Strasbourg. It was also important that Barroso explicitly linked the promotion of EU democracy to the development of European political parties and to the Europeanisation of the European Parliament's elections' campaign:

> An important means to deepen the pan-European political debate would be the presentation by European political parties of their candidate for the post of Commission President at the European Parliament elections already in 2014. This can be done without Treaty change. This would be a decisive step to make the possibility of a European choice offered by these elections even clearer. I call on the political parties to commit to this step and thus to further Europeanise these European elections (Barroso 2012).

In perfect tune with Barroso's position, the EP and in particular the EPP Group took it upon themselves to promote the *Spitzenkandidaten* initiative.[51] EPP MEP Carlo Casini, on behalf of the Constitutional Affairs Committee he chaired, tabled a motion that "[u]rge[d] the European political families to nominate candidates for the Presidency of the Commission and expect[ed] those candidates to play a leading role in the parliamentary electoral campaign; stresse[d] the importance of reinforcing the political legitimacy of both Parliament and the Commission by connecting their respective elections more directly to the choice of the voters" (European Parliament 2014a). The motion eventually resulted, with minor changes in

---

49 EPP Group Archives, N.1.1.8, EPP Party, "A Constitution for a Strong Europe", Adopted at the EPP Congress, Estoril, 18 October 2002.

50 Although the word *Spitzenkandidaten* was not used until the 2014 elections campaign it is already being used here for simplicity and consistency with the rest of the analysis.

51 When it accepted Barroso's candidacy in Warsaw in April 2009, the EPP already used the rhetoric of Spitzenkandidaten.

European Parliament resolution of 22 November 2012 on the elections to the European Parliament in 2014 (European Parliament 2014b).

Five European Parties eventually nominated *Spitzenkandidaten* in 2014: besides the EPP, the PES, the ALDE, the Greens and the GUE/NGL. The EPP Congress that was held in Dublin in March 2014 elected Jean-Claude Juncker as its candidate. An EPP press release confidently asserted that "upon winning the elections, Jean Claude-Juncker will have the democratic mandate to assume the Presidency of the European Commission". It is questionable whether the EPP's 2014 electoral result could be construed as having been a victory. But the eventual nomination of Juncker as President of the Commission appeared at the time to be even more significant than if it had resulted from an outright absolute majority of the EPP in the European elections. Juncker's success was in fact based on a politicisation of the nomination process, whereby the three core EP groups formed a coalition to support him. The EPP, S&D and ALDE Groups, in announcing their coalition supporting Jean-Claude Juncker as would-be European Commission President, issued a joint statement in which they claimed it was their aim to "secur[e] a wider base for building a stable majority for the forthcoming European Commission" and that they had "decided to co-operate for creating a stable pro-Europe majority at the Parliament, for defending the values and the principles of European integration, still trying – jointly – to obtain reform reinforcing and improving the functioning and the transparency of institutions, as well as their efficacy in creating economic growth and facing the future challenges of the Union." (EU News 2014).

Whereas the EPP Party's role was more pronounced than the EPP Group's in the 2014 election of the Commission's President, the latter demonstrated a renewed relevance in the 2019 campaign. Over one year ahead of the beginning of the 2019 campaign, in February 2018, the EPP Group issued a Group information note in which it claimed, amongst other things, that "the leading candidate process idea emerged in 1997 and was supported by Helmut Kohl and Wilfried Martens" and that the EPP Group was the driving force in bringing the leading candidate process idea to political reality in 2014 in the conviction of it not being "just an experiment but an additional irreversible step in fermenting democratic legitimacy at European level".[52]

A few months later, the EPP Group's Chair Manfred Weber was elected as the EPP's candidate for President of the European Commission at the

52 EPP Group Archives, 47 Strategie politique, Group information notes, 2018.

EPP 2018 Congress in Helsinki, with 492 of the 619 valid votes. Although the candidate's election is clearly a prerogative of the party, the choice of Manfred Weber stressed the relevance and the involvement of the EPP Group as well. The President of the EPP Joseph Daul saluted Manfred Weber as

> a candidate with integrity and experience, who brings innovative ideas and the vision needed to defend our values, build bridges and shape the future of Europe. … With him, we look forward to the campaign; the chance to uphold our accomplishments, to preserve the European project and lead the way for a strong and united Europe with EPP at the helm. *(EPP 2018).*

In this statement, there is a clear acknowledgement of the importance for a candidate to have had previous political experience at European level, namely in this case, in the EPP political group. But the actual process that on 2 July 2019 led the European Council to the appointment of Ursula von der Leyen to the Presidency of the Commission tells a very different story as it appears to have been totally divergent from what had been hoped for less than eight months before by Joseph Daul.

The other groups' unwillingness to give Manfred Weber their wholehearted support made it very clear, rather soon after the EP elections and the rather disappointing showing of the EPP and of the other core parties, that his chances of becoming Commission President were practically non-existent. Just prior to the June 2019 Brussels European Council meeting in Brussels, Weber was informed by his S&D and ALDE/Renew Europe colleagues that he would not have their backing. This in itself was enough to pre-empt Weber's chances. Moreover, at the meeting, Emmanuel Macron made it very clear that it was the European Council's privilege to appoint a candidate of their choice, according to the current treaties, which do not provide for the appointment of a top candidate in EP elections, even if he did not exclude the possibility of direct universal suffrage elections of the Commission's President in the future.

A few days later, at a G20 meeting in Osaka, Angela Merkel indicated her support for the idea of appointing a *Spitzenkandidat* to the Commission's Presidency but allowed for the possibility that the S&D candidate, Frans Timmermans, and not only Manfred Weber, could be chosen. This appeared to be a tactical move to return to 'backroom' negotiations in the Council. It was clear that Timmermans would never get the qualified majority required in the Council either because of the Visegrad Member States' and Italy's opposition to a Socialist. The negotiations took place at the Special European Council meeting of 30 June-2 July 2019 in Brussels.

The appointments of Ursula von der Leyen (German, EPP) to the Presidency of the Commission, Christine Lagarde (French, close to ALDE/ Renew Europe) to the Presidency of the European Central Bank (ECB), Josep Borrell (Spanish, S&D) as 'foreign policy chief', the journalistic shorthand for High Representative of the Union for Foreign Affairs and Security Policy, Charles Michel (Belgian, ALDE/Renew Europe) to the Presidency of the Council as well as that of David Sassoli (Italian, S&D) to the Presidency of the European Parliament stemmed from an old-fashioned package deal that took into account most of the criteria, special requests and vetoes that are typical of such negotiations.

The Berlin-Paris axis emerged as the clear winner. Not only because Angela Merkel and Emmanuel Macron obtained the two most important positions at stake, and clearly the ones they respectively wanted, but also because the system that has governed the EU for decades was strengthened in the process. The five appointees came from MS that had been historically central to the EU project, including the relative newcomer Spain. They also belonged to or were very close to one of the three core parties of the EU party system. Perhaps more importantly, no concessions were made to the Visegrad countries, even if they had the evident merit for the winners of having contributed decisively to fending off the *Spitzenkandidaten* threat. Poland was the only Member State of the remaining big ones not to obtain an important EU position. Even the designation of David Sassoli, against the wishes of the Eurosceptic, sovereignist Italian government of the time, was a clear warning to those who were hoping to change the rules of the game at EU level.

What emerges from all of this is evident continuity in the protagonists and procedures of EU decision-making, a remarkable and unexpected outcome of what were supposed to be the elections that would change the EU. The EPP Group and its Chair, Manfred Weber, were 'collateral damage' in this battle, along with the hope for an institutionalisation of the political group's strategy to determine the choice of President of the Commission by appointing their *Spitzenkandidaten*. Despite this setback, however, the EPP Group remains the most influential in the EP, as shown in previous sections. Its biggest challenge will be to maintain the internal unity that is necessary to elaborate political strategies suitable for leadership in the EP.

The *Spitzenkandidaten* strategy, on the other hand, is for all practical purposes a missed opportunity that may not present itself again in the near future. But the fact that the President of the Commission did not participate in the electoral race and had no previous experience at EU level is clearly revealing of how unsuccessful the leading candidate strategy was in 2019 and, prospectively, will be in the future. The only hope for its revival may, paradoxically, come from the S&D and ALDE Groups' refusal to endorse Manfred Weber's bid for the Commission's Presidency. At the time of the next elections, this could allow for a retrospective interpretation that would put the blame for the failure of the *Spitzenkandidaten* strategy on the core groups' inability to build a coalition, thus implying that it could be tried again under more favourable circumstances. However, for this to be possible it might be necessary for the three core groups, and possibly the Greens, to agree on a much more explicit pre-electoral pact and programme, something that could be problematic. Even so, it would be very unlikely that the European Council, and most importantly the leading governments within it, would agree not to exercise their privilege after having rightfully taken it back from the European parties.

### *The EPP Group's role in the EP's relations with the Commission and the Council*

The European Parliament's powers have always been at the crux of the debate over how supranational and democratic the European Union really is. Such powers do not depend only on legal attributions and other formal arrangements, but also on the complex set of formal and informal relations with the other major EU institutions: the Commission and the Council[53].

The nature of the relationships between the EP and the Commission and the Council is respectively very different. The EP and the Commission belong to the same institutional circuit in the EU: the supranational one. At least in theory, they both respond to the European electorate as a whole, albeit in a less than direct way for the Commission. Conversely, the Council belongs to the intergovernmental institutional circuit and its national ministerial components respond directly to the citizens in their respective Member States. This being the case, not only is the relationship between the EP and the Commission more formalised institutionally (consisting of the procedures for the approval and the possible censure of the Commission), but it is also, broadly speaking, politically more intense and co-operative, in the pursuit of what has always been a common European mission. The idea, which has already been encountered in the analysis, that the EU could make substantial progress through a parliamentarisation of

---

53 The term Council(s) is used in the literature to designate the European Council of Ministers in its various incarnations and often to include the European Council as well. This term is being used less and less since the Treaty of Lisbon introduced a new figure, the President of the European Council, maintaining the Council of Ministers rotating Presidency, de facto separating the two.

its political system is based on the notion that the political link between the EP and the Commission should be made stronger. Indeed, the change imparted by the European political parties' decision to appoint *Spitzenkandidaten* to the Presidency of the Commission in 2014 and 2019 was meant to go in that direction. But the outcome of the 2019 elections confirmed that a parliamentarisation of the Commission's President's appointment will only be possible with a specific treaty reform.

In any event, however, for the first thirty years of its existence, until the Single European Act entered into force in 1987, that is, the governance of the EU was dominated by the technocratic, and for some excessively bureaucratic, guidance of the Commission, with the EP being relegated to little more than an advisory role. Unfortunately, EC decision-making appeared to have been severely hampered by the "general phenomenon of an excessive load of business aggravated by slow and confused handling (which) may be summed up in the one French word lordeur" (Council of the European Communities 1980: 11). These difficulties led the European Commission to appoint a Working Party in 1971, under the Chairmanship of Professor Georges Vedel, Honorary Dean of the Paris Faculty of Law and Economic Sciences, with the main task of considering a new position for the EP in the EC's overall institutional architecture on the basis of extended budgetary and legislative powers. The Commission's attention to the idea of streamlining the EC's working methods was evidenced again by the decision in 1979 to establish the Group of Five under the leadership of Dirk Spierenburg, a Dutch diplomat and former President of the High Authority of the European Coal and Steel Community (ECSC), whose Report focussed on a reorganisation of the Commission itself and its procedures.[54]

In a parallel move, the European Council set up a committee of 'Three Wise Men' (Barend Biesheuvel, former Dutch Prime Minister, Edmund Dell, former British Minister for Trade, and Robert Marjolin, French and former Vice-President of the European Commission) with the task of drafting proposals likely to rationalise and expedite the EC's decision-making. The Three Wise Men's recommendations concerned all major EC institutions and specifically suggested the desirability of improving co-ordination between the Commission and the newly elected EP.

However, the character of the relationship between the EP and the Council(s) is very different from the one between the EP and the Commission. To be sure, the EP and the Council of Ministers share a very impor-

---

54 Besides Spierenburg the Group included Karl Buschmann, Paul Delouvrier, Giuseppe Petrilli and Dick Taverne.

tant function: that of co-legislators. As fundamental as such a function may be, its character is very procedural. Thus, the EP/Council relationship is less an expression of a political convergence between the two institutions than that between the EP and the Commission. This does not necessarily mean that the relationship between the EP and the Council is adversarial or prevalently conflictual. Although "there is a high potential for conflict between the Council and the EP … day-to-day decision-making is found to be characterised by a high level of consensus, not only within, but also between the institutions. Despite initial controversies, most EU legislative procedures are concluded at a very early stage … and a procedure hardly ever fails completely". The reasons for this are paradoxically similar to those that would predict conflict between the two institutions: rationally driven behaviour does not necessarily stem from concerns over individual institutions' prerogatives but rather from a desire for "more efficiency … to avoid lengthy and cumbersome decision-making processes" (Mühlböck and Rittberger 2015: 2-5).

The Treaty of Lisbon added one more area of co-operation between the EP and the European Council, arguably the highest incarnation of the Council of Ministers. The annexed Declaration 11 on Article 17(6) and (7) of the Treaty on European Union recites: "The Conference considers that, in accordance with the provisions of the Treaties, *the European Parliament and the European Council are jointly responsible for the smooth running of the process leading to the election of the President of the European Commission*" (emphasis ours). This goes beyond the simple conferral to the EP of the prerogative to elect the President of the Commission, as it creates the conditions for an involvement of the Parliament in the nomination process *prior* to the nomination of a candidate by the European Council. This innovation of the Lisbon Treaty has been exploited to justify the presentation of *Spitzenkandidaten* by the EP political groups, but it has also created a new area of EP/EC co-operation irrespective of the EP political groups' strategic decision.

The first area in which the Parliament was given effective powers vis-à-vis the Commission and, less directly, also vis-à-vis the Council, was that of budgetary control, stemming from the approval of the 1970 Treaty of Luxembourg, which gave the EC its own resources. Indeed "the adoption of the Luxembourg Treaty in 1970 enabled the EP to play an increasingly influential role in the Community's budgetary process" (Rittberger 2005). Such powers were further strengthened with the 1975 Treaty of Brussels. Although no change was introduced on the revenue side, the role of the EP and its President (who was given the power to declare and sign the adoption of the annual budget) was significantly enhanced. In particular, the EP was formally given the power to reject the budget[55] and "entrusted with the sole authority for discharge" (De Feo 2017: 39-40). This normative framework remained unchanged until the approval of the Lisbon Treaty in 2007 when, with the abolition of the distinction between compulsory and non-compulsory expenditures, the EP was given a power of co-decision with the Council over the entire EU budget.

According to an empirical study on EU budgetary politics, the EP took a very active role in that field very early on, albeit tempered by the strategic convergence between the EP and the Commission. Based on observations of the values of four different indicators[56], Johannes Lindner (2006) established that rather significant levels of conflict in the assessment approval of and compliance with the budget occurred rather often, not least for the active role taken by the EP. Beginning with a first occurrence in 1978, when the EP approved a budgetary amendment, specifically concerning provisions in the Regional Fund, that pushed non-compulsory expenditures in the 1979 budget "considerably above the maximum rates of increase as calculated by the Commission" (Lindner 2006: 82), conflict on budgetary issues intensified in the following years when "four budgets (1980, 1985, 1986 and 1988) ... were not adopted ... according to the Treaty calendar". In particular "the EP rejected the [1980] budget in December [1979]" which "was operated, for the first time, under the provisional twelfths rule until its final adoption in July 1980" (De Feo 2017: 47). Subsequently, the Parliament refused to grant discharge to the European Commission twice, in 1984 (for financial year 1982) and in 1998 (for financial year 1996). In this latter case, the EP's refusal ultimately led to the resignation of the Commission headed by Jacques Santer (European Parliament 2015f)[57].

---

55 "Parliament considered this power already implicit in the 1970 Treaty, but the Council opposed this interpretation. The new Treaty makes the principle clear" (De Feo 2017: 40).

56 1) Actors' inability to abide by the budgetary timetable, as laid down in the Treaty (including the enactment of the provisional twelfths rule); 2) actions taken before the European Court of Justice (against the EP); 3) rejection of the general budget or a supplementary and amending budget by the EP; 4) Member States' refusal to pay their share of the enacted budget (Lindner 2006: 28).

57 The dispute over the budget raised questions about nepotism and financial mismanagement, mostly concerning the behaviour of Édith Cresson, European Commissioner for Research, Science and Technology. These induced the EP to table a motion of censure of the Commission. After a first vote in the EP against the censure, a report by a Committee of Independent Experts reiterated the indictment of Cresson's actions and paved the conditions for another motion of censure, which was pre-empted by the Santer's Commission's resignation.

This last episode is considered the most telling example of the EP's empowerment vis-à-vis the Commission resulting from its role in budgetary control, but a cumulative analysis of the various conflicts over the EU budget that are listed above also testifies to the ability of the EP to exercise a more significant role vis-à-vis the Council as well. For example, the Regional Fund decision in the revision of the 1979 budget stemmed from the EP regarding "budgetary powers as a lever for influencing legislative decisions", something it alleged to be implicit in the Treaty; "due to the upcoming direct election, Parliament was determined to stand firmly by its [T]reaty interpretation to a greater extent than it had been in previous years". This position was met in the Council by the negative reaction of Denmark, France and UK. Such "disunity among Member States weakened the Council" and ultimately led to the compromise adoption of a "supplementary and amending budget" which would not have occurred otherwise (Lindner 2006: 51-56).

The other area in which the EP increased its powers in absolute terms as well as in relation to the other major institutions is legislation. In this area, the EP improved its position much more markedly vis-à-vis the Council, as it progressively acquired co-decisional status, but made very little progress in terms of legislative initiative powers, which to an almost exclusive extent still belong to the Commission. This process had a belated start (considering that an increase in the EP's legislative powers had already been recommended in the 1971 Vedel report) but came to full fruition in the relatively short time span between the 1987 Single European Act and the 2007 Treaty of Lisbon, when co-decision between the EP and Parliament became the feature of the Ordinary Legislative Procedure (see Johansson in Chapter 2 of this book). Carine Germond's analysis in Chapter 3 of this book provides good examples of how the combined use of its budgetary and legislative powers allowed the EP to exercise considerable influence in internal policy areas, especially in the context of the last reform of the CAP in which "EPP Group members and Rapporteurs were influential in toning down the most radical of the Commission's proposals and enforcing a relatively conservatist EP position". Similarly, with the approval of the Maastricht Treaty, the EPP Group's positions on European Monetary Union, on the extension of co-decision powers for the EP and on the creation of an independent ECB were accepted. Symbolically even more important was the acceptance of the subsidiarity principle, amenable to the party's Christian vision of Europe, as posed by Wolfram Kaiser in Chapter 1 of this book.

It comes as no surprise that the EPP Group's position on the enhancement of the EP's financial and, more specifically, budgetary powers was always favourable and positive. EPP Group Member Heinrich Aigner, who was also instrumental in the attribution to the EP of a role in the appointment of members of the Court of Auditors, made it very clear in an open plenary debate held in July 1972 that the Group considered "the question of budgetary power as a cornerstone of the democratic development of the Communities" (Fontaine 2009: 94). This is consistent with the Group's European ambition as it was taking shape at the time and can be seen as the first concrete manifestation of the relentless commitment of the EPP, Party and Group, to the enhancement of the EP's role in European level democracy until the approval of the Treaty of Lisbon. But taking positions on the EP's use of budgetary powers has proven to be less simple for the EPP Group than one might expect. The institutional and political context in which such decisions have to be taken is very complex.

Institutionally, the power of (dis)approval of the budget can create tensions if not outright conflicts with the Commission, as well as with the Council. The relationship with the Commission in particular is one the EP and the EPP Group, as its foremost political component, value very much and are not very keen to compromise. The power of giving or denying discharge of the budget is potentially even more conflictual, as it can imply a negative judgement on how the Commission has operated and not simply be seen as a benevolent, albeit firm, suggestion for the Commission to revise the budget, as could be in case of a rejection. Politically the picture is even more complex, as the EPP's interests do not necessarily coincide with the rest of the EP, given the different positions that the other political groups, most notably the PES/S&D, can take. Moreover, fellow party members are at any given time in relevant positions within the Commission (often as Presidents) and the Council, as Heads of Government. These circumstances certainly limit or at least condition the ability of the EPP Group to take adversarial positions vis-à-vis the other two institutions.

A good case in point was the discharge of the 1996 budget, a process that eventually led to the resignation of the Commission headed by Jacques Santer, a Christian Democrat from Luxembourg. EPP-ED MEP James Elles, Rapporteur for the 1996 EU budget, indicated that "the EP had been hindered in obtaining access to information by the Commission and that the latter had shown itself to be totally incapable of accepting such responsibilities … [and that], the only possible course was to refuse discharge". The Group's President, Martens, however, "said that no voting instructions would be given to the EPP members of the Committee on Budgetary Control. They would vote according to their conscience and on the basis of their knowledge of the issue as a whole".[58] As the debate focused on how to behave in plenary, EPP MEPs' intentions to vote were split between discharge and censure. In December 1998, the EP "refused to grant discharge to the Commission for the 1996 budget", with the EPP Group's favourable vote. In response to this, the PES/S&D "lodged a motion of no-confidence against the European Commission" (Fontaine 2009: 413). A similar motion was lodged by the ENF Group.

An especially appointed own Working Group recommended that the EPP Group should not take part in the vote on the motion of censure tabled by the PES/S&D and should abstain on the ENF Group's one. It appeared that the Group's main preoccupation was not to facilitate the PES' strategy to divert the attention from the responsibilities of the two Socialist Commissioners, Cresson and Marin. It was felt that "the PES Group wanted to protect the Socialist Commissioners concerned by tabling a motion of censure whose rejection would be tantamount to a vote of confidence in the Commission. It was necessary [for the EPP Group] to avoid lending credibility to the motion of censure, in order to marginalise the PES. The EPP Group had to present itself as the group which genuinely wished to address the problem of fraud and misappropriation, by tabling an oral question and a resolution".[59]

Clearly this position reveals the complexity of the concerns that were behind it. Paradoxically, it might have been easier for the EPP to take a stronger position on "fraud and misappropriation" if the two Commissioners had belonged to a party other than the PES. The "EPP Group ... still maintained confidence in the Commission and would confirm this by their behaviour in the vote of no confidence, as there was no provision in the Treaties for a vote of confidence. The Commission had inherited an unfortunate legacy from the past but should now take the responsibility for finding practicable solutions. ... Moreover, "[t]here was no provision in the treaties for declarations of no confidence against individual Commissioners; [thus] it was not possible to go along with the Socialist motion of no confidence".[60] With 43 votes against and 39 in favour, the EPP Group decided not to support the censure motion[61], contributing to its rejection by 293 votes to 232 (Fontaine 2009, p. 413). The eventual resignation *in toto* of the Santer Commission, made necessary by the threat of another motion of censure,

58 EPP Group Archives, A.1.46, Group meeting minutes 9 December 1998.
59 EPP Group Archives, A.1.46, Group meeting minutes 6-7.01.1999.
60 EPP Group Archives, A.1.47, Group meeting minutes 11.01.1999.
61 EPP Group Archives, A.1.47, Group meeting minutes 14.01.1999.

very likely to be successful this time due to the conclusions of a group of 'wise men' especially appointed for the purpose, was a less than ideal outcome for the EPP Group. As stated by its President Wilfried Martens: "I did everything I could to save Santer and his Commission, but my efforts were in vain. It was a very difficult time" (cited in Fontaine 2009: 414).

Beyond these often politically laden aspects of the relationships between the EP and the other two institutions, there are more routine, but by no means unimportant, aspects that concern all levels of their apparatuses. The EP/Commission relationship was codified in 2000 in the "Framework Agreement on relations between the European Parliament and the Commission", in which, to better reflect the new 'special partnership' between Parliament and the Commission, the two institutions agreed on a number of measures "to strengthen the political responsibility and legitimacy of the Commission, extend constructive dialogue, improve the flow of information between the two institutions and improve co-operation on procedures and planning"[62].

The EPP Group has always been at the forefront of initiatives and negotiations on these matters. The Group's Vice-Chair at the time, Paulo Rangel, drafted the report that amended "The framework agreement on relations between the European Parliament and the European Commission". With the amended framework, according to Rangel, "the European Parliament seized [a] historical opportunity [...] It reinforced its role as the main political actor of the European Union. During the negotiations ... we opted for a wide interpretation of the Treaty of Lisbon. [...] The European project undoubtedly wins with this agreement".[63] Furthermore, by recognising the "first line institutional role of the 'house of the citizens'," the framework agreement deepened "the democratisation of the European Union". At the same time, the EP "gave a strong sign that [it] want[ed] to continue consolidating the principle of the division of powers."[64] Paulo Rangel was also Rapporteur on the revision of the framework (European Parliament 2010b). Another EPP MEP, Danuta Maria Hübner, took the role of Rapporteur on the Interinstitutional Agreement on Better Law-Making between the three institutions: Parliament, the Council of the European Union and the European Commission. According to Hübner, "elements of particular importance for the European Parliament of the

62 OJ C 121, 24.4.2001.

63 EPP Group Archives, D.1.2010.7-0005, press release, Parliament-Commission framework agreement: Green light to Paulo Rangel MEP to start his report.

64 EPP Group Archives, D.1.2010.10-0049, press release, framework agreement between Parliament and Commission adopted. Paulo Rangel MEP.

content of the new agreement … included multiannual and annual programming; the Commission's follow-up to Parliament's legislative initiative requests and justifications for and consultations on envisaged withdrawals of legislative proposals; better law-making tools – … important for a well-informed, inclusive and transparent decision-making process – and the impact assessment issue" (European Parliament 2016).

Other initiatives were stimulated by the provisions for the enactment of the Treaty of Lisbon. Again, Paulo Rangel was the author of the own-initiative report on the implementation of the Treaty of Lisbon with respect to the European Parliament. In connection with Rangel's report, the Constitutional Affairs Committee organised a public hearing on 20 January 2014 on the "Relations between the European Parliament and the European Commission: Parliamentarism or Presidentialism?", in which the discussion was focused, amongst other things, on the accountability and the legitimacy of EU institutions within the framework of separation of powers, already stressed by Rangel in his 2010 commentary on the amended framework, as the cornerstone principle of any democratic system.

Two prominent EPP Group exponents (Director for Relations with National Parliaments Beatrice Scarascia Mugnozza and former Director of EPP Group Presidency Johan Ryngaert) confirmed the importance of informal day-to-day relations between the Group and fonctionnaires and/or political exponents of the various institutions for the smooth running of operations in which they are jointly involved (Interviews Scarascia Mugnozza, 2-4.04.2019; Ryngaert, 3.04.2019;). They also confirmed that such links are more developed as well as easier to establish and maintain with the Commission than with the Council, not least on account of the difficulties posed by the Council's six-month rotating Presidency. EPP Group officials routinely interact with members of Commissioners' cabinets on matters of mutual concern. Similar interactions also take place in Working Groups, where Commissioners' cabinet staff and EPP Group staff meet and discuss Commission's documents and proposals (Interview Ryngaert, 3.04.2019). The EPP Group, however, was always supportive of all initiatives intended to improve links between EU institutions even if not spearheaded by one of its representatives, as was the case in favour of Martin Schulz' successful position on the 2016 Framework Agreement, on which the Council had initially been very cautious. Following the same logic, as indicated by Johan Ryngaert, EPP Group-Commission relations are entertained at a very high level at work dinners held regularly on one Tuesday night a month in Brussels. On such occasions, the participants, the EPP Group's President and all Commissioners belonging to the EPP, discuss an agenda prepared ahead of time. These work dinners are also attended by the EPP Party's President and Secretary-

General which, according to Ryngaert, adds to their political significance, as what is being discussed can be transmitted through the EPP Party to Member States' parties and Ministers and even Prime Ministers at times (on Tuesday work dinners see also Kaiser in Chapter 1 and Johansson in Chapter 2 of this book). The G5 meetings are a version of this at an even higher level, at which the President and First Vice-President of the Commission participate with the President of the EP as well as the Presidents of the EPP Group and of the S&D Group (see also Schackleton 2017).

## *Conclusion*

During the 40 years of the elected European Parliament's history, the EPP Group's importance and influence have often fluctuated. At the same time, the Group's composition and organisational structure have undergone significant changes. To a large extent, the two sets of phenomena go hand in hand, although, whilst the latter were forced upon the Group by external factors such as EU enlargements and important security and socio-economic challenges that have occurred at European and even global level throughout this period, the former were the product of the Group's own ability to respond to the challenges. Indeed, the EPP Group has adapted its ideological and overall political outlook to the different priorities and concerns expressed by new national parties from incoming Member States and to the new socio-economic and political scenarios brought on by the impact of international and domestic terrorism, migration, as well as global financial and economic crises. Somewhat connected to all of this is the (re-)emergence of sovereignist, if not outright nationalist and secessionist, positions in Member States. By doing so, the EPP Group was able to maintain, with only occasional setbacks, its strong representation in the EP and a pervasive organisational presence in the EU as a whole. It goes without saying that throughout the EP's elected history these dynamics have strongly influenced, for better or for worse, the modalities and efficacy of the EPP Group's quest for what we have called its European ambition.

It would be wrong, however, not to consider factors other than numerical strength, organisational resilience and ideological/political outlook. The Group's strategic vision and institutional presence deserve as much attention. The one element that has remained practically unchanged in the EPP Group's strategy throughout the elected EP's history is the reliance on the unity of the EP party system's core, especially on crucial institutional and constitutional issues. This has been of fundamental importance especially when, in the course of the first four elected terms, the EPP Group was not the largest one in the EP. Being part of the core always allowed it to be a driving force within what was, with minor differences, a strong Europeanist majority. At the same time, the Group's institutional presence, not only in terms of Presidencies (7 out of 17 so far), but also of important committee Chairmanships and Rapporteurships as well as other key positions, such as even simple membership in crucially important committees (see Germond in Chapter 3 and Gagatek in Chapter 4 of this book), was almost always higher than would have been granted by its sheer numerical strength, as the analysis of the IR index has shown in this chapter.

EU enlargements have significantly affected the EP party system and the EPP Group throughout the period on which this analysis is focused. The very transition from the appointed to the elected Parliament was much conditioned by the first enlargement, especially in terms of its impact on the EPP Group, which found no representation in two of the most recent Member States at the time, Denmark and, above all, the UK. To a large extent because of this, the EPP Group was relegated to a subordinate position vis-à-vis the PES/S&D Group for the first four elected terms. During this initial period, the internal structuring of the Group was characterised by the strong prevalence of the German delegation, with the Italian one often a close second[65]. All the other successive enlargements had very important combined effects. For one, the EP, with 705 MEPs instead of the initial 410, is now much larger[66]. At the same time, the size of the largest national delegations, has been reduced in absolute terms (except Germany's) and, more visibly, relative terms[67]. The EP is now much more fragmented, and therefore more difficult to manage politically, even if the number of political groups has remained more or less constant.

The fragmentation is much more evident within the political groups, including or even especially, the EPP, as demonstrated by the decline in the relative size of the historically strongest national delegations, prominently the German one, which constituted the Group's veritable driving forces. This fact alone has made it progressively more difficult to maintain the Group's almost single-minded unity and come to reach common positions

65 Italy's was the second largest delegation within the EPP Group in the first three elections and was replaced by Spain's in the fourth one (Fontaine 2009: 593-598).

66 See note 9 above.

67 The four largest delegations accounted for a total of 324 out of 410 seats (79% of the total) as opposed to 316 out of 751 (42% of the total) in 2019. After Brexit and the UK's replacement with Spain's delegation as the fourth largest MS delegation, these numbers have marginally dropped in absolute terms (310) and improved in relative terms (44% of the new total of 705).

on crucial questions swiftly and smoothly. This has certainly had an impact on the further advancement of the once dominant federalist ambition, at least from the Treaty of Lisbon onwards. The effects of the Group's numerical fragmentation have been enhanced by the increasing heterogeneity, in terms of history, ideology and values, of the newly incorporated national delegations. To fully understand the reasons for and the implications of this particular aspect, other exogenous factors have to be taken into account. The momentous political and socio-economic transformations of the second half of the last forty years have profoundly transformed European societies and their value systems. The collapse of the Soviet Union and what was known as the Eastern Bloc brought into the Western-based economic system, and eventually into the European Union, an unprecedented number of new protagonists, with traditions, values and socio-economic characteristics that were very different from those of the existing Member States. The rejection of post-communism, often also in the form of more moderate socialism, in the former Eastern Bloc countries certainly contributed to the success of moderate parties, often amenable to the EPP, even if not necessarily to its Christian democratic foundations.

As a matter of fact, the process of absorption of former Eastern Bloc delegations has profoundly diluted the original Christian democratic identity and values of the Group, to an extent that has gone far beyond the effects of the initial incorporation of non-denominational conservative parties from new Western Member States (beginning with Greece, Portugal and Spain) as well as, for a time, from the UK. This is not only posing difficulties in terms of reaching common positions and ensuring the smooth running of internal decision-making processes, but it is also potentially creating the conditions for significant changes in the Group's political positioning and strategic outlook.

It emerges rather clearly from this analysis that the incorporation of sister parties from the Visegrad group of countries has posed serious challenges not only to the Group's original Christian democratic identity but also to its historical and unconditional Europeanism. For example, although the reasons for the Group's reversal of positions on transnational lists in EP elections can be manifold, the fact that the arguments used by EPP Group exponents called to provide explanations were very reminiscent of those used by Eurosceptic parties and governments suggests the emergence of more ambivalent positions on Europe within the Group. These difficulties, however, are also due to factors over which the EPP, Party and Group, has very little control, as further federalist advancements would require treaty reforms which the aforementioned sovereignist positions in several Member States make almost impossible.

What might appear as an increasing acceptability of albeit mild Eurosceptic or sovereignist positions within the Group could also be taken as potentially leading to a change in its overall strategy and positioning within the EP party system. However, it is difficult at this time to even imagine the possibility of a new understanding with the ID Group and/or Eurosceptic parties now in the NI, as it would be numerically infeasible. Moreover, toning down the current understanding with the S&D and ALDE on institutional and strategic political decisions is only a distant possibility as it would weaken the Group's importance in the EP. In any event, the Group is still displaying remarkable resilience and the ability to respond to all the ideological, organisational and political challenges it has been called to face. This has been pointed out in a previous section and in Chapters 3 and 4 of this book. Especially in the latter, in the context of the Transatlantic Trade and Investment Partnership, the analysis has revealed that the EPP Group has continued to exert considerable influence in EU policy making vis-à-vis the other components of the EP party system. The EPP Group maintains its primacy also in the more general institutional context of the Union, as demonstrated by its unsurpassed institutional relevance scores. All of these achievements are made possible by its continuing status as the largest group in the EP and by its superior inclusiveness, which, with the addition of Estonia's extra post-Brexit MEP (see note 21), allows it to have direct links with all of the EU's 27 Member States.

This clean bill of health notwithstanding, the EPP Group's quest for more Europe seems to be on hold. The challenges posed by internal and external security, societal and economic constraints, as well as, most recently, by the Covid-19 pandemic are daunting and, for the moment, apparently impossible to face. But the pandemic has once again exposed the inadequacy of EU and non-EU nation states' responses to global crises and their consequences. These reverberate in the EU's dominant intergovernmental decision-making approach, especially on questions concerning the appropriation and allocation of the funds required to respond to the crisis. These limits are not offset but only mitigated by the responses provided by supranational institutions such as the ECB and the Commission, as the EU is not yet endowed with its own resources and supranational institutions must rely on Member States' governments' decisions for the funding of their initiatives. The need to find solutions apt to face potential new challenges similar to those posed by the global financial crisis or the post-pandemic recovery may show the way for future European progress. The EPP Group and the other groups in the EP party system core will be called upon to prove they can be a very important part of it.

*APPENDIX*

*Table A1 Weighting of institutional positions in the EP*

| | |
|---|---|
| **EP Presidency** | 60pts |
| **EP Vice Presidency** | 10pts |
| **Quaestor** | 8pts |
| **Chair High Importance Committees**[68] | 12pts |
| **Vice-Chair High Importance Committees** | 6pts |
| **Chair Medium Importance Committees** | 8pts |
| **Vice Chair Medium Importance Committees** | 4pts |
| **Chair Limited Importance committees** | 5pts |
| **Vice Chair Limited Importance committees** | 2pts |
| **Chair High Importance delegations**[69] | 6pts |
| **Vice-Chair Most Importance Delegations** | 3pts |
| **Chair Medium Importance Delegations** | 4pts |
| **Vice Chair Medium Importance Delegations** | 2pts |
| **Chair Limited Importance Delegations** | 3pts |
| **Vice Chair Limited Importance Committees. And delegations** | 1pts |

68 The logic behind distinguishing more and less important committees is based on the likelihood that the actions of a committee (e.g. reports) can have relevant consequences in terms of future legislation. This largely depends on the EU's spheres of policy-competence. The high-medium-limited importance scale, thereby, aims to contrapose areas in which the EU can produce binding legislation for its Member states to areas in which it can only recommend legislation. Most committees have received a score of medium importance: in these areas there is binding EU legislation but national interests still play in important role in the definition of policy. High importance has only been assigned to those committees operating in areas wherein the EU has an exclusive competence, i.e. the rules at the heart of the functioning of the EU. Limited importance has been assigned to those committees operating in areas in which the EU can only recommend legislation to the Member states.

69 Importance has been given in relation to countries' size and proximity to the EU. The underlying reasoning is that the function of delegations is to foster relationship with big (potential) trading partners (e.g. US-China) and to test the ground for enlargement in neighbouring countries. High importance: G20 countries + neighbouring countries that are either economically strong or have potential for enlargement. Medium importance: Relatively big countries/regions in the rest of the world + small neighbouring countries. Limited importance: Small countries/ regions in the rest of the world.

*Table A2 Seat percentages and IR scores per political group and EP term*

| EP term | Party | Seats (%) | Inst. Score (%) | IR/Seat differential |
|---|---|---|---|---|
| 1 | EPP | 26.34 | 27.34 | 1.00 |
| | S&D | 27.32 | 34.95 | 7.63 |
| | ALDE | 9.76 | 13.34 | 3.58 |
| | **TOTAL DIFFERENCE** | | | **12.22** |
| | COMM ALL | 10.73 | 7,17 | |
| | ED | 15.37 | 12.68 | |
| | *Other* | 10.24 | 4.52 | |
| 2 | EPP | 25.35 | 28.24 | 2.89 |
| | S&D | 29.95 | 32.42 | 2.47 |
| | ALDE | 7.14 | 7.88 | 0.74 |
| | **TOTAL DIFFERENCE** | | | **6.10** |
| | COMM ALL | 9.45 | 9.09 | |
| | ED | 11.52 | 14.56 | |
| | *Other* | 16.59 | 7.80 | |
| 3 | EPP | 23.36 | 30.81 | 7.45 |
| | S&D | 34.75 | 43.15 | 8.40 |
| | ALDE | 9.46 | 5.94 | -3.52 |
| | **TOTAL DIFFERENCE** | | | **12.33** |
| | ED | 6.56 | 4.59 | |
| | Greens-EFA | 5.79 | 4.70 | |
| | GUE & Far left | 8.11 | 5.29 | |
| | *Other* | 11.97 | 5.53 | |
| 4 | EPP | 27.51 | 32.44 | 4.92 |
| | S&D | 34.92 | 42.64 | 7.72 |
| | ALDE | 7.76 | 11.17 | 3.41 |
| | **TOTAL DIFFERENCE** | | | **16.05** |
| | GUE-NGL | 4.94 | 5.28 | |
| | UEN | 4.76 | 4.57 | |
| | Greens-EFA | 4.06 | 2.89 | |
| | *Other* | 16.05 | 1.02 | |
| 5 | EPP | 37.22 | 43.07 | 5.85 |
| | S&D | 28.75 | 30.20 | 1.45 |
| | ALDE | 7.99 | 10.66 | 2.67 |
| | **TOTAL DIFFERENCE** | | | **9.97** |

| EP term | Party | Seats (%) | Inst. Score (%) | IR/Seat differential |
|---|---|---|---|---|
| | Greens-EFA | 7.67 | 6.46 | |
| | GUE-NGL | 6.71 | 6.04 | |
| | *Other* | 11.66 | 3.57 | |
| 6 | EPP | 36.61 | 36.85 | 0.24 |
| | S&D | 27.32 | 31.64 | 4.32 |
| | ALDE | 12.02 | 13.84 | 1.82 |
| | **TOTAL DIFFERENCE** | | | **6.38** |
| | Greens-EFA | 5.74 | 5.17 | |
| | GUE-NGL | 5.60 | 4.94 | |
| | UEN | 3.69 | 4.66 | |
| | *Other* | 9.02 | 2.91 | |
| 7 | EPP | 36.01 | 37.80 | 1.79 |
| | S&D | 25.00 | 28.11 | 3.11 |
| | ALDE | 11.41 | 13.60 | 2.19 |
| | **TOTAL DIFFERENCE** | | | **7.09** |
| | ECR | 7.34 | 6.54 | |
| | Greens-EFA | 7.47 | 7.49 | |
| | GUE-NGL | 4.76 | 4.22 | |
| | *Other* | 8.02 | 2.24 | |
| 8 | EPP | 29.43 | 36.51 | 7.08 |
| | S&D | 25.43 | 29.20 | 3.76 |
| | ALDE | 8.92 | 11.77 | 2.85 |
| | **TOTAL DIFFERENCE** | | | **13.69** |
| | ECR | 9.32 | 10,28 | |
| | Greens-EFA | 6.66 | 5,78 | |
| | GUE-NGL | 6.92 | 5,95 | |
| | *Other* | 13.32 | 0,51 | |
| 9 | EPP | 24.23 | 29.21 | 4.98 |
| | S&D | 20.51 | 29.12 | 8.61 |
| | ALDE | 14.38 | 16.91 | 2.53 |
| | **TOTAL DIFFERENCE** | | | **16.11** |
| | ECR | 8.26 | 8.71 | |
| | Greens-EFA | 9.85 | 9.56 | |
| | GUE-NGL | 5.46 | 5.64 | |
| | *Other* | 17.31 | 0.85 | |

*Table A3 Seats % and Institutional index score (IR) % by National Delegation within the EPP: EP terms 1–8*

| | MS | A | | B | | BG | | CY | | CZ | | DK | | EST | | FIN | | F | | D | | GR | | H | | IRL | | I | |
|---|---|---|---|---|---|---|---|---|---|---|---|---|---|---|---|---|---|---|---|---|---|---|---|---|---|---|---|---|---|---|---|
| Term | | | | | | | | | | | | | | | | | | | | | | | | | | | | | | | |
| 1 | | | | 8.00 | 9.16 | | | | | | | 1.00 | 0.00 | | | | | 7.00 | 8.78 | 35.00 | 35.11 | 12.0 | 4.58 | | | 3.00 | 6.49 | 25.00 | 24.43 |
| 2 | | | | 5.00 | 3.04 | | | | | | | 2.00 | 2.39 | | | | | 9.00 | 20.44 | 36.00 | 32.32 | 7.00 | 7.73 | | | 5.00 | 4.14 | 23.00 | 17.68 |
| 3 | | | | 6.00 | 0.00 | | | | | | | 2.00 | 1.54 | | | | | 5.00 | 7.71 | 27.00 | 31.74 | 8.00 | 6.24 | | | 3.00 | 1.47 | 23.00 | 19.63 |
| 4 | | 3.00 | 1.23 | 4.00 | 0.92 | | | | | | | 0.00 | 0.00 | | | 2.00 | 0.61 | 8.00 | 8.60 | 28.00 | 32.10 | 5.00 | 6.76 | | | 2.00 | 1.84 | 7.00 | 7.68 |
| 5 | | 3.00 | 1.74 | 3.00 | 2.20 | | | | | | | 0.00 | 0.00 | | | 2.00 | 1.16 | 9.00 | 12.41 | 22.00 | 25.64 | 4.00 | 3.71 | | | 2.00 | 3.83 | 15.00 | 12.88 |
| 6 | | 2.00 | 0.95 | 2.00 | 0.71 | 1.00 | 0.00 | 1.00 | 0.48 | 5.00 | 6.90 | 0.36 | 0.00 | 0.00 | 0.00 | 1.00 | 0.48 | 6.00 | 3.57 | 18.00 | 28.78 | 4.00 | 4.52 | 5.00 | 2.73 | 2.00 | 1.07 | 9.00 | 8.80 |
| 7 | | 2.19 | 1.55 | 1.82 | 1.32 | 2.55 | 1.55 | 0.73 | 0.00 | 0.73 | 0.00 | 0.46 | 0.00 | 0.36 | 0.00 | 1.46 | 0.88 | 12.0 | 10.15 | 15.33 | 18.32 | 2.55 | 3.53 | 5.11 | 5.30 | 1.46 | 3.31 | 9.49 | 15.23 |
| 8 | | 2.28 | 1.80 | 1.83 | 1.58 | 3.20 | 3.38 | 0.46 | 0.00 | 3.20 | 4.06 | 1.00 | 0.00 | 0.46 | 0.00 | 1.37 | 2.48 | 9.13 | 13.08 | 10.96 | 16.57 | 2.28 | 1.35 | 5.48 | 5.41 | 1.83 | 3.16 | 6.85 | 11.72 |

| | MS | LV | | LT | | L | | M | | NL | | PL | | P | | RO | | SK | | SLO | | ESP | | S | | GB | | HR | |
|---|---|---|---|---|---|---|---|---|---|---|---|---|---|---|---|---|---|---|---|---|---|---|---|---|---|---|---|---|---|---|---|
| Term | | | | | | | | | | | | | | | | | | | | | | | | | | | | | | | |
| 1 | | | | | | 2.00 | 5.34 | | | 8.00 | 6.11 | | | | | | | | | | | | | | | | | | |
| 2 | | | | | | 3.00 | 0.83 | | | 7.00 | 8.84 | | | 3.00 | 0.00 | | | | | | | 1.00 | 4.97 | | | | | | |
| 3 | | | | | | 2.00 | 4.04 | | | 8.00 | 6.42 | | | 2.00 | 0.73 | | | | | | | 13.0 | 11.56 | | | 1.00 | 8.07 | | |
| 4 | | | | | | 1.00 | 0.92 | | | 6.00 | 3.53 | | | 1.00 | 1.23 | | | | | | | 17.0 | 24.73 | 3.00 | 1.23 | 11.0 | 7.07 | | |
| 5 | | | | | | 1.00 | 0.00 | | | 4.00 | 1.51 | | | 4.00 | 4.06 | | | | | | | 12.0 | 12.41 | 3.00 | 1.97 | 16.0 | 16.47 | | |
| 6 | | 1.00 | 0.48 | 1.00 | 0.48 | 1.00 | 3.57 | 1.00 | 0.48 | 3.00 | 2.14 | 5.00 | 7.02 | 3.00 | 1.55 | 3.00 | 0.48 | 3.00 | 1.66 | 1.00 | 1.43 | 9.00 | 9.04 | 2.00 | 0.48 | 10.0 | 12.25 | | |
| 7 | | 1.46 | 0.66 | 1.46 | 0.88 | 1.09 | 3.31 | 0.73 | 0.00 | 1.82 | 0.44 | 10.58 | 17.22 | 3.65 | 1.55 | 5.47 | 3.53 | 1.46 | 1.32 | 1.46 | 0.66 | 8.76 | 7.95 | 1.82 | 1.32 | 0.00 | 0.00 | 1.82 | 0.00 |
| 8 | | 1.83 | 0.00 | 1.37 | 0.45 | 1.37 | 0.68 | 1.37 | 0.90 | 2.28 | 1.35 | 10.05 | 12.85 | 3.65 | 1.58 | 5.94 | 4.28 | 2.74 | 2.48 | 2.28 | 2.25 | 7.76 | 5.19 | 1.83 | 1.35 | 0.91 | 0.00 | 2.28 | 0.00 |

*Table A4 Total scores per party*

| | | |
|---|---|---|
| EPP | 5326 | 34.72 % |
| S&D | 5017 | 32.70 % |
| ALDE | 1721 | 11.22 % |
| COMM ALL | 206 | 1.34 % |
| ECR | 426 | 2.78 % |
| ED | 409 | 2.67 % |
| EDA | 124 | 0.81 % |
| Greens-EFA | 682 | 4.45 % |
| GUE-NGL | 699 | 4.56 % |
| Other Formations | 490 | 3.19 % |
| UEN | 242 | 1.58 % |
| ***TOTAL*** | **15342** | **100.00 %** |

*Table A5 Scores per party for Quaestors*

| | | |
|---|---|---|
| EPP | 450 | 37.04 % |
| S&D | 330 | 27.16 % |
| ALDE | 165 | 13.58 % |
| COMM ALL | 45 | 3.70 % |
| ECR | 30 | 2.47 % |
| ED | 75 | 6.17 % |
| EDA | 15 | 1.23 % |
| EPD | 15 | 1.23 % |
| GUE-NGL | 90 | 7.41 % |
| ***TOTAL*** | **1215** | **100.00 %** |

*Table A6 Scores per party in Presidency*

| | | |
|---|---|---|
| EPP | 1200 | 37.56 % |
| S&D | 1190 | 37.25 % |
| ALDE | 350 | 10.95 % |
| COMM ALL | 40 | 1.25 % |
| ECR | 30 | 0.94 % |
| ED | 140 | 4.38 % |
| EDA | 30 | 0.94 % |
| Greens-EFA | 90 | 2.82 % |
| GUE-NGL | 80 | 2.50 % |
| RG | 15 | 0.47 % |
| UEN | 15 | 0.47 % |
| UEN-EPP* | 15 | 0.47 % |
| ***TOTAL*** | ***3195*** | ***100.00 %*** |

*Table A7 Party Scores in Committee*

| Party | Scores | Percentage |
|---|---|---|
| EPP | 2123 | 34.78 % |
| S&D | 2026 | 33.19 % |
| ALDE | 674 | 11.04 % |
| COMM ALL | 52 | 0.85 % |
| ECR | 206 | 3.37 % |
| ED | 90 | 1.47 % |
| EDA | 28 | 0.46 % |
| EDD | 14 | 0.23 % |
| EFDD | 28 | 0.46 % |
| EN | 14 | 0.23 % |
| EPD | 10 | 0.16 % |
| ERA | 10 | 0.13 % |
| FE | 14 | 0.23 % |
| Greens-EFA | 337 | 5.52 % |
| GUE-NGL | 293 | 4.80 % |
| INDDEM | 30 | 0.49 % |
| LU | 4 | 0.07 % |
| RG | 12 | 0.20 % |
| UEN | 139 | 2.78 % |
| ***TOTAL*** | 6104 | 100.46 % |

*Table A8 Party scores in delegations*

| Party | Scores | Percentage |
|---|---|---|
| EPP | 1553 | 33.04 % |
| S&D | 1471 | 31.29 % |
| ALDE | 532 | 11.32 % |
| COMM ALL | 69 | 1.47 % |
| ECR | 160 | 3.40 % |
| ED | 104 | 2.21 % |
| EDA | 51 | 1.08 % |
| EDD | 14 | 0.30 % |
| EFDD | 28 | 0.60 % |
| EN | 9 | 0.19 % |
| EPD | 8 | 0.17 % |
| ER | 17 | 0.36 % |
| ERA | 18 | 0.38 % |
| FE | 14 | 0.30 % |

| Party | Scores | Percentage |
|---|---|---|
| Greens-EFA | 255 | 5.42 % |
| GUE-NGL | 236 | 5.02 % |
| INDDEM | 17 | 0.36 % |
| RG | 45 | 0.96 % |
| UEN | 88 | 1.87 % |
| UFE | 12 | 0.25 % |
| ***TOTAL*** | 4701 | 99.99 % |

*Table A9 EPP Group 1979–2019: List of Chairs and Secretary-Generals by nationality*

| Name | Position | Nationality | National Party | Legislature/ Time in office |
|---|---|---|---|---|
| Klepsch, Egon | Chair | Germany | CDU | 1 |
| Barbi, Paolo | Chair | Italy | DC | 1 |
| Klepsch, Egon | Chair | Germany | CDU | 2 |
| Klepsch, Egon | Chair | Germany | CDU | 2 |
| Klepsch, Egon | Chair | Germany | CDU | 3 |
| Tindemans, Leo | Chair | Belgium | CVP | 3 |
| Martens, Wilfried | Chair | Belgium | CVP | 4 |
| Martens, Wilfried | Chair | Belgium | CVP | 4 |
| Pöttering, Hans-Gert | Chair | Germany | CDU | 5 |
| Pöttering, Hans-Gert | Chair | Germany | CDU | 5 |
| Pöttering, Hans-Gert | Chair | Germany | CDU | 6 |
| Daul, Joseph | Chair | France | UMP | 6 |
| Daul, Joseph | Chair | France | UMP | 7 |
| Daul, Joseph | Chair | France | UMP | 7 |
| Weber, Manfred | Chair | Germany | CDU | 8 |
| Weber, Manfred | Chair | Germany | CDU | 8 |
| Weber, Manfred | Chair | Germany | CDU | 9 |
| Bettamio, Giampaolo | Secretary General | Italy | DC | 01/07/1979–31/01/1986* |
| Guccione, Sergio | Secretary General | Italy | DC | 15/03/1986–31/12/1990 |
| Guckenberger, Gerhard | Secretary General | Germany | CDU | 24/01/1991–09/04/1997 |
| David, Mario | Secretary General | Portugal | PSD | 10/04/1997–07/02/1999 |
| Welle, Klaus | Secretary General | Germany | CDU | 08/02/1999–31/12/2003 |
| Pedersen, Niels | Secretary General | Denmark | DFK | 01/01/2004–31/08/2007 |

| Name | Position | Nationality | National Party | Legislature/ Time in office |
|---|---|---|---|---|
| Kamp, Martin | Secretary General | Germany | CDU | 01/09/2007–30/04/2020 |
| Busuttil, Simon | Secretary General | Malta | NP | 01/05/2020 - |

*Bettamio was appointed Secretary-General on 1/10/1976 and simply continued in office after the first direct elections of the EP

*Table A10 Presidents of the elected Parliament*

| Name | Term of office | | Party | Group | Country | EP term |
|---|---|---|---|---|---|---|
| Simone Veil | July 1979 | Jan. 1982 | UDF | LD | France | 1st |
| Piet Dankert | Jan. 1982 | July 1984 | PvdA | SOC | Netherlands | |
| Pierre Pflimlin | July 1984 | Jan. 1987 | UDF/RPR | EPP | France | 2nd |
| Henry Plumb | Jan. 1987 | July 1989 | Con | ED | United Kingdom | |
| Enrique Barón Crespo | July 1989 | Jan. 1992 | PSOE | SOC | Spain | 3rd |
| Egon Klepsch | Jan. 1992 | July 1994 | CDU | EPP | Germany | |
| Klaus Hänsch | July 1994 | Jan. 1997 | SPD | PES/S&D | Germany | 4th |
| José María Gil-Robles | Jan. 1997 | July 1999 | PP | EPP | Spain | |
| Nicole Fontaine | July 1999 | Jan. 2002 | UMP | EPP | France | 5th |
| Pat Cox | Jan. 2002 | July 2004 | Ind | ELDR | Ireland | |
| Josep Borrell | July 2004 | Jan. 2007 | PSOE | PES/S&D | Spain | 6th |
| Hans-Gert Pöttering | Jan. 2007 | July 2009 | CDU | EPP | Germany | |
| Jerzy Buzek | July 2009 | Jan. 2012 | PO | EPP | Poland | 7th |
| Martin Schulz | Jan. 2012 | July 2014 | SPD | S&D | Germany | |
| | July 2014 | Jan. 2017 | | | | 8th |
| Antonio Tajani | Jan. 2017 | July 2019 | FI | EPP | Italy | |
| David Sassoli | July 2019 | Jan. 2022 | PD | S&D | Italy | 9th |

# The Authors

**Luciano Bardi** (PhD: The Johns Hopkins University, Baltimore) is Part-time Professor at the European University Institute's Alcide De Gasperi Research Centre (ADGRC) in Florence, Italy; he is also the Co-Founder (with Peter Mair) of the OPPR formerly at the European University Institute and now at the University of Pisa.
His research activities focus on elections, democracy and representation in the European Parliament, policies and democratic governance of the European Union, foreign policy, Euroscepticism, as well as political parties and party systems especially at European Union level.
He is Project director of "PartAdapt – The adaptation of party organizations at national and European level"; and President of "Navigatore Elettorale".

**Wojciech Gagatek** is Assistant Professor at the Faculty of Political Science and International Studies, University of Warsaw, Poland. In the past, he has published extensively on party politics at the European level, in particular about the role of the EPP, led and participated in international research projects, and carried out wide-ranging field research in EU institutions, such archive research, legislative analysis and elite interviews. Furthermore, he co-authored two reports commissioned by the European Parliament.

**Carine Germond** is Professor of European Studies at NTNU, Norway. She has held competitive and prestigious research grants, fellowships and positions at multiple institutions across Europe and in the USA. In her publications, she has examined Franco-German bilateral relations and their role in European integration during the Cold War period and the role of transnational societal actors in European policy-making processes within the EU's Common Agricultural Policy and in the European Parliament.

**Karl Magnus Johansson** is Professor of Political Science at Södertörn University, Stockholm, Sweden. His research interests include the intersection between EU-level political parties/groups and constitutional reform in the EU. He has published widely on various aspects of transnational party co-operation within and throughout the EU and on EU politics, as well as on questions related to Sweden's membership in the EU.

**Wolfram Kaiser** is Professor of European Studies at the University of Portsmouth, UK, and Visiting Professor at the College of Europe in Bruges, Belgium. He has published widely on European integration and transnational and global networks. His most recent books include *Shaping European Union* (2018), *Writing the Rules for Europe* (2014, with J. Schot) and *Exhibiting Europe in Museums* (2014, with S. Krankenhagen and K. Poehls).

**Silvia Sassano** is a researcher in History of European Integration. She is a post-doctoral Fellow at the Alcide De Gasperi Research Centre of the European University Institute in Florence, Italy. Since 2018 she has been collaborating with the International Studies Institute of Florence as guest speaker for the "The European Union" course. Her main research interests and publications deal with the History of the EC/EU Policies and History of the EC/EU institutions, with a particular focus on European Territorial Co-operation, European Cohesion Policy and EC/EU enlargements.

# General Appendix

*List of Abbreviations*

| | |
|---|---|
| AFET | EP Committee on Foreign Affairs |
| AFCO | EP Committee on Constitutional Affairs |
| AGRI | EP Committee on Agriculture and Rural Development |
| ALDE | Alliance of Liberals and Democrats for Europe |
| AP | Alianza Popular |
| CAP | Common Agricultural Policy |
| CD Group | Christian Democratic Group |
| CDU | Christlich Demokratische Union Deutschlands (Christian Democratic Union) |
| CFSP | Common Foreign and Security Policy |
| CSU | Christlich-Soziale Union in Bayern (Christian Social Union) |
| CLIM | EP Temporary Committee on Climate Change |
| COP | Conferences of Parties |
| COPA-COGECA | Comité des organisations professionnelles agricoles-Comité général de la coopération agricole de l'Union européenne (Committee of agricultural professional organizations-General Confederation of Agricultural Cooperatives) |
| CSDP | Common Security and Defence Policy |
| DC | Democrazia Cristiana |
| DEVE | EP Committee on Development |
| DROI | AFET subcommittee on Human Rights |
| EC | European Communities |
| ECB | European Central Bank |
| ECJ | European Court of Justice |
| ECOFIN | Economic and Financial Affairs Council configuration |
| ECON | EP Committee on Economic and Monetary Affairs |
| ECR | European Conservatives and Reformists Group |
| ECSC | European Coal and Steel Community |
| ECU | European Currency Unit |
| ED | European Democrats |
| EDC | Equipo Demócratico Cristiano |
| EEA | European Economic Area |
| EEAS | European External Action Service |
| EEC | European Economic Community |
| EFDD | Europe of Freedom and Direct Democracy Group |
| EMPL | EP Committee on Employment and Social Affairs |
| EMU | Economic and Monetary Union |

| | |
|---|---|
| EMS | European Monetary System |
| ENF | Europe of Nations and Freedom Group |
| EP | European Parliament |
| EPC | European Political Community |
| EPP | European People's Party |
| EPRG | Energy Policy Research Group |
| ERM | Exchange Rate Mechanism |
| ESM | European Stability Mechanism |
| ETS | Emissions Trading Scheme |
| ETUC | European Trade Union Conferederation |
| EU | European Union |
| EUCD | European Union of Christian Democrats |
| FTA | Free Trade Agreements |
| GATT | General Agreement on Tariffs and Trade |
| Greens-EFA | Greens – European Free Alliance |
| GUE-NGL | European United Left – Nordic Green Left |
| HR/VP | EU's High Representative for Foreign Affairs and Security Policy |
| ID | Identity and Democracy Group |
| IGC | Intergovernmental Conference |
| INTA | EP Committee on International Trade |
| ISDS | Investor-state dispute settlement |
| JHA | Justice and Home Affairs |
| JPC | EU-Turkish Joint Parliamentary Committee |
| KVP | Katholieke Volkspartij (Catholic People's Party) |
| LIBE | EP Committee on Civil Liberties, Justice and Home Affairs |
| MEP | Member of European Parliament |
| MRP | Mouvement Républicain Populaire |
| NEI | Nouvelles Equipes Internationales |
| NI | Non-Inscrits (Non-Attached) |
| NGOs | Non-Governmental Organizations |
| OECD | Organisation for Economic Co-operation and Development |
| OLP | Ordinary legislative procedure |
| QMV | Qualified majority voting |
| PES | Party of European Socialists |
| PFELs | European Political Foundations |
| PDP | Parti Démocrate Populaire |
| PP | Partido Popular |
| PCI | Partito Comunista Italiano (Italian Communist Party) |
| PSI | Partito Socialista Italiano (Italian Socialist Party) |
| RQMV | Reversed Qualified Majority Voting |
| SEA | Single European Act |
| SGP | Stability and Growth Pact |
| SFP | Single Farm Payment |

| | |
|---|---|
| SIPDIC | Sécretariat International des Partis Démocratiques d'Inspiration Chrétienne |
| S&D | Socialists and Democrats |
| TEU | Treaty on European Union |
| TFEU | Treaty on the Functioning of the European Union |
| TTIP | Transatlantic Trade and Investment Partnership |
| UKIP | United Kingdom Independence Party |

# General Appendix

## List of Archives

Archives Nationales, Paris, France.

Bundesarchiv, Koblenz, Germany.

EPP Group Archives, Brussels, Belgium.

Historical Archives of the European Union (HAEU), Florence, Italy.

Katholiek Documentatie- en Onderzoekscentrum (KADOC), Leuven, Belgium.

Archiv für Christlich-demokratische Politik (ACDP), Konrad Adenauer Stiftung (KAS), Sankt Augustin, Germany.

Österreiches Staatsarchiv, Vienna, Austria.

University College Dublin (UCD) Archives, Dublin, Ireland.

*List of Interviews*

**Bettamio, Giampaolo**, Rome, 9.11.2018 (Wolfram Kaiser)

**Brok, Elmar**, Phone, 10.12.2018 (Wojciech Gagatek); Berlin, 23.03.2018 (Dietmar Nickel, HAEU Oral History Collections); Brussels, 25.02.1998 (Karl Magnus Johansson)

**Dastoli, Virgilio**, Phone, 10.10.2017 (Wolfram Kaiser)

**Engel, Frank**, Phone, 5.02.2019 (Wojciech Gagatek)

**Fjellner, Christofer**, Phone, 16.01.2019 (Wojciech Gagatek)

**Grzyb, Andrzej**, Brussels, 25.09.2018 (Wojciech Gagatek)

**Jacqué, Jean-Paul**, Bruges, 17.10.2017 (Wolfram Kaiser)

**Jansen, Thomas**, Phone, 13.6.2018 (Wolfram Kaiser); Lund, 27.10.1995 (Karl Magnus Johansson)

**Kaczmarek, Filip**, Poznań, 8.09.2018 (Wojciech Gagatek)

**Kalniete, Sandra**, Brussels, 10.10.2018 (Wojciech Gagatek)

**Kamp, Martin**, Phone, 16.12.2019 (Karl Magnus Johansson); Phone, 3.10.2019 (Wojciech Gagatek)

**Martens, Wilfried**, Brussels, 30.03.2000 (Karl Magnus Johansson)

**McAllister, David**, Brussels, 10.10.2018 (Wojciech Gagatek)

**Méndez de Vigo, Íñigo**, Phone, 11.05.2000 (Karl Magnus Johansson); Fiesole, 23.11.2018 (Alfredo De Feo, HAEU Oral History Collection)

**Nickel, Dietmar**, Skype, 27.10.2017 (Wolfram Kaiser)

**Pöttering, Hans-Gert**, Brussels, 26.6.2018 (Wolfram Kaiser); Brussels, 25.02.1998 (Karl Magnus Johansson)

**Preda, Cristian**, Brussels, 10.10.2018 (Wojciech Gagatek)

**Quisthoudt-Rowohl, Godelieve**, Brussels, 29.11.2018 (Wojciech Gagatek)

**Ribera d'Alcalá, Riccardo**, Brussels, 26.9.2018 (Wolfram Kaiser)

**Ryngaert, Johan**, Brussels, 5.12.2019 and 3.04.2019 (Luciano Bardi)

**Salafranca, Juan**, Brussels, 9.07.2018 (Wojciech Gagatek)

**Salafranca Sanchez-Neyra, Jose Ignacio**, Brussels, 10.10.2018 (Wojciech Gagatek)

**Saryusz-Wolski, Jacek**, Brussels, 4.09.2018 (Wojciech Gagatek)

**Scarascia Mugnozza, Beatrice**, Brussels, 2-4.04.2019 (Luciano Bardi); Brussels, 26.6.2018 (Wolfram Kaiser); Phone, 17.12.2019 (Karl Magnus Johansson)

**Schoutheete, Philippe de**, Stockholm, 8.04.1999 (Karl Magnus Johansson)

**Welle, Klaus**, Brussels, 24.02.1998 and 3.12.2002 (Karl Magnus Johansson)

**Wenta, Bogdan**, Brussels, 25.09.2018 (Wojciech Gagatek)

## Bibliography

Anderson, Karen M. (2015) *Social Policy in the European Union*. London: Palgrave.

Andrlik, Erich (1981) The Farmers and the State: Agricultural Interests in West German Politics. *West European Politics* 4, 104-19.

Appeldoorn, Bastiaan van (2002) *Transnational Capitalism and the Struggle over European Integration*. London: Routledge.

Attinà, Fulvio (1990) The Voting Behaviour of European Parliament Members and the Problem of the Europarties. *European Journal of Political Research* 17, 557-79.

Aydın-Düzgit, Senem (2012) *Constructions of European Identity: Debates and Discourses on Turkey and the EU*. London: Palgrave Macmillan.

Bajon, Philip (2012) *Europapolitik "am Abgrund": Die Krise des "leeren Stuhls" 1965-66*. Stuttgart: Franz Steiner.

Balfour, Rosa (2013) *Human Rights and Democracy in EU Foreign Policy: The Cases of Ukraine and Egypt*. London: Routledge.

Bardi, Luciano (2014) *The Evolution of the Europarty System after the 2014 Elections of the European Parliament.* Directorate General for Internal Policies, Policy Department C: Citizens' Rights and Constitutional Affairs.

Bardi, Luciano (2008) Party Responses to new Challenges. In: Karina Kosara-Pedersen and Peter Kurrild-Klitgaard (eds.) *Partier og Partisystemer i Forandering: Festskrift til Lars Bille*. Odense: Syddansk Universitetsforlag, 127-48.

Bardi Luciano (2004) European Political Parties. A (Timidly) Rising Actor in the EU Political System. *The International Spectator* 39/2, 17-30.

Bardi, Luciano (2002) Parties and Party Systems in the European Union. In: Kurt Richard Luther and Ferdinand Müller-Rommel (eds.) *Political Parties in a Changing Europe: Political and Analytical Challenges*. Oxford: Oxford University Press, 292-322.

Bardi, Luciano (1994) Transnational Party Federations, European Parliament Party Groups, and the Building of Europarties. In: Richard Katz and Peter Mair (eds.) *How Parties Organize: Adaptation and Change in Party Organizations in Western Democracies*. Beverly Hills and London: Sage Publications, 357-373.

Bardi, Luciano (1990) The Harmonisation of European Electoral Law. In: Serge Noiret (ed.), *The Comparative Study of European Electoral Reforms*. Baden-Baden: Nomos, 503-29.

Bardi, Luciano, Katz, Richard S. and Peter Mair (2015) Towards a European Politics. In: Richard Johnston and Campbell Sharman (eds.) *Parties and Party Systems: Structure and Context*. Vancouver: University of British Columbia Press, 127-47.

Bardi, Luciano and Enrico Calossi (2009) Models of Party Organisation and Europarties. In: Bill Cross, Joan DeBardeleben and Jon Pammett (eds.) *Activating the Citizen: Dilemmas of Citizen Participation in Europe and Canada*. London: Palgrave Macmillan, 151-72.

Barroso, José Manuel Durão (2012) State of the Union 2012 Address, Plenary session of the European Parliament, 12 September 2012, Strasbourg. https://ec.europa.eu/commission/presscorner/detail/en/SPEECH_12_596 (accessed 31 May 2020)

Bates, Robert H., Greif, Avner, Levi, Margaret and Jean-Laurent Rosenthal (1998) *Analytic Narratives*. Princeton: Princeton University Press.

BBC (1971) *Jean Monnet, Father of Europe*. The 1971 BBC Documentary. https://www.brookings.edu/blog/brookings-now/2014/03/14/jean-monnet-father-of-europe-the-1971-bbc-documentary/ (accessed 31 May 2020).

Beach, Derek (2012) The Constitutional Treaty. The Failed Formal Constitutionalisation. In: Finn Laursen (ed.) *Designing the European Union: From Paris to Lisbon*. London: Palgrave Macmillan, 217–43.

Beach, Derek (2007) The European Parliament in the 2000 IGC and the Constitutional Treaty Negotiations: From Loser to Winner. *Journal of European Public Policy* 14/8, 1271-92.

Bengtsson, Rikard and Ole Elgström (2012) Conflicting Role Conceptions? The European Union in Global Politics. *Foreign Policy Analysis* 8/1, 93-108.

Best, Edward, Gray, Mark and Alexander Stubb (eds.) (2000) *Rethinking the European Union: IGC 2000 and Beyond*. Maastricht: European Institute of Public Administration.

Bicchi, Federica and Sandra Lavenex (2015) The European Neighbourhood: Between European Integration and International Relations. In: Knud Erik Jorgensen et al. (eds.), *The SAGE Handbook of European Foreign Policy*. London: SAGE, 868-83.

Bickerton, Christopher J., Hodson, Dermot and Uwe Puetter (2015) The New Intergovernmentalism: European integration in the post-Maastricht era. *Journal of Common Market Studies* 53/4, 703-22.

Bickerton, Chistopher J. (2011) *European Union Foreign Policy: From Effectiveness to Functionality*. London: Palgrave MacMillan.

Boassson, Elin Lerum and Jorgen Wettestad (2014) Policy Invention and Entrepreneurship: Bankrolling the Burying of Carbon in the EU. *Global Environmental Change* 29, 404-12.

Bomsdorf, Eckart (1980) Die Kräfteverteilung im Europa-Parlament nach Fraktionen und Ländern. *Zeitschrift für Parlamentsfragen* 11, 396-403.

Bongardt, Annette and Francesco Torres (2012) The Lisbon Strategy. In: Erik Jones, Anand Menon and Stephen Weatherhill (eds.) *The Oxford Handbook of the European Union*. Oxford: Oxford University Press, 468-83.

Bösch, Frank (2001) *Die Adenauer-CDU: Gründung, Aufstieg und Krise einer Erfolgspartei 1945-1969*. Stuttgart: DVA.

Botsiou, Konstantina E. (2009) The European Centre-Right and European Integration: The Formative Years. In: Constantine Arvanitopoulos (ed.) *Reforming Europe. The Role of the Centre-Right*. Berlin: Springer, 173-206.

Bouwen, Pieter (2004) The Logic of Access to the European Parliament: Business Lobbying in the Committee on Economic and Monetary Affairs. *Journal of Common Market Studies* 42, 473-95.

Bowler, Shaun and Gail McElroy (2015) Political Group Cohesion and 'Hurrah' Voting in the European Parliament. *Journal of European Public Policy* 22/9, 1355–65.

Braghiroli, Stefano (2012) Je t'aime… moi non plus! An Empirical Assessment of Euro-Parliamentarians' Voting Behaviour on Turkey and Turkish Membership. *Southeast European and Black Sea Studies* 12/1, 1–24.

Braun, Mats (2016) *Europeanization of Environmental Policy in the New Europe: Beyond Conditionality*. London: Routledge.

Bressanelli, Edoardo (2014) *Europarties after Enlargement: Organization, Ideology and Competition*. London: Palgrave Macmillan.

Bressanelli, Edoardo and Nicola Chelotti (2018) The European Parliament and Economic Governance: Explaining a Case of Limited Influence. *The Journal of Legislative Studies* 24, 72-89.

Brok, Elmar and Guy Verhofstadt (2010) *Proposal for the Establishment of the EEAS*. Working document 6. Brussels: European Parliament.

Buchanan, Tom, and Martin Conway (eds.) (1996) *Political Catholicism in Europe, 1918-1965*. Oxford: Oxford University Press.

Budden, Philip (2002) Observations on the Single European Act and "Relaunch of Europe": a less "Intergovernmental" Reading of the 1985 Intergovernmental Conference. *Journal of European Public Policy* 9/1, 76–97.

Budden, Philip (1994) *The Making of the Single European Act: The United Kingdom and the European Community: 1979–1986*. Unpublished thesis presented to the Faculty of Modern History at the University of Oxford.

Burns, Charlotte (2016) The European Parliament and Climate Change: A Constrained Leader? In: Rüdiger K.W. Wurzel and James Connelly (eds.) *The European Union as a Leader in International Climate Change Politics: Still Taking a Lead?* London: Routledge, 76-89.

Burns, Charlotte (2013) Consensus and Compromise Become Ordinary – but at What Cost? A Critical Analysis of the Impact of the Changing Norms of Codecision upon European Parliament Committees. *Journal of European Public Policy* 20, 988-1005.

Burns, Charlotte (2005) The European Parliament: The European Union's Environmental Champion? In: Andrew Jordan and Camilla Adelle (eds.) *Environmental Policy in the EU: Actors, Institutions and Processes*. London: Earthscan.

Burns, Charlotte, Paul Tobin and Sebastian Sewerin (eds.) (2015) *The Impact of the Economic Crisis on European Environmental Policy*. Oxford: Oxford University Press.

Burns, Charlotte, and Neil Carter (2010a) The European Parliament and Climate Change: From Symbolism to Heroism and Back Again. In: Rüdiger K.W. Wurzel and James Connelly (eds.) *The European Union as a Leader in International Climate Change Politics.* London: Routledge, 78-93.

Burns, Charlotte, and Neil Carter (2010b) Is Codecision Good for the Environment? *Political Studies* 58, 128-42.

Calligaro, Oriane (2013) *Negotiating Europe: EU Promotion of Europeaness since the 1970s*. London: Palgrave Macmillan.

Cellini, Jacopo (2018) The Idea of Europe at the Origins of the European People's Party: the Making of the European Manifesto and of the EPP's Political Programme. *Journal of European Integration History* 24/1, 79-94.

Cicchi, Lorenzo (2016) *Is Euro-Voting Truly Supranational? National Affiliation and Political Group Membership in the European Parliament*. Pisa: Pisa University Press.

Cini, Michelle and Lee McGowan (1998) *Competition Policy in the European Union*. London: Macmillan.

Chang, Michele (2009) *Monetary Integration in the European Union*. London: Palgrave Macmillan.

Christiansen, Thomas and Christine Reh (2009) *Constitutionalizing the European Union*. London: Palgrave Macmillan.

Christiansen, Thomas and Simona Piattoni (eds.) (2003) *Informal Governance in the European Union*. Cheltenham: Edward Elgar.

Claeys, Paul-H. and Nicole Loeb-Mayer (1979) Trans-European Party Groupings: Emergence of New and Alignment of Old Parties in the Light of the Direct Elections to the European Parliament. *Government and Opposition* 14, 455-78.

Clark, Christopher (2013) The New Catholicism and the European Culture Wars. In: Christopher Clark and Wolfram Kaiser (eds.) *Culture Wars: Secular-Catholic Conflict in Nineteenth-Century Europe*. Cambridge: Cambridge University Press, 11-46.

Coen, David and Katsaitis, Alexander (2013) Chameleon Pluralism in the EU: An Empirical Study of the European Commission Interest Group Density and Diversity across Policy Domains. *Journal of European Public Policy* 20, 1104-19.

Commission of the European Communities (1991a) Communication of the Commission to the Council. *The Development and Future of the CAP: Reflections Paper of the Commission*. COM(91)100 final. Brussels: CEC.

Commission of the European Communities (1991b) *The Development and Future of the CAP. Follow-Up to the Reflections Paper COM(91)100 of 1 February 1991*. Brussels: CEC.

Conway, Martin (2004) The Rise and Fall of Western Europe's Democratic Age, 1945-1973. *Contemporary European History* 13/1, 67-88.

Copeland, Paul and Dimitris Papadimitriou (eds.) (2012) *The EU's Lisbon Strategy: Evaluating Success, Understanding Failure*. London: Palgrave.

Corbett, Richard (2012) The Evolving Roles of the European Parliament and of National Parliaments. In: Andrea Biondi, Piet Eeckhout and Stefanie Ripley (eds.) *EU law after Lisbon*. Oxford: Oxford University Press.

Corbett, Richard (1998) *The European Parliament's Role in Closer EU Integration*. London: Palgrave.

Corbett, Richard (1993) *The Treaty of Maastricht: From Conception to Ratification. A Comprehensive Reference Guide*. Harlow: Longman.

Corbett, Richard (1987) The 1985 Intergovernmental Conference and the Single European Act. In: Roy Pryce (ed.) *The Dynamics of European Union*. London: Croom Helm, 238–72.

Corbett, Richard, Jacobs, Francis and Darren Neville (2016). *The European Parliament*. 9th ed. London: John Harper Publishing.

CORDIS (2004) EPP group "revisits" the Lisbon agenda. https://cordis.europa.eu/article/rcn/22857/en (accessed 31 May 2020).

CORDIS (2005) Political groups split over revised Lisbon strategy. https://cordis.europa.eu/article/id/23312-political-groups-split-over-revised-lisbon-strategy/en (accessed 31 May 2020).

Costello, Roy and Robert Thomson (2016) Bicameralism, Nationality and Party Cohesion in the European Parliament. *Party Politics* 22/6, 773-83.

Costello, Roy and Robert Thomson (2010) The Policy Impact of Leadership in Committees: Rapporteurs' Influence on the European Parliament's Opinions. *European Union Politics* 11/2, 219-40.

Council (1992) Council directive 92/43/EEC of 21 May 1992 on the conservation of natural habitats and of wild fauna and flora.

Council of the European Communities (1980) Three Wise Men's Report on European Institutions. Bruxelles: Council of the European Communities.

Cox, Graham, Lowe, Philip and Michael Winter (1987) Farmers and the States: A Crisis for Corporatism. *The Political Quarterly* 58, 73-81.

Cox, Graham, Lowe, Philip and Michael Winter (1986) From State Direction to Self-Regulation: The Historical Development of Corporatism in British Agriculture. *Policy & Politics* 14, 475-90.

Crowson, Nick J. (2007) *The Conservative Party and European Integration since 1945*. London: Routledge.

Culpepper, Pepper D. (1993) Organisational Competition and the Neo-Corporatist Fallacy in French Agriculture. *West European Politics* 16, 295-315.

Dakowska, Dorota (2009a) Networks of Foundations as Norm Entrepreneurs: Between Politics and Policies in EU Decision-Making. *Journal of Public Policy* 29/2, 201-21.

Dakowska, Dorota (2009b) The Emergence of European Political Foundations: Political Entrepreneurs and Transnational Transfers. *GSPE Working Paper*. http://aei.pitt.edu/12443/ (accessed 31 May 2020).

Daugbjerg, Carstens (1999) Reforming the CAP: Policy Networks and Broader Institutional Structures. *Journal of Common Market Studies* 37, 407-28.

De Feo, Alfredo (2017) The European Budget. Motor or Brake of European Integration? A Walk through 40 Years of Budgetary Decisions. In: Stefan Becker, Michael W. Bauer and Alfredo De Feo (eds.) *The New Politics of the European Union Budget*. Baden-Baden: Nomos, 33-82.

de Ruiter, Rik and Christine Neuhold (2016) The Winner Takes It All? The Implications of the Lisbon Treaty for the EPs Legislative Role in Co-decision. In: Finn Laursen (ed.) *The EU's Lisbon Treaty: Institutional Choices and Implementation*. London: Routledge, 103-18.

de Vreese, Claes H., Boomgaarden, Hajo G. and Holli A. Semetko (2008) Hard and Soft: Public Support for Turkish Membership in the EU. *European Union Politics* 9/4, 511-30.

Delreux, Tom and Sander Happaerts (2012) *Environmental Policy and the politics in the European Union*. London: Palgrave Macmillan.

Dinan, Desmond (2018) *The Historiography of the European Parliament: Changing Perceptions of the Institution from the 1950s to Today*. Brussels: EPRS European Parliament History Series.

Dinan, Desmond (2012) The Single European Act: Revitalising European Integration. In: Finn Laursen (ed.) *Designing the European Union. From Paris to Lisbon*. London: Palgrave Macmillan, 124–46.

Dinan, Desmond (1999). *Ever Closer Union? An Introduction to European Integration*. London: Palgrave Macmillan.

Dinan, Desmond and Sophie Vanhoonacker (2000) IGC 2000 Watch (Part 2): The Opening Round. *ECSA Review* 13/3, 1 and 8–9.

Djankov, Simeon (2014) *Inside the Euro Crisis: An Eyewitness Account*. Washington, DC: Peterson Institute for International Economics.

Dodo, Mahamat K. (2014) Historical Evolution of the Social Dimension of the European Integration: Issues and Future Prospects of the European Social Model. *L'Europe en Formation* 372, 51-66.

Duchêne, François (1994) *Jean Monnet: The First Statesman of Interdependence*. New York: Norton.

Duranti, Marco (2017) *The Conservative Human Rights Revolution: European Identity, Transnational Politics, and the Origins of the European Convention*. Oxford: Oxford University Press.

Dyson, Kenneth (1994) *Elusive Union: The Process of Economic and Monetary Union*. London: Longman.

Dyson, Kenneth and Kevin Featherstone (1999) *The Road to Maastricht: Negotiating Economic and Monetary Union*. Oxford: Oxford University Press.

EPP (2018) Press Release 8 November 2018. Manfred Weber elected as EPP candidate for the President of the European Commission. https://www.epp.eu/press-releases/manfred-weber-elected-as-epp-candidate-for-the-president-of-the-european-commission/ (accessed 31 May 2020)

EPP (2007) *EPP in Action. EPP Yearbook 2007*. Brussels: European People's Party.

EPP/EUCD (1997) *EPP/EUCD Yearbook '96*. Brussel: European People's Party.

EPP Group (2020a) Letter to Presidents of EU Commission and European Council. https://www.eppgroup.eu/sites/default/files/attachments/2020/05/epptovdlmichelonmff_0.pdf (accessed 31 May 2020)

EPP Group (2020b) EPP Group threatens to veto EU budget if Parliament is sidelined. https://www.eppgroup.eu/newsroom/news/epp-group-to-veto-eu-budget-if-parliament-is-sidelined (accessed 31 May 2020)

EPP Group (2018) Press release 7 February 2018. EPP Group votes down transnational lists. https://www.eppgroup.eu/newsroom/news/epp-group-votes-down-transnational-lists (accessed 31 May 2020)

EPP Group (2017) Press release 20 June 2017. Human rights crucial to evaluation of new EU-Cuba agreement. https://www.eppgroup.eu/newsroom/news/human-rights-crucial-to-evaluation-of-new-eu-cuba-agreement (accessed 31 May 2020)

EPP Group (2014) Press release 16 April 2014. Statute and funding Regulation for European political parties adopted in plenary. https://www.eppgroup.eu/newsroom/news/regulation-on-european-political-parties-adopted-in-plenary (accessed 31 May 2020)

EPP Group (2013) 2-Pack: Strengthening the Economic and Budgetary Surveillance of Euro Area Member States Requesting or Receiving Financial Assistance. https://www.eppgroup.eu/newsroom/news/2-pack-strengthening-economic-and-budgetary-surveillance (accessed 31 May 2020)

Eriksen, Erik Oddvar (2011) Governance between Expertise and Democracy: The Case of European Security. *Journal of European Public Policy* 18/8, 1169–89.

Erkelens, Leendert and Steven F. Blockmans (2012) Setting up the European External Action Service: An Institutional Act of Balance. *CLEER Working Papers* 1, 1–32.

EU News (2014) The socialists – populars coalition at the European Parliament extended to liberals. https://www.eunews.it/en/2014/06/26/the-socialists-populars-coalition-at-the-european-parliament-extended-to-liberals/18228 (accessed 31 May 2020)

Euractiv (2016) Socialist MEPs visit Cuba, plead for stronger ties. https://www.euractiv.com/section/development-policy/news/socialist-meps-visit-cuba-plead-for-stronger-ties/ (accessed 31 May 2020)

European Commission (2010a) Communication from the Commission to the European Parliament, the Council, the European Economic and Social Committee and the Committee of the Regions, The CAP towards 2020: Meeting the food, natural resources and territorial challenges of the future. COM(2010) 672 final.

European Commission (2010b) Commission staff working document, Lisbon Strategy evaluation document. SEC(2010) 114 final.

European Consensus (2006) Joint statement by the Council and the representatives of the governments of the Member States meeting within the Council, the European Parliament and the Commission on European Union Development Policy: The European Consensus. OJ C 46/1, 24.2.2006.

European Parliament (2018) Resolution of 12 September 2018 on the state of EU-US relations (2017/2271(INI)), Doc. A8-0251/2018.

European Parliament (2017a) Resolution of 14 February 2017 on the revision of the European Consensus on Development (2016/2094(INI)), Doc. A8-0020/2017.

European Parliament (2017b) Report on the proposal for a regulation of the European Parliament and of the Council amending Regulation (EU, Euratom) No. 1141/2014 of the European Parliament and the Council of 22 October 2014 on the statute and funding of European political parties and European political foundations (COM(2017)0481 – C8-0307/2017 – 2017/0219(COD)), Doc. A8-0373/2017.

European Parliament (2016) Report on the conclusion of an Interinstitutional Agreement on Better Law-Making between the European Parliament, the Council of the European Union and the European Commission (2016/2005(ACI)), Doc. A8-0039/2016.

European Parliament (2015a) Draft report of 5 February 2015 containing the European Parliament's recommendations to the Commission on the negotiations for the Transatlantic Trade and Investment Partnership (TTIP) (2014/2228(INI)).

European Parliament (2015b) Resolution of 8 July 2015 containing the European Parliament's recommendations to the European Commission on the negotiations for the Transatlantic Trade and Investment Partnership (TTIP) (2014/2228(INI)), Doc. A8-0175/2015.

European Parliament (2015c) Resolution of 10 June 2015 on the state of EU-Russia relations (2015/2001(INI)), Doc. A8-0162/2015.

European Parliament (2015d) Results of votes, 8.07.2015. P8_PV(2015)07-08(VOT)_EN.doc, PE 564.811. http://www.europarl.europa.eu/sides/getDoc.do?type=PV&reference=20150708&secondRef=TOC&language=en (accessed on 31 May 2020)

European Parliament (2015e) Report on the reform of the electoral law of the European Union (2015/2035(INL)), Doc. A8-0286/2015.

European Parliament (2015f) EP news – Eu Affairs https://www.europarl.europa.eu/news/en/headlines/eu-affairs/20150427STO46470/discharge-procedure-how-parliament-scrutinises-the-eu-budget (accessed 31 May 2020)

European Parliament (2014a) Motion for a resolution to wind up the debate on the statement by the Commission pursuant to Rule 110(2) of the Rules of Procedure on the elections to the European Parliament in 2014 (2012/2829(RSP)), Doc. B7-0520/2012.

European Parliament (2014b) Resolution of 22 November 2012 on the elections to the European Parliament in 2014 (2012/2829(RSP)), Doc. B7-0520/2012.

European Parliament (2013a) Resolution of 23 May 2013 on EU trade and investment negotiations with the United States of America (2013/2558(RSP)), Doc. B7-0187/2013.

European Parliament (2013b) Results of votes, PV 23/05/2013—13.11, PE 511.455. http://www.europarl.europa.eu/sides/getDoc.do?type=PV&reference=20130523&secondRef=TOC&language=en (accessed 31 May 2020)

European Parliament (2013c) Report on the proposal for a regulation of the European Parliament and of the Council on the statute and funding of European political parties and European political foundations (COM(2012)0499 – C7-0288/2012 – 2012/0237(COD), Doc. A7-0140/2013.

European Parliament (2012) Draft report on the proposal for a regulation of the European Parliament and of the Council on the strengthening of economic and budgetary surveillance of Member States experiencing or threatened with serious difficulties with respect to their financial stability in the euro area. 2011/0385(COD).

European Parliament (2011a) Report on the CAP towards 2020: meeting the food, natural resources and territorial challenges of the future (2011/2051(INI)), Doc. A7-0202/2011.

European Parliament (2011b) Communiqué de Presse. http://www.europarl.europa.eu/sides/getDoc.do?type=IM-PRESS&reference=20111010IPR28832&language=EN. (accessed 31 May 2020)

European Parliament (2011c) Report on increasing the impact of EU development policy (2011/2047(INI)), Doc. A7-0205/2011.

European Parliament (2011c) Report on Political parties at European level and rules regarding their funding (2010/2201(INI)), Doc. A7-0062/2011.

European Parliament (2010a) Resolution of 8 July 2010 on the future of the Common Agricultural Policy after 2013 (2009/2236(INI)), Doc. A7-0204/2010.

European Parliament (2010b) Report on the revision of the framework agreement on relations between the European Parliament and the Commission (2010/2118(ACI)), Doc. A7-0279/2010.

European Parliament (2009a) *Building Parliament. Fifty Years of European Parliament History 1958-2008*. Luxembourg: Office for Official Publications of the European Communities.

European Parliament (2009b) 2050: The future begins today – recommendations for the EU's future integrated policy on climate change, Doc. A6-0495/2008.

European Parliament (2009c) Report on the institutional aspects of setting up the European External Action Service (2009/2133(INI)), Doc. A7-0041/2009.

European Parliament (2008) Compromise Amendments 1-25 on the proposal for a directive of the European Parliament and of the Council amending Directive 2003/87/EC so as to improve and extend greenhouse gas emission allowance trading system of the Community. Draft report Avril Doyle: 2008/0013 (COD).

European Parliament. (2007a) Resolution of 26 September 2007 on towards a common European foreign policy on energy (2007/2000(INI)), Doc. A6-0312/2007.

European Parliament (2007b) Report on the composition of the European Parliament (2007/2169(INI)), Doc. A6-0351/2007.

European Parliament (2007c) Report on the proposal for a regulation of the European Parliament and of the Council amending Regulation (EC) No 2004/2003 on the regulations governing political parties at European level and the rules regarding their funding (COM(2007)0364 – C6-0202/2007 – 2007/0130(COD)), Doc. A6-0412/2007.

European Parliament (2007d) Report on the roadmap for the Union's Constitutional Process (2007/2087(INI), Doc. A6-0197/2007.

European Parliament (2005) Minutes of proceedings, Result of roll-call votes – Annex 2 (9/3/2005). https://www.europarl.europa.eu/sides/getDoc.do?pubRef=-//EP//NONSGML+PV+20050309+RES-RCV+DOC+PDF+V0//EN&language=EN (accessed 31 May 2020)

European Parliament (2004) Report on the amendments to the European Parliament's Rules of Procedure following the adoption of the Regulation governing the statute and the financing of political parties at European level (2003/2205(REG)), Doc. A5-0071/2004.

European Parliament (2003) Report on the proposal for a European Parliament and Council regulation on the statute and financing of European political parties
(COM(2003) 77 – C5-0059/2003 – 2003/0039(COD)), Doc. A5-0170/2003.

European Parliament (2002a) Report on the division of competences between the European Union and the Member States (2001/2024(INI)), Doc. A5-0133/2002.

European Parliament (2002b) Report on enlargement: Progress report (COM(2002) 700 – C5 0474/2002 – 2002/2160(INI)), Doc. A5-0371/2002.

European Parliament (2000a) Report on the reinforced cooperation (2000/2162(INI)), Doc. A5-0288/2000.

European Parliament (2000b) Resolution on the convening of the Intergovernmental Conference, Doc. A5-0018/2000.

European Parliament (2000c) Resolution containing the European Parliament's proposals for the Intergovernmental Conference, Doc. A5-0086/2000.

European Parliament (2000d) Report on the enlargement of the European Union (COM(1999) 500 – C5 0341/2000 – 2171/2000 (COS)), Doc. A5-0250/2000.

European Parliament (1999) Final report on the preparation of the reform of the Treaties and the next Intergovernmental Conference, Doc. A5–0058/1999.

European Parliament (1997a) Resolution of 19 November 1997 on the Amsterdam Treaty, Doc. A4-0347/1997.

European Parliament (1997b) Report on the proposal of the European Parliament to the Extraordinary European Council Summit on Employment (20-21 November 1997), Doc. C4-0389/97.

European Parliament (1996) Resolution of 13 March 1996 on the convening of the IGC, evaluation of the work of the Reflection Group and definition of the political priorities of the European Parliament with a view to the Intergovernmental Conference, Doc. A4-0068/96.

European Parliament (1995) Resolution on the functioning of the Treaty on European Union with a view to the 1996 Intergovernmental Conference – implementation and development of the Union, Doc. A4-0102/95.

European Parliament (1994) Resolution of 10 February 1994 on the Constitution of the European Union, Doc. A3-64/94.

European Parliament (1992) Resolution of 7 April 1992 on the results of the Intergovernmental Conferences, Doc. A3-0123/1992.

European Parliament (1990a) Resolution of 11 July 1990 on the European Parliament's guidelines for a draft constitution for the European Union, Doc. A3-0165/1990.

European Parliament (1990b) Resolution of 12 December 1990 on the constitutional basis of European Union, Doc. A3-0301/1990.

European Parliament (1989a) Resolution on the strategy of the European Parliament for achieving European Union, Doc. A 2-332/88.

European Parliament (1989b) Report on Economic and Monetary Union, Doc. A3-0223/90.

European Parliament (1987) Resolution on the strategy of the European Parliament for achieving European Union, Doc. A 2-28/87.

European Parliament (1985a) Debates of the European Parliament of 12 December 1985, No 2-333/281.

European Parliament (1985b) Report on the state of the development of the electoral procedure for the election of the Members of the European Parliament, Doc. A 2-1/85.

European Parliament (1982a) Motion for a resolution, Doc. 1-940/81.

European Parliament (1982b) Report drawn up on behalf of the Political Affairs Committee on a draft uniform electoral procedure for the election of Members of the European Parliament, Doc. 1-988/81/A.

European Parliament (1981a) Report on the relation between the European Parliament and the national Parliaments, Doc. 1-206/81.

European Parliament (1981b) Report on the relations between the European Parliament and the European Council, Doc. 1-739/81.

European Parliament (1981c) Report on the role of the European Parliament in the negotiation and ratification of treaties of accession and of other treaties and agreements between the European Community and third countries, Doc. 1-685.

European Parliament (1981d) Motion for a resolution, Doc. 1-347/79.

European Parliament (1972) Report on the competences and powers of the European Parliament, Doc. 28.266/rev.

European Parliament (No date) Briefing note for the meeting of the EMPL Committee 5 October 2009 regarding the exchange of views on the Lisbon Strategy and the EU cooperation in the field of social inclusion. 2009-2014. https://www.europarl.europa.eu/meetdocs/2009_2014/documents/empl/dv/lisbonstrategybn_/lisbonstrategybn_en.pdf. (accessed 31 May 2020)

Express (2020) EU divided: Bloc's budget row EXPLODES as von der Leyen allies threaten to sink her plans. https://www.express.co.uk/news/world/1279175/EU-news-budget-Ursula-von-der-Leyen-coronavirus-rescue-fund-plans-latest-update (accessed 31 May 2020)

Fabbrini, Federico (2016) *Economic Governance in Europe: Comparative Paradoxes and Constitutional Challenges*. Oxford: Oxford University Press.

Falkner, Gerda (1998) *EU Social Policy in the 1990s: Towards a Corporatist Policy Community*. London: Routledge.

Farrell, Henry and Adrienne Héritier (2003). Formal and Informal Institutions under Codecision: Continuous Constitution-Building in Europe. *Governance* 16/4, 577–600.

Fasone, Cristina (2014) European Economic Governance and Parliamentary Representation: What Place for the European Parliament? *European Law Journal* 20, 164-85.

Feliu, Laura and Francesc Serra (2015) The European Union as a "Normative Power" and the Normative Voice of the European Parliament. In: Stelios Stavridis and Daniela Irrera (eds.) *The European Parliament and its International Relations*. London: Routledge, 17-34.

Fiott, Daniel (2015) The Diplomatic Role of the European Parliament's Parliamentary Groups. *SIEPS European Policy Analysis* 3.

Fontaine, Pascal (2009) *Voyage to the Heart of Europe 1953-2009: A History of the Christian-Democratic Group and the Group of the European People's Party in the European Parliament*. Brussels: Racine.

Fontaine, Pascal (2009) *Herzenssache Europa: Eine Zeitreise 1953-2009*. Brussels: Racine.

Forsyth, Murray (1964) *The Parliament of the European Communities*. London: PEP.

Frantescu, Doru Peter (2016) *Who is for and against free trade in the European Parliament*. https://www.votewatch.eu/blog/who-is-for-and-against-free-trade-in-the-european-parliament/ (accessed 31 May 2020)

Fouilleux, Eve (1996) *La Cogestion à la française à l'épreuve de l'Europe: L'exemple de la réforme de la Politique Agricole Commune*. Grenoble: CERAT-IEP.

Fowler, Linda, Polhuis, Pieter and Scott C. Paine (1983) Changing Patterns of Voting Strength in the European Parliament. *Comparative Politics* 15/2, 159-75.

Fraktion der EVP/ED im Europäischen Parlament (ed.) (2000) *Liber Amicorum: Für Egon Klepsch zum 70. Geburtstag am 30. Januar 2000*. Trier: Paulinus.

Gagatek, Wojciech and Steven Van Hecke (2014) The Development of European Political Foundations and Their Role in Strengthening Europarties. *Acta Politica* 49/1, 86-104.

Gagatek, Wojciech (2009). The European People's Party and the Party of European Socialists: Government and opposition? *European View* 8/2, 301-11.

Garavini, Giuliano (2012) *European Integration, Decolonization, and the Challenge from the Global South 1957-1986*. Oxford: Oxford University Press.

Garzia, Diego, Trechsel, Alexander and Lorenzo de Sio (2017) Party Placement in Supranational Elections: An Introduction to the Euandi 2014 Dataset. *Party Politics* 23/4, 333-41.

Garzon, Isabelle (2006) *Reforming the Common Agricultural Policy: History of a Paradigm Change*. London: Palgrave Macmillan.

Geary, Michael, Germond, Carine, and Kiran K. Patel (2013) The Maastricht Treaty: Negotiations and Consequences in Historical Perspective. *Journal of European Integration History* 19 (special issue).

Gehler, Michael (2001) Der "Genfer Kreis": Christdemokratische Parteienkooperation und Vertrauensbildung im Zeichen der deutsch-französischen Annäherung 1947–1955. *Zeitschrift für Geschichtswissenschaft* 49/7, 599–625.

Gehler, Michael, Gonschor, Marcus, Meyer, Hinnerk and Hannes Schönner (eds.) (2018) *Transnationale Parteienkooperation der Europäischen Christdemokraten und Konservativen*. Berlin: de Gruyter.

Gehler, Michael and Wolfram Kaiser (eds.) (2004a) *Christian Democracy in Europe since 1945*. London: Routledge.

Gehler, Michael and Wolfram Kaiser (eds.) (2004b) *Transnationale Parteienkooperation der europäischen Christdemokraten. Dokumente 1945-1965*. Munich: K.G. Saur.

Germond, Carine (2013) Preventing Reform? Agricultural Interest Groups and the Common Agricultural Policy. In: Wolfram Kaiser and Jan-Henrik Meyer (eds.) *Societal Actors in European Integration: Polity-Building and Policy-Making 1958-92*. London: Palgrave Macmillan.

Germond, Carine and Henning Türk (eds.) (2008) *A History of Franco-German Relations in Europe: From "Hereditary Enemies" to Partners*. London: Palgrave Macmillan.

Germond, Carine. 2015. An Emerging Anti-Reform Green Front? Farm Interest Groups Fighting the 'Agriculture 1980' Project, 1958-1972. *European Review of History* 22/3, 433-50.

Gheyle, Niels and Ferdi De Ville (2019) Outside Lobbying and the Politicization of the Transatlantic Trade and Investment Partnership. In: Doris Dialer and Margarethe Richter (eds.) *Lobbying in the European Union: Strategies, Dynamics and Trends*. Berlin: Springer, 339-54.

Graaf, Jan de (2019) *Socialism across the Iron Curtain: Socialist parties in East and West and the Reconstruction of Europe after 1945*. Cambridge: Cambridge University Press.

Grant, Win (1997) *The Common Agricultural Policy*. London: Palgrave Macmillan.

Green Cowles, Maria (1995) Setting the Agenda for a New Europe: The ERT and the EC 1992. *Journal of Common Market Studies* 33/4, 501-26.

Green Cowles, Maria (1994) *The Politics of Big Business in the European Community: Setting the Agenda for a New Europe*. Washington DC: American University.

Greenpeace (2018) *Out of Balance: Industry Links in the European Parliament Agriculture Committee*. Brussels: Greenpeace European Unit. https://www.greenpeace.de/sites/www.greenpeace.de/files/publications/out_of_balance_-_industry_links_in_the_european_parliament_agri_committe.pdf (accessed 31 May 2020)

Greer, Alan and Thomas Hind (2012) Inter-institutional Decision-Making: The Case of the Common Agricultural Policy. *Policy and Society* 31/4, 331-341.

Griffiths, Richard and Brian Girvin (eds.) (1995) *The Green Pool and the Origins of the Common Agricultural Policy*. London: Bloomsbury.

Grunert, Thomas (1990) The European Parliament in Search of a Uniform Electoral Procedure. In: Serge Noiret (ed.) *The Comparative Study of European Electoral Reforms*. Baden-Baden: Nomos, 487-502.

Gualerzi, Giorgio (1959) *La politica estera dei popolari*. Rome: Cinque lune.

Guerrieri, Sandro (2015) The Genesis of a Supranational Representation: The Formation of Political Groups at the Common Assembly of the ECSC, 1952-1958. In: Lucia Bonfreschi, Giovanni Orsina and Antonio Varsori (eds.), *European Parties and the European Integration Process, 1945-1992*. Brussels: Peter Lang, 393-410.

Guerrieri, Sandro (2011) La délégation italienne au Parlement européen (1952-1979). *Journal of European Integration History* 17/1, 47-59.

Gürkan, Seda (2018) The Role of the European Parliament in Turkey-EU Relations: A Troublemaker or a Useful Normative Actor? *Southeast European and Black Sea Studies* 18/1, 107–25.

Haas, Ernst B. (1958) *The Uniting of Europe: Political, Social and Economical Forces 1950-1957*. London: Stevens and Sons.

Hänggi, Heiner (2004) The Use of Force Under International Auspices: Parliamentary Accountability and "Democratic Deficits". In: Heiner Hänggi and Hans Born (eds.) *The "Double Democratic Deficit": Parliamentary Accountability and the Use of Force under International Auspices*. Farnham: Ashgate, 3-18.

Hantrais, Linda (2007) *Social Policy in the European Union*. 3rd edition. London: Palgrave.

Heard-Lauréote, Karen (2010) *European Union Governance: Effectiveness and Legitimacy in European Commission Committees*. London: Routledge.

Hendricks, Gisela (1988) Germany and the CAP: National Interests and the European Community. *International Affairs* 65, 75-87.

Hendriks, Gisela (1991) *Germany and European Integration, the Common Agricultural Policy: An Area of Conflict*. New York: Berg.

Heinelt, Hubert, Tanja Malek, Randall Smith and Annette E. Töller (eds.) (2018) (or. ed. 2001). *European Union Environmental Policy and New Forms of Government: A Study of the Implementation of the Environmental Impact Assessment Directive and the Eco-Management and Audit Scheme Regulation in Three Member States*. London: Routledge.

Héritier, Adrienne (2017) *The Increasing Institutional Power of the European Parliament and EU Policy Making*. Institute for European Integration Research, Working Series.

Herman, Valentine and Juliet Lodge (1978) *The European Parliament and the European Community*. London and New York: Macmillan and St.Martin's Press.

Herranz-Surrallés, Anna (2014) The EU's Multilevel Parliamentary (Battle)field: Inter-Parliamentary Cooperation and Conflict in Foreign and Security Policy. *West European Politics* 37/5, 957-75.

Heumen, Lennaert van and Mechthild Roos (eds.) (2019) *The Informal Construction of Europe*. London: Routledge.

Hill, Christopher (2003) *The Changing Politics of Foreign Policy*. London: Palgrave Macmillan.

Hill, Christopher (2002) The Geopolitical Implications of Enlargement. In: Jan Zielonka (ed.) *Europe Unbound: Enlarging and Reshaping the Boundaries of the European Union*. London: Routledge, 95–116.

Hix, Simon (2002a) Constitutional Agenda-Setting Through Discretion in Rule Interpretation: Why the European Parliament Won at Amsterdam. *British Journal of Political Science* 32/2, 259–80.

Hix, Simon (2002b) Parties at the European Level. In: Paul Webb, David Farrell and Ian Holliday (eds.) *Political Parties in Advanced Industrial Democracies*. Oxford: Oxford University Press.

Hix, Simon, Noury, Abdul G. and Gérard Roland (2007) *Democratic Politics in the European Parliament*. Cambridge: Cambridge University Press.

Hix, Simon, Noury, Abdul G. and Gérard Roland (2006) Dimensions of Politics in the European Parliament. *American Journal of Political Science* 50/2, 494-520.

Hix, Simon, Noury, Abdul G. and Gérard Roland (2005) Power to the Parties: Cohesion and Competition in the European Parliament, 1979-2001. *British Journal of Political Science* 35/2, 209-34.

Hix, Simon, Raunio, Tapio and Roger Scully (2003) Fifty years on: Research on the European Parliament. *Journal of Common Market Studies* 41, 191-202.

Hix, Simon and Christopher Lord (1997) *Political Parties in the European Union*. London: Macmillan.

Houdbine, Anne-Marie and Jean-Raymond Vergès (1966) *Le Parlement Européen dans la construction de l'Europe des six*. Paris: Presses Universitaire de France.

Ishiyama, John, Pace, Christopher and Brandon Stewart (2018) Foreign Threat and Political Party Change: Russia and Changes in Party Manifestos. *Communist and Post-Communist Studies* 51/4, 325-35.

Jackson, Andrew L. R. (2018) *Conserving Europe's Wildlife, Law and Policy of the Natura 2000 Network of Protected Areas*. London: Routledge.

Jacobs, Francis B. (1991) The European Parliament and Economic and Monetary Union. *Common Market Law Review* 28, 361-82.

Jacobs, Francis B., Corbett, Richard and Michael Shackleton (2003) *The European Parliament*. 5th edition. London: Cartermill.

Jančić, Davor (2017) TTIP and Legislative-Executive Relations in EU Trade Policy. *West European Politics* 40/1, 202-21.

Jančić, Davor (2016) World Diplomacy of the European Parliament. *The Hague Journal of Diplomacy* 11, 121-43.

Jansen, Thomas (1998) *The European People's Party: Origins and Development*. London: Macmillan.

Jansen, Thomas and Steven Van Hecke (2011) *At Europe's Service: The Origins and Evolution of the European People's Party*. Berlin: Springer.

Johansson, Karl Magnus (2017) The Role of Europarties in EU Treaty Reform: Theory and Practice. *Acta Politica* 52/3, 286–305.

Johansson, Karl Magnus (2016) Europarty Influence and Its Limits: The Case of the European People's Party and the Amsterdam Treaty. *Journal of European Integration* 38/1, 79–94.

Johansson, Karl Magnus (2015) The European People's Party and the Amsterdam Treaty. *Journal of European Integration History* 21/2, 269-86.

Johansson, Karl Magnus (2003) *Förberedelser inför regeringskonferenser – framtidskonventet i sitt sammanhang*. Stockholm: Svenska institutet för Europapolitiska studier (Sieps).

Johansson, Karl Magnus (2002a) Another Road to Maastricht: The Christian Democrat Coalition and the Quest for European Union. *Journal of Common Market Studies* 40/5, 871-93.

Johansson, Karl Magnus (2002b) Party Elites in Multilevel Europe: The Christian Democrats and the Single European Act. *Party Politics* 8/4, 423-39.

Johansson, Karl Magnus and Tapio Raunio (2019) *Political Parties in the European Union*. Oxford Research Encyclopedia of Politics. New York: Oxford University Press, 1-19.

Johansson, Karl Magnus and Tapio Raunio (2005) Regulating Europarties: Cross-Party Coalitions Capitalizing on Incomplete Contracts. *Party Politics* 11/5, 515–34.

Johansson, Karl Magnus and Tapio Raunio (2004) *Politiska partier i den europeiska författningen*. Stockholm: SNS Förlag.

Johansson-Nogués, Elisabeth (2015) Enlargement. In: Knud Erik Jorgensen et al. (eds.), *The SAGE Handbook of European Foreign Policy*. London: SAGE, 853-66.

Judge, David (1992) "Predestined to Save the Earth": The Environment Committee of the European Parliament. *Environmental Politics* 1, 186-212.

Judge, David and David Earnshaw (2008) *The European Parliament*. 2nd edition. London: Palgrave Macmillan.

Judt, Tony (2005) *Postwar: A History of Europe since 1945*. New York: Penguin.

Kaeding, Michael (2005) The World of Committee Reports: Rapporteurship Assignment in the European Parliament. *The Journal of Legislative Studies* 11/1, 82-104.

Kaiser, Wolfram (2020) "Allmächtige Spinne im Netz"? Egon A. Klepsch als EVP-Fraktionsvorsitzender im Europäischen Parlament 1977-82 und 1984-92. In: Michael Borchard (ed.) *Deutsche Christliche Demokraten in europäischen Institutionen*. Düsseldorf: Droste (in press).

Kaiser, Wolfram (2018a) *Shaping European Union: The European Parliament and Institutional Reform, 1979-1989*. Brussels: EPRS European Union History Series.

Kaiser, Wolfram (2018b) Transnational Practices Governing European Integration: Executive Autonomy and Neo-Corporatist Concertation in the Steel Sector. *Contemporary European History* 27/2, 239-57.

Kaiser, Wolfram (2013) Europeanization of Christian Democracy? Negotiating Organization, Enlargement, Policy and Allegiance in the European People's Party. In: Wolfram Kaiser and Jan-Henrik Meyer (eds.) *Societal Actors in European Integration: Polity-Building and Policy-Making 1958-1992*. London: Palgrave Macmillan, 15-37.

Kaiser, Wolfram (2012) Political Parties in the European Polity: Eastern Enlargement in Historical Perspective. In: Bruno Arcidiacono et al. (ed.) *Europe Twenty Years after the End of the Cold War: The New Europe, New Europes?* Brussels: P.I.E. Peter Lang, 33-45.

Kaiser, Wolfram (2007) *Christian Democracy and the Origins of European Union*. Cambridge: Cambridge University Press.

Kaiser, Wolfram (2005) Political Dynamics in an Emerging Polity: Globalisation, Transnational Relations and Europeanisation. In: Johnny Laursen (ed.) *The Institutions and Dynamics of the European Community, 1973-1983*. Baden-Baden: Nomos, 51-75.

Kaiser, Wolfram (2000) Cooperation of European Catholic Politicians in Exile in Britain and the United States during World War II. *Journal of Contemporary History* 35/3, 439-65.

Kaiser, Wolfram (1999) *Using Europe, Abusing the Europeans: Britain and European Integration 1945-63*. London: Palgrave Macmillan.

Kaiser, Wolfram and Piotr Kosicki (eds.) (2021) *Christian Democrats in Political Exile: People, Networks, and Ideas in the Global Twentieth Century*. Leuven: Leuven University Press.

Kaiser, Wolfram, and Jan-Henrik Meyer (2017) *International Organizations & Environmental Protection: Conservation and Globalization in the Twentieth Century*. New York: Berghahn.

Kaiser, Wolfram and Kiran K. Patel (2017) Multiple Connections in European Cooperation: International Organizations, Policy Ideas, Practices and Transfers 1967–1992. *European Review of History* 24/3, 337-57.

Kaiser, Wolfram and Johan Schot (2014) *Writing the Rules for Europe: Experts, Cartels and International Organizations*. London: Palgrave Macmillan.

Kaiser, Wolfram, Leucht, Brigitte and Michael Gehler (eds.) (2010) *Transnational Networks in Regional Integration: Governing Europe 1945-83*. London: Palgrave Macmillan.

Kaiser, Wolfram, and Christian Salm (2009) Transition und Europäisierung in Spanien und Portugal: Sozial- und christdemokratische Netzwerke im Übergang von der Diktatur zur parlamentarischen Demokratie. *Archiv für Sozialgeschichte* 49, 259-82.

Katz, Richard S. and Peter Mair (1995) Changing Models of Party Organisation and Party Democracy: The Emergence of the Cartel Party. *Party Politics* 1, 5-28.

Kay, Adrian (2003) Path Dependency and the CAP. *Journal of European Public Policy* 10, 405-20.

Keeler, John T.S (1987) *The Politics of Neo-Corporatism in France: Farmers, the State, and Agricultural Policy-Making in the Fifth Republic*. Oxford: Oxford University Press.

Kelemen, R. Daniel, Menon, Anand and Jonatham Slapin (2014) Wider and Deeper? Enlargement and Integration in the European Union. *Journal of European Public Policy* 21/5, 647-63.

Kerr, Henry H. (1973) Changing Attitudes through International Participation: European Parliamentarians and Integration. *International Organization* 27/1, 45-83.

Kerremans, Bart and Yf Reykers (2015) Political Parties and Interest Groups. In: Knud Erik Jorgensen et al. (eds.) *The SAGE Handbook of European Foreign Policy*. London: SAGE, 429-41.

King, Anthony (1969) Political Parties in Western Democracies: Some Sceptical Reflections. *Polity* 2, 111-41.

Kingston, Suzanne, Heyvaert, Veerle and Aleksandra Čavoški (2017) *European Environmental Law*. Cambridge: Cambridge University Press.

Kissack, Robert (2015) The EU and Human-Rights Promotion. In: Knud Erik Jorgensen et al. (eds.) *The SAGE Handbook of European Foreign Policy*. London: SAGE, 822–36.

Kleimann, David (2011) Taking stock: EU Common Commercial Policy in the Lisbon Era. *CEPS Working Document* 346.

Klingemann, Hans Dieter et al. (2006) *Mapping Policy Preferences: Estimates for Parties, Electors, and Governments in Eastern Europe, the European Union and OECD 1990-2003*. Oxford: Oxford Univeristy Press.

Klüver, Heike and Jae-Jae Spoon (2015) Bringing Salience Back In: Explaining Voting Defection in the European Parliament. *Party Politics* 21/4, 553-64.

Knudsen, Ann Kristina (2012) The 1970 and 1975 Budget Treaties: Enhancing the Democratic Architecture of the Community. In: Finn Laursen (ed.) *Designing the European Union: From Paris to Lisbon*. London: Palgrave Macmillan, 98-123.

Knudsen, Ann-Christina L. (2009) *Farmers on Welfare: The Making of Europe's Common Agricultural Policy*. Ithaca/NY: Cornell University Press.

König, Thomas (2008) Why Do Member States Empower the European Parliament? *Journal of European Public Policy* 15/2, 167-88.

Koop, Christel, Reh, Christine and Edoardo Bressanelli (2018) When Politics Prevails: Parties, Elections and Loyalty in the European Parliament. *European Journal of Political Research* 57/3, 563-86.

Kreppel, Amie (2002) *The European Parliament and Supranational Party System: A Study in Institutional Development*. Cambridge: Cambridge University Press.

Kurtzer, Paulette and Alice Cooper (2013) Biased or Not? Organized interests and the Case for the EU Food Information Labelling. *Journal of European Public Policy* 20, 722-40.

Laakso, Markku and Rein Taagepera (1979) "Effective" Number of Parties: A Measure with Application to West Europe. *Comparative Political Studies* 12, 3-27.

Laffan, Brigid and Pierre Schlosser (2016) Public Finances in Europe: Fortifying EU Economic Governance in the Shadow of the Crisis. *Journal of European Integration* 38, 237-49.

Lamassoure, Alain (2004) *Histoire secrète de la Convention Européenne*. Paris: Fondation Robert Schuman/Éditions Albin Michel.

Lamberts, Emiel (ed.) (2002) *The Black International*. Leuven: Leuven University Press.

Laurent, Pierre-Henri and Marc Maresceau (eds.) (1998) *The State of the European Union*. Vol. 4: *Deepening and Widening*. Boulder/CO: Lynne Rienner Publishers.

Laursen, Finn (ed.) (2016a) *The EU's Lisbon Treaty: Institutional Choices and Implementation*. London: Routledge.

Laursen, Finn (2016b) *The Founding Treaties of the European Union and Their Reform*. Oxford Research Encyclopedia of Politics. New York: Oxford University Press.

Laursen, Finn (ed.) (2012a) *Designing the European Union: From Paris to Lisbon*. London: Palgrave Macmillan.

Laursen, Finn (2012b) The Treaty of Nice: The Inadequate Preparation of Enlargement. In: Laursen Finn (ed.) *Designing the European Union: From Paris to Lisbon*. London: Palgrave Macmillan, 196–216.

Laursen, Finn (ed.) (2006) *The Treaty of Nice: Actor Preferences, Bargaining and Institutional Choice*. Leiden: Martinus Nijhoff Publishers.

Lees, Emma and Jorge E. Viñuales (eds.) (2019) *The Oxford Handbook of Comparative Environmental Law*. Oxford: Oxford University Press.

Lenschow, Andrea (2005) Environmental Policy: Contending Dynamics of Policy Change. In: Helen S. Wallace, William Wallace and Mark E. Pollack (eds) *Policy-Making in the European Union*. Oxford: Oxford University Press, 305-27.

Leopold, Patricia M. (1982) Community Law-making: Opinions of the European Parliament. *Oxford Journal of Legal Studies* 2/3, 454-59.

Leucht, Brigitte (2018) The Policy Origins of the European Economic Constitution. *European Law Journal* 24/2-3, 191-205.

Leucht, Brigitte, and Katja Seidel (2008) Du Traité de Paris au règlement 17/1962: ruptures et continuités dans la politique européenne de concurrence, 1950-1962. *Histoire, Économie et Société* 27/1, 35-46.

Lindner, Johannes (2006) *Conflict and Change in EU Budgetary Politics*. London: Routledge.

Lindstädt, René, Slapin, Jonathan B. and Ryan J.V. Wielen (2012) Adaptive Behaviour in the European Parliament: Learning to Balance Competing Demands. *European Union Politics* 13/4, 465-86.

Lodge, Juliet (1985) Euro-Elections and the European Parliament: The Dilemma over Turnout and Powers. *Parliamentary Affairs* 38/1, 40-55.

Lord, Christopher (2011) The Political Theory and Practice of Parliamentary Participation in the Common Security and Defence Policy. *Journal of European Public Policy* 18/8, 1133-50.

Lord, Christopher (2008) Is There a Role for Parliamentary Participation in European Security Co-ordination? In: Dirk Peters and Wolfgang Wagner (eds.) *The Parliamentary Control of European Security Policy*. Oslo: Arena, 29-49.

Lovec, Marko and Emil Erjavec (2015) The Co-decision Trap: How the Co-decision Procedure Hindered CAP Reform. *Intereconomics* 50, 52-8. https://archive.intereconomics.eu/year/2015/1/the-co-decision-trap-how-the-co-decision-procedure-hindered-cap-reform/ (accessed 31 May 2020).

Luster, Rudolf (ed.) (1988) *Bundesstaat Europäische Union: Ein Verfassungsentwurf*. Sindelfingen: Libertas Verlag.

Lynch, Frances M.B. (1997) *France and the International Economy: From Vichy to the Treaty of Rome*. London: Routledge.

Mair, Peter (2007) Political Opposition and the European Union. *Government and Opposition* 42/1, 1-17.

Marks, Gary et al. (eds.) (2007) Crossvalidating Data on Party Positioning on European Integration. *Electoral Studies* 26/1, 23-38.

Marks, Gary and Carole J. Wilson (2000) The Past in the Present: A Cleavage Theory of Party Response to European Integration. *British Journal of Political Science* 30/3, 433-59.

Marquand, David (1979) *Parliament for Europe*. London: Cape.

Martens, Wilfried (2008) *Europe: I Struggle, I Overcome*. Dordrecht: Springer.

Maurer, Andreas (2013) From EMU to DEMU: The Democratic Legitimacy of the EU and the European Parliament. IAI Working Papers 13/11. http://iaitestnew.asw.bz/sites/default/files/iaiwp1311.pdf (acccessed 31 May 2020)

McElroy, Gail and Kenneth Benoit (2012) Policy Positioning in the European Parliament. *European Union Politics* 13/1, 150-67.

Merkel, Angela (2010) Foreword. In: Jean-Claude Piris, *The Lisbon Treaty: A Legal and Political Analysis*. Cambridge: Cambridge University Press, xv.

Meyer, Jan-Henrik (2017) Making the Polluter Pay: How the European Communities Established Environmental Protection. In: Wolfram Kaiser and Jan-Henrik Meyer (eds.) *International Organizations & Environmental Protection: Conservation and Globalization in the Twentieth Century*. New York: Berghahn, 182-210.

Meyer, Jan-Henrik (2014) Getting Started: Agenda-Setting in European Environmental Policy in the 1970s. In: Johnny Laursen (ed.) *The Institutions and Dynamics of the European Community, 1973-83*. Baden-Baden: Nomos, 221-24.

Meyer, Jan-Henrik (2013) Saving Migrants: A Transnational Network Supporting Supranational Bird Protection Policy in the 1970s. In: Wolfram Kaiser, Brigitte Leucht and Michael Gehler (eds.) *Transnational Networks in Regional Integration: Governing Europe 1945-83*. London: Palgrave Macmillan, 176-98.

Meyer, Jan-Henrik (2012) A Good European? Hans-Edgar Jahn – Anti-Boshevist, Cold Warrior, Environmentalist. In: Ann-Christina L. Knudsen and Karen Gram-Skjoldager (eds.) *Living Political Biography: Narrating 20th Century European Lives*. Aarhus: Aarhus University Press, 137-59.

Meyer, Jan-Henrik (2011) Green Activism: The European Parliament's Environmental Committee Promoting a European Environmental Policy in the 1970s. *Journal of European Integration History* 17/1, 73-85.

Middlemas, Keith (1995) *Orchestrating Europe: The Informal Politics of the European Union 1973–1995*. London: Fontana Press.

Milward, Alan S. (1992) *The European Rescue of the Nation-State*. London: Routledge.

Mittag, Jürgen (2011) Die Politisierung der Gemeinsamen Versammlung der Europäischen Gemeinschaft für Kohle und Stahl: Anfänge transnationaler Fraktionsbildung im Europäischen Parlament. *Journal of European Integration History* 17/1, 13-30.

Monar, Jörg and Wolfgang Wessels (eds.) (2001) *The European Union after the Treaty of Amsterdam*. London: Continuum.

Moravcsik, Andrew (1998) *The Choice for Europe: Social Purpose and State Power from Messina to Maastricht*. Ithaca/NY: Cornell University Press.

Mourlon-Druol, Emmanuel (2012) *A Europe made of Money? The Emergence of the European Monetary System*. Ithaca/NY: Cornell University Press.

Mühlböck, Monika and Berthold Rittberger (2015) The Council, the European Parliament, and the Paradox of Inter-Institutional Cooperation. In: Christine Neuhold and SophieVanhoonacker (eds.) Dynamics of Institutional Cooperation in the European Union: Dimensions and Effects. *European Integration online Papers (EIoP)* 19/1, Special issue, 1-20. http://eiop.or.at/eiop/texte/2015-004a.htm (accessed 31 May 2020).

Neuhold, Christine (2006) The European Parliament and the European Commission: "You Can't Always Get What You Want". In: Finn Laursen (ed.) *The Treaty of Nice: Actor Preferences, Bargaining and Institutional Choice*. Leiden: Martinus Nijhoff Publishers, 351-67.

Neuhold, Christine (2001) The "Legislative Backbone" Keeping the Institution Upright? The Role of European Parliament Committees in the EU Policy-Making Process. *European Integration Online Papers* 5. http://eiop.or.at/eiop/texte/2001-010a.htm (accessed 31 May 2020).

Nicolas, J. (1981) Le Parlement élu et le processus législatif de la Communauté. *Revue du Marché Commun* 251, 491-503.

Niemann, Arne (2013) EU External Trade and the Treaty of Lisbon: A Revised Neofunctionalist Approach. *Journal of Contemporary European Research* 9/4, 633-58.

Norman, Peter (2003) *The Accidental Constitution: The Story of the European Convention*. Brussels: EuroComment.

O'Keeffe, Mícheál, Salines, Marion and Marta Wieczorek (2016) The European Parliament's Strategy in EU Economic and Financial Reform. *Journal of European Public Policy* 23, 217-35.

Palmer, Michael (1983) The Development of the European Parliament's Institutional Role within the European Community, 1974-1983. *Journal of European Integration* 6/2-3, 183-202.

Peñalver García, Nereo, and Julian Priestley, (2015) *The Making of a European President*. London: Palgrave Macmillan.

Pardo, Sharon and Neve Gordon (2018) Euroscepticism as an Instrument of Foreign Policy. *Middle East Critique* 27/4, 399-412.

Pasquinucci, Daniele (2013) *Uniti dal voto? Storia delle elezioni europee 1948-2009*. Milan: Franco Angeli.

Patel, Kiran K. (ed.) (2013) *The Cultural Politics of Europe. European Capitals of Culture and European Union since the 1980s*. London: Routledge.

Patel, Kiran K. (2009) *Europäisierung wider Willen: Die Bundesrepublik Deutschland in der Agrarintegration der EWG, 1955-73*. Munich: Oldenbourg.

Patel, Kiran K. and Heike Schweitzer (eds.) (2013) *The Historical Foundations of EU Competition Law*. Oxford: Oxford University Press.

Patterson, Lee Ann (1993) A three-level game approach to understanding agricultural policy in the European Union: A study of the 1988 stabilizers agreement and the 1992 MacSharry reform package. http://aei.pitt.edu/7140/1/002374_1.PDF (accessed 31 May 2020).

Pempel, T. John (ed.) (1990) *Uncommon Democracies: The One Party Dominant Regimes*. Cornell: Cornell University Press.

Peterson, John and Elizabeth Bomberg (1999) *Decision-Making in the European Union*. London: Palgrave Macmillan.

Pierson, Paul (2000) Increasing Returns, Path Dependence, and the Study of Politics. *American Political Science Review* 94/2, 251-67.

Piris, Jean-Claude (2010) *The Lisbon Treaty: A Legal and Political Analysis*. Cambridge: Cambridge University Press.

Plumb, Henry (2001) *The Plumb Line: A Journey through Agriculture and Politics*. London: Greycoat Press.

Pollack, Mark A. (1997) Representing Diffuse Interests in EC Policy-Making. *Journal of European Public Policy* 4, 572–90.

Polk, Jonathan et al. (2017) Explaining the Salience of Anti-Elitism and Reducing Political Corruption for Political Parties in Europe with the 2014 Chapel Hill Expert Survey Data. *Research & Politics* 4/1, 1-9.

Pons, Silvio (2010) The Rise and Fall of Eurocommunism. In: Melvyn P. Leffler and Odd Arne Westad (eds.) *The Cambridge History of the Cold War*. Cambridge: Cambridge University Press, 45-65.

Poptcheva Eva-Maria (2016) *Understanding the d'Hondt method Allocation of Parliamentary Seats and Leadership Positions*. Brussels: EPRS.

Pöttering, Hans-Gert (2016) *United for the Better: My European Way*. London: John Harper Publishing.

Pöttering, Hans-Gert (2006) The EPP and the EPP-ED Group. Success through Synergy. *European View* 3/1: 111-19.

Pridham, Geoffrey and Pippa Pridham (1981) *Transnational Party Co-operation and European Integration: The Process towards Direct Elections*. London: Allen & Unwin.

Priestley, Julian (2008) *Six Battles that Shaped Europe's Parliament*. London: John Harper Publishing.

Ramírez Pérez, Sigfrido M. (2010) The European Committee for Economic and Social Progress: Business Networks between Atlantic and European Communities. In: Wolfram Kaiser, Brigitte Leucht and Michael Gehler (eds.) *Transnational Networks in Regional Integration. Governing Europe 1945-83*. London: Palgrave, 61-84.

Raube, Kolja (2014) Parliamentarization Approaches: Parliamentary Control in EU Foreign Policy. In: Maciej Wilga and Ireneusz Pawel Karolewski (eds.) *New Approaches to EU Foreign Policy*. London: Routledge, 125-42.

Raube, Kolja (2012) The European External Action Service and the European Parliament. *The Hague Journal of Diplomacy* 7/1, 65-80.

Raunio, Tapio and Wolfgang Wagner (2017) Towards Parliamentarisation of Foreign and Security Policy? *West European Politics* 40/1, 1-19.

Raunio, Tapio (1997) *The European Perspective: Transnational Political Groups in the 1989-1994 European Parliament*. Aldershot: Ashgate.

Rassmussen, Maja K. (2015) The Battle for Influence: The Politics of Business Lobbying in the European Parliament. *Journal of Common Market Studies* 53, 365-82.

Rasmusseen, Maja K. (2012) Is the European Parliament Still a Policy Champion for Environmental Interests? *Interest Groups and Advocacy* 1, 239–59.

Rattinger, Hans (1982) Abstimmungsmacht, politische Distanzen und Abstimmungskoalitionen zwischen den Fraktionen im Europäischen Parlament. *Zeitschrift für Soziologie* 11/2, 133-49.

Ringe, Nils (2010) *Who Decides, and How? Preferences, Uncertainty, and Policy Choice in the European Parliament*. Oxford: Oxford University Press.

Rittberger, Berthold (2014) Integration without Representation? The European Parliament and the Reform of Economic Governance in the EU. *Journal of common market Studies* 52, 1174–83.

Rittberger, Berthold (2005) *Building Europe's Parliament: Democratic Representation Beyond the Nation-State*. Oxford: Oxford University Press.

Rittberger, Berthold (2003) The Creation and Empowerment of the European Parliament. *Journal of Common Market Studies* 41, 203-25.

Roederer-Rynning, Christilla (2017) Parliamentary Assertion and Deep Integration: The European Parliament in the CETA and TTIP Negotiations. *Cambridge Review of International Affairs* 30/5-6, 507-26.

Roederer-Rynning, Christilla (2015) The Common Agricultural Policy: The Fortress Challenged. In: Helen Wallace, Mark A. Pollack and Alasdair R. Young (eds.) *Policy-Making in the European Union*. Oxford: Oxford University Press, 181-205.

Roederer-Rynning, Christilla (2002) Farm Conflict in France and the Europeanisation of Agricultural Policy. *West European Politics* 25, 105-24.

Roederer-Rynning, Christilla (2003) From "Talking Shop" to "Working Parliament"? The European Parliament and agricultural change. *Journal of Common Market Studies* 41, 113–35.

Roederer-Rynning, Cristilla and Frank Schimmelfennig (2012) Bringing Co-Decision to Agriculture: A Hard Case of Parliamentarization. *Journal of European Public Policy* 19, 951–68.

Roos, Mechthild (2017) Far Beyond the Treaties' Clauses: The European Parliament's Gain in Power, 1952-1979. *Journal of Contemporary European Research* 13, 1055-75.

Roos, Mechthild and David Howarth (2017) Pushing the Boundaries: New Research on the Activism of EU Supranational Institutions. *Journal of Contemporary European Research* 13, 1007-24.

Rosén, Guri (2015a) EU Confidential: The European Parliament's Involvement in EU Security and Defence Policy. *Journal of Common Market Studies* 53/2, 383-98.

Rosén, Guri (2015b). *Striving for Influence: The European Parliament in EU Foreign Policy*. Oslo: Arena.

Salm, Christian (2017) *Impact of the ECSC Common Assembly on the Politics, Negotiation and Content of the Rome Treaties*. Brussels: EPRS European Parliament History Series.

Sartori, Giovanni (1976) *Parties and Party Systems: A Framework for Analysis*. Cambridge: Cambridge University Press.

Scalingi, Paula (1980) *The European Parliament: The Three-Decade Search for a United Europe*. London: Aldwych.

Scharpf, Fritz (2002) The European Social Model: Coping with the Challenges of Diversity. *Journal of Common Market Studies* 40, 645-70.

Schattschneider, Elmer E. (2004) *Party Government: American Government in Action*. New Brunswick: Transaction. Originally published in New York: Farrar and Rinehart, c1942.

Schmidt-Drüner, Marion (2014) *Employment and Social Affairs in the European Parliament*. Brussels: European Parliament.

Schmitt, Herman and Jacques Thomassen (2009) The European Party System after Enlargement. In: Jacques Thomassen (ed.) *The Legitimacy of the European Union After Enlargement*. Oxford: Oxford University Press, 23-43.

Schoutheete, Philippe de (1986) Le rapport Tindemans: dix ans après. *Politique étrangère* 51/2, 527-38.

Schulz, Stefan (2019) *Social and employment policy: general principles*. https://www.europarl.europa.eu/factsheets/en/sheet/52/social-and-employment-policy-general-principles (accessed 31 May 2020)

Schwartz, Michael (2018) The European Parliament's Standing Committees: Patterns of Behaviour and Modes of Functioning After the Treaty of Lisbon. *Bruges Political Research Papers* 69.

Selck, Torsten J. and Bernard Steunenberg (2004) Between Power and Luck: The European Parliament in the EU Legislative Process. *European Union Politics* 5/1, 25-46.

Servent, Ariadna Ripoll (2018) *The European Parliament*. London: Palgrave Macmillan.

Servent, Ariadna Ripoll (2014) The Role of the European Parliament in International Negotiations after Lisbon. *Journal of European Public Policy* 21/4, 568-86.

Shackleton, Michael (2017) Transforming Representative Democracy in the EU? The Role of the European Parliament. *Journal of European Integration* 39/2, 191-205.

Shaw, Jo (2002) *Process, Responsibility and Inclusion in EU Constitutionalism: The Challenge for the Convention on the Future of the Union*. Updated Version: September 2002. London: The Federal Trust.

Sidjanski, Dusan (1984) Le Parlement Européen et les groupes d'intérêt. In: Hrbek Rudolf, Jospeh Jamar and Wolfgang Wessels (eds.) *The European Parliament on the Eve of the Second Direct Election: Balance Sheet and Prospects*. Bruges: De Tempel, 520-53.

Siles-Brügge, Gabriel (2017) Transatlantic Investor Protection as a Threat to Democracy: The Potency and Limits of an Emotive Frame. *Cambridge Review of International Affairs* 30/5-6, 464-88.

Sjursen, Helene (2011) The EU's Common Foreign and Security Policy: The Quest for Democracy. *Journal of European Public Policy* 18/8, 1069-77.

Sorauf, Frank J, (1964) *Political Parties in the American System*. Boston: Little Brown.

Soriano, Victor Fernández (2017) Facing the Greek Junta: The European Community, the Council of Europe and the Rise of Human-Rights Politics in Europe. *European Review of History* 24/3, 358-76.

Stavridis, Stelios and Daniela Irrera (eds.) (2015) *The European Parliament and its International Relations*. London: Routledge.

Stur, Beata (2017) *New rules in funding European political parties*. https://www.neweurope.eu/article/new-rules-funding-european-political-parties/ (accessed 31 May 2020).

Swinnen, Johan F.M and Louise Knops (2012) *CAP Reform: Will the European Parliament take the bull by the horns?* CEPS Commentary https://www.ceps.eu/system/files/Commentary%20Co-decision.pdf (accessed 31 May 2020)

Tallberg, Jonas and Karl Magnus Johansson (2008) Party Politics in the European Council. *Journal of European Public Policy* 15/8, 1222–42.

Taviani, Paolo Emilio (1954) *Solidarietà atlantica e Comunità Europea*. Florence: Le Monnier.

Thiemeyer, Guido (1999) *Vom "Pool Vert" zur Europäischen Wirtschaftsgemeinschaft: Europäische Integration, Kalter Krieg und die Anfänge der Gemeinsamen Europäischen Agrarpolitik 1950-57*. Munich: Oldenbourg.

Trocini, Federico (2012) Italian Reactions to German unification: Prejudice and Reciprocal Misunderstandings. *Mémoire(s), identité(s), marginalité(s) dans le monde occidental contemporain* 8. https://journals.openedition.org/mimmoc/1066 (accessed 31 May 2020)

Trouwborst, Arie (2011) Conserving European Biodiversity in a Changing Climate: The Bern Convention, the European Union Birds and Habitats Directives and the Adaptation of Nature to Climate Change. *Review of European Community & International Environmental Law* 20, 62-77.

Tsebelis, George et al. (2001) Legislative Procedures in the European Union: An Empirical Analysis. *British Journal of Political Science* 31/4, 573-99.

Tulli, Umberto (2017) *Un Parlamento per l'Europa. Il Parlamento europeo e la battaglia per la sua elezione (1948-1979)*. Milan: Mondadori.

Vaniomäki, Päivi and Étienne Deschamps (2018) *30 years of the Sakharov Prize: The European Parliament Upholding Freedom of Thought*. Brussels: EPRS.

Varsori, Antonio (2010) Le développement d'une politique sociale européenne. In: Gérard Bossuat et al. (eds.) *L'expérience européenne: 50 ans de construction de l'Europe 1957-2007. Des historiens en dialogue*. Baden Baden: Nomos.

Türkeş-Kılıç, Selin (2019) Justifying Privileged Partnership with Turkey: An analysis of Debates in the European Parliament. *Turkish Studies* 21/1, 29-55.

Van den Putte, Lore, Ville, Ferdi D. and Jan Orbie (2015) The European Parliament as an International Actor in Trade. From Power to Impact. In: Stelios Stavridis and Daniela Irrera (eds.) *The European Parliament and its International Relations*. London: Routledge, 84-101.

Van Hecke, Steven (2012) Polity-Building in the Constitutional Convention: Transnational Party Groups in European Union Institutional Reform. *Journal of Common Market Studies* 50/5: 837–52.

Van Hecke, Steven (2010) Do Transnational Party Federations Matter? (... and Why Should We Care?) *Journal of Contemporary European Research* 6/3, 395-411.

Van Hecke, Steven (2004) Christian Democratic Parties and Europeanisation. In: Steven Van Hecke and Emmanuel Gerard (eds.) *Christian Democratic Parties in Europe since the End of the Cold War*. Leuven: Leuven University Press, 43–54.

Vanhoonacker, Sophie (2012) The Amsterdam Treaty: Modest reforms. In: Finn Laursen (ed.) *Designing the European Union: From Paris to Lisbon*. London: Palgrave Macmillan, 180–95.

Verschaeve, Joren and Sarah Delputte (2015) The Role of the European Parliament in EU Development Policy. In: Stelios Stavridis and Daniela Irrera (eds.) *The European Parliament and its International Relations*. London: Routledge, 67-83.

Vincenti, Daniela (2015) *MEPs give TTIP proposal a second try*. https://www.euractiv.com/section/trade-society/news/meps-give-ttip-proposal-a-second-try/ (accessed 31 May 2020).

Voerman, Gerrit and Jan van der Harst (2015) Conclusion. In: Jan van der Harst and Gerrit Voerman (eds.) *An Impossible Job?: The Presidents of the European Commission, 1958–2014*. London: John Harper Publishing, 277-98.

Von Beyme, Klaus (1985) *Political Parties in Western Democracies*. Aldershot: Gower.

Wagner, Wolfgang (2006) The Democratic Control of Military Power Europe. *Journal of European Public Policy* 13/2, 200-16.

Warlouzet, Laurent (2020) *Completing the Single Market: The European Parliament and Economic Integration, 1979-1989*. Brussels: EPRS European Union History Series.

Warlouzet, Laurent (2018) *Governing Europe in a Globalizing World: Neoliberalism and its Alternatives following the 1973 Oil Crisis*. London: Routledge.

Warlouzet, Laurent (2016) The Centralization of EU Competition Policy: Historical Institutionalist Dynamics from Cartel Monitoring to Merger Control (1956-91). *Journal of Common Market Studies* 54/3, 725-41.

Warren, Thomas (2018) The European Parliament and the Eurozone Crisis: An Exceptional Actor? *The British Journal of Politics and International Relations* 20, 632-51.

Weale, Albert et al. (2000) *Environmental Governance in Europe: An Ever Closer Ecological Union?* Oxford: Oxford University Press.

Webb, Paul David Farrell and Ian Holliday (eds.) (2002) *Political Parties in Advanced Industrial Democracies*. Oxford: Oxford University Press.

Wessels, Wolfgang and Franziska Bopp (2008) The Institutional Architecture of CFSP after the Lisbon Treaty: Constitutional Breakthrough or Challenges Ahead? *CEPS Challenge Paper* 10.

Westlake, Martin 1994. *A Modern Guide to the European Parliament*. London: Pinter.

Whitaker, Richard (2011) *The European Parliament's Committees: National Party Influence and Legislative Empowerment*. London: Routledge.

Whitaker, Richard, Hix, Simon and Galina Zapryanova (2016) *EPRG MEP Survey Dataset 2016 Release*. https://mepsurvey.eu/data-objects/data/ (accessed 31 May 2020).

Wisniewski, Elisabeth (2013) The Influence of the European Parliament on the European External Action Service. *European Foreign Affairs Review* 18/1, 81-101.

Wódka, Jakub (2016) Transnational Cooperation of Turkish Political Parties as an Ineffective Tool of Europeanization. *Southeast European and Black Sea Studies* 16/2, 295-315.

Woolcock, Stephen (2018). European Union (EU) Trade Policy. In: *The New Palgrave Dictionary of Economics*. London: Palgrave Macmillan, 4047-53.

Wortmann-Kool, Corien and Maarten Willemen (2013) The EPP Group: Bold Measures in Response to the Crisis. In: Vít Novotný (ed.) *From Reform to Growth: Managing the Economic Crisis in Europe*. Delft: Eburon Uitgeverij BV, 489-506.

Yordanova, Nikoleta (2013) *Organising the European Parliament: The Role of the Committees and their Legislative Influence*. Brussels: ECPR Press.

Yordanova, Nikoleta (2009) The Rationale behind Committee Assignment in the European Parliament: Distributive, Informational and Partisan Perspectives. *European Union Politics* 10, 253-80.

Young, Alasdair and John Peterson (2015) Trade. In: Knud Erik Jorgensen et al. (eds.) *The SAGE Handbook of European Foreign Policy*. London: SAGE.

Ziller, Jacques. 2012. The Treaty of Lisbon: Constitutional Treaty, Episode II. In: Finn Laursen (ed.) *Designing the European Union. From Paris to Lisbon*. London: Palgrave Macmillan, 244–68.

# List of Figures


| | | |
|---|---|---|
| Figure 3.1 | The evolution of EPP membership in the AGRI, ECON, EMPL and ENVI Standing Committees in comparison, by EP term | 151 |
| Figure 3.2 | Chairmanship of AGRI, ECON, EMPL and ENVI Standing Committees, 1979–2019 | 153 |
| Figure 3.3 | Vice-Chairmanship of AGRI, ECON and EMPL Standing Committees, 1979–2019 | 153 |
| Figure 3.4 | Political group membership in the AGRI Standing Committee, 1979–2019 | 155 |
| Figure 3.5 | Political Group membership in the ECON Standing Committee, 1979–2019 | 158 |
| Figure 3.6 | Political Group membership in the EMPL Standing Committee, 1979–2019 | 160 |
| Figure 3.7 | Political group membership in the ENVI Standing Committee, 1979–2019 | 161 |
| Figure 4.1 | EPP parties' positions on EU's defence and security policy (as of 2014) | 221 |
| Figure 4.2 | Scatterplot: the overall position toward European integration by the position toward EU foreign and security policy | 223 |
| Figure 4.3 | Policy attitudes on five topics of the EU External Relations | 225 |
| Figure 4.4 | Vote on EU strategic communication to counteract anti-EU propaganda by third parties (14 October 2016, (2016/2030(INI)) | 232 |

Figure 4.5 Vote on European Parliament resolution on the human rights situation in Cuba (15 November 2018, 2018/2926(RSP)) 233

Figure 4.6 Vote on European Parliament resolution of 8 July 2015 containing the European Parliament's recommendations to the European Commission on the negotiations for the Transatlantic Trade and Investment Partnership (TTIP) (2014/2228(INI)) 239

Figure 4.7 Histogram illustrating the positions of the EPP Group member parties on the question of the EU enlargement to Turkey 246

Figure 4.8 Scatterplot: the overall position toward European integration by the position on the EU membership of Turkey 247

Figure 5.1 Seats percentages for EP political groups by EP term* 262

Figure 5.2 Correlation between EP political groups seat percentages and IR values 280

Figure 5.3 Institutional Relevance (IR) Index per legislature: trends for EPP, S&D and ALDE 281

Figure 5.4 EPP: comparison between IR values and seat percentage trends 282

Figure 5.5 The EPP Group's internal balance. National delegations seat percentages 1979–2019 288

Figure 5.6 Institutional Relevance Index per legislature: trends for the delegations of Germany, Italy, Spain, Poland and UK 289

Figure 5.7 Germany: comparison between IR values and seat percentages 291

Figure 5.8 Italy: comparison between IR values and seat percentages 292

Figure 5.9 Benelux: comparison between IR values and seat percentages 292

Figure 5.11 UK: IR values and seat percentages 293

Figure 5.12 Spain: IR values and seat percentages 294

Figure 5.13 Poland: IR values and seat percentages 294

Figure 5.14 Seats and IR scores. Comparison between the German national delegation and the whole EPP 297

Figure 5.15 Replacement rate of EPP MEPs 298

Figure 5.[illegible] Boxplot comparison between [illegible] values and seat per[illegible] [illegible] 2[illegible]

Figure [illegible] [illegible] [illegible]

Figure [illegible] [illegible] R values and seat percentages [illegible]

Figure [illegible] Rooted R values and seat percentages [illegible]

Figure [illegible] [illegible] R values: Comparison between [illegible] [illegible] 2[illegible]

Figure [illegible] [illegible] [illegible]

# List of Tables


| | | |
|---|---|---|
| Table 3.1 | Composition of the AGRI, ECON, EMPL and ENVI Standing Committees, by political group and EP term | 197 |
| Table 4.1 | Composition of AFET, DEVE, INTA by political group and EP term | 209 |
| Table 4.2 | Descriptive statistics on the selected policy positions of the EPP Group member parties | 222 |
| Table 4.3 | Frequency of receiving voting instructions | 224 |
| Table 4.4 | Frequency of receiving voting instructions (II) | 224 |
| Table 4.5 | The level of agreement between the EPP Group line and members (in percentages) in relation to the EPP Group line | 227 |
| Table 5.1 | EP political groups seat % by EP term* | 264 |
| Table 5.2 | Number of total Member states represented in the EP political groups by EP term | 271 |
| Table 5.3 | The EPP Group in the Europarty system: indicators by EP term | 273 |
| Table 5.4 | Vote against transnational lists by EP political group* | 302 |
| Table A1 | Weighting of institutional positions in the EP | 327 |
| Table A2 | Seat percentages and IR scores per political group and EP term | 328 |
| Table A3 | Seats % and Institutional index score (IR) % by National Delegation within the EPP: EP terms 1–8 | 330 |
| Table A4 | Total scores per party | 331 |

| | | |
|---|---|---|
| Table A5 | Scores per party for Quaestors | 331 |
| Table A6 | Scores per party in Presidency | 331 |
| Table A7 | Party Scores in Committee | 332 |
| Table A8 | Party scores in delegations | 332 |
| Table A9 | EPP Group 1979–2019: List of Chairs and Secretary-Generals by nationality | 333 |
| Table A10 | Presidents of the elected Parliament | 334 |

# Index of Names


Adenauer, Konrad 29, 30, 33, 42, 43, 51, 61, 68, 163
Adonnino, Pietro 59
Aigner, Heinrich 319
Alber, Siegbert 93
Álvarez de Miranda, Fernando 54
Amato, Giuliano 114, 126
Andreotti, Giulio 29, 40, 93, 94
Antoniozzi, Dario 65
Arndt, Rudi 56, 57
Arnold, Karl 33
Ashton, Catherine 233, 234
Aznar, José Maria 54

Balz, Burkhard 178
Bangemann, Martin 49, 66
Barbi, Paolo 39, 40, 43, 93, 333
Barnier, Michael 116, 126
Barón Crespo, Enrique 57, 99, 126
Barroso, José Manuel 127, 176, 185, 283, 309, 310
Battista, Emilio 63
Berendt, Walter 49
Berlusconi, Silvio 122, 266
Bersani, Giovanni 39, 40, 42
Bertrand, Alfred 39, 43, 55, 64, 65, 73, 84
Bettamio, Giampaolo 40, 43, 45–47, 93, 333, 334
Bidault, Georges 30, 33, 61
Biedenkopf, Kurt 37
Biesheuvel, Barend 315
Blumenfeld, Erik 65, 67
Bocklet, Reinhold 166–168, 300
Boersma, Jacob 80, 81, 187
Boeselager, Damian 272
Bonsignore, Vito 213
Borrell, Josep 126, 313, 334
Boscary-Monsservin, Roland 75
Bourlanges, Jean-Louis 99, 104
Brandt, Willy 56
Bresso, Mercedes 307
Briand, Aristide 28
Brok, Elmar 41, 99, 104–106, 109, 110, 115–120, 122–127, 205, 211, 212, 215, 232, 234, 237
Bruton, John 116
Bukman, Piet 47
Buschmann, Karl 315
Busuttil, Simon 296, 334
Buttiglione, Rocco 309

Casini, Carlo 310
Caspary, David 241
Cellini, Jacopo 89, 197
Chirac, Jacques 111
Churchill, Winston 23
Cockfield, Arthur 78
Colin, André 41
Colombo, Emilio 39, 49, 50, 56, 84, 93, 99, 282
Conway, Martin 23, 24
Corbett, Richard 67
Cortivo, Maria Louisa 38, 46
Cresson, Édith 317, 320
Croux, Lambert 44, 92

Dakowska, Dorota 305
Dankert, Piet 50, 279, 334
Daul, Joseph 126, 127, 185, 220, 287, 312, 333
David, Mario 333
Davies, Chris 192

de Castro, Paolo 169
de Ferranti, Basil 79
De Gasperi, Alcide 7
De Gaulle, Charles 42, 43, 48, 62–64, 84, 287
de Menthon, François 62, 73
de Palacio, Ana 116
Debatisse, Michel 155, 156, 163
Dehaene, Jean-Luc 114, 116, 126, 306
Dell, Edmund 315
Delors, Jacques 69, 78, 79, 145, 147
Delouvrier, Paul 315
Deringer, Arved 41, 73, 74, 78, 83, 84, 86
Dess, Albert 169, 170
di Poi, Alfredo 43
Dichgans, Hans 72
Diligent, André 65
Dimitrakopoulos, Giorgos 109, 111, 305
Dooge, James 52, 172
Doyle, Avril 192
Duff, Andrew 115, 127, 301
Duisenberg, Wim 176
Dury, Raymonde 106

Elles, James 319
Engel, Frank 209, 214, 220, 235, 236
Erhard, Ludwig 72
Essayah, Sari 178

Fanfani, Amintore 37
Feio, Diogo 178
Ferragni, Arnaldo 43, 47
FitzGerald, Garret 93
Fjellner, Christofer 219, 220, 242
Florenz, Karl-Heinz 162, 192
Fontaine, Nicole 108–110, 334
Fontaine, Pascal 243, 248
Foot, Michael 61
Forlani, Arnaldo 93
Fraga Iribarne, Manuel 54
Franco, Francisco 28, 54
Franz, Otmar 173, 175
Froment-Meurice, François 104
Fugmann, Friedrich 69
Furler, Hans 37, 39, 41, 42, 49, 59, 63

Gauzès, Jean-Paul 179
Gerokostopoulos, Achillefs 44
Giannakou, Marietta 306, 307
Giavazzi, Giovanni 93
Gil-Robles, José María 99, 295
Giscard d'Estaing, Valéry 116–119
Goebbels, Robert 185
Grzimek, Bernhard 82
Gualtieri, Roberto 211
Guccione, Sergio 43, 333
Guckenberger, Gerhard 43, 47, 333
Guglielmone, Teresio 63
Guigou, Elisabeth 105

Hallstein, Walter 58, 72, 73
Hänsch, Klaus 104, 115, 122, 127, 334
Herman, Fernand 79, 84, 92, 93, 95, 97–99, 102, 104, 172, 175
Heseltine, Michael 52
Houben, Robert 32, 73
Howe, Geoffrey 52
Hübner, Danuta Maria 301, 321
Hurd, Douglas 52

Jahn, Hans Edgar 37, 39, 80–84, 187, 189
Jansen, Thomas 45, 47, 94, 106, 118
Johnson, Stanley 189
Jonker, Sjouke 44, 66, 67
Juncker, Jean-Claude 176, 182, 256, 311

Kaczmarek, Filip 209, 214, 217, 219, 220, 234, 236
Kaiser, Jacob 37
Kalniete, Sandra 206, 217, 219, 232, 238, 246

Kamp, Martin 89, 116, 120, 290, 334
Karamanlis, Konstantin 53
Karas, Othmar 178, 186
Karremans, Johannes 9, 89
Katzer, Hans 50
Kelly, Petra 80
Kinnock, Neil 56
Klepsch, Egon 36, 38–40, 43, 45–54, 56, 57, 65, 66, 68, 76, 77, 85, 93, 95–99, 101, 102, 175, 279, 333, 334
Klompé, Margaretha 63
Kohl, Helmut 36, 46–48, 51, 52, 56, 57, 85, 93–95, 100, 105, 116, 119, 164, 182, 296, 311
Kok, Wim 185
Kopf, Herman 63
Korhola, Eija-Ritta 188
Köstinger, Elisabeth 171
Kremer, Christian 116

La Via, Giovanni 171
Lagarde, Christine 313
Lamassoure, Alain 301, 302
Lambrias, Panayotis 93
Lange, Bernd 241, 242
Langen, Werner 178
Langes, Horst 46
Lefèvre, Théo 47
Lehne, Klaus-Heiner 185, 186
Leinen, Jo 109, 111, 301, 305, 306
Lenz, Otto 42, 43
Lindner, Johannes 317, 318
Lubbers, Ruud 93, 101
Lücker, Hans August 39, 41, 55, 58, 66, 74–76, 83, 84, 163

Macron, Emmanuel 263, 312, 313
MacSharry, Ray 133, 143, 165, 166, 168
Maij-Weggen, Hanja 104, 106, 107, 110, 115
Mallström, Cecilia 242
Mansholt, Sicco 74, 80
Marjolin, Robert 315
Martens, Wilfried 11, 92, 93, 104, 107, 111, 114, 118, 120, 126, 127, 243, 244, 249, 296, 311, 319, 321, 333
Martin, David 102, 104, 174
Martino, Edoardo 63
Marx, Karl 24
Mathieu, Véronique 306
McAllister, David 219, 220, 230, 231, 246
McGuinness, Mairead 171
Méndez de Vigo, Íñigo 104, 107, 110, 114–116, 118, 120, 122, 125
Merkel, Angela 124, 126, 127, 176, 312, 313
Michel, Charles 21, 313
Milinkevich, Aleksandr 215, 238
Milward, Alan S. 28
Mitterrand, François 50, 61, 65, 100
Mogherini, Federica 233, 234
Monnet, Jean 14, 31, 32
Monti, Mario 116
Moreau, Jacques 69, 79
Moro, Aldo 41
Müller, Josef 62
Muntingh, Hemmo 189
Mussolini, Benito 27

Opitz, Hans-Joachim 32, 42, 43
Oreja, Marcelino 99
Osman, Salih Mahmoud 215
Owen, David 65

Patten, Chris 52
Paya, Oswaldo 215
Pedersen, Niels 296, 333
Pella, Giuseppe 39, 63
Petrilli, Giuseppe 315
Pezet, Ernest 31, 33
Pfennig, Gero 69
Pflimlin, Pierre 52, 74, 84, 295, 334

Plumb, Henry 50, 52, 155, 163, 164, 279, 334
Poher, Alain 42, 47, 63
Pohle, Wolfgang 73
Pope Pius XII 24
Pöttering, Hans-Gert 38, 41, 106–112, 114–116, 118, 120, 125–127, 184, 243, 244, 333, 334
Preda, Cristian 209, 214, 217, 219, 220, 230, 234
Priestley, Julian 105, 121, 122
Prodi, Romano 111, 116, 309
Pronk, Bartho 182

Quisthoudt-Rowohl, Godelieve 219, 237, 240, 242

Rangel, Paulo 321, 322
Ribera d'Alcalá, Riccardo 45
Richarts, Hans 187
Rifkind, Malcolm 52
Rogalla, Dieter 79
Rubinacci, Leopoldo 72
Rumor, Mariano 44
Ryngaert, Johan 283, 303, 322, 323

Sakharov, Andriej 208, 215, 237, 251
Salafranca Sanchez-Neyra, Jose Ignazio 213
Salazar, António de Oliveira 54
Santer, Jacques 19, 47, 93, 95, 309, 317, 319–321
Sarkozy, Nicholas 176
Sassen, Emmanuel 32
Sassoli, David 281, 313, 334
Scarascia Mugnozza, Beatrice 44, 117, 118, 120, 322
Scarascia Mugnozza, Carlo 63, 73
Scelba, Mario 39, 40, 58, 63
Schäuble, Wolfgang 116, 118, 120
Schleicher, Ursula 111, 305
Schöpflin, György 302, 303
Schuijt, Willem 64
Schulz, Martin 279, 322, 334
Schuman, Robert 14, 32, 33, 41, 61, 68
Scrivener, Christine 79
Seitlinger, Jean 44, 47, 300
Selmayr, Martin 116
Sentsov, Oleg 215, 238
Serrarens, P.J.S. 30
Severin, Adrian 301
Spaak, Paul-Henri 49, 92
Spinelli, Altiero 17, 65–70, 79, 80, 256, 300
Sturzo, Luigi 27
Suárez, Adolfo 54

Tajani, Antonio 290, 296, 334
Taverne, Dick 315
Taviani, Paolo Emilio 30, 62, 84
Teitgen, Pierre-Henri 31, 62, 63, 84
Thatcher, Margaret 50, 52, 53, 265
Thyssen, Marianne 185, 186
Timmermans, Frans 312
Timoshenko, Julia 233
Tindemans, Leo 39, 47, 50, 53, 65, 66, 80, 84, 93, 99, 102, 103, 243, 333
Tolman, Teun 156
Tsatsos, Dimitris 107, 109, 110

van Velzen, Wim 182
Vedel, Georges 315, 318
Veil, Simone 50, 67, 282, 283, 334
Ventre, Riccardo 125
Vergeer, Willem 93
Verhofstadt, Guy 205, 211, 283
von Brentano, Heinrich 31, 33, 62, 84
von der Groeben, Hans 74, 78, 86
von der Leyen, Ursula 21, 256, 309, 312, 313
von Habsburg, Otto 44
von Wogau, Karl 79, 172

Wahl, Jürgen 45

Weber, Manfred 21, 219, 252, 256, 290, 311–314, 333
Welle, Klaus 107, 113, 114, 116, 296, 333
Werner, Pierre 79, 144, 172
Wieland, Rainer 307
Wigny, Pierre 63, 73, 84
Wortmann-Kool, Corien 178

Yousafzai, Malala 215

Zaccagnini, Benigno 35